FLORIDA STATE
UNIVERSITY LIBRARIES

JUN 19 1996

TALLAHASSEE, FLORIDA

# GHANA

## SAIS African Studies Library

General Editor
*I. William Zartman*

# GHANA

## The Political Economy of Recovery

edited by
Donald Rothchild

Lynne Rienner Publishers • Boulder & London

Published in the United States of America in 1991 by
Lynne Rienner Publishers, Inc.
1800 30th Street, Boulder, Colorado 80301

and in the United Kingdom by
Lynne Rienner Publishers, Inc.
3 Henrietta Street, Covent Garden, London WC2E 8LU

© 1991 by Lynne Rienner Publishers, Inc. All rights reserved

**Library of Congress Cataloging-in-Publication Data**
Ghana : the political economy of recovery / edited by Donald
   Rothchild.
      p. cm.—(SAIS African studies library)
   Includes bibliographical references and index.
   ISBN 1-55587-237-9 (h/c)
   ISBN 1-55587-284-0 (p/b)
   1. Ghana—Economic conditions—1979– 2. Ghana—Economic policy.
3. Ghana—Politics and government—1979– 4. Economic stabilization—
Ghana. I. Rothchild, Donald S. II. Series.
HC1060.G43 191
338.9667—dc20                                                    90-26072
                                                                     CIP

**British Cataloguing in Publication Data**
A Cataloguing in Publication record for this book
is available from the British Library.


Printed and bound in the United States of America

The paper used in this publication meets the requirements
of the American National Standard for Permanence of
Paper for Printed Library Materials Z39.48-1984.
5 4 3 2 1

*To*
*Victor A. Olorunsola,*
*for his excellent scholarship,*
*integrity, and close friendship*

# Contents

| | |
|---|---|
| List of Tables and Figures | ix |
| List of Acronyms | xi |
| Acknowledgments | xv |
| Map of Ghana | xvi |

## PART 1   INTRODUCTION

1 Ghana and Structural Adjustment: An Overview
   *Donald Rothchild* — 3

## PART 2   THE POLITICAL AND SOCIAL ENVIRONMENT

2 The Political Transformation of Ghana Under the PNDC
   *Naomi Chazan* — 21
3 The PNDC and the Problem of Legitimacy
   *Kwame A. Ninsin* — 49
4 Educating Rawlings: The Evolution of Government Strategy Toward Smuggling
   *Paul Nugent* — 69
5 Equity Issues in Ghana's Rural Development
   *Gwendolyn Mikell* — 85
6 The Political Economy of Education Reform in Ghana
   *James Cobbe* — 101

## PART 3  THE CHALLENGE OF POLITICAL AND ECONOMIC REFORM

7  The Political Economy of Stabilization and Structural Adjustment in Ghana
   *Jon Kraus* — 119
8  Leadership Commitment and Political Opposition to Structural Adjustment in Ghana
   *Richard Jeffries* — 157
9  Labor in Ghana Under Structural Adjustment: The Politics of Acquiescence
   *Jeffrey Herbst* — 173
10  State Enterprises Divestiture: Recent Ghanaian Experiences
   *E. Gyimah-Boadi* — 193
11  Export Diversification Under the Economic Recovery Program
   *Kwasi Anyemedu* — 209
12  Reviving Cocoa: Policies and Perspectives on Structural Adjustment in Ghana's Key Agricultural Sector
   *Cord Jakobeit* — 221

## PART 4  THE CHALLENGE OF INTERNATIONAL NEGOTIATIONS

13  Negotiating Adjustment and External Finance: Ghana and the International Community, 1982–1989
   *Matthew Martin* — 235

*Selected Bibliography* — 265
*About the Contributors* — 271
*Index* — 275
*About the Book* — 285

# Tables and Figures

## ■ Tables

| | | |
|---|---|---|
| 4.1 | The Rewards of Cocoa Smuggling into Togo and Côte d'Ivoire | 72 |
| 4.2 | Estimated Losses of Cocoa Through Smuggling | 72 |
| 4.3 | The Trend in Cocoa Prices | 78 |
| 4.4 | Profits from Smuggling of Petroleum Products | 80 |
| 6.1 | Economically Active Population by Employment Status and Education | 101 |
| 6.2 | Characteristics of Households by Quintiles | 102 |
| 6.3 | Education and the Poor | 103 |
| 6.4 | 1988–1989 Junior and Senior Secondary School Data | 113 |
| 6.5 | Access to Primary School by Region | 113 |
| 6.6 | Indicators of Regional Disparity in Primary Schools | 114 |
| 7.1 | Ghana: Selected Production Indicators | 122 |
| 7.2 | Cocoa Prices, Inflation Rates, Real Minimum Wages, and Terms of Trade | 123 |
| 7.3 | Ghana Economic Indicators | 128 |
| 7.4 | Devaluation of the Cedi | 137 |
| 11.1 | Value of Nontraditional Experts | 215 |
| 12.1 | Cocoa Producer Prices and the Development of Real Income | 224 |
| 12.2 | Development of Cocoa Revenue for the Government | 228 |
| 12.3 | Cocoa Projects by the World Bank and Other Donors Since 1980 | 231 |
| 13.1 | Ghana's Policy-Based Loans | 236 |
| 13.2 | Ghana—Main Economic Indicators | 245 |
| 13.3 | Ghana—Debt and External Finance | 253 |

## ■ Figures

| | | |
|---|---|---|
| 9.1 | Work Days Lost Due to Strikes | 179 |
| 9.2 | Real Per Capita Income | 187 |
| 10.1 | The Organizational Structure of the Divestiture Program | 199 |

# Acronyms

| | |
|---|---|
| ADC | Agricultural Development Corporation |
| AFRC | Armed Forces Revolutionary Council |
| AGC | Ashanti Goldfields Corporation |
| AGI | Association of Ghana Industries |
| ALU | Association of Local Unions |
| | |
| BMB | Borenschot-Moret-Bosboom |
| | |
| CDO | Civil Defence Organisation |
| CDR | Committees for the Defence of the Revolution |
| CEPS | Customs, Excise and Preventive Services |
| CMB | Cocoa Marketing Board |
| COMECON | Council for Mutual Economic Assistance |
| CPI | consumer price index |
| CPP | Convention People's Party |
| CSD | Cocoa Services Division |
| CVC | Citizens Vetting Committee |
| | |
| DA | District Assembly |
| DANIDA | Danish International Development Agency |
| DIC | Divestiture Implementation Committee |
| | |
| ECA | Economic Commission for Africa |
| ECOWAS | Economic Community of West African States |
| EDSAC | Educational Sector Adjustment Credit |
| EFF | Extended Fund Facility |
| ERP | Economic Recovery Program |
| ESAF | Enhanced Structural Adjustment Facility |

| | |
|---|---|
| FOB | free on board |
| | |
| GBC | Ghana Broadcasting Corporation |
| GDP | gross domestic product |
| GES | Ghana Education Service |
| GIHOC | Ghana Industrial Holding Corporation |
| GIMPA | Ghana Institute of Management and Public Administration |
| GLSS | Ghana Living Standards Survey |
| GPRTU | Ghana Private Road Transport Union |
| GTP | Ghana Textile Printing |
| | |
| IBRD | International Bank for Reconstruction and Development |
| ICO | International Cocoa Organization |
| ICU | Industrial and Commercial Workers Union |
| IDA | International Development Association |
| IDC | Industrial Development Corporation |
| IFC | International Finance Corporation |
| IMF | International Monetary Fund |
| | |
| JFM | June Fourth Movement |
| JSS | Junior Secondary Schools |
| | |
| KNRG | Kwame Nkrumah Revolutionary Guards |
| | |
| LDC | less developed country |
| LVB | Land Valuation Board |
| | |
| MDPI | Management Development and Productivity Institute |
| MDU | Maritime and Dockworkers Union |
| MIGA | Multilateral Investment Guarantee Agency |
| | |
| NBER | National Bureau of Economic Research |
| NCD | National Commission on Democracy |
| NCWD | National Council on Women in Development |
| NDC | National Defence Committee |
| NDM | New Democratic Movement |
| NIC | National Industrial Companies |
| NIC | National Investigations Committee |
| NLC | National Liberation Council |
| NRC | National Redemption Council |
| NSC | Negotiating Sub-Committee |
| NUGS | National Union of Ghana Students |

| | |
|---|---|
| OECD | Organization for Economic Cooperation and Development |
| OFY | Operation-Feed-Yourself |
| PAMSCAD | Programme of Actions to Mitigate the Social Costs of Adjustment |
| PDC | People's Defence Committees |
| PIB | Prices and Incomes Board |
| PNDC | Provisional National Defence Council |
| PS | principal secretary |
| RCC | Regional Coordinating Committee |
| SAF | Structural Adjustment Facility |
| SAP | Structural Adjustment Program |
| SDA | Social Dimensions of Adjustment |
| SDR | special drawing rights |
| SEC | State Enterprises Commission |
| SES | State Enterprises Secretariat |
| SFC | State Fishing Corporation |
| SGMC | State Gold Mining Corporation |
| SMC | Supreme Military Council |
| SOE | state-owned enterprise |
| SPA | Special Program of Assistance |
| SSNIT | Social Security and National Insurance Trust |
| SSS | Senior Secondary Schools |
| TSC | Technical Sub-Committee |
| TUC | Trades Union Congress |
| UGFC | United Ghana Farmers' Council |
| UNDP | United Nations Development Program |
| UNICEF | United Nations International Children's Emergency Fund |
| USAID | United States Agency for International Development |
| WDC | Workers' Defence Committees |
| WID | Women in Development |

# Acknowledgments

An editor is necessarily a facilitator who relies on a wide gamut of cooperation and support from a variety of sources. In this undertaking, I have indeed been very fortunate. The organization of the conference on Ghana on April 6 and 7, 1990, at the Johns Hopkins Nitze School of Advanced International Studies in Washington, D.C., fell very heavily on the capable shoulders of I. William Zartman, the director of the African Studies Program, and Theresa Simmons. Not only did they guide me through the intricacies of planning and arranging the meeting, but they secured the financial backing so indispensable for a project of this sort. The meeting proved more than worth the effort, for a large group of participants with widely differing views debated the issues of governance and structural adjustment in an intense but highly constructive manner. The results, I feel, deserve the attention of a broad audience of scholars and practitioners concerned with the problems of development in the Third World.

Following the Washington meeting, I also had the advantage of being able to consult a variety of scholars for help in analyzing and evaluating the papers. Again, I. William Zartman was particularly supportive. In addition, I received important assistance from Naomi Chazan, E. Gyimah-Boadi, Jeffrey Herbst, Michael Lofchie, Matthew Martin, and Joan M. Nelson. Finally, Caroline Hartzell and Pamela Evans proved keen and conscientious editors, and Linda Potoski and Kathi Miller were most patient in typing and revising the manuscripts.

*Donald Rothchild*

Source: U.S. Department of State, Bureau of Public Affairs.

# PART 1
## INTRODUCTION

# 1

# Ghana and Structural Adjustment: An Overview

*Donald Rothchild*

Ghana, the pacesetter of African independence from colonial rule, has now emerged as the test case of structural adjustment. A program of structural reform has both economic and political dimensions. It is characterized, on the economic side, by a reliance on market mechanisms, the promotion of exports, reduction in the size and functions of the civil service, privatization, the elimination of marketing boards, and currency devaluation. On the political side, it involves a shift in the role and functions of government; as the World Bank puts it, a structural adjustment program (SAP) implies "not just less government but better government—government that concentrates its efforts less on direct interventions and more on enabling others to be productive."[1]

What can such a reform program be expected to achieve in overcoming Ghana's economic stagnation and what the Bank calls the "failure of governance"?[2] In the short term, the economic indicators are most encouraging. Ghana's estimated annual growth rate of 6 to 7 percent of gross domestic product (GDP) during the 1984–1988 period certainly was one of the highest reported in sub-Saharan Africa at that time.[3] Reacting enthusiastically to this performance, the World Bank's representative on the scene concluded that "if it can happen in Ghana, it can happen in any African country."[4] Has Ghana in fact become a model for its neighbors? Is its experience generalizable? And what are the broader implications that follow from this reform process?

To gain an insight into the problems and prospects of Ghana's experiment with structural adjustment, a number of questions were posed at the Johns Hopkins Nitze School of Advanced International Studies; they deserve repetition here.

1. *To what extent do authoritarian regimes provide a shortcut for overcoming harsh political and economic constraints on development?* As

Jeffrey Herbst observes, structural adjustment measures "are extremely controversial because they involve large changes in the distribution of resources which are certain to leave some people worse off in the short run."[5] In light of President K. A. Busia's overthrow in 1972 following an attempt to devalue the currency, ought one to conclude that a highly centralized regime, military or otherwise, is indispensable to a process of change in current Ghanaian circumstances?

2. *In the short term, will the articulate public acquiesce in, even accept, the necessary hardships involved in a program of structural reforms? And in the long term, will the regime be able to build an adequate support base to maintain the current reform program intact?* Clearly, public acquiescence is essential if the regime is to avoid active protest and be able to attract international lending and assistance as well as foreign investment. In the long term, however, coercion must give way to legitimacy, and regime survival and performance must depend upon a reasonably broad base of support.

3. *What are the implications of economic rehabilitation for a strengthening and reform of the state?* Put another way, will a pruning of the state and its functions, as intended by many proponents of Ghana's SAP, lead to more effective governance? And is there a threshold beyond which such a pruning will prove counterproductive? Clearly, if limited state resources were directed away from civil service benefits and salaries and toward the development of certain of the more productive sectors in the country's economy, the overall results might be very favorable for Ghana as a whole.

4. *Have the relatively disadvantaged classes and regions benefited from structural adjustment?* Although improvements in welfare have taken place under the SAP, the results have been uneven and modest thus far. Who has benefited from the recovery effort? In raising this question, important distinctions must be made between different socioeconomic classes in the rural areas and the poor as well as the poorest of the poor in the urban areas. Moreover, if structural adjustment exacerbates existing interregional discrepancies, it can cause competition and conflict that may become pronounced in the years ahead.

5. *What would a successfully adjusted economy look like in ten years' time?* Is the process likely to result in higher levels of manufacturing and agricultural productivity? Can diversification of exports be anticipated? Will the present pace of timber cutting lead to adverse environmental consequences? And, on the political side, will the reforms promote a supportive coalition of major interest groups?

6. *Is there any thinking in Ghana at the present time about an alternative economic and political agenda?* In the past, Ghana appears to have swung back and forth between the alternatives of Nkrumah-styled "socialism" and welfare capitalism. If the current experiment with structural reform

proves unable to provide the country with self-sustaining growth and development, is some other option or set of options likely to engender mass support?

### ■ The Background to Reform

From 1974 to the early 1980s, the Ghanaian economy and polity was in decline, unable, for a combination of structural and policy-based reasons, to seize the initiative and overcome the constraints on choice. By 1981, for example, the real GDP had fallen by as much as 15 percent compared to 1974.[6] Certainly, some of the problems were external and therefore lay beyond the country's control. A small state heavily dependent upon external sources for its imports of petroleum, machinery, and manufactured items and on foreign markets for its exports of cocoa, timber, and diamonds, Ghana is perceived by many as remaining firmly linked to a powerful international capitalistic economy.

To a significant extent, the Ghanaian economy does reflect the expansion and contraction that takes place in the core countries of Western Europe, North America, and the Pacific Rim. The effect is to leave its citizens feeling exposed and vulnerable, dependent upon world market forces and upon multinational companies, foreign governments, and multilateral organizations for its interactions with the wider world community. Delinkage from international capitalism is not a feasible option (and, in fact, it was some of the international banks and Western-based corporations such as the Firestone Company, rather than the Ghanaian state, that reduced their loans or severed their ties with Ghana in the early 1980s); yet, not surprisingly, Ghanaians view external reliance as resulting in unequal terms of exchange. Rawlings's repeated references, therefore, to "neocolonialism" as one of the causes of the country's present difficulties have struck a strong emotional chord among local audiences.[7]

Although Ghana is constrained by the external environment, this is hardly the full explanation for the country's difficulties. Declining agricultural and industrial productivity, in some cases despite rising international market prices, contributed substantially to the country's economic malaise during the 1970s and 1980s.[8] Thus, diamond, manganese, and bauxite exports fell heavily in this period, and even though the output of gold dropped from 15,973 grams in 1975 to 10,764 grams in 1981, the value of this export in cedis (¢) rose impressively as a consequence of higher world market prices. Cocoa exports, which normally accounted for 60 percent of foreign exchange revenues, did poorly in these years, plummeting from a high of 557,000 long tons in the 1964/65 crop year to 185,000 in 1980/81, resulting in a net deficit in the budget in 1981 and 1982.[9] Between 1970 and

1980, moreover, Ghana's share of world cocoa exports fell from 33 to 17 percent.[10] Declining productivity was in part attributable to policy failures and bureaucratic mismanagement. Overstaffed and inefficient parastatals (see Chapter 10), poor infrastructure, low producer prices, overpricing of the local currency, budgetary imbalances, skewed sectoral and regional allocations, inadequate agricultural research, ineffective disease control, a declining quality in extension services, and so forth all played a part in the falloff in the production of minerals, manufactured goods, and food and cash crops. To be sure, a portion of the drop in production may be accounted for by activity in the parallel economy, but this still leaves open a broad area of lost capacity.

In brief, when Rawlings assumed power in December 1981, the economy was indeed in dire straits. The reasons were multiple and overlapping and included international constraints, drought, policy failures, and bureaucratic mismanagement. To unleash the forces of recovery, it was necessary for Rawlings to take drastic action, first in the direction of radical populism and then by an externally induced structural adjustment program. The benefits and costs arising from this experiment with structural reforms in Ghana are sufficiently complex and important to warrant the attention of a wide array of observers.

## ■ The Rawlings Revolution and Economic Reform

After an initial fifteen-month period of populist mobilization and experimentation, the Rawlings regime, determined to secure international resources for the country's development and under heavy pressure from the urban middle classes and wage earners, moved to a more pragmatic stance on economic and political issues. The rhetoric of populism became linked with a rather conventional economic approach.[11] The establishment of a military-led populist regime provided Rawlings with considerable room to maneuver, enabling him to impose a variety of harsh measures intended to rehabilitate the economy. And his adoption of a conventional view of economic reform helped him attract the necessary external support to implement a program of structural adjustment. But the political and economic resources gained by such a strategy were necessarily short-lived, requiring that Rawlings move swiftly to set the basis for self-sustaining growth and development. Over the long term, the challenges of legitimacy, the building of a coalition of supporting interests, and the achievement of effective political and economic development cannot be put off without creating an element of uncertainty about the future.

Certainly Rawlings's cautiousness on economic matters became evident by 1983. The April 1983 budget adopted a rather pragmatic approach to

Ghana's economic problems, including such austerity measures [as restricting] transactions utilizing foreign exchange, increasing indirect taxes [and] duties, and boosting the prices of essential goods and services; i[t] established a system of bonuses for exporters and surcharges for imports that raised the effective cedi/dollar rate from 2.75 to approximately 25 (an implied devaluation of 89 percent).[12] International Monetary Fund (IMF) officials, not surprisingly, responded favorably to such measures. Subsequently, the ruling Provisional National Defence Council (PNDC) approved a number of policies intended to reduce the rate of inflation and the level of governmental expenditures. These policies included restrictions on the money supply, new controls on expenditures, and initiatives intended to increase the state's capacity to collect taxes.

In addition, the PNDC sought to improve the country's productive base, allocating increased resources to the agricultural sector, raising the producer prices of such export crops as cocoa, taking steps to rehabilitate the mining industry and to negotiate oil-prospecting concessions, and making efforts to provide a greater array of consumer goods in the rural areas. In August, the IMF agreed to lend Ghana special drawing rights (SDR) of 359 million, with another SDR of 120 million pending. Moreover, the World Bank, through its International Development Association (IDA) soft loan affiliate, provided Ghana with a grant of $65 million. Then, in October 1983, the government eliminated the various bonuses for exporters and surcharges for importers and further devalued the cedi, lowering the rate to ¢30 to the dollar, a move that appeared to earn further approval for the PNDC from IMF and World Bank observers. Rawlings's economic pragmatism, fortuitously combined with the rhetoric of populist assertion, had struck a sufficient balance between domestic aspirations and international objectives to allow for a new initiative to achieve national recovery. Thomas Callaghy points out just how critical this reconciliation is for development under current circumstances:

> The ability of Third World governments to engage in sustained economic adjustment—caught as they are between strong and often contradictory internal and external pressures and economic and political logics—depends in large part on the technocratic and bureaucratic capabilities of the state apparatus and the ability of leaders to use these capabilities effectively. This means coping with the complex two-level negotiating "games"—economic and political games played simultaneously at domestic and international levels.[13]

For the moment at least, the Rawlings regime had succeeded in managing the complex and reinforcing logics of the political and economic games, facilitating the adoption and implementation of a structural reform program that was both innovative and far-reaching.

## ■ Ghana's Structural Adjustment Program: Aims and Objectives

By 1983, then, the Rawlings administration had concluded that there was no real alternative to structural reforms. "The analysis of both the historical development and the existing situation made it obvious," the government declared, "that a large part of the resources necessary for investment to rehabilitate the productive and social infrastructure would have to be mobilised from external sources. *In simple terms, we had to look quickly for financial* help from the international community on [a] bilateral as well as [a] multilateral basis."[14] In Kwame Ninsin's words (Chapter 3 in this book), the reality of the country's peripheral position "had overwhelmed it."

Such a change of short-term preferences from radical populism to liberal reform was no doubt difficult in the extreme; yet, given the shortcomings of past policy (in particular, the lack of fiscal and monetary responsibility) and the severity of the international environment, there was no obvious alternative. Thus, the largely internal, populist thrust had to be complemented with a pragmatic approach at both the domestic and international levels.[15] And once the decision to experiment with structural adjustment was taken, there was no turning back. With the presentation of the 1990 budget, the PNDC secretary for Finance and Economic Planning, Kwesi Botchwey, ruled out any "relapse into the careless populism of the past that all but destroyed our national economy."[16]

The Ghana government formally launched its Economic Recovery Program (ERP) in April 1983. The first phase of the program (1983–1986) concentrated on halting the decline in industrial production and commodity exports; its second phase (1987–1989) focused on economic development. The program had as its guiding objective "the realignment of the price and incentive system in the economy in favour of the productive, particularly the export, sectors."[17] The exchange system was to be progressively liberalized, price controls eliminated, and producer prices for cash crops increased significantly. The ERP also entailed a concerted effort to restore fiscal and monetary discipline, in part to encourage savings and investment and in part to lessen the overhang of domestic and international imbalances. To implement this, the state and its institutions were to be reorganized and, where necessary, reduced in size and function. In place of an overconcern with regulating every aspect of economic relations (something that was bound to prove ineffective under the conditions of weak state capacity prevailing in the country), the bureaucracy would, it was hoped, concentrate to a greater extent on the rehabilitation of Ghana's productive and social infrastructure.[18]

The Rawlings regime moved swiftly to adjust the exchange rate from ₵2.75 to the dollar in 1983 to ₵90 to the dollar in 1986. It also set up an auction system in September of that year, which allocated scarce foreign exchange holdings to the highest bidders. Moreover, by establishing foreign exchange bureaus in 1988, the government was able to create an entirely new structure that ensured an ongoing process of devaluations over time.[19] As a consequence, the cedi continued to adjust to market forces, falling to an official rate of ¢330 to the dollar by July 1990. Other reforms included introducing import liberalization; tightening financial accountability; reducing deficit financing; increasing producer prices for cocoa; and cutting back on the size of the public service, marketing boards, and parastatal bodies (an estimated 53,000 civil servants were let go by the end of 1989). As E. Gyimah-Boadi shows, some thirty-two state-owned enterprises (SOEs) were scheduled for privatization; in addition to this list of SOEs initially put up for sale, the government has indicated that it is prepared to accept bids on any SOE (some 185 in all), barring only the eighteen that have been declared strategic (such as Ghana Airways). Such reforms were not without their adverse implications, however, for the government also took steps to curtail expenditures by making people pay part of the cost of much-needed social services (see Chapter 6).[20]

On the whole, the IMF/World Bank response to these initiatives was highly positive. To be sure, their officials did not see all their recommendations put into effect, for the Rawlings administration softened the impact of the reforms by maintaining some price controls, allowing some moderate wage increases, and implementing devaluation by phases. Even so, the donor countries reacted favorably to the general thrust of the Rawlings reform package. A Consultative Group of Donors, long dormant regarding assistance to Ghana, reassembled in Paris in November 1983.[21] Responding in an affirmative manner to Ghana's SAP, they began a process that led to regular meetings. The result, as Matthew Martin shows in Chapter 13, has been a steadily climbing pattern of annual commitments, rising to a high of $900 million in 1989.

## ■ Ghana's Performance in Implementing Its SAP

In assessing performance it is necessary to examine whether the Ghanaian government has achieved its objectives under the reform program and what costs such an approach has entailed. Certainly, a number of economic indicators point to some significant, even if essentially short-term, achievements from structural adjustment. The SAP reversed the decline of recent years and recovered at least some of the lost ground of the last decade. Although the statistics lack precision, the trend is nonetheless encouraging: an annual growth in the GDP of 6 percent or more in the 1984–1988 period; an estimated increase in agricultural production of 3.6 percent in 1988; an estimated increase in the industrial sector of 10.3 percent in 1988; an estimated inflation rate of 31 percent in 1988; an increase in the rate of domestic savings from ¢62.5 billion in 1987 to ¢84.8 billion in 1988; decreases in budget deficits to ¢7.5 billion in 1985, ¢2 billion in 1986, and a balanced budget in 1986; and an overall balance of payments surplus of more than ¢22.5 million in 1987.[22] In addition, as Kwasi Anyemedu suggests in Chapter 11, some initial progress has been made in diversifying exports away from the long-term reliance upon cocoa. However, that the earnings from gold production and exports will equal those of cocoa by 1995, as Anyemedu suggests, has been questioned by Cord Jakobeit and other contributors to this book.

Despite the impressiveness of Ghana's performance record, it remains unclear whether the same rate of expansion could be sustained into the mid-1990s. The structural reform program began to encounter various constraining factors by the end of the ERP's second phase. First, there were signs in 1988 of a falloff in local private investment in Ghana's economy.[23] Second, and related to this, foreign investors and commercial lenders continued to hold back, wary of the country's political stability and investment opportunities. Third, there can be no guarantee that external aid and lending agencies will continue their present rate of support for Ghana. As Matthew Martin notes, the negotiating procedure and system of external finance in place at the present time is a most uncertain basis on which to build self-sustaining development. Among African states, Ghana indeed remains a favorite of the international donor community at this time, but how long can such a status last? Resources remain tight. As other African countries adopt attractive structural reform programs of their own and compete for IMF and World Bank backing, the temptation to "satisfice" by spreading some of the funds among a number of credible claimants may indeed prove great. The result of such a process could well be a general underfunding of many programs, including Ghana's.

Fourth, Ghana's recovery remains vulnerable to international commodity price changes. While the value of exports declined in 1989 from $881 million to $816 million, the cost of imports (most notably, petroleum products) rose by nearly 20 percent, to $1.108 billion.[24] The resulting trade deficits largely reflected the effects of declining world market prices on such commodities as cocoa. Thus, even though Ghana's cocoa production rose from 153,000 metric tons in 1984 to 300,000 metric tons in 1989, the net benefit of increased production was more than offset by the decline in world market prices.[25] Without the rise in cocoa exports, however, the international trade results might have proved adverse indeed.

Fifth, Ghana's heavy external indebtedness continues to act as a constraint on economic growth. In this regard, Kodwo Ewusi notes that "the ERP has not only increased the level of indebtedness but has increased debt servicing to unrealistically high levels. One major problem resulting from the ERP is the increasing dependency and vulnerability of the economy to external economic factors."[26] Certainly, Ghana's debt problems were exacerbated by the fall of cocoa and gold prices on the international market in 1988/89, which had the effect of raising the debt service to export ratio. It may be, however, that the debt service to export ratio will fall slightly in the 1990s, assuming that export earnings will continue to rise.[27]

Finally, the falloff in economic and social opportunities for substantial numbers of Ghanaians may lead over time to a backlash effect. A new assertiveness in the face of hardship may place limitations on the pursuit of further policies of austerity, devaluation, and the application of market economy formulas. Cutbacks in the civil service have contributed to the unemployment problem. Many of the people declared redundant were already living in the urban areas, and they represent a disaffected interest group capable of bringing significant pressure to bear on those in power. Jeffrey Herbst, in Chapter 9, explains the lack of current urban worker unrest despite significant income losses brought on by the implementation of the ERP in terms of such factors as chance, the undermining of traditional union leadership, government repression, delays in implementation, and the support of some workers for PNDC reform policies. Whether this quiescence on the part of the workers will endure, however, remains to be seen.

Clearly, relative declines in the quality of life for many members of the urban working class may create an environment in which a seemingly insignificant change of policy can trigger broad protest. In Captain Kojo Tsikata's words, "life is tough for the common man in Ghana."[28] The average worker's national minimum daily wage of ¢218 (as of March 1990) is barely enough to pay for such basic expenses as housing, food, electricity, and clothing. In addition, the urban worker must now pay school fees and medical expenses, costs that are not very burdensome for the relatively advantaged but that represent a definite hardship for most citizens. As Jon Kraus contends in Chapter 7, the benefits of devaluation, infrastructural support, higher cocoa and other export prices, and so forth, real as they may be as stimulants of economic activity, involve substantial sacrifices on the part of the relatively disadvantaged in terms of consumption and social opportunities. Expensive consumer goods are on display in the shops, but the average Ghanaian often lacks the disposable resources to purchase them.

The possibilities for rural discontent, as Gwendolyn Mikell shows in Chapter 5, also remain a factor in any situation marked by the kinds of inequalities evident on the Ghanaian scene. In absolute terms, the standard of life of rural dwellers remains very low compared with that of Accra residents. In 1988, for example, 47 percent of the people living in Accra had access to indoor plumbing, whereas only 1 percent of urban dwellers did; moreover, 77.8 percent of the people in Accra could expect to utilize electricity in their homes, while in the rural areas only 7.7 percent of the inhabitants had similar opportunities.[29] The structural reform program had indeed altered the rural-urban terms of trade to the advantage of the rural parts of the country; nevertheless, the country's growth under the SAP has not yet reached all groups and has not proceeded rapidly enough to erase the legacy of fifteen years of decline. As a consequence, the ordinary rural person has remained poor with respect to socially related outputs and outcomes.

In an attempt to ease the worst effects of a market-oriented approach on Ghana's population, the government created the Programme of Actions to Mitigate the Social Costs of Adjustment (PAMSCAD) in 1988. With funds from the donor countries, the PAMSCAD has undertaken a number of social projects intended to meet the basic needs of the poorest citizens—nonformal education, rudimentary health projects, feeder road construction, and training for the unemployed.[30] Because of the government's limited ability to implement these programs, and because donors have made commitments of only some $85 million to the program and have been generally slow in making their payments, progress has not been very impressive thus far. As of the end of 1989, according to World Bank sources, some twenty community-initiative projects had been completed and another 198 projects started; nevertheless, in light of the overwhelming needs of the society, this record seems an inadequate response to the problem on the part of the donor community and local officials.

Impressive as the growth statistics appear to be, then, it remains unclear whether the pace of Ghana's current recovery can be sustained under the present structural adjustment plan. The domestic and international investor communities remain wary, the external lending base remains uncertain, external indebtedness is rising, and the value of exports is declining. At home, there is an increasing problem with unemployment (especially as civil servants are struck off the public rolls); class, regional, and gender inequalities remain stubbornly in evidence; and the quality of life for the ordinary worker and farmer has improved little. The effect is to create strains on the Ghanaian state as it proceeds with its recovery program. The ERP approach clearly involves a difficult (even potentially dangerous) transition between the overextended state structures of the past and the leaner and hopefully more focused state structures of the future. A radical approach intended to unleash new energies and create new expectations, this process of reducing state responsibilities and controls necessarily entails careful fine-tuning and readjustment by those in power. Hence, to orchestrate its own retreat, while avoiding the extremes of economic hardship and social incoherence, the state must remain active and provide leadership.

In pursuing structural adjustment, then, the state as economic n is heavily constrained by a variety of forces over which it has control. This situation is further complicated by its capacity as political manager, that is, its ability to organize the interactions among various interests in the society and to regulate the political order in an authoritative and effective manner.[31] Thus, proficiency at establishing new organizing principles of economic relations must be complemented by a capacity for governance, which I would define as the development of political routines by state, societal, and international actors that buttress patterns of reciprocity and political exchange relations among them.[32] The Ghanaian state displays less skill in its domestic political relations than it does as an economic manager and international negotiator. In part, as Naomi Chazan suggests in Chapter 2, this reflects a number of factors: the pressing nature of economic reforms, external donor agency influences, the state's insulation from society and its capacity to resist interest group demands, and so forth. The results of this asymmetry in the state's economic and political management, however, have created a disequilibrium in the development process. Economic growth has not been paralleled by progress in developing responsive state structures, creating an imbalance that could prove threatening to sustained economic development over time.

The indicators of low political responsiveness are readily apparent in the latter years of PNDC rule. First, and most important, are the increasing challenges to regime legitimacy. Rawlings himself points to the problem when he attests to the disturbing growth of what he calls "the culture of silence." For one of Ghana's leading academicians, Adu Boahen, the origins of the culture of silence are not mysterious but reflect the general public's "fear" of the PNDC government and its misgivings over the heavy social costs of the ERP program. To quote Boahen:

> We have not protested or staged riots not because we *trust* the PNDC but because we *fear* the PNDC! We are afraid of being detained, liquidated or dragged before the CVC [Citizens Vetting Committee] or NIC [National Investigations Committee] or being subjected to all sorts of molestation.[33]

Indeed, Boahen had substantial grounds for being apprehensive. Among the indicators were the heavy fines and jail sentences handed out by the tribunals, especially in the early years of the regime; the killing of three judges and a retired army officer in June 1982; the cancellation in 1989, without formal explanation by the government, of the Sixth Biennial Conference of the African Bar Association; and the banning of the activities of two indigenous religious groups and of the Jehovah's Witnesses and the Church of Jesus Christ of Latter-Day Saints.[34]

But, as Kwame Ninsin and other authors in this book show, the problem of legitimacy went deeper than the issue of civil liberties. Other important dimensions included continuing manifestations of domestic and international exploitation and, related to this, corrupt practices by the dominant political and economic classes. Rawlings's personal integrity, higher commodity producer prices, and a variety of monetarist policies have led to a decline in some of the most abusive forms of corruption (on smuggling activities, see Chapter 4); but the structure of class exploitation remains as apparent as ever to many observers of the Ghana scene. Structural adjustment, argues Adebayo Adedeji, executive secretary of the UN Economic Commission for Africa (ECA), "has produced little enduring poverty alleviation and certain [of its] policies have worked against the poor."[35] Whether accurate or not, so long as members of the public regard structural reforms as dealing mainly with the challenge of production and not that of distribution and external dependence, they are not likely to view as valid those governments that impose the harsh logic of austerity and "skewed" allocations upon them.

The challenge of governance includes other features as well. For one thing, maintaining a demanding reform program such as Ghana's ERP means building an adequate coalition support base. Certainly, as Richard Jeffries and others note in this book, the Ghanaian state is somewhat insulated from society, allowing it considerable autonomy from domestic pressures. Such an aloof posture facilitates the implementation of programs that lack wide popular support, but at the cost of seeming to be unresponsive to the preferences of its citizens. For another thing, the Rawlings regime has failed thus far to produce any kind of blueprint outlining its plans for a return to civilian government. Ghanaians, says Boahen, want a return to multiparty politics, and beyond that he asks whether, in light of strong ethnic and regionalist feelings, it is not time to look again at the question of federal government.[36] So far, the government's moves toward setting out its ideas on the future political system seem tentative and improvised. In this respect, the 1988–1989 district assembly elections, where some 59 percent of the registered voters participated in selecting members for Ghana's 110 assemblies on a nonpartisan basis, can be interpreted either as part of the "legitimacy phase," to adopt Naomi Chazan's term, or as a stopgap measure that does little to ensure the flow of information from the regions to the political center. Certainly, the staggered timetable of the elections and the role of the National Commission on Democracy in organizing and supervising the campaign have raised some questions about the fairness of the process.[37] Either way, what exists so far hardly amounts to an outline of the political system to come. This means that the economic reform program remains to be complemented by an equally focused political reform program.

## ■ Conclusion

To achieve self-sustaining development, the state as a political manager must complement and reinforce the state as an economic manager. This is necessarily a complex task involving complicated trade-offs between productionist and distributional goals. The Ghanaian experience points to a limited economic recovery, no mean feat in light of the ruinous economic situation of the 1970s and early 1980s. Yet the economic benefits of a reduced state and monetarist approach are not shared equitably and do not hold out any certain vision of continued economic expansion in the years ahead. For some, the ERP program justified the regime's harsh austerity measures. Yet what is necessary may not be sufficient to ensure genuine development, and the economic recovery has certainly not been matched by a political recovery that accepts the transition from coercion to legitimate power and that establishes a responsive state.

To examine Ghana's particular trade-off between economic and political goals under its rather distinctive Structural Adjustment Program in the 1980s and 1990s, it is time now to turn to the various chapter authors. Part 2 analyzes the political and social context in which choice occurs; Part 3 focuses on various elements in the political economy of reform; and Part 4 concentrates on the process of negotiations that have taken place between Ghana and the international community. Taken together, what emerges is a complex picture of one regime's efforts to establish a strategy for recovery under conditions of turbulence.

In some respects Ghana's experience with structural adjustment seems unique: in the extent of the political and economic collapse that preceded its SAP, the commitment and unity of its government, the regime's determination to change the rural-urban terms of trade, the amount of money the international community was prepared to provide, the availability of skills, the influx of labor, and the ability of producers to respond to price incentives in the short term (see Chapter 13). The overall implication seems clear: Ghana's experience with structural adjustment is not easily transferable to the rest of Africa. At the same time, it does resemble other programs in its domestic distributional imbalances (class, regional, gender) and temporal imbalances (the sacrifices of long-term natural resources for short-term growth, notably with respect to timber exports).[38] Ruling out the alternative economic agenda of self-reliance as infeasible in Ghana and elsewhere on the continent—because of these countries' external dependence and limited support base for a strategy of radical restructuring—what seems necessary is to design structural adjustment in such a way as to reconcile political, distributional, environmental, and international objectives more effectively with productionist aims. We have yet to develop a political and economic blueprint to achieve these diverse goals in Ghana, or elsewhere in Africa.

## ■ Notes

I wish to express my appreciation to Naomi Chazan, E. Gyimah-Boadi, Caroline Hartzell, Jeffrey Herbst, Matthew Martin, and Joan M. Nelson for comments on the first draft of this chapter.

1. World Bank, *Sub-Saharan Africa: From Crisis to Sustainable Growth* (Washington, D.C.: World Bank, 1989), p. 5.
2. Ibid., p. 5.
3. Republic of Ghana, *Towards a New Dynamism*, report prepared by the government of Ghana for the Fifth Meeting of the Consultative Group for Ghana, Paris, February 28–March 1, 1989 (Accra: Government Printer, 1989), p. 4; also see Ernest Harsch, "On the Road to Recovery," *Africa Report* 34, 4 (July–August 1989), p. 22.
4. Quoted in James Brooke, "In Western Eyes, Ghana Is Regarded As African Model," *New York Times*, January 3, 1988, p. 1. Also see *The Post* (Accra), no. 23 (1989), pp. 1–3.
5. Jeffrey Herbst, "Economic Reform in Africa: The Lessons of Ghana," *UFS Field Staff Reports*, Africa/Middle East 1989–90, No. 15 (Indianapolis: Universities Field Staff International, 1990), p. 1.
6. Quoted in Donald Rothchild and E. Gyimah-Boadi, "Ghana's Economic Decline and Development Strategies," in John Ravenhill (ed.), *Africa in Economic Crisis* (New York: Columbia University Press, 1986), pp. 256–257.
7. Ibid., pp. 257–258.
8. See Robert M. Price, "Neo-Colonialism and Ghana's Economic Decline: A Critical Assessment," *Canadian Journal of African Studies* 18, 1 (1984), pp. 163–193; and James C. W. Ahiakpor, "The Success and Failure of Dependency Theory: The Experience of Ghana," International Organization 39, 3 (1985).
9. Kodwo Ewusi, *Trends in the Economy of Ghana, 1986–88* (Legon, Ghana: Institute of Statistical, Social and Economic Research, 1988), p. 9.
10. Herbst, "Economic Reform in Africa," p. 4.
11. Donald Rothchild, "The Rawlings Revolution in Ghana: Pragmatism with Populist Rhetoric," *CSIS Africa Notes*, no. 42 (May 2, 1985), pp. 1–6.
12. Herbst, "Economic Reform in Africa," p. 4.
13. Thomas M. Callaghy, "Toward State Capability and Embedded Liberalism in the Third World: Lessons for Economic Adjustment," in Joan M. Nelson (ed.), *Fragile Coalitions: The Politics of Economic Adjustment* (New Brunswick, N.J.: Transaction Books, 1989), p. 120.
14. Republic of Ghana, *National Programme for Economic Development* (Accra: Ghana Publishing Corporation, 1987), p. 3. Italics in text.
15. On parallel experiences in the region, see Donald Rothchild and E. Gyimah-Boadi, "Populism in Ghana and Burkina Faso," *Current History* 88, 538 (May 1989), pp. 221–224, 241–244.
16. Ben Ephson, "Targets Revised," *West Africa* (London), January 22–28, 1990, p. 85.
17. Republic of Ghana, *Towards a New Dynamism*, p. 2.
18. Republic of Ghana, *Revolution Brings Progress to Ghana* (Accra: Information Services Department, 1988), p. 11.
19. Herbst, "Economic Reform in Africa," p. 6.
20. For an excellent description of the deterioration at Ghana's universities, see Merrick Posnansky, "Towards Excellence in Higher Education—Ghana," an

open lecture presented at the University of Ghana, Legon, March 9, 1989, esp. pp. 1–5. Typescript copy.

21. For a study of IMF/World Bank negotiations with Ghana following the fall of Kwame Nkrumah's government in 1966, see Eboe Hutchful (ed.), *The IMF and Ghana: The Confidential Record* (London: Zed Books, 1987).

22. Data compiled from *Towards a New Dynamism*, p. 28; Ewusi, *Trends in the Economy of Ghana*; and the World Bank.

23. *West Africa*, December 25–January 7, 1989, p. 2165.

24. See Colin Legum, "Ghana: Where All Is Gold That Glitters, but Oil Costs Retard Recovery," *Third World Reports*, N.H/2 (February 21, 1990), p. 2.

25. See the interview with P. V. Obeng, chairman of the Committee of Secretaries, in *West Africa*, March 5–11, 1990, p. 359.

26. Ewusi, *Trends in the Economy of Ghana*, p. 60.

27. Letter from Matthew Martin, July 27, 1990.

28. *New African* (London), no. 269 (February 1990), p. 30.

29. Republic of Ghana, *Ghana Living Standards Survey: Preliminary Results 1988* (Accra: Statistical Service, 1988), pp. 50, 53.

30. Republic of Ghana, *Programme of Actions to Mitigate the Social Costs of Adjustment* (Accra: Government Printer, 1987).

31. On the constraints on the performance of the civil service, see E. Gyimah-Boadi and Donald Rothchild, "Ghana," in V. Subramaniam (ed.), *Public Administration in the Third World* (New York: Greenwood Press, 1990), pp. 229–257.

32. On this, see Goran Hyden, "Reciprocity and Governance in Africa," in James S. Wunsch and Dele Olowu (eds.), *The Failure of the Centralized State* (Boulder: Westview Press, 1990), ch. 11.

33. Albert Adu Boahen, "The Ghana Sphinx: Reflections on the Contemporary History of Ghana: 1972–1987" (Accra: Ghana Academy of Arts and Sciences, 1989), pp. 51–52.

34. *West Africa*, November 20–26, 1989, p. 1925.

35. Quoted in Adebayo Adedeji, "Lessons for the 1990s," *West Africa*, January 8–14, 1990, p. 14.

36. Boahen, "The Ghana Sphinx," p. 64.

37. The election process was staggered over a three-month period, from December 6, 1988, to February 27, 1989. The country's ten regions were grouped into three electoral zones and, for administrative and logistical reasons, each zone voted at a separate time. This electoral timetable did awaken some fears among observers that the results in one zone would influence those in another zone. See National Commission for Democracy, *The District Assembly Elections Report* (Summary), mimeo; and Colleen Lowe Morna, "Ghana: Election Aftermath," *New African*, no. 259 (April 1989), pp. 24–25.

38. For comparative data on structural adjustment programs, see Nelson, *Fragile Coalitions*; and Joan M. Nelson (ed.), *Economic Crisis and Policy Choice: The Politics of Adjustment in the Third World* (Princeton: Princeton University Press, 1990).

# PART 2
# THE POLITICAL AND SOCIAL ENVIRONMENT

# 2

# The Political Transformation of Ghana Under the PNDC

*Naomi Chazan*

## ■ The PNDC and Political Transformation

Ghanaian politics underwent three distinct phases during the course of the 1980s. The first—populist—phase (1982–1983) coincided with severe social and economic upheavals that, when coupled with drought and the massive influx of Ghanaians expelled from Nigeria, led Ghana to the brink of total collapse.[1] The second—adjustment—phase (1983–1987) was dominated by the adoption of a rigorous economic stabilization and rehabilitation program, which augmented state capabilities and enhanced the political space available to social institutions. The third—consolidation—phase (1987– ) has been punctuated by regime efforts (as yet only partial) to mold political institutions and by an increasing number of debates over preferred norms and mechanisms of political interaction. In the following pages, the composition, predilections, interests, decisions, and actions of political agents at each of these stages will be scrutinized in light of changes in institutional capabilities and in underlying socioeconomic structures. On this basis, some of the ramifications of these dynamics for Ghana and for comparative political processes will be discussed.

The main contention of this investigation is that the political logic guiding Ghanaian politics in the postcolonial period was dramatically revised in the course of the 1980s. The urban bias that predetermined the state-centric hegemonic propensities of successive regimes in Ghana[2] was no longer viable after the PNDC, through its initial actions, completed the process of state deflation and encouraged the dispersion of power in society. The crisis of the early 1980s was a necessary precondition for the reorganization of formal and social institutions.[3]

The Structural Adjustment Program contributed significantly to the revival of state capacities and to the consolidation of civil society. In Ghana, the resurgence of associational life and the growth in the informal economy came together with an increase in the measure of stateness in the mid-1980s,[4] suggesting that the fortification of the state apparatus is related to the crystallization of a distinct arena of societal exchange.[5] The reform in agriculture not only altered the terms of trade between rural and urban areas, but, by expanding the political definition of the people in spatial terms to encompass residents of the countryside, also provided the necessary impetus for a change in the relationship between state and social groups.[6] In the process, political and economic rationality became more closely aligned.[7] The interaction between the state and social groups in Ghana during this period has thus been a mutually transforming experience.[8]

In this context, the durability of the PNDC may be related to the ability of its leaders to constantly adapt policy in light of changing events and needs. The consistency of the regime's goals enhanced the rulers' commitment to socioeconomic and political reform, while the absence of a detailed program of action enabled the pursuit of a series of piecemeal—at times even contradictory—moves that maintained a dynamic of action and response throughout the decade of the 1980s. Stability has therefore come to be associated with the crucial leadership skills of flexibility and persistence.[9] The survival of the government has not, however, brought about a substantive change in the rules of the political game and the vehicles for effective participation, representation, and communication. Although incipient steps have been taken to reconstruct the polity from below, these have yet to be translated into new norms of political conduct or appropriate institutional mediations.[10] In these circumstances, the exercise of power follows familiar patterns of officially sanctioned repression, intolerance, and exclusion.

The challenge facing Ghanaians today is therefore different from that of yesteryear. From issues of governance and economic rehabilitation they are presently confronted with the task of creating frameworks that can give concrete expression to the changing bases of state-society relations and that can help to promote a new rhythm of political life in the country. Until the connection between official agencies and civil society is articulated in political terms, the transformation of the past decade will remain, perforce, ambiguous and incomplete.[11]

## ■ The Dynamics of Political Transformation

When the PNDC assumed power on December 31, 1981, Ghana was in the midst of a multifaceted crisis of political enfeeblement, social fragmentation, and economic decline. The retrogressive cycle launched at the beginning of independence resulted in the consistent loss of autonomy by the state, which had been penetrated by increasingly particularistic and personal interests. At the same time, state agencies had been misused by a series of weak and capricious leaders, by an overbloated bureaucracy, and by avaricious and contentious patrons.[12] Problems of state autonomy were consequently compounded by state incapacitation. Since many individuals and social groups no longer viewed the state as an important source of benefits, they devised means to avoid its extractive reach. State-society relations were in almost total disrepair, and the country was impoverished. The statist rationales developed during decolonization and institutionalized in the early independence period had the cumulative effect of undermining socioeconomic progress and promoting immeasurable turmoil and widespread misery.

☐ *The Populist Phase*

The 31st December takeover was an act of rebellion against the postindependence leadership generation. It was "an integral part of a long popular, so far frustrated historical struggle against oppressive, corrupt, autocratic and exploitative rule."[13] The underlying premise of Jerry Rawlings and the first members of the PNDC was that the civilian and military establishment that had ruled the country for close to a quarter of a decade had pursued its own interests at the expense of the bulk of the population; thus, the elimination of this group and its replacement by alternative rulers representing popular concerns could pave the way to social justice and economic growth. The thrust of the second Rawlings coup was therefore highly personalistic: who ruled was seen as the answer to the country's ills. The first phase of the PNDC was the last full-fledged attempt to employ the postcolonial political logic, this time in the name of the (mostly urban) masses previously excluded from the state nexus.[14]

The initial composition of the PNDC reflected a commitment to rebellion and reform within the reigning statist paradigm. The ruling coalition was made up of some radical intellectuals, student leaders, and a few soldiers who had maintained contact with Jerry Rawlings after Hilla Limann forced his retirement from the armed forces in November 1979. Its membership reflected the organizational links that Rawlings had established with the June Fourth Movement (JFM), the New Democratic Movement (NDM), the socialist student movement, and militant trade unionists between 1979 and 1981.[15] This constellation was not dependent on any of the key organized professional groups in the country, and its youthful complexion highlighted its renunciation of established authority. At the same time, however, it drew its backing almost exclusively from urban quarters: workers, students, and a young neo-Marxist intelligentsia.[16] In a very different way, its initial pronouncements (including calls for nationalization) reflected the state-centric bias of preceding governments.

Jerry Rawlings charted the broad agenda of the "31st December Revolution" when he defined the goals of the PNDC as the rearrangement of the foundations of Ghanaian politics through the transformation of social, economic, and political relationships. This grand reformist vision, repeated on numerous occasions, was presented as the only viable alternative to the venality of former rulers. The specific themes elaborated at this juncture highlighted the need to eradicate elite privilege, transfer power to the people by bringing the masses into the decisionmaking process, establish a new democratic order based on social equality and justice, and maintain vigilance against manifestations of imperialism and neocolonialism.[17] The PNDC, by making an ideological break with the past, thus reinterpreted the focus of political life and placed a strongly populist perspective at the center of the Ghanaian political stage.[18]

There was, however, a subtle but vital difference between the positions of the ideologues of PNDC I, who stressed the significance of the capture of the state as the first step toward revolutionary change, and the emphasis placed by Rawlings on moral rectitude, accountability, reciprocity, and ethical reform. While other leaders of the PNDC underlined the revolutionary nature of the regime, Rawlings expressed himself in missionary and prophetic terms.[19] The former employed the tools of class analysis, whereas Rawlings consistently focused on the people in relation to officialdom.[20] But since the influence of the neo-Marxist intelligentsia on the political education of Jerry Rawlings was still strong at this time, the class-based view, with all its statist presumptions, prevailed.[21]

The PNDC pursued a three-pronged policy during its first year in office. First, it launched an all-out campaign against those it defined as members of privileged groups. These included former politicians, government officials, executives in state corporations, traders, professionals, and entrepreneurs. Hastily assembled Citizens Vetting Committees, Public Tribunals, and investigative bodies hauled in purported offenders and meted out stiff sentences without due process. Specific individuals were hounded and their property was confiscated, and evidence of harassments, beatings, and even official killings mounted.[22] Second, the government created an entire network of popular institutions in an attempt to incorporate the people into the governing process. These included People's Defence Committees (PDCs) and Workers' Defence Committees (WDCs). Official backing was granted to a variety of ideological movements, including the JFM, the NDM, and the Kwame Nkrumah Revolutionary Guards. These popular frameworks were designed to coexist with, rather than displace, the formal administration, thus inducing a form of institutional dualism that made any form of coordinated decisionmaking virtually impossible.[23] And third, the PNDC attempted to translate dependency theory into policy terms by imposing a wage and price freeze, exhorting militants to help in the evacuation of cocoa, and advocating self-reliance.²⁴ These measures frightened away what few prospective investors existed and further weakened Ghana's bargaining position in the international economic community. The substance of the measures adopted by the PNDC and the violent manner in which they were carried out contributed substantially to the turmoil and upheaval associated with this period.

The first PNDC's version of the statist formula had a devastating effect on the official and social structures of power in Ghana and on the extent of their interaction. During its first eighteen months in office the Rawlings government systematically undermined already weakened state agencies. In its attempt to rid the formal apparatus of corrupt elements, the PNDC divested these institutions of almost all of their skilled personnel (by the beginning of 1983 barely one-third of Ghana's top-level professionals were still in the country).²⁵ The dualistic decisionmaking structures made policy erratic and frequently contradictory. And the absence of resources magnified the limited capabilities of formal structures. In a very real sense, the Ghanaian state lost almost all capacity to design, let alone implement, its programs.²⁶

State enfeeblement came together with the dismantling of previous instruments of social control. No corporatist bodies were established on a countrywide basis at this time. More to the point, the direct attack on the patronage network was not accompanied by the creation of alternative forms of social mediation capable of linking the rural population to government officials. To be sure, the divided elites of yesteryear, themselves responsible for a great deal of the retrogressive cycle that peaked at the beginning of the 1980s, had been excluded from state power. But in the early phase of PNDC rule, no alternative ruling group was consolidated. As a result, the state apparatus lost any ability to penetrate to the local level.²⁷

The amorphousness of the PNDC program, together with the sharp disagreements it evoked, left the government with very little palpable support in the country. Indeed, the regime itself, populist rhetoric notwithstanding, became increasingly impenetrable for most Ghanaians. Moreover, just as the regime became more autonomous, the last vestiges of state autonomy were eroded. By opening up the bureaucracy and the parastatal sector to popular participation, Rawlings and his associates not only exposed the state as an institution to a broad spectrum of demands, but they also provided some of the tools for the realization of those demands. The populist notion of the desirability of the people capturing the state and transforming it was effectively disproven as wholesale and unregulated access effectively stripped the state of any semblance of structural independence. By the beginning of 1983, the Ghanaian state had become effectively delegitimated and incapacitated.²⁸

The activities of the PNDC in its populist phase also significantly altered the shape of civil society. Since the leaders of established intermediate groups (including lecturers, lawyers, doctors, market women, key church personalities) were ridiculed and their access to official resources curtailed, and since umbrella organizations and overarching structures were almost nonexistent at this time, most people sought protection from official abuses and growing poverty in smaller, more localized frameworks.

The beginning of the 1980s witnessed a proliferation of economic, religious, and communal networks. Local groups were augmented by a second generation of mutual aid societies, trading networks, self-defense groups, women's organizations, youth movements, and village improvement societies. As spiritual, pentecostal, and charismatic movements blossomed,[29] established churches provided guidance and imposed their own codes of economic conduct on their members. Entrepreneurial, credit, banking, and barter groups were set up alongside new welfare associations.

The salience of these groups, together with the reaffirmation of communal and ascriptive links, placed renewed emphasis on reciprocal forms of exchange and norms of accountability, while acknowledging the need for watchfulness based on considerable doses of suspicion and cynicism.[30] These social associations served as vehicles for the expression of alienation from the existing political order and as breeding grounds for the construction or reinforcement of alternative value systems. On a small, but extremely disparate, scale, nonhegemonic rules of social interaction were explored.

The activities of these groups focused primarily on concrete attempts to fulfill basic needs in the face of enormous poverty. They differed qualitatively from previous kinds of informal activities in that they directly related to scarcity, to the absence of basic commodities, to the withdrawal of state services, and to very real threats to physical survival.[31]

The coping strategies honed at this juncture assumed four main forms.[32] First, some people designed spiritual and social techniques to make do with less and adopted attitudes ranging from fatalism to indifference as a means of accommodating to increased suffering. Second, many individuals (both professionals and unskilled laborers) chose to emigrate in search of employment. Nigeria and other West African countries were the most important targets of this migration, but Ghanaians also moved to Europe, the Middle East, and North America in search of work. Third, the informal sector expanded rapidly. The elaborate, and at the time also explicitly illegal, parallel market became the most important funnel for the distribution of goods. It also constituted a critical setting for petty manufacturing and small-scale agricultural production.[33] Within this increasingly organized sector, new norms and directions of interchange developed, carefully enforced by popularly backed arbiters.[34] And, finally, in some rural communities self-encapsulation techniques were explored as villagers stepped up food-gathering activities, experimented with marginal varieties of plants, engaged in additional processing of food crops, and expanded village exchange networks.[35]

The adoption of these heterogeneous survival stratagems accentuated social fragmentation. The destruction of patronage networks and the emphasis on communal and personal links reduced both the need and the feasibility of operating beyond the local level. Since coping techniques had become an absolute necessity and horizontal ties were rudimentary at best, social life took on an extremely parochial complexion.[36] The political significance of these measures rested, at this juncture, more in the rupture of old lines of social communication than in the reorganization of the social order.

The shrinkage of the formal political arena and the simultaneous enclosure of social groups reduced interactions between state and society to a minimum. Where these did occur they frequently took violent forms. Mutual detachment became the norm and both state organs and social aggregations narrowed their spheres of reference. Consequently, the scope of institutional activities diminished. The unraveling of state and societal structures during the early tenure of the PNDC was the culmination of processes that began long before Jerry Rawlings's rise to power. The policies advocated by the PNDC did, however, serve to intensify the pace of social and formal disintegration. The outcome of the combination of regime agency and longer-term trends was to deinstitutionalize the structures that had propelled the postcolonial political logic.

By the end of the first year of PNDC rule, the resource base that had supported the urban preferences of the past had also collapsed. Economic conditions were simply disastrous. Total food availability was barely 68 percent of minimal caloric requirements. Medical facilities could not offer even the most basic services. Infant mortality had risen from 80 per 1,000 to 120 per 1,000 in seven years, the roads were often impassable, the phone system didn't work, food supplies were unpredictable, and production levels were at an all-time low.[37] To further complicate matters, drought conditions had developed, and in January 1983 over a million Ghanaians expelled from Nigeria began to make their way back to a country that could not support those who had remained.[38] The question was no longer where resources were located but if they existed at all.

The survival of the government at this stage was surprising. In all probability, Rawlings succeeded in weathering the crisis partly because several coup attempts (launched first by remnants of the elite and later by left-wing opponents) were amateurish and poorly executed; partly because the opposition was even weaker than the government; and mostly because other preoccupations were so overriding and control of the state apparatus so uninviting that the locus of activities had shifted elsewhere.

In these circumstances, a power vacuum emerged at the state core. The limited amount of power that existed before the launching of the populist experiment had been reduced, and what remained was dispersed to other locations. The decay of the structures of the statist system and the social and economic recession had rendered the postcolonial logic meaningless. The extent of the crisis and the depth of the trough in Ghana were a reflection of the severity of the shredding of the fabric of social and political life in the country.[39]

## ☐ The Adjustment Phase

The disintegration of the hegemonic system and the political logic on which it depended paved the way for Ghana's gradual extrication from the postcolonial syndrome.[40] The beginnings of this process lay in the amplification of an approach to deal with the twin crises of economic production and political authority.[41] Emphasis shifted from questions of who held power to issues of how power was to be used and to what ends. During the first six months of 1983, a substantive reevaluation took place, broad revolutionary goals were injected with specific programmatic contents, and guidelines were designed for their realization.

Jerry Rawlings launched the move from rebellion to rehabilitation in a series of speeches decrying the irresponsibility of some militants and calling for the determination of priorities and the design of specific policies in the social, economic, and political spheres.[42] Rawlings repeatedly justified the new orientation of the PNDC in terms, first, of the need to adjust policies in order to fulfill the purposes of the 31st December takeover. "Certainly this is a revolutionary situation. We are engaged in a process of social transformation. Those who think that this must necessarily be accompanied by wild rhetoric and civil confusion in order to qualify for the name 'revolutionary' may, of course, have different opinions. Perhaps we can call it a common sense revolution."[43] Second, he highlighted the need to get down to the brass tacks of rebuilding the society and the economy. "Our objectives have never changed. There are those who talk about deviation and 'U-turns,' but they are the impractical theorists, the impatient ideologists who expect to attain their goals overnight, but who are unable to contribute to the practical day to day drudgery of working towards these goals."[44] And third, he continuously highlighted the shift to concrete programs in terms of moral imperatives. If probity, accountability, and reciprocity were to be attained, then it followed in his view that citizens should bear a measure of responsibility as well.[45]

Rawlings's ability to guide the transition from the populist to the adjustment phase of PNDC rule rested on a combination of leadership traits and environmental conditions. On the personal side, Rawlings himself, despite the turbulence around him, retained considerable popularity, enjoying a reputation for honesty, dedication, and commitment to justice. He also adhered closely to his self-proclaimed purpose of bringing about a societal reordering without being overly bound to any particular plan to achieve this goal or too closely tied to a specific conception of "the people." With his astute mind and pragmatic bent, he could oversee the general direction of regime policy but did not necessarily delve into specifics.[46] Politically, Rawlings at this time was not subject to serious social pressures, except for those emanating from radical political groups. He understood that the social constituency of this portion of the intelligentsia was extremely limited, and, unlike these ideologues, he had no vested interest in the statist paradigm.[47] Since Rawlings had retained his own independence while representatives of these circles were part of the ruling coalition, he did not feel obliged, given the circumstances, to continue to uphold their policies. And finally, needless to say, the chaotic situation in Ghana demanded a forceful and detailed response.

The stage was thus set for the introduction of a series of policy initiatives. These revolved around three main axes. The first, and undoubtedly the best known, was the introduction of the Economic Recovery Program, involving the acceptance of the conditionalities of the International Monetary Fund and the World Bank and the adoption of a rigorous stabilization regimen and structural adjustment plan based on market principles.[48] The second concerned the establishment of a framework for the redesign of the political structure of the country. The National Commission on Democracy was established, headed by Justice D. F. Annan, and charged with the task of formulating what the government termed a "true" democracy (as opposed to the notion of a "new" democracy propounded during the first phase of PNDC rule).[49] By relegating the political task to the drawing board, an attempt was made to highlight economic priorities at the expense of political ones.[50]

The third (and most immediate) move involved a governmental restructuring. By late 1983, all the original members of the PNDC except Rawlings had been replaced. The new PNDC consisted of the heads of the major official agencies, public corporations, and the army. With the addition of P. V. Obeng, the coordinating secretary (roughly equivalent to the prime minister), in July 1985, greater harmony was achieved between the political, military, and administrative wings of the regime.[51] The PNDC was essentially institutionalized in the process.

The network of popular organizations was also revamped. The National Defence Committee (NDC) was dismantled and the PDCs and WDCs reorganized as Committees for the Defence of the Revolution (CDRs). Members of all classes were invited to participate (although most did not actually join).[52] The National Mobilisation Programme was charged with the task of promoting local development, and its local auxiliaries (Mobisquads) were directed to assist in community welfare efforts.[53] Although the Public Tribunals were not disbanded, the centrality of the civilian courts was reaffirmed. A campaign was also launched to lure skilled Ghanaians residing abroad back to the country, and the position of chiefs was revived as a focus of social action.[54] The results of these measures were threefold: political representation was effectively foreclosed; specifically political institutions were separated from bureaucratic and judicial ones; and the witch hunt against educated groups was denounced in an effort to reestablish a technocratic core at the center.

The salience of the economic recovery program became particularly apparent during implementation. The PNDC scrupulously pursued the provisions of its own plan and in return received significant capital injections from abroad. The technical team headed by Kwesi Botchwey, secretary of finance, and Joe Abbey was protected by the government, and by 1985 economic indicators showed some improvement. The GDP had increased by 13 percent, inflation was reduced in that year to 20 percent, exports had risen by 76 percent, the transportation system was being repaired, and government expenditures were down. Significantly, goods were available in the market, food was plentiful, and though income disparities grew, the PNDC had begun to turn the economy around.[55]

Achievements in the political arena were far more ambiguous. Populist rhetoric persisted, but the CDRs hardly constituted attractive vehicles for political participation. The NCD devoted more attention to redrawing electoral districts than to elaborating a new model of democratic rule. In fact, when asked about the timetable for the return to civilian rule, Justice Annan stated that this would "be determined by the speed with which Ghanaians came to realize the meaning of democracy."[56]

There are a variety of reasons for the more systematic implementation of the economic package. First and foremost, economic concerns were more pressing, and some amelioration had to be achieved quickly. Second, international donor agencies made the continuous flow of resources contingent on progress. Since in many respects Ghana was a test case for SAPs in general, careful attention was given to monitoring the execution of specific steps. Third, while the government could control fiscal and adjustment measures, it was not in a position to carry out ambitious programs in other spheres. Fourth, as repeatedly mentioned by observers, the PNDC continued to be insulated from the demands of strong sectors, partly because of its break with postcolonial elites and partly because social groups were fragmented and dispersed.[57] Fifth, the administrative needs of economic reform, at least at the initial stage, were not necessarily compatible with new schemes for participatory politics.[58] Finally, and not coincidentally, since the future of the PNDC depended in no small measure on its capacity to pursue its economic strategy, the government exhibited a strong commitment to its successful implementation.[59]

PNDC moves, economic accomplishments notwithstanding, continued to be greeted with large doses of skepticism. The middle class urban groups, still smarting from the indignities suffered after the 1981 takeover and resentful of the influx of expatriates in the form of IMF and World Bank consultants, were not anxious to cooperate with the government. The ERP/SAP adversely affected the population in the cities and particularly antagonized the workers and the urban poor. They were joined by students and by the neo-Marxist intelligentsia (who opposed what they considered to be the ideological betrayal of Jerry Rawlings).[60] Thus, the transition to the adjustment phase of the PNDC undermined the regime's original support base but did not provide any real alternatives.[61] The main beneficiaries of the new economic measures were the rural dwellers, but their support for the government was diffuse and unorganized.

In these circumstances, the regime had to devise means to govern the country without any visible backing. A mixture of techniques was employed, all of a strongly authoritarian sort.[62] First, decisionmaking became heavily centralized, consultation ground to a halt, a series of hidden advisers was brought in, and intrigues in "the Castle" proliferated. Second, Rawlings's idiosyncratic political style dominated and was used as a substitute for the creation of institutionalized forms of political interaction. Third, the security apparatus, controlled by Rawlings's close associate and chief strategist, Kojo Tsikata, was used with abandon. Fourth, the government continued to employ violent techniques (including torture and summary executions) to suppress any sign of opposition. And finally, some rudimentary neocorporatist measures were introduced to create the illusion of a modicum of social depth. Thus, if the PNDC's policies changed in the second stage of its tenure, its practices continued to be coercive and capricious.

The disorder that marked PNDC I was replaced under PNDC II by a calmer, although hardly more equitable, political climate. Structural adjustment was accompanied by the creation of an administrative regime that did not encourage any significant movement toward political reform. A "culture of silence" had set in, one that left the government aloof from the people and the vision of popular rule perhaps even more remote than in the past.

The policies of the PNDC at this juncture nevertheless had an important impact on state and social institutions. The adoption of the SAP package contributed significantly to the restructuring of the Ghanaian state and to the redefinition of its role in society. The first visible change occurred in the size of the official apparatus. The reduction in government expenditures led to retrenchment in the civil service and to the laying off of over 12,000 employees. The implementation of privatization schemes meant that the number of parastatals was reduced and that employment in surviving corporations was restricted.[63]

The second, and perhaps most prominent, change took place in the internal organization of the state apparatus. During this time, the various institutions of government at the center were more clearly demarcated, and the spheres of influence of the political, administrative, military, and judicial branches spelled out with greater precision.[64] The foundations were thus laid for a more effective administration.[65] The internal restructuring in the state apparatus not only imposed a degree of order in the heretofore unwieldy public sector, but also augmented the capacity of state institutions.[66]

The third element of change in the state arena related to shifts in the proclaimed spheres of official activity. Areas of state intervention were specified. The state shed some of its welfare character and purposely adopted a policy of nonintervention in certain fields (such as production). In other spheres (health, education) it sought to recover costs through the imposition of user fees. Although this self-imposed constraint was partly dictated by financial considerations, the net effect was to reduce expectations by purposely narrowing the functions of the state in Ghanaian society.[67] These developments, while limiting the reach of the state in specific subject areas, actually augmented its ability to act in other spheres, thus simultaneously increasing and defining its extractive capacities.

The fourth, and final, aspect of change in the state arena concerned the reassertion of a measure of autonomy. The emphasis in the ERP on technocratic skills and the premium placed on attracting qualified human resources led to the beginning of the creation of a new and fairly cohesive state elite. The size of this group was small (as most Ghanaian professionals stayed away from the country or pursued careers outside the formal sector), and its bureaucratic code was still amorphous. But since access to these state administrators was blocked, they did succeed in maintaining a greater degree of independence than many of their predecessors.

Developments at the state level between 1983 and 1987 had important repercussions for social relations. In Ghana, as elsewhere, the IMF package implicitly favored the creation of institutions independent of state control. And precisely because formal structures were initially enfeebled, and, when reorganized, their penetrative capacities were curtailed, more room was available for a variety of activities at the societal level.

One major social consequence of the Structural Adjustment Program and the changes it entailed was to further expand the network of voluntary and local associations. As occupational, service, community, and religious organizations grew substantially, new interest groups emerged (human rights associations, for one). The diversification of the associational landscape and its gradual institutionalization was augmented by the flow of resources from abroad.[68] Within these frameworks specific notions of authority, community, distributive justice, and conflict resolution were defined. Moreover, participatory values were inculcated and experience gained on a small scale. Since many of the new groups were created at the intermediate level, the associational boom also possessed the potential of aggregating local interests.[69] In political terms, the increased pace of associational growth served to pluralize institutional life in the country.[70]

Another effect of the new policy orientation in the societal sphere was evident in the burgeoning informal sector.[71] Economic activities in this realm included the development of microindustries and small manufacturing cooperatives, the revival of local markets, shifts in patterns of agricultural production, and the creation of new distribution networks. By the mid-1980s, it was estimated that the informal sector accounted for fully 85 percent of employment in the country.[72] Social service activities began to develop around the second economy. Some of the new associations entered the housing field, and others dealt with health, education, sanitation, and infrastructure development. Despite the social inequalities that emerged in the informal sector, in many respects the vibrancy of activities in the parallel market was in itself an act of political assertion.[73]

The combination of associational growth and informal economic activity also produced a different breed of elites. These entrepreneurs were, unlike many of their predecessors, neither linked to the state nor dependent on its resources. Alternative avenues of accumulation and social stratification developed, leading to the emergence of a new group of upwardly mobile Ghanaians who flourished in comparison with salaried employees.[74] The elites that coalesced at the middle level of social organization shared many interests and possessed some of the means for the realization of these interests. These elites began to serve as an important political counterweight to state-based strata, thereby suggesting new bargaining possibilities absent in clientelistic frameworks.

The variety evident in the informal sector pointed to an important restructuring of social life. While specific groups carved out their own spheres of autonomous action and began to amass resources and capital independently, they also encouraged the development of wider communication networks based on lateral transactions.[75] The emergence of organizational forms of pluralism thus led to a greater degree of societal interlocking at the grassroots as well as intermediate level. With straddling widespread, vertical and horizontal exchanges intersected at the middle level of social organization in a symbiotic relationship reflecting the demarcation of new political spaces that implied neither state domination nor local subordination.[76]

Interactions between the redrawn social order and state institutions during the second phase of PNDC rule were sparse, as few mechanisms for interchange existed and mutual distrust prevailed. The expansion of the associational realm was not, however, necessarily disruptive to the policies or concerns of state agencies. The activities of civil society relieved Ghanaian officials of some of their obligations to divert resources for daily consumption, thereby releasing state-controlled funds for other projects.

Thus, if the ERP encouraged the proliferation of social organizations, associational activity also contributed to the implementation of the government's economic program. In very important respects, the strengthening of civil society had the effect of fortifying both the capacity and the autonomy of the state. Despite the clear separation between state and civil society, developments in each of these realms were in many senses mutually reinforcing.

The trends evident in the institutional sphere were buttressed by the most notable outcome of the Structural Adjustment Program: the reversal of the terms of trade between the rural and urban areas. Hikes in producer prices and infrastructural rehabilitation meant that the lot of many rural communities improved, while residents of the cities carried the burden of the reform program.[77] Statistics showed that the exodus from the rural areas had been halted and that people were returning to the countryside.[78] The socioeconomic processes that had supported the urban bias of the past had been replaced by a more dispersed pattern of resource allocation. The stage was thus set for the elaboration of a political logic based on spatial rather than zero-sum concepts of power.

By the close of the first phase of the ERP, economic conditions in the country had clearly improved, but the external debt had grown and income disparities had become more pronounced. "More poor and vulnerable people have been made less poor and/or vulnerable since 1983 than the reverse. But that defence is not good enough. The absence of integrating human imbalance stabilization into the programme's core strategy was—and to a large extent remains—a basic flaw."[79] Urban discontent was expressed in a series of strikes that commenced in 1986. The PNDC found it difficult to explain that without its economic liberalization scheme the situation would be considerably worse.[80] As the SAP entered a new phase, the government could no longer avoid coming to terms with some of the social and political by-products of its economic reform.

☐ *The Consolidation Phase*

The dilemmas facing Ghanaians in 1987 were different from those they had confronted five years earlier. Economic liberalization, far from increasing popular involvement in government, actually exacerbated social cleavages and delayed political reform. The problem of regime legitimacy loomed large as the decade drew to a close.

The PNDC, confronted with rising disaffection in urban quarters and with growing evidence of social inequalities, faced the challenge of devising viable means to manage social relations more effectively. Jerry Rawlings decided once again to reevaluate the PNDC's course in light of these changing realities. In his ongoing search for a way to change popular expectations of government and link development opportunities to greater responsibility, he attempted to capitalize on rural support (and deflect attention from growing tensions in the cities) by rearranging priorities and placing political and social concerns on a par with economic ones. The third phase of the PNDC has entailed a "political structural adjustment."[81]

The decision to launch a program of political reform was in all probability prompted by a growing awareness that the government's stability could not be guaranteed unless some changes were made on the political front. But it was also patently evident that further economic progress depended on "getting politics right."[82] In this, as in previous policy alterations, Rawlings displayed a combination of astuteness and self-preservation on the one hand and consistency in the pursuit of his transforming mission on the other. In the process, his role on the Ghanaian political scene changed from that of remote manager to one of uncertain—and all too human—head of state.

The reordering of the foci of PNDC efforts was articulated in two major policy instruments promulgated on July 1, 1987. The first, the National Programme for Economic Development, set out targets for economic growth in the post-ERP era. Besides detailing production goals, the new plan underlined the need to deal with the social facets of structural adjustment. It suggested that "sustained work at both economic and political levels will be required" in order to attain social and general well-being.[83] The revived emphasis on issues of social equity was further expounded in the adoption of the Programme of Actions to Mitigate the Social Costs of Adjustment, backed by specially earmarked funds from foreign sources.

The second document enunciated the PNDC's decision to begin political reform at the local level. The "Blue Book" on local government authority spelled out the limitations of the period of "true" democracy and called for a new phase of "real" democracy commencing with elections for District Assemblies (DAs).[84] The DAs were presented as "the bodies exercising state power as the people's local government." The declared purpose of the proposed elections was to "democratize state power and advance participatory democracy and collective decision-making at the grassroots," and they were heralded as "an important step in the PNDC's programme of evolving national political authority through democratic processes."[85] The plan delineated means for ongoing participation at the local level; included specific provisions for monitoring, recalling, and rejuvenating leadership; and expanded the role of local government in development efforts. Particular attention was paid to designing procedures for consultation and interaction between elected officials and their constituencies.[86]

The plans initiated in mid-1987 not only constituted another example of the PNDC's preference for piecemeal policy adjustments, but, like previous shifts, also contained important substantive dimensions. The definition of "the people," perceived in the populist phase as referring to the dispossessed and in the adjustment phase as encompassing the poor, was reformulated to give prominence to residents of the countryside at the expense of those living in the cities. The stress placed on creating channels of participation first at the local level was hardly unreasonable given the shift in the location of resources that had taken place in the preceding period and the need to defuse growing criticism. The bottom-up approach to political reform reflected changing conceptions and processes, while simultaneously serving the regime's need to secure its hold on power through the creation of a visible and cohesive support base.

Preparations for the local elections, which included a prolonged voter registration and district demarcation exercise, took more than eighteen months. During this period, many of the adverse effects of structural adjustment became more salient (the growing debt burden, gross discrepancies in income, the perpetuation of pockets of abject poverty, and rising prices).[87] Evidence of official malpractices mounted. And although external allocations did increase, foreign government credits did not reach the levels expected by economic planners. Throughout this period, the PNDC continued to employ repressive measures, violate human rights, silence its opponents, and curtail basic civic freedoms. The elections were hardly conducted in a democratic atmosphere.

In December 1988, the first set of elections took place in the Ashanti, Western, Eastern, and Central regions (designated as zone 1 of three electoral zones). The last round of balloting was completed on February 23, 1989. The final results revealed that a record number of candidates stood for office in the 110 districts (12,842), including more women and previously underrepresented occupational groups.[88] Fewer seats were uncontested than anticipated. And with all the reservations with which the district assembly proposal was greeted initially, the elections did arouse a measure of enthusiasm, at least in the rural areas.

Electoral patterns in the district assembly ballot revealed key features of state-society relations at the end of the decade. In the first place, participation rates were extraordinarily high (59.1 percent).[89] Although the government did everything possible to bring out the vote, the response was still well above recent ballots. If in the 1970s low turnouts (35.25 percent in the parliamentary elections of 1979 and 18.4 percent in the district council elections of 1978) were correlated with a lack of interest in events at the national level and with diminishing state legitimacy,[90] then the 1988–1989 ballot was indicative of a revised trend in some quarters toward engagement in formal politics. The district assembly elections showed that for many citizens the Ghanaian state had been recognized as an acceptable (albeit not exclusive) arena of political interaction.

Second, for the first time in postcolonial Ghanaian history, a regime derived its support primarily from rural constituencies. Participation rates were higher in the largely rural Upper East (62 percent), Upper West (67.4 percent), Northern (60.6 percent), Ashanti (60.8 percent), Brong Afhafo (60.2 percent), and Eastern (60.8 percent) regions than in the more urbanized Western (55.3 percent) and Greater Accra (44.3 percent) regions. Indeed, voter participation in the large cities was much below national and regional averages: Kumasi attracted only a 45 percent turnout and Legon a dismal 11 percent. This distribution was indicative of the relative strength of the PNDC in the countryside and its waning credibility in the cities. The government could justly lay claim to having gone far beyond previous regimes in incorporating the previously excluded rural voters into the state orbit.[91] It could not, however, overcome urban disaffection via the local polls.

Finally, new arenas of political competition were opened up at the district level, signaling a move away from state-centric patterns of political contestation. Elected councilors (including older farmers, traders, service workers, and youth) mingled with appointed representatives (consisting mostly of a mixture of chiefs, retired civil servants, entrepreneurs, professionals, and CDR activists) in the district assemblies. Initial assessments indicate that DAs have become the center of a great deal of political, if not administrative, activity.[92]

The district assembly elections undoubtedly contributed to stabilizing PNDC rule and granted the Rawlings government much-needed breathing space.[93] During the grace period in the aftermath of the elections, the regime has attempted to consolidate a political machine in the rural areas, composed of rural activists concentrated in the DAs and regime loyalists in local CDR and Mobisquad branches. It has also continued its effort to gain the cooperation of old elites through a process of cooptation. More significantly, Rawlings and his advisers have been given some time to consider how to proceed with the next stages of the democratization process begun at the grassroots level without forfeiting the gains achieved in the rural areas.

The PNDC has had to contend, however, with the insistent pressures of organized social groups at the intermediate level. Many associations rejected the regime's local government reforms (which in all probability were designed, inter alia, to bypass them), claiming that these constituted a fragmented response to the much broader need for democratization, which their spokespersons implied must involve nationwide elections.[94] In attempting to quell these voices, Rawlings not only has exposed himself to charges of power monopolization, but has also fostered a growing contradiction between the PNDC's policy of political liberalization at the local level and its closure of opportunities for public involvement nationally.

Rawlings has shown signs of being keenly aware of the political price of ignoring the deeply entrenched norms of public scrutiny and demands for official probity that had propelled him to power. On the tenth anniversary of the June 4 uprising, speaking again in normative phraseology, he asked Ghanaians to make accountability an "irrevocable, non-negotiable policy of Ghana."[95] But slogans such as "Freedom, Justice and Accountability for a Greater Tomorrow" cannot erase the growing impatience with populist and local substitutes for meaningful participation.

The post-ERP structure of power distribution has generated persistent calls for a viable formula for power sharing. People are "waiting for populist spectacles to be replaced with the structures and substance of democracy."[96] In stark contrast to the tenor of similar demands in the past, the thrust of social concerns appears to be not control of the state but the removal of official restrictions and the molding of frameworks that can safeguard social spaces and permit adequate representation. The government has yet to design regular mechanisms of interaction or formulate mutually acceptable rules of the political game.

The current consolidation phase in Ghanaian politics has been accompanied by the augmentation of the penetrative capacities of the state. But it has also magnified the problems of legitimacy and, especially, authority that induced the transition to PNDC III. Rawlings has been unable to translate his proclaimed concern for political rectitude into a detailed concept of democratic government for the country. He has also been reluctant to reveal how the local democratization process is to be pursued at all levels of social exchange. Politically, at the turn of the decade Ghana was faced with more questions than answers. The preservation of the PNDC had come to depend on its capacity to translate regime consolidation into legitimation.

At this juncture, a new political architecture is called for, one that respects autonomous spaces and takes into consideration the pluralism that has emerged on the Ghanaian scene during the course of the 1980s. The political dynamic of regime reformulation is an integral part of economic rehabilitation and social reconstruction. Until a binding formula is devised to regulate political conduct and adequate arrangements are designed for political communication, the shifts in socioeconomic processes and in power structures at the state and societal levels will remain uninstitutionalized. The economic recovery of Ghana in these circumstances is partial, and the political transformation of the country under the aegis of the PNDC incomplete.

■ **Political Change and Political Transformation: Some Implications**

The foundations of Ghanaian politics were altered in the 1980s under PNDC rule. Periodic changes in regime orientations mirrored more elemental processes of resource redistribution and institutional remolding in the arenas of the state and civil society. The disaggregation of power in the early part of the decade paved the way for its reaggregation in redefined social and political spaces. Successive adjustments in regime policy outlooks in response to immediate challenges established a momentum of change with broad social and political ramifications. The stability of a change-oriented leadership throughout the decade, with all its frailties, provided a necessary framework for maintaining a rhythm of innovation. By the beginning of the 1990s, however, there was too great a gap between the authoritarian practices of the government and the pluralist distribution of power in society. This situation raised a new, and possibly insurmountable, dilemma for Jerry Rawlings and the PNDC. The issue was how to pursue the process of political reform by creating political institutions endowed with new rules of conduct without relinquishing power. This task necessitates a flexibility far beyond that required in the past.

The political challenge confronting Ghana today is daunting. Three possible immediate courses of action exist. First, Jerry Rawlings may decide to pursue the democratization process to its logical conclusion, following up the district assembly elections with a comprehensive program for civilianization. Second, under the present circumstances, he may opt to retreat from the path of economic liberalization, abandon the structural adjustment program, and reinstate hegemonic principles as a means of appearing to show regime responsiveness to popular concerns. Or third, Rawlings and the other leaders of the PNDC may, as they have three times in the past, devise another (as yet unclear) ingenious scheme involving a further reshuffling of priorities and a specific program of action. Whatever direction policy takes in the coming years, it is evident that the PNDC (or its successors) cannot avoid coming to terms with the intricacies of political reconstruction indefinitely.

The dynamics of political transformation in the PNDC's Ghana have several important analytical and comparative ramifications. The process of political change has involved the constant interaction of long-term social and economic processes with changing institutional capabilities and short-term reactions to specific problems. On the level of political agency, recent events in Ghana have accentuated the contribution of leadership vision, programmatic pragmatism, and determination in the formulation and implementation of policy. In this connection, the Ghanaian experience demonstrates that economic liberalization may induce substantial changes in the structure of the state and civil society, but these do not necessarily lead to shifts in the conduct or mechanisms of political relations. Thus, while the substance of plans continues to be central, in conditions of flux the capacity to deal with the unintended consequences of policy designs is equally vital.

Processes of state empowerment and the evolution of civil society occurred in tandem in Ghana. This pattern raises the possibility that the precise contours of contemporary states cannot be adequately determined until the various parameters of civil society are identified and their institutional, material, and symbolic dimensions explored more carefully. This requires a closer look at the loci of power in society. The Ghanaian experiment of the 1980s highlights the intimate connection between institutional characteristics and the distribution of resources. During the 1980s, the accumulation of capital both formally and informally redirected socioeconomic interests away from monolithic dependence on the state and the capital city, thereby undermining the postcolonial logic that had dominated politics in the first three decades of independence.

These dynamics refocused attention on the task of regime reordering: on the construction of political (as opposed to administrative or social) institutions within which different norms of conduct could develop over time. The Ghanaian case does not yet provide adequate answers to how effective regime engineering takes place, although it does suggest that a constructive rhythm requires a renewed emphasis not only on the augmentation of institutional capacities and the reallocation of power, but also on the details of political mechanics.

Ghana, like many other countries, is in the midst of a comprehensive social, economic, and political reevaluation. Its recent experiences, while hardly as dramatic as those taking place in Europe and portions of Asia and Central and South America, are nevertheless no less significant or instructive. In all probability, the lessons gleaned from the close analysis of recent developments in Ghana can yield important insights into similar processes occurring elsewhere. But in order for these dynamics to be fully grasped, it is necessary to further hone the conceptual and theoretical implements used to illuminate political processes and to uncover political trends. This chapter has attempted to make a small contribution in this direction by merging the analysis of structures, policy, and processes in a dynamic framework designed to explore the political transformation of Ghana in the 1980s.

## ■ Notes

My thanks to Donald Rothchild for his careful comments on the initial draft of this paper, and to the participants of the International Conference on the Political Economy of Ghana for their thoughtful suggestions. The Harry S. Truman Research Institute of the Hebrew University of Jerusalem provided the facilities and support that enabled the preparation of this paper.

1. Richard Hodder-Williams, *An Introduction to the Politics of Tropical Africa* (London: George Allen and Unwin, 1984), p. 233, claims that by 1982 the Ghanaian state had essentially disintegrated.

2. Richard Rathbone, "Ghana," in John Dunn (ed.), *West African States: Failure and Promise* (London: Cambridge University Press, 1978), pp. 31–32.

3. This is a critical part of the argument in Joel Migdal, *Strong Societies and Weak States: State-Society Relations and State Capabilities in the Third World* (Princeton: Princeton University Press, 1988), esp. pp. 249–271.

4. On the notion of stateness see Otwin Marenin, "The Managerial State in Africa: A Conflict Coalition Perspective," in Zaki Ergas (ed.), *The African State in Transition* (London: Macmillan, 1987), p. 61.

5. See Vivienne Shue, "State Power and Social Organization in China: From Revolution to Reform," paper presented at the workshop "State Power and Social Forces: Domination and Transformation in the Third World," Austin, February 1990, p. 3. This analysis differs from that of Robert Fatton, Jr., "The State of African Studies and Studies of the African State: The Theoretical Softness of the 'Soft State,'" *Journal of Asian and African Studies* 24, 3–4 (1989), pp. 170–187.

6. Michael Ford and Frank Holmquist, "Crisis and Reform," in Naomi Chazan and Timothy M. Shaw (eds.), *Coping with Africa's Food Crisis* (Boulder: Lynne Rienner Publishers, 1988), p. 229, correctly anticipated these developments.

7. On this point see John Ravenhill, "The Elusiveness of Development," in John Ravenhill (ed.), *Africa in Economic Crisis* (New York: Columbia University Press, 1986), p. 13.

8. Joel Migdal, "The State in Society: An Approach to Struggles for Domination," paper presented at the workshop "State Power and Social Forces: Domination and Transformation in the Third World," Seattle, December 1989, p. 4.

9. Migdal, *Strong Societies and Weak States*, p. 275.

10. Jean-François Bayart, "Civil Society in Africa," in Patrick Chabal (ed.), *Political Domination in Africa: Reflections on the Limits of Power* (London: Cambridge University Press, 1986), pp. 109–125. For a more detailed analysis see Jean-François Bayart, *L'Etat en Afrique: La Politique du Ventre* (Paris: Fayard, 1989), esp. pp. 19–31.

11. Michael Bratton, "Peasant-State Relations in Post-Colonial Africa: Engagement or Disengagement?" paper presented at the workshop "State Power and Social Forces: Domination and Transformation in the Third World," Seattle, December 1989), p. 35, suggests that little transformation has taken place. During the past decade, however, evidence of power redistribution suggests that a new foundation for political reordering may have been created, although scarcely institutionalized, in some parts of sub-Saharan Africa.

12. Douglas Rimmer, "Ghana's Economic Decline," *Africa Insight* 18, 3 (1988), pp. 119–123, suggests that governments and leaders were directly responsible for the economic collapse of the country at this juncture. This point is highlighted in numerous works. The best statement of the paradox of patronage is an unpublished piece by Chris Allen, "Staying Put: Handy Hints for Heads of State," paper presented at the symposium "Authority and Legitimacy in Africa," University of Stirling, May 1986.

13. Maxwell Owusu, "Rebellion, Revolution and Tradition: Reinterpreting Coups in Ghana," *Comparative Studies in Society and History* 31, 2 (1989), p. 383. Also see his "Customs and Coups in Africa: Toward a Juridical Interpretation of Civil Order and Disorder in Ghana," *Journal of Modern African Studies* 23, 4 (1985), esp. p. 3.

14. The limited revolutionary potential of this approach is discussed in Martin Kilson, "Anatomy of African Class Consciousness: Agrarian Populism in Ghana from 1915 to the 1940s and Beyond," in I. L. Markovitz (ed.), *Studies in*

*Power and Class in Africa* (London: Oxford University Press, 1987), pp. 50–66.

15. Quite clearly, this constellation diverged drastically from the composition of all military or civilian ruling alliances in the past. The unpredictability of military leadership in Ghana is highlighted in Dennis Austin, "The Ghana Armed Forces and Ghanaian Society," *Third World Quarterly* 7, 1 (1985), pp. 97–111.

16. Richard Jeffries, "Ghana: Jerry Rawlings ou un Populisme à Deux Coups," *Politique Africaine* 2, 8 (1982), esp. pp. 16–17.

17. See Deborah Pellow and Naomi Chazan, *Ghana: Coping with Uncertainty* (Boulder: Westview Press, 1986), pp. 78–79.

18. See Edmond Jouvé, "L'Idéologies des Armées Populistes en Afrique," *Revue Internationale de Stratégie* 32 (1987), esp. p. 35.

19. For one example: "Ghana may not be that rich but she is the political light of Africa." Jerry John Rawlings, *A Revolutionary Journey: Selected Speeches of Flt.-Lt. Jerry John Rawlings*, vol. I (Accra: Ghana Publishing Corporation, n.d.), p. 1.

20. Eme Ndu, "Ghana: Transition to Socialism?" *Labour, Capital and Society* 21, 1 (1988), pp. 40–43. This difference has also been noted by Emmanuel Hansen, "The State and Popular Struggles in Ghana, 1982–1986," in Peter Anayang' Nyong'o (ed.), *Popular Struggles for Democracy in Africa* (London: Zed Press, 1987), pp. 170–208.

21. Some of this ambiguity is articulated in the essays included in Kwame Ninsin and F. K. Drah (eds.), *The Search for Democracy in Ghana* (Accra: Assempa Publishers, 1987).

22. These actions have been documented in great detail. For one example see E. Gyimah-Boadi and Donald Rothchild, "Rawlings, Populism and the Civil Liberties Tradition in Ghana," *Issue* 12, 3–4 (1982), pp. 64–69.

23. The most detailed account of these institutions may be found in Donald I. Ray, *Ghana: Politics, Economics and Society* (Boulder: Lynne Rienner Publishers; London: Frances Pinter, 1986). Also see Adotey Bing, "Popular Participation Versus People's Power: Notes on Politics and Power Struggles in Ghana," *Review of African Political Economy* 31 (1984), pp. 91–104, and Zaya Yeebo, "Ghana: Defence Committees and the Class Struggle," *Review of African Political Economy* 32 (1985), pp. 64–72.

24. See James C. W. Ahiakpor, "The Success and Failure of Dependency Theory: The Experience of Ghana," *International Organization* 39, 3 (1985), pp. 535–552.

25. See Emil Rado, "Notes Towards a Political Economy of Ghana Today," *African Affairs* 85, 341 (1986), p. 563. Kwesi Jonah of the University of Ghana in Legon confirms these findings in the first draft of his Ph.D. dissertation, "The Politics of the Brain-drain in Ghana" (Jerusalem: Hebrew University, 1990).

26. The importance of state capacities in maintaining a developmental cycle is stressed, for Côte d'Ivoire, by Richard Crook, "Patrimonialism, Administrative Effectiveness and Economic Development in Côte d'Ivoire," *African Affairs* 88, 351 (1989), pp. 205–228.

27. Robert Fatton, Jr., "Bringing the Ruling Class Back In: Class, State and Hegemony in Africa," *Comparative Politics* 20, 3 (1988), p. 254, sees this as part of a general phenomenon of incomplete hegemonic control by the African ruling classes.

28. These features of stateness are analyzed masterfully in Joshua Forrest,

"The Quest for State 'Hardness' in Africa," *Comparative Politics* 22, 4 (1988), pp. 423-442.

29. Kwesi Jonah, "Crisis and Response in Ghana" (Kingston, Jamaica: University of the West Indies, Institute of Social and Economic Research, April 1989), p. 34.

30. Baffour Agyeman-Duah, "Ghana, 1982-1986: The Politics of the P.N.D.C.," *Journal of Modern African Studies* 25, 4 (1987), p. 620.

31. See an alternative interpretation by Jeffrey Herbst, "The Exit Option and the Politics of Protest in Africa," draft ms., 1988, pp. 15-16. Herbst's analysis of the limitations of the exit option may be correct for the mid-1980s, but was not an accurate reflection of activities in the early part of the decade.

32. These strategies have been discussed at length in Victor Azarya and Naomi Chazan, "Disengagement from the State in Africa: Reflections on the Experience of Ghana and Guinea," *Comparative Studies in Society and History* 19, 1 (1987), pp. 106-131. This summary is necessarily brief to avoid undue repetition.

33. See Cyril Kofie Daddieh, "Economic Development and the Informal Sector in Ghana Reconsidered: Notes Towards a Reconceptualization" (Harvard University, Africa Research Program, April 1987).

34. This system is described in depth by Gracia Clark, "Price Control of Local Foodstuffs in Kumasi, Ghana," in Gracia Clark (ed.), *Traders Versus the State: Anthropological Approaches to Unofficial Economies* (Boulder: Westview Press, 1988), pp. 57-58.

35. George J. S. Dei, "Coping with the Effects of the 1982-83 Drought in Ghana: The View from the Village," *Africa Development* 13, 1 (1988), pp. 107-122. Also see Merrick Posnansky, "Ghana: Hardships of a Village," *West Africa* (October 29, 1984), p. 2161.

36. This point is made superbly for other parts of Africa in René Lemarchand, "The State, the Parallel Economy and the Changing Structure of Patronage Systems," in Donald Rothchild and Naomi Chazan (eds.), *The Precarious Balance: State and Society in Africa* (Boulder: Westview Press, 1988), pp. 149-170.

37. UNICEF, *Ghana: Adjustment Policies and Programmes to Protect Children and Other Vulnerable Groups* (Accra: UNICEF Office, n.d), provides an excellent capsule summary of the situation. For an analysis see Donald Rothchild and E. Gyimah-Boadi, "Ghana's Economic Decline and Development Strategies," in Ravenhill, *Africa in Economic Crisis*, pp. 254-285, and Jon Kraus, "The Political Economy of Food in Ghana," in Naomi Chazan and Timothy M. Shaw (eds.), *Coping with Africa's Food Crisis* (Boulder: Lynne Rienner Publishers, 1988), pp. 75-118.

38. See Roger Gravil, "The Nigerian Aliens Expulsion Order of 1983," *African Affairs* 84, 337 (1985), pp. 523-559, and Lynne Brydon, "Ghanaian Responses to the Nigerian Expulsion of 1983," *African Affairs* 84, 337 (1985), pp. 561-578.

39. This terminology is derived from Thomas M. Callaghy, "Lost Between State and Market: The Politics of Economic Adjustment in Ghana, Zambia and Nigeria," in Joan M. Nelson (ed.), *The Politics of Economic Adjustment in Developing Nations* (Princeton: Princeton University Press, 1990). All references to this work are from the original manuscript.

40. This point is made emphatically by Ford and Holmquist, "Crisis and Reform," pp. 231-232.

41. Michael Bratton gives a very compelling summary of the problematics

in "Beyond the State: Civil Society and Associational Life in Africa," *World Politics* 41, 3 (1989), pp. 407–410.

42. The groundwork was laid in a major speech by Jerry Rawlings, "Discipline and Productivity: Radio and Television Broadcast, Sunday, August 28, 1983" (Accra: Government Printer, 1983).

43. "Interview with Jerry Rawlings," *New African* 220 (1986), p. 61. This is the position taken in several analyses of this period as well. See Don Robotham, "The Ghana Problem," *Labour, Capital and Society* 21, 1 (1988), pp. 12–35.

44. "Interview with Jerry Rawlings," *Africa* 175 (1986), p. 17. Rawlings was referring to suggestions that the regime had begun to execute a reversal of policy objectives. For an analysis see Donald Rothchild and E. Gyimah-Boadi, "Populism in Ghana and Burkina Faso," *Current History* 88, 538 (1989), pp. 221–224, 241–244.

45. Margaret Novicki, "Interview with Rawlings," *Africa Report* 29, 2 (1984), p. 4.

46. Although much has been written in the popular press on Rawlings, no serious work has been carried out on his leadership style. Many studies of Ghana in the 1980s simply ignore the personal factor entirely, in stark contrast to analyses of Ghanaian politics in the 1970s, such as Mike Oquaye, *Politics in Ghana, 1972–1979* (Accra: Tornado Publications, 1980).

47. In many respects Rawlings claimed that his radical advisers had only themselves to blame for forcing a policy shift, since their moves had led directly to the crisis. See Novicki, "Interview with Rawlings," 1984, pp. 4–8. This accusation has aroused numerous reactions. See the debate between Kwame Ninsin and James Ahiakpor. Kwame A. Ninsin, "Ghanaian Politics After 1981: Revolution or Evolution?" *Canadian Journal of African Studies* 21, 1 (1987), pp. 17–31; James C. W. Ahiakpor, "Recognizing Left from Right in Ghana," *Canadian Journal of African Studies* 22, 1 (1988), pp. 132–136; and Kwame A. Ninsin, "Recognizing Left from Right in Ghanaian Politics: A Reply to Ahiakpor," *Canadian Journal of African Studies* 22, 1 (1988), pp. 137–139.

48. Since many of the other chapters in this book deal with the specifics of the Structural Adjustment Program, I will not go into an in-depth analysis of its provisions. For the basic documents see: Republic of Ghana, *Economic Recovery Programme, 1984–1986* (Accra: Government Printer, 1983); *Summary of the PNDC's Budget Statement and Economic Policy for 1983* (Accra: Government Printer, 1983); and periodic annual reviews of the progress of the plan in 1984, 1985, and 1986.

49. Republic of Ghana, "The Search for True Democracy in Ghana" (Accra: Information Services Department, n.d.).

50. For specifics see Naomi Chazan, "Planning Democracy in Africa: A Comparative Perspective on Nigeria and Ghana," *Policy Sciences* 22 (1989), pp. 325–327.

51. The Economist Intelligence Unit, *Country Profile: Ghana* (London: The Economist, 1987), p. 5.

52. Committee for the Defence of the Revolution, *Guidelines* (Accra: Government Printer, 1986).

53. The activities of the Mobisquads are discussed in Gwendolyn Mikell, "The State, Local Resources and Political Participation in Ghana," paper presented at the Thirty-second Annual Meeting of the African Studies Association, Atlanta, November 1989.

54. Ninsin, "Ghanaian Politics After 1981," bemoans this trend. For a case study of the role of chiefs in the crisis, see Donald I. Ray, "Evaluation of

Traditional Rulers as a Policy Instrument for Managing the Food Crisis: The Case of Northern Ghana," *Geneva-Africa* 25, 1 (1987), pp. 7–24.

55. World Bank, *Ghana: Towards Structural Adjustment* (Washington, D.C.: World Bank, 1986). Inflation rates fluctuated substantially during the first phase of the ERP, reaching 31 percent in 1988.

56. *West Africa* (October 27, 1986), p. 2255, as quoted in Agyeman-Duah, "Ghana, 1982–1986," p. 622.

57. Henry Bienen has shown that subsidy cuts have not created undue turmoil. See Henry S. Bienen and Mark Gersovitz, "Consumer Subsidy Cuts, Violence and Political Stability," *Comparative Politics* 19, 1 (1986), pp. 25–44. Also see Henry Bienen, "Populist Military Regimes in West Africa," *Armed Forces and Society* 11 (1985), pp. 357–377.

58. This point is made superbly by Joan M. Nelson, "The Politics of Long-Haul Economic Reform," in Joan M. Nelson et al., *Fragile Coalitions: The Politics of Economic Adjustment* (New Brunswick: Transaction Books, 1989), pp. 3–26.

59. This point is stressed by IMF and World Bank sources. See Sheetal K. Chand and Reinold van Til, "Toward Successful Stabilization and Recovery," *Finance and Development* 25, 1 (1988), p. 35: "In Ghana the Government's strong political will was instrumental both in shaping the adjustment strategy and in successfully implementing it."

60. For one example see Chris B. Atim and Ahmed S. Gariba, "Ghana's Revolution or Counter-Revolution?" *Journal of African Marxism* 10 (1987), pp. 90–105.

61. E. Gyimah-Boadi, "Economic Recovery and Politics in the PNDC's Ghana," paper delivered at an Inter-Faculty Lecture, University of Ghana, Legon, August 1989, pp. 11–13.

62. The following analysis is based on the masterful exposition in ibid., pp. 14–20. Richard Jeffries, in Chapter 8 of this book, reinforces these points.

63. Information culled from *AED* (November 23, 1985), p. 7. Also see Callaghy, "Lost Between State and Market," p. 25. For more details see E. Gyimah-Boadi's chapter in this book.

64. This constituted a major deviation from the alternating military-party system that had existed since independence. See Robert Pinkney, "Ghana: An Alternating Military/Party System," in Vicky Randall (ed.), *Political Parties in the Third World* (London: Sage, 1988), pp. 33–56.

65. The need for greater efficiency is underlined in John Dunn, "The Politics of Representation and Good Government in Post-Colonial Africa," in Chabal, *Political Domination in Africa*, pp. 158–174.

66. This reordering was incomplete, as the issue of decentralization, crucial for rearranging the relationship between the administrative center and local communities, was tackled only on paper. See Republic of Ghana, "Decentralisation in Ghana" (Accra: Information Services Department, n.d.).

67. Jonah, "Crisis and Response in Ghana," p. 51.

68. Anne Drabek (ed.), "Development Alternatives: The Challenge for NGO's," *World Development*, Special Supplement, 15 (1987), p. 2.

69. Some scholars have expressed doubts about the aggregative capacity of the new associations. See "Perestroika Without Glasnost in Africa" (Atlanta: The Carter Center, Conference Report Series, 2, 1, February 1989), pp. 5–6.

70. This point is emphasized in Michael Bratton, "The Politics of Government-NGO Relations in Africa," *World Development* 17, 4 (1989), pp. 569–587.

71. Since this topic is dealt with in another chapter, I will confine myself to a brief sketch.//
72. Jonah, "Crisis and Response in Ghana," p. 15. Incomes in the informal economy were usually lower than in the formal sector in the urban areas (see UNICEF, Ghana, pp. 8–9).
73. Richard L. Sklar, "Developmental Democracy," *Comparative Studies in Society and History* 19, 4 (1987), p. 712, claims that the informal sector is directly related to new modes of democratic assertion.
74. Ahwireng-Obeng, "Entrepreneurial Revolution for the African Third World: The Case of Ghana," *Canadian Journal of Development Studies* 9, 1 (1988), pp. 19–35.
75. Naomi Chazan and Donald Rothchild, "Corporatism and Political Transactions: Some Ruminations on the Ghanaian Experience," in Julius E. Nayong'oro and Timothy M. Shaw (eds.), *Corporatism in Africa: Comparative Analysis and Practice* (Boulder: Westview Press, 1989), pp. 167–193.
76. A fuller discussion of political spaces in Ghana may be found in Naomi Chazan, "Liberalization, Governance and Political Space in Ghana," in Michael Bratton and Goran Hyden (eds.), *Governance and Politics in Africa* (Boulder: Lynne Rienner Publishers, forthcoming).
77. Callaghy, "Lost Between State and Market," p. 28.
78. Kodwo Ewusi, *Statistical Tables on the Economy of Ghana, 1950–1985* (Legon: Institute for Statistical, Social and Economic Research, 1986).
79. Reginald Herbold Green, "Ghana: Progress, Problematics and Limitations of the Success Story," *IDS Bulletin* 19, 1 (1988), p. 11. For another view see Yao Graham, "Ghana: The IMF's African Success Story?" *Race and Class* 29, 3 (1988), pp. 41–52.
80. Callaghy, "Lost Between State and Market," calls this the "politics of counterfactuals," p. 29.
81. Jerry Rawlings as quoted in Colleen Lowe Morna, "A Grassroots Democracy," *Africa Report* 34, 4 (1989), p. 20.
82. Goran Hyden, "Governance: A New Approach to Comparative Politics," paper presented at the Thirty-first Annual Meeting of the African Studies Association, Chicago, October 1988, p. 23.
83. Republic of Ghana, *National Programme for Economic Development (Revised)* (Accra: Ghana Publishing Corporation, 1987), p. 21.
84. Republic of Ghana, *District Political Authority and Modalities for District Level Elections* (Accra: Ghana Publishing Corporation, July 1, 1987). Also see PNDCL 207, "Local Government Law (1988)."
85. Ibid., pp. 1–2.
86. Joseph R. A. Ayee, "The Provisional National Defence Council's 'Blue Book' on District Political Authority and the Future of Local Government in Ghana," *The Journal of Management Studies* 4 (1988), pp. 25–39.
87. For some social indicators see Republic of Ghana Statistical Service and the World Bank, *Ghana Living Standards Survey: Preliminary Results* (Accra: Social Dimensions of Adjustment Project Unit, October 1988).
88. Kojo T-Vieta, "Ghana: Mixed Results," *West Africa* 3737 (March 27, 1989), pp. 510–511.
89. All statistics are based on Republic of Ghana, Ministry of Local Government, *Information Digest*, nos. 3 and 5 (1989), which contain a complete breakdown of voting figures. The comparative figures for the 1978 district council election and the 1979 parliamentary elections were generously supplied by Joseph Ayee.

90. Naomi Chazan, "The Anomalies of Continuity: Perspectives on Ghanaian Elections Since Independence," in Fred M. Hayward (ed.), *Elections in Independent Africa* (Boulder: Westview Press, 1986), pp. 61–86.

91. For an evaluation of past voting patterns see Peter Osei-Kwame and Peter J. Taylor, "A Politics of Failure: The Political Geography of Ghanaian Elections, 1954–1979," *Annals of the Association of American Geographers* 74, 4 (1984), pp. 574–589.

92. Mikell, "The State, Local Resources, and Political Participation in Ghana," p. 11. Also see the last sections of her broad historical study: Gwendolyn Mikell, *Cocoa and Chaos in Ghana* (New York: Paragon House, 1989).

93. The following discussion is based on the perceptive analysis in Gyimah-Boadi, "Economic Recovery and Politics in the PNDC's Ghana," pp. 27–28.

94. For one example, see *The Path: Newsletter of the Kwame Nkrumah Revolutionary Guards* (Accra: n.d.), p. 7: "We believe that the state of Ghana was born out of the ballot box and any search for political alternatives which does not recognize the indispensable role of the ballot box as the most rational democratic process, is to our mind an exercise in futility."

95. As quoted in Ben Ephson, "People Are Watching," *West Africa* 3747 (June 12, 1989), p. 952.

96. Nii K. Bentsi-Enchill, "The Storm of June 4," *West Africa* 3747 (June 12, 1989), p. 953.

# 3
# The PNDC and the Problem of Legitimacy

*Kwame A. Ninsin*

A regime can achieve a measure of legitimacy if it can convince critical social classes of its ability and determination to (1) master the processes of accumulation and (2) ensure reasonable access to the economic surplus. The first condition is normally about the expectations shared by industrialists, merchants, and other capitalists (in general, the ruling class, as well as its functionaries within the middle class) that the state will provide them with adequate protection and guarantees to enhance opportunities for profit and private accumulation. The second, the problem of access, pertains to the claim of the noncapitalist strata of society for guaranteed access to the economic surplus. Access, which Geoff Lamb has defined as a function of the power relations prevailing in a society, refers to who controls and who secures the right to use part of the scarce social resources.[1] Where the state is unable to secure what either or both clusters of social classes regard as their rights, it stands in danger of forfeiting the support of the relevant social classes.

In Ghana, as in other developing countries, the process of legitimating a government is affected by accumulation trends in the economy. For it is in the economy that the state's incapacity to master the accumulation process and create equitable access to the economic surplus is exposed.[2] This weakness stems from the colonial origins of both the state and ruling classes.[3] In the case of Ghana, the ruling class had, by the 1980s, become "compradorized," while the economy had become heavily dependent on inflows of external resources to generate growth. These developments are important in two ways. First, they draw attention to the extent to which external economic interests have strengthened their presence in the economy and thereby undermined the prospects for regime autonomy and legitimacy.[4] Second, they highlight the recurrence of the accumulation crisis because of the growing extroversion and fragility of the economy. In a nutshell, success in legitimating the regime of a developing country is bound to be strongly affected by the country's external economic relations.

The problem of legitimacy is a more serious one for military governments because they lack the necessary constitutional and legal sanctions that form the usual basis for modern government. The government of the PNDC, which came to power by a coup d'état, naturally raised constitutional and legal questions about its claim to govern. Furthermore, the PNDC took power when the country's economic crisis had become so severe[5] that the ruling class had, out of desperation, resorted to corruption as a means of accumulation,[6] while the material conditions of the lower classes deteriorated sharply. As a result of the grave social inequalities arising from the economic crisis, radical political organizations, which derived their support mainly from the lower classes, had emerged and had fiercely attacked leading state institutions.[7] The political situation was therefore extremely unstable. And then the government departed from the tradition whereby the leaders of successful coups had courted the support of sections of the ruling class: it claimed—rhetorically at least—the moral and political right to jettison the ruling class from political and economic power. The result was the political buffeting experienced by that government during the 1982–1984 period.

In what follows I examine the PNDC government's attempts to grapple with this legitimacy crisis. I argue that the PNDC inserted itself in a very unstable political situation where the organized sections of the lower classes appeared to be winning sizable political space in a free-for-all struggle against the political representatives of the ruling classes. Because of their growing political strength, the lower classes (as represented by their more organized sections, particularly the urban working classes) became a critical social force in any attempt to stabilize the political situation.[8] The PNDC responded to that situation by reorganizing the state to incorporate the lower classes through organized labor.[9] The government created new political structures as the principal means for incorporating the lower classes in the prevailing power relations; it did not restructure state power. That partial reorganization of state institutions threatened the political and economic position of the ruling class and its functionaries as well as the country's external trading partners. The political reactions of the ruling classes considerably jeopardized the government's position until the Economic Recovery Program came into force.

The implementation of the ERP assured these socioeconomic interests (both internal and external) of the PNDC government's inclination to create the necessary conditions for accumulation. Even though the guarantees contained in the ERP fell short of the transfer of political power to the political representatives of the ruling classes, they nonetheless restored a fragile equilibrium against the background of alienated urban-based support.

The primary concern of the government, especially since 1985, has been the establishment of a stable basis of social support.

This chapter is divided into four sections. The first deals with attempts to solve the legitimacy crisis through the reorganization of the Ghanaian state and the political struggle arising from these efforts. The second addresses the resurgence and exacerbation of the legitimacy crisis as a result of the ERP. The third section raises doubts about the government's rural support, and the fourth examines attempts to develop alternative bases of support.

## ■ State Reorganization

On the assumption of power, the PNDC government attempted to anchor its rule in the support of the lower classes, whose organized urban-based sections had been engaged in a series of political confrontations since the mid-1960s.[10] The call for the formation of defense committees was the first bold step in this direction. By the end of 1982, a number of new and important state institutions had been established. These included the National Defence Committee—established to advise the PNDC in the exercise of its functions and also to initiate measures aimed at promoting the objectives of the revolution; the Citizens Vetting Committee and the National Investigations Committee—formed to investigate the assets of people suspected of living beyond their legal means, and economic crimes, respectively; and Public Tribunals—which were to avoid the delays and technicalities of the existing judicial system by dealing expeditiously with various criminal cases brought before them.[11] Even at the institutional level of the state, the creation of such new institutions constituted a formidable inroad into the prevailing state system.

This notwithstanding, the new institutions did not create a niche in the edifice of state power for the lower classes. For example, the highest organ of the defense committees was the National Defence Committee, which was to advise the PNDC and also implement its political program. Yet, this body was not part of the decisionmaking body. Nor did it have direct input into the decisions taken by the PNDC government. It merely had a member of the PNDC as its chairman. The NDC was represented on other new bodies like the National Economic Review Committee, the National Policy Implementation Monitoring Secretariat, and the State Commission for Economic Cooperation. But it appears that the potential influence of the representatives of the NDC on these bodies was neutralized by the superior representation of the ruling class on those same bodies. In general, communication between the NDC and the PNDC appears to have been blocked as early as 1982. Thus, by the close of 1982 there were complaints from some radical organizations concerning the lack of communication with the PNDC and the need, therefore, to establish "more systematic channels of communication and consultation between the progressive tendency of the highest levels of state power, and the progressive organizations."[12]

Even though this institutional reorganization did not give the lower classes any foothold in the center of power, the intensity of the political struggles they waged through the defense committees against the ruling class for ultimate control of state power became a key source of concern for the government during the 1982–1983 period. It should be recalled that the defense committees had come into being independent of the PNDC government, even though they enjoyed the moral and political support of the government until their political demise in 1984. The lower classes, especially organized labor, took advantage of (1) the freedom to engage in militant political action, which the independence of the defense committees provided them,[13] and (2) the government's declarations of intent to create a truly popular democratic basis of political power to wage a fierce struggle against the institutions, practices, ideas, and values of the ruling class. The ruling class responded through associations, nonstate institutions, and state institutions—like the judiciary—that it controlled. It attacked and resisted the government in general and the defense committees in particular.[14]

It was obvious from the reactions of the ruling class that the changes the PNDC had sought to effect in the institutional setup of the state, on the one hand, and what the lower classes sought to achieve in the structure of state power and production relations, on the other, were illegitimate. Hence, the collective political actions of the lower classes to correct perceived inequalities appeared to the ruling class as revolutionary. For example, the form of political action initiated by the lower classes (as well as the underlying ideological positions) conflicted with the liberal democratic forms and beliefs that have become part of the ideology of the ruling class— including its attitude toward private property and a free-market economy, the rule of law and the position of the judiciary, freedom of worship, and freedom of association. Such contradictory positions offended the received norms, values, and patterns of democratic political behavior known to the ruling class. As such they were interpreted as an assault on the key political and social institutions and norms that define political practice and the structure of Ghanaian society.[15]

Three forms of internal opposition to the politics of the PNDC and the defense committees may be identified. One was the open and rancorous agitation against the government that emanated from the nonstate political institutions that the ruling class dominated, namely, the Christian churches, the bar and bench, the independent press, and professional associations. The other was the covert actions of top bureaucrats within the financial and economic ministries—both old and new—in either frustrating new policy directions initiated by the new government or shaping policy in a direction consistent with the material interests of the ruling class. A classic case was the heated controversy over whether or not the new government should negotiate with the IMF for support in reviving the economy. The top bureaucrats and technocrats of these ministries, who were obviously hostile to the anti-IMF position of the left-wing and radical elements within the defense committees, used their position to persuade the PNDC to negotiate with the IMF.[16] This is what Peter Bachrach and Morton Baratz would describe as the mobilization of bias.[17]

The third strategy of internal opposition was far more covert than the second. It entailed the mobilization of deep-seated prejudices in the social structure to displace or suppress the conflict being fanned by the defense committees.[18] The ruling class so effectively mobilized bias against the radical political activities of the defense committees that public opinion was turned against the alleged excesses—including acts committed against chiefs and managers in state enterprises; against market women, some of whom had been flogged in public; and against legitimately acquired wealth—and destabilizing activities of the defense committees. The rumors that were peddled about the conduct of the defense committees were effective enough to discredit them and radical lower-class politics as a whole. Moreover, they succeeded in jeopardizing the continued exercise of political power by the PNDC. Hence, Chairman Rawlings could openly castigate the defense committees and their leaders for indulging in acts calculated to alienate support for his government.[19]

By then the PNDC was poised to retreat from its radical populist politics as well as its tirade against imperialism and capitalism.[20] The political implications of the country's economic crisis were becoming clearer: if the economic situation did not stabilize and if a measure of security for accumulation was not ensured, there would be no political peace. It had become equally clear that if militant political activities were not curtailed, the financial and other resources needed to revitalize the economy would not be forthcoming. The shortage of capital for reviving the economy, for financing even the barest minimum of consumer imports, and for servicing the country's external debt had been compounded by the insistence of the country's creditors and the World Bank that the government should agree to implement the IMF's conditionalities before any relief in the form of new loans could be expected from the international financial community.[21] Furthermore, an unofficial trade embargo by the country's traditional trading partners—including the government of the country's West African neighbor, Nigeria—had also been imposed. These actions exposed the grim reality of the regime's helpless dependence on external economic interests to manage its relations with internal political forces. They showed beyond a doubt that without the tacit approval of such external interests the government could not consolidate its rule. Such actions also emphasized the fact that the conditions for the government's legitimacy were as much internally rooted as they were external.

The acceptance of IMF conditionalities via the implementation of the economic recovery program from the first quarter of 1983 met the demands of external capitalist interests. The substantial inflow of external financial resources following the implementation of that economic reform package also assured sections of the ruling class that the government would not destroy the economic basis of its domination. But the economic reform measures satisfied the country's ruling classes only partially. Furthermore, they deprived the government of its urban-based lower-class support. Therefore, by the beginning of 1985, the government had lost substantial support among the urban-based lower classes without securing the total support of the ruling class.

## ■ The ERP and the PNDC's Isolation

Because the Economic Recovery Program was based on neoclassical economic doctrines of free trade, comparative advantage in international trade, monetary and fiscal policies, etc., the country's capitalist elements, especially those based in the external trade sector of the economy, would benefit immensely from the ERP's emphasis on export promotion. On the other hand, most local manufacturers would have to compete with massive imports resulting from the liberalization of trade. There would be others, probably the majority of the capitalist class, who would have to contend with the gamut of stringent requirements of the ERP's fiscal, monetary, and trade policies. That is, ultimately, the reform policies would perforce disregard the interests of some of the politically strategic social groups—including sections of the capitalist class, all those who depended on wages and salaries, and, in particular, the lower classes. In general, this group would include all those who were engaged in sectors of the economy that did not contribute directly to strengthening the economy's external sector. Such groups, as well as others who suffered adverse effects from the ERP, would not, to say the least, lend unqualified support to the government. Some sections of the capitalist class would simply acquiesce to the government of the PNDC, while other social groups would tend to demonstrate their displeasure with government policies in the form of open protest or opposition. I would therefore argue that the problem of legitimacy arising from the ERP lay in the fact that the weakness of the Ghanaian economy had obliged the PNDC government to comply with the conditionalities[22] of foreign capitalist interests to implement those economic reform policies in a manner that gave primacy to the interests of such external economic forces.

In short, the reform policies, as structured, benefited mostly external economic interests. The success of these policies was measured by the extent to which the country could (1) repay its external debt; (2) balance its external trade accounts (that is, continue to participate in global trade as an importer of manufactured goods and exporter of primary products); (3) balance its budget as a way of restraining the inflationary pressures within the economy; and (4) maintain an internationally acceptable exchange rate to ensure profitable investment.[23] Insofar as the function of the ERP was to strengthen the economy's external sector, there would be little regard for the interests of key social classes.[24]

The external orientation of the ERP had a significant impact on internal politics. By its nature, the ERP required the imposition of a strong government as the precondition for success. That meant mastery and use of the coercive organs of the Ghanaian state against all opposition groups. However, the government combined authoritarian rule with a policy of "divide and rule" toward strategically placed social classes.[25] A few instances of these strategies will provide useful examples. Between 1982 and 1984, the government exploited the support it enjoyed from labor as organized under the defense committees to contain opposition from the ruling class. Once the PNDC had subdued the organized and articulate sections of this class, it turned around to attack labor (under the leadership of the defense committees) for its alleged militancy and for "regarding itself as a parallel or alternative power."[26] After 1985, the government relentlessly ferreted out and detained or intimidated critics and organized opposition within the Trades Union Congress (TUC); radical organizations such as the New Democratic Movement (NDM), the Kwame Nkrumah Revolutionary Guards (KNRG), and others that operated clandestinely or from exile; and the National Union of Ghana Students (NUGS), the student organization based in the country's three universities. As punishment for potential critics and opposition groups within the labor movement, the government pursued a policy of denying some unions access to resources under the ERP while giving preferential treatment to others by improving salaries and benefits or assuring them access to resources under the ERP. The Civil Servants' Association, railway workers, and mine workers have benefited from such special treatment, as has the Ghana Private Road Transport Union (GPRTU). The first three of these workers' groups have a tradition of militancy. The last is important by virtue of its numbers and the branches it has in every corner of the country.

The case of the GPRTU requires additional comment. The mutual trust between this union and the government was so strong that, during the district-level elections held in December 1988 to February 1989, the union provided vehicles to convey election officials and voters in some electoral districts to the voting areas. It has also been collecting taxes from all commercial vehicle operators for the government. And in May 1990, the government used public money to import 100 Autosan buses from Poland (under a barter trade agreement with that country) for the GPRTU. The union was to repay the cost in thirty-six months. It was also announced at the presentation ceremony that the government would soon import Benz buses from Germany and Toyota Corona cars from Japan for the union. These, it was stated, were an affirmation of the government's confidence in the union.[27]

But most unions did not enjoy such government confidence. The government was not just hostile to some of the other unions—it also embarked on a deliberate policy of de-unionizing them. For example, workers of the Customs, Excise and Preventive Services (CEPS), who belong to the Public Service Workers' Union, lost their union membership when the government turned the CEPS into a security agency of the government. Similarly, workers of the Ghana Broadcasting Corporation (GBC) were literally deprived of their right to form a union when the GBC was declared a security zone following a fracas between the union and management. And the membership of the Industrial and Commercial Workers Union (ICU) was systematically depleted through retrenchment, privatization of state enterprises, and—in cases like the Ghana Textile Printing (GTP)—through the suppression of an experiment in worker self-management.[28] Meanwhile, key union leaders—like the secretary-general of the TUC and other general secretaries—have been offered sinecure appointments.[29]

The government's relationship with groups within urban-based non–lower class circles also reflected the level of benefit one group or the other derived either directly or indirectly from ERP policies. Its relations with professional groups like the bar association and university teachers were characterized by either latent or open hostility. Other professionals, especially those with special technical expertise, were euphoric about the sudden growth of the consultancy industry under the government's ERP; exporters received constant encouragement, monetary rewards, and incentives, while manufacturers were blamed for the problems of the manufacturing sector and urged to be more efficient and competitive with imported merchandise; and timber merchants received generous financial and technical support to decimate the country's forest resources. And while a core group of economic technocrats in the financial bureaucracies enjoyed considerable monetary rewards and a boost in status through regular attendance at international conferences, workshops, etc., the bulk of the middle class that depended entirely on salaries from both the public and private sectors could not recover financially from the depressed state of the pre-ERP era.

The policy of divide and rule is remarkable for its inefficiency as a strategy for securing stable social support for government. Thus, between 1985 and 1988, the government had to contend with demands from almost all the key political groups in the country, including labor and students, manufacturers, and professional politicians. Workers backed their demand for a living wage and improved working conditions with severe criticisms of the government's economic and social policies and a demand for constitutional rule as well as protection for civil liberties. Students of the country's three universities criticized the government's educational and economic reform policies and demanded a return to constitutional rule. Neither was the business community, especially manufacturers, happy with the government's open trade regime, which hurt local industry. Similarly, the political elite of the Ghanaian establishment was not enthusiastic about the government's continued monopoly of state power, which meant its exclusion from the direct exercise of political power.[30]

For the Ghanaian capitalist class and its political elite it was not the basic philosophy and outlines of the ERP that were in question. Rather, they were worried about the ERP's scope and the political framework for its implementation. And that is what they contested in a rather covert way.

In a nutshell, the redistributive effect of the ERP policies on critical urban-based classes was not entirely supportive of the government. As is the logical consequence of all structural adjustment programs, small groups within these classes benefited from the economic reform policies of the PNDC government, while the majority suffered relative deprivation. The result was considerable dissatisfaction among the deprived strata of urban-based classes.

Therefore, by 1987 the PNDC had not been able to resolve satisfactorily the problem of legitimacy that confronted it on the assumption of power. Its urban support base remained quite fragmented and frail. Given the fact that nonelectoral politics in Ghana is largely urban-centered, the PNDC's loss of decisive support among the urban-based classes (a loss that was confirmed in the low voter turnout at the district assembly election) created a thorny political problem.[31]

## ■ Precarious Rural Support

As the government alienated substantial sections of the urban-based classes, it could not be complacent about its support among the nonurban classes. Agricultural producers who were alleged to be among the leading beneficiaries of the ERP—e.g., the producers of cocoa, coffee, cereals, and other export crops—found that the benefits that accrued to them from ERP policies were tentative. It is true, for example, that the nominal producer price of cocoa rose considerably during the period.[32] But as a percentage of FOB (free on board), at the official exchange rate, the nominal producer price declined from 38.0 percent in the 1982/83 main crop season to below 20.0 percent through 1986/87, rising to 33.2 percent in the 1987/88 main crop season.[33]

There were other adverse economic factors that affected the government's chances of securing unqualified support from the rural classes. These included the burden of taxation that certain reform measures entailed for the rural population (like the decentralization measures that shifted a considerable tax burden onto them) and the educational reforms that imposed on parents additional financial responsibilities for educating a child. Other factors included the reversal in rural-urban terms of trade in favor of the rural population. The reversal was neither spectacular nor stable (116.5 percent in 1983; 114.5 percent in 1984; 110.8 percent in 1985; and 104.9 percent in 1986 [1970=100]);[34] and a rate of price inflation that was higher for rural dwellers (6,590.6) than for urbanites (6,118.7) (1977=100).[35] These factors would suggest that the government could not be confident of securing appreciable support from the rural classes, because for them also the material payoffs from the ERP were not substantial.

As a recent report to the United States Committee on Foreign Affairs of the House of Representatives pointed out, the ERP had adverse effects on the material conditions of the rural population.[36] The gains from producer price increases went mainly to a minority of large-scale farmers. Quoting from a recent survey by a combined team of Overseas Development Institute and University of Ghana researchers, the report noted that 32 percent of the rural households known to grow cocoa received as much as 94 percent of the gross income from cocoa. The remaining 68 percent received a mere 6 percent of the cocoa income. For the 82 percent of rural households that do not grow cocoa, real per capita income stagnated. In brief, the majority of farmers—mostly peasants—were losers.

This pattern of income distribution was the direct result of the monetarist policies implemented under the ERP so that the government could regain access to the international financial markets irrespective of the domestic social and political costs. The loss of reliable urban support and the intense criticism and political agitations the ERP had generated during the late 1980s, coupled with the adverse social effects of the ERP on the rural populations and its potentially dangerous political ramifications in that social sector, obliged the government to attempt to institutionalize its relationship with the rural people. The focus on the rural population appears to have been a prudent option because, apart from the loss of its urban lower-class support, (1) Rawlings's own populism inclined him toward the rural producers, whom he referred to as the "real" and "exploited" workers of the country; and (2) their generally low level of political organization and consciousness made them vulnerable to political manipulation.

## ■ The Search for Alternative Support

The government's decision to organize local elections in 1988–1989 for the establishment of district assemblies/councils has been interpreted in several ways. One popular view is that it was aimed at securing nonurban support. This interpretation has been questioned on the grounds that the government's electoral achievement concealed several political difficulties.[37] It must be conceded that the government achieved tremendous success in realizing a 59.0 percent voter turnout; of a total of 9,680 assembly members, 7,260 elected were representatives and 2,420 appointed members. In relation to the population of about 14 million, the assembly members constitute a potentially formidable political resource that can be employed to mobilize support for the regime.

However, there were serious obstacles to the full realization of this potential. First, even though the elections to the district assemblies/councils were controlled, it would appear that they succeeded in reproducing existing grassroots political conflicts—a situation that also affected the Convention People's party (CPP) in the 1950s.[38] Hence, there were persistent reports about assembly members getting engaged in chieftaincy and land disputes as well as other local conflicts. Second, in the case of the PNDC government, the district assemblies appear to have become captives also of the existing political alignments in the country—namely, political coalitions of the Convention People's Party–National Alliance of Liberals tradition; the United Party–Progress Party tradition; and the more recent coalition of radicals, socialists, and populist groupings, including pro-PNDC supporters. It is therefore questionable whether the PNDC could capture and control these contradictory political forces prevailing at the grassroots.

Third, reports about developments at the district level suggest that some of these political forces were determined to assert the independence of the District Assemblies from the central government. This often took the form of persistent quarrels and struggles for power between certain elected representatives to the DAs and their presiding member (or president), or the district secretary (who is appointed by the central government), or the district or local branch of the Committees for the Defence of the Revolution. It is remarkable that the power struggles were against district officers who were mainly government appointees. For example, about 62 percent of the presiding members of the assemblies were government appointees. The district secretary is also appointed by the government. The struggles, which were essentially struggles to control local resources, centered on the power of taxation, control over finance and land, and the right to settle land disputes.

Furthermore, some assembly members were reported to have arrogated to themselves the power to dissolve the local CDRs. In a more extreme case, one DA in the Volta Region was recently reprimanded for resolving to change the name of the district it serves, alter its boundaries, and then take over all government property within its jurisdiction.[39] In the course of this contest between the district assembly members and the PNDC government, most assembly members have been constrained by the rather fragile financial position of their districts from transforming the assemblies/councils into independent centers of political power.

These and other factors that were yet to surface severely limited the government's ability to use the DAs as instruments of legitimation. Above all, the government is disadvantaged by the fact that the assembly members contested the elections as independent candidates because the government insisted on organizing the elections on a nonparty basis. This denied the government the organizational means for controlling the elected members in competition with other party representatives.

Because of the political cost of the ERP and the constraints inherent in the limited political reforms that culminated in the establishment of the DAs, the government appears to have used other methods to secure support in both the urban and rural areas of the country. Two principal means have been identified: corporatism[40] and populism.[41] In the first instance, the government actively cultivated the support of existing organizations, or created new ones for the same purpose. We have already drawn attention to attempts to gain the support of existing organizations, especially the GPRTU, the Railway Workers' Union, the Mine Workers' Union, and the Civil Servants' Association—all traditional labor unions. The new ones include the 31st December Women's Movement and the Mobisquads. Since the government came to power, numerous other occupationally based associations of petty commodity producers have also been formed. But most of these have been engineered into existence mainly to facilitate tax collection from the mass of small-scale business operators by the Internal Revenue Department.

Especially in its relations with peasant farmers, the government projected an image of determination to correct the problem of access[42] created for it by the so-called urban-based parasitic and bureaucratic elites.[43] In this respect the government achieved a major success in the introduction of the Akuafo Cheque System. By this system cocoa farmers could be paid by check for the cocoa they sold to the marketing agency of COCOBOD. This reduced the practice whereby cocoa purchasing clerks cheated farmers of considerable amounts of money.

But in the main, the government appears to be handicapped in its attempt to incorporate certain social groups into the prevailing power structure. There are two explanations for this. First, corporatism, as known in the political practice of Latin American countries, is underpinned by a "legal system based on a particular view of the foundation and source of law."[44] This is conspicuously absent from the Ghanaian situation.

Furthermore, this legal system has produced a definitive political identity and organization of society. According to Weinstein:

> One of the most significant dimensions of corporate identity is the vertical nature of solidarity patterns and the concomitant lack of horizontal (cross-cutting) solidarity with a consequent societal inability to achieve a synthesizing consensus based on a commitment to basic equality. . . . Two key aspects of corporatively organized societies are the class-striated, hierarchically ordered relationships within each corporate pillar and the relative lack of interaction between the individuals in each pillar, except at the elite level. Man in a corporative world can look up and down, but not across.[45]

In contrast to the political strategies of the PNDC government, one can isolate nothing more than ad hoc attempts to coopt groups and individuals into the power structure. Apart from the 31st December Women's Movement, there was no serious attempt to build a corporate societal structure in its support. The absence of these two salient features of corporatist politics makes the application of the concept of corporatism to current Ghanaian political practice very inappropriate. The PNDC government simply did not have the ideological and organizational means to build a corporatist political structure.

The government's political practice toward the lower classes—especially those based in the rural areas—appears to be influenced by a certain vague sense of social justice that requires that the wealth of society should benefit its real producers—namely, rural producers. But even in this regard the government was constrained by the fact that the economic crisis had considerably reduced the resources available to the state for distribution to such disadvantaged groups. Consequently, it was obliged to depend largely on the generosity of foreign donors for the necessary resources before it could provide the necessary credit and development assistance to the rural people.

A key foreign-based resource of the government is the Programme of Actions to Mitigate the Social Costs of Adjustment.[46] The program "seeks to address the needs of vulnerable groups who are in a precarious condition due to the adjustment program or due to the earlier period of economic decline."[47] However, "projects were included in the proposed portfolio if they had a strong poverty focus; high economic and social rates of return; modest institutional requirements to ensure ease and speed in implementation; and *in sensitive areas, high visibility to enhance confidence in and sustainability of the ERP*."[48] The government actively maximized local support for this program. In fact, it was the principal source of funds for its rural/community development program.

As might be expected, the emphasis was on community development— and not politics. Communities were urged to initiate "self-help" projects as a condition for securing government support under the PAMSCAD to develop their locality. But, of course, the usual political gain—namely, support for the government or a positive image for it—was expected from such material assistance to rural communities.

However, because the PAMSCAD was not a liberally funded government-initiated program, there were obvious difficulties in its full implementation. For instance, there was a gap between enthusiastic pledges by the country's foreign donors and actual disbursements. There were also administrative bottlenecks that delayed project identification and implementation.[49] Because of such bottlenecks associated with foreign aid–related projects, the potential political benefits from the PAMSCAD could not be fully exploited.

Evidently, the severity of the economic crisis and the fact that the government had to solicit external financial support before it could cope with rural needs placed considerable constraint on its ability to nurture or buy social support. This left the government in a rather weak bargaining position, especially as several critical social groups continued to make economic, social, and political demands.

The occasional appeals that Rawlings made directly to the rural people were an attempt to transcend the limitations imposed by a weak economy. Even though Rawlings was known for his charismatic appeal as far back as June 1979, during the post-1985 period he developed a strong inclination to interact more with rural populations. In more dramatic instances he camped by villages, worked with them on community projects, and held durbars with them.[50] To win the support of sections of the urban-based classes, especially those that had traditionally subscribed to the African policy of Nkrumah's CPP, the government intensified its militant stand on African issues, and tried to rehabilitate Kwame Nkrumah.[51]

## ■ Conclusion

If the problem of legitimacy is rooted in the weakness of the Ghanaian economy, especially its dependent character, then the PNDC government could cultivate and retain substantial political support at home only if the economy could achieve long-term growth, and foreign assistance would not be of the type that would compel it to ignore the interest of critical domestic classes. This would give the government the necessary material resources and freedom to handle demands from such classes. For, in the final analysis, Ghanaian politics is governed by instrumentalist considerations. This is not to say, however, that there were no Ghanaians who were sincerely committed to certain political ideals.

Maxwell Owusu draws attention to the fact that the legitimacy of the

CPP regime began to crumble in the 1962–1965 period, when the economic situation deteriorated sharply.[52] During this period the potential effect of the mobilization drive of the party was neutralized by individual calculations of material disadvantage at a time when the distributive mechanisms of the state were being warped under pressure from the mounting crisis.[53] If the economic foundations of the state remain weak, the PNDC government could not be expected to succeed where others had failed.

It is equally significant that Nkrumah's charisma could not mitigate the legitimacy crisis that confronted his regime during the 1962–1965 period. It is therefore doubtful that the populist charisma of Rawlings could galvanize solid social support for stable and democratic governance. The use of excessive force in politics does not guarantee political stability. More especially, it destroys democratic structures wherever they exist.

The problem is, indeed, tantalizing. Kwame Nkrumah's government had the supreme advantage of a political party, and yet it could not institutionalize its rule on a democratic basis. The Rawlings government has not had this advantage. Nor has it been able to initiate a populist social movement similar, for example, to Peronism in Argentina. Furthermore, from all indications it abhors the clientelist politics (with its attendant official political corruption) that characterized previous regimes. But even if it did not, corruption could not be used as an efficient means of redistributing the social wealth where there was too little wealth to be distributed.[54] This is where the PNDC has been handicapped: the economy remains as fragile as it was in the 1950s. Accordingly, the state cannot accumulate enough surplus for the benefit of critical social groups. And the ERP has not secured the PNDC any permanent friends.

## ■ Notes

1. Geoff Lamb, "Marxism, Access and the State," *Development and Change* 6, 2 (April 1975), p. 119.
2. Samir Amin, "Democracy and National Strategy in the Periphery," *Third World Quarterly* 9, 4 (October 1987), p. 1130.
3. The state in colonial Ghana was an extension of the British imperial state. Political independence meant the establishment of a separate and independent state—but not necessarily an autonomous state.
4. For developing economies the internationalization of capital has extended the basis of state legitimacy beyond the boundaries of the nation-state into the dominant centers of wealth and power within the world economy. See Bill Jordan, *The State: Authority and Autonomy* (Oxford: Basil Blackwell, 1985).
5. A fair knowledge of the extent of the economic crisis can be obtained from *The Economic Survey, 1981* (Accra: Central Bureau of Statistics [now Statistical Service], 1983).
6. Kwame A. Ninsin, "The Roots of Corruption: A Dissenting View," *Journal of Management Studies*, 3d series, vol. 1 (March 1984).

7. The agitations of organized labor during the 1967–1981 period have been analyzed in Kwame A. Ninsin, *Political Struggles in Ghana* (Accra: Tornado Publications, forthcoming).

8. The situation was similar to that in 1948–1950. For a discussion of the revolutionary situation created by the emergence of the masses as an independent political force in Ghana's independence struggle, see C. L. R. James, *Nkrumah and the Ghana Revolution* (London: Allison and Busby, 1977).

9. Issa Shivji discusses this theoretical issue in "The Reorganization of the State and the Working People in Tanzania," paper presented at the Conference on State and Society in Africa, Oaxtepec, Morelos, October 23–29, 1983. I find the analytical distinction he makes between *state power* and *state apparatus* quite germane to our understanding of Ghanaian politics during the 1950s and 1980s.

10. See Ninsin, *Political Struggles in Ghana*.

11. These new institutions were established, respectively, under the *Provisional National Defence Council (Establishment) Proclamation* (1981); *Citizens Vetting Committee Law*, 1982 PNDCL 1; *National Investigations Committee Law*, 1982 PNDCL 2; and the *Public Tribunals Law*, 1982 PNDCL 24.

12. Reported in Kwame A. Ninsin, "Ghanaian Politics After 1981: Revolution of Evolution?" *Canadian Journal of African Studies* 21, 1 (1987), p. 26.

13. The significance of the defense committees as an independent weapon in the working class struggles of the 1982–1984 period is the subject of an essay by Yao Graham, "From GTP to Assene: Aspects of Industrial Working Class Struggles, 1982–1987," in E. Hansen and K. A. Ninsin (eds.), *The State, Development and Politics In Ghana* (London: Codesria Book Series, 1989).

14. The conflicting positions of the protagonists in the struggles of the 1982–1984 period have also been analyzed in Ninsin, "Ghanaian Politics After 1981."

15. George M. Thomas et al. explain why this should be the conclusion. They point out that "change in action presupposes change in the legitimating frame to which the collective action is oriented and within which action is constituted. Consequently, many (attempted) changes . . . are viewed as simply disruptive and disorderly." See George M. Thomas et al., "Legitimacy and Collective Action," *Social Forces* 65, 2 (December 1986).

16. Hence the June Fourth Movement (one of the radical organizations that was closer to the PNDC at the time) would denounce in its organ *The Workers Banner* (September 6–23, 1982) people the JFM regarded as internal collaborators (of the IMF) and reactionaries who had infiltrated the PNDC and secured its acceptance of the IMF-sponsored package of economic reform policies and programs.

17. Peter Bachrach and Morton S. Baratz, "Two Faces of Power," *American Political Science Review* 56, 4 (December 1962); Peter Bachrach and Morton S. Baratz, "Decision and Non-decision: An Analytical Framework," *American Political Science Review* 57, 3 (September 1963).

18. See E. E. Schattschneider, *The Semisovereign People* (New York: Rinehart & Winston, 1960), pp. 70–71.

19. Rawlings radio and television broadcasts following the abortive coup d' état on June 19.

20. The politics of the PNDC's populism have been analyzed in Kwame A. Ninsin, "From the Defence Committees to the District Assembly Elections: Strategies of Mobilisation Under the PNDC," paper presented at the Conference of

the Ghana National Committee of CODESRIA, University of Legon, March 1–3, 1990.

21. This is a familiar weapon of foreign capital currently being employed on its behalf by the IMF and the World Bank. It is aimed at ensuring compliance with the worldwide accumulation imperative inherent in the world economy. See C. Palliox, "The Self-Expansion of Capital on a World Scale," *Review of Radical Political Economics* 9, 2 (1977), for an analysis of the dynamics of this global movement. See also Ronald T. Libby, "The International Monetary Fund's 'Rehabilitation' of Ghana, 1966–69," *The African Review* 6, 4 (1976); Ronald T. Libby, "External Cooptation of a Less Developed Country's Policy-Making: The Case of Ghana, 1969–72," *World Politics* 29, 1 (October 1976); Eboe Hutchful (ed.), *The IMF and Ghana: The Confidential Record* (London: Zed Books, 1987); and Kwesi Jonah, "Changing Relations Between the IMF and the Government of Ghana, 1960–1987," in E. Hansen and K. A. Ninsin (eds.), *The State, Development and Politics in Ghana* (London: Codesria Book Series, 1989).

22. This was especially true of the IMF conditionalities. These are consistent with the position of the World Bank as amplified in the Berg Report as well as the positions of other donor agencies and governments that come together at the annual Paris debt rescheduling conference. *Accelerated Development in Sub-Saharan Africa* (Washington, D.C.: World Bank, 1981)—also known as the Berg Report.

23. M. G. de Vries discusses some of the policy options implied by the IMF conditionalities in his *Balance of Payments Adjustment, 1945 to 1986: The IMF Experience* (Washington, D.C.: International Monetary Fund, 1987), pp. 203–207. As pointed out, the conditionalities are designed to correct the disequilibrium in the external economic transactions of developing countries, in particular, and therefore do not necessarily strengthen their internal capacities for sustainable growth.

24. In practical terms, strengthening the external sector meant externalizing a developing country's economic surplus. According to a recent announcement by the secretary for Finance and Economic Development made at a special press conference in the "Meet-the-Press" series of the Ministry of Information, the country had reduced the external debt of $600 million, which it inherited, to $200 million during the period of the ERP (1983–1989). But more significantly, during this period gross capital inflows—including purchases from the IMF, grants, concessional loans, and borrowings—amounted to $4.3 billion; outflows—including payments for long-term debt and payments made to the IMF—totaled $3.0 billion. Net inflows therefore stood at just $1.3 billion. Because of the government's heavy reliance on such external transactions, the country's external debt stood at $3.0 billion (in January 1990). During the same period the country's balance of external trade showed a deficit of $800 million: imports were valued at $5.9 billion, while exports were valued at $5.1 billion. *Ghanaian Times*, January 13, 1990, p. 1.

25. According to Bill Jordan, the policy of divide-and-rule is characteristic of governments that depend on external economic interests to strengthen and legitimate their rule at home. See Jordan, *The State: Authority and Autonomy*, p. 159.

26. This change was made by Rawlings in his inaugural address to the Western Region Consultative Committee, December 7, 1984. The speech has been reprinted as "Defending the Revolution" in *The Process of Consolidation*, selected speeches and interviews of Flt. Lt. J. J. Rawlings (Accra: Information Services Dept., 1985, January 1, 1984–December 31, 1984, vol. 3).

27. See *People's Daily Graphic*, May 5, 1990, p. 1.

28. For the background to the PNDC government's relations with the Ghana Textiles Printing, see Yao Graham, "From GTP to Assene."

29. For example, the secretary-general of the TUC, A. K. Yankey, was appointed a member of the National Commission for Democracy, a department of state created by the PNDC government to be responsible for the formulation of a new constitutional and political arrangement for the country, as well as the conduct of elections. Since about 1987, Mr. Yankey's public pronouncements were more supportive of various government positions than the TUC's. Some have alleged that he might be protecting his office, which had attracted unusually generous perquisites. See, for example, E. Dagadu, "Labour Under Fire," *West Africa*, June 5–11, 1989, pp. 918–919.

30. Because of the government's tight control over nonofficial political activities, these groups could not openly express their grievances. Accordingly, the associations of workers, university students, and lawyers, for example, could only take advantage of their respective congresses to define their positions on relevant government policies. See, for example, *The Final Communiqué of the 23rd Annual Congress of the National Union of Ghana Students held at the UST Kumasi*, April 17–23, 1988; see also the NUGS's statement at the end of their March 1990 congress and the *Resolution Adopted by the 3rd Quadrennial Delegates Congress of the Trades Union Congress (Ghana)* held at the University of Cape Coast, March 16–18, 1988. Invariably, however, such resolutions would not be published by the state-owned media, which monopolized the national communications network.

31. There is a concise analysis of the rural-urban distribution of the votes cast at the district assembly elections in Ninsin, "From the Defence Committees to the District Assembly Elections."

32. Kodwo Ewusi, *Structural Adjustment and Stabilisation Policies in Developing Countries: A Case Study of Ghana's Experience in 1983–1986* (Legon, Ghana: Institute of Statistical, Social, and Economic Research, 1987), p. 56.

33. World Bank, *Ghana: Structural Adjustment for Growth*, Report No. 7515-GH (Washington, D.C.: World Bank, 1989), p. 20.

34. Ewusi, *Structural Adjustment*, p. 56.

35. World Bank, *Ghana: Structural Adjustment for Growth*, p. 167.

36. United States Government, *Report of a Staff Study Mission to Great Britain, Ghana, Senegal, Côte d'Ivoire, and France, November 29–December 20, 1988, to the Committee on Foreign Affairs, U.S. House of Representatives* (Washington, D.C.: U.S. Government Printing Office, 1989).

37. Ninsin, "From the Defence Committees to the District Assembly Elections."

38. See Dennis Austin, *Politics in Ghana* (London: Oxford University Press, 1966), pp. 1–152, for an account of how such local conflicts were politicized and transferred into the CPP.

39. See *Ghanaian Times*, June 27, 1990, p. 1, for the report on this particular District Assembly.

40. E. Gyimah-Boadi, "Economic Recovery and Politics in the PNDC's Ghana," paper read at the Inter-Faculty Lecture, University of Ghana, Legon, August 3, 1989, pp. 17–24.

41. Ninsin, "From the Defence Committees to the District Assembly Elections."

42. In this regard, the government was simply exploiting the usual problem

created by bureaucratized and imperfect market systems for distributing social resources like credit, farm inputs, income, and development projects that favored those with influence, status, experience and education, strategic connections, and luck. The problem of access created for the lower classes through such bureaucratic and imperfect market systems is discussed in B. B. Schaffer and Wen-hsien Huang, "Distribution and the Theory of Access," *Development and Change* 6, 2 (April 1975).

43. In Rawlings's prorural, antiurban populist pronouncements, he described rural-urban relations as essentially exploitative, with urban dwellers being the exploiters.

44. Martin Weinstein, "Corporatist Ideology in Latin America: Implications of the Uruguayan Case," in M. J. Blachman and R. G. Hellman (eds.), *Terms of Conflict: Ideology in Latin American Politics* (Philadelphia: ISHI, 1977), p. 68.

45. Ibid., p. 66.

46. Republic of Ghana. *Programme of Actions to Mitigate the Social Costs of Adjustment* (Accra: Government Printer, November 1987).

47. Ibid., p. 1.

48. Ibid. Emphasis is mine.

49. World Bank, *Ghana: Structural Adjustment for Growth*, p. 41.

50. More recent cases were the two successive visits within two weeks that Rawlings paid to the Afram Plains. For coverage of those visits see *People's Daily Graphic*, February 17 and 26, 1990, and *The Ghanaian Times*, February 17, 19, and 24, 1990. Establishing such personal links with the masses is part of the leadership style of populists. See Nicos Mouzelis, *Politics in the Periphery* (London: Macmillan, 1986), pp. 3–72.

51. To mark the eightieth birthday of Kwame Nkrumah, on September 21, 1989, the PNDC government organized a highly publicized international conference in Accra. That was the first of its kind since Nkrumah's death, and the first event of such grandeur since the regime came to power. The use of Nkrumah's image and his legacy of militant pan-Africanist, antiapartheid, and proliberation African policy are inextricably linked.

52. This is the main thesis of Maxwell Owusu, *Uses and Abuses of Political Power* (Chicago: University of Chicago Press, 1970).

53. See the speech delivered by Nkrumah in 1961 at the Kwame Nkrumah Ideological Institute at Winneba, in which he called for "cipipification," that is, spreading branches of the CPP to all parts of the country.

54. A good example of how political corruption or patronage could be used to redistribute the economic surplus for the benefit of the socially disadvantaged, and also to secure social stability and legitimacy, is provided by U.S. social history during the period of industrialization and massive immigration from Europe. See, for example, Richard Hofstadter, *The Age of Reform* (London: Jonathan Cape, 1962), pp. 173–254.

# 4

# Educating Rawlings: The Evolution of Government Strategy Toward Smuggling

*Paul Nugent*

The ongoing debate about the merits of the Structural Adjustment Program and its political consequences has for the most part failed to address basic questions about the capacities of the Ghanaian state. The Rawlings regime has itself made a series of tacit admissions about the limits to its control over the social and economic activities of its citizens. Local government reforms should perhaps be seen as an attempt to hitch the wagon of the state to functioning institutions and political networks at the grassroots level. Similarly, the legalization of small-scale mining, or *galamsey*, is an admission of defeat for state authorities after decades of trying to stamp out illegal operations. One of the most intriguing turnabouts is reflected in government strategies to deal with smuggling. Few issues have as consistently dominated the official media over the last two decades as this alleged "scourge." On coming to power, the PNDC promised tough new measures to finally eradicate what it regarded as the most serious economic crime of all. The experience of 1982/83 brought home to the Rawlings regime just how difficult this would be to achieve. However, it was also a positive learning experience in the sense that the government discovered not only some of the advantages of market forces, but also more novel ways of asserting control over border communities. This chapter is about the dawning of this awareness.[1] In what follows, I shall focus on three sets of issues, namely:

- The factors that contributed to the smuggling problem in the decade preceding the December 1981 coup
- The evolution of PNDC strategy since 1982
- The successes that can be claimed for a more imaginative approach to the problem

## ■ The Historical Roots of Smuggling

Smuggling is a topic for research that yields few certainties.[2] However, one point about which we can feel confident is that smuggling has a history that antedates independence. Throughout Africa, the demarcation of colonial frontiers was followed by the introduction of duties and trade restrictions, which provided financial rewards for those who were willing to risk evading border controls. Smuggling was sometimes merely a term expressing official disapproval for trade that was carried out along precolonial routes in defiance of the newly imposed frontiers. Commonly, however, it was the different economic regimes that prevailed on either side of a boundary that made certain forms of trade profitable for the first time. It is this category of smuggling that became more pronounced in the 1970s, especially in regions where francophone states bordered countries that were not connected to the franc zone. In the case of Ghana, this was a decade when the flow of illicit trade increased markedly. Whereas produce had been smuggled into Ghana as recently as the 1950s, twenty years later the pattern was reversed. Now cocoa, foodstuffs, minerals, and timber began to leave Ghana in substantial quantities for Côte d'Ivoire, Upper Volta (now Burkina Faso), and Togo.[3] At a time when foreign exchange was desperately short, the cumulative effect of smuggling on the Ghanaian economy and the financial health of the state was profound. In the space available, it is possible to do no more than simply isolate the most important factors in the equation.

Undoubtedly, the single most important contributing factor was the overvalued cedi. Prior to 1961, Ghana, like neighboring countries, was tied to the former imperial currency zone, which limited room for maneuver but guaranteed the convertibility of the currency. Whereas francophone neighbors continued to use the CFA franc, Ghana decided to break the link with sterling. In subsequent years, the cedi was pegged against the dollar at a rate that was at variance with the real rate of exchange. The options of floating the cedi or at least adjusting its value were equally unpopular because they would push up the cost of imports and generally raise consumer prices. The overthrow of the Busia regime in 1971, following the introduction of a devaluation package, revealed precisely how politically sensitive the matter had become and served as a lesson to successor governments. The Acheampong regime compounded the problem by not only revaluing the cedi, but also by recklessly printing more money whenever budgetary constraints loomed. As the gap between the official and real rates of exchange widened, an extensive currency black market emerged. Whereas the parallel rate had stood at 1.3 times the official rate in 1972, by 1981 it was 9.6 times higher.[4] This stimulated smuggling because Ghanaians who had anything to sell could multiply their earnings severalfold by selling their goods in the francophone countries and then changing the CFA francs into cedis at black market rates. Almost every town located near a border had its currency changers, who were often strangers (commonly Hausa or Yoruba traders) connected to transnational commercial networks. Smuggling was a relatively democratic activity in the sense that it included both the well-to-do, such as wealthy rice farmers in the north during the Acheampong years,[5] and ordinary peasants. Whereas the former confidently dispatched their trucks across the borders once they had paid the requisite bribe, the mass of petty smugglers preferred to headload their goods along secret bush paths.

The range of smuggled goods was extensive. However, it was the loss of cocoa that government officials most often complained about. Apart from the operation of the black market, there were additional reasons why many cocoa farmers chose to smuggle their beans. As is well known, the fiscal base of the Ghanaian state has rested upon the use of the Cocoa Marketing Board to tax the farmers.[6] Ghana was not, of course, alone in doing this. During the 1970s, the Togolese government similarly squeezed the farmers to a level that the World Bank believed was detrimental to the long-term viability of the industry.[7] Nevertheless, the Togolese and the Ivorians continued to offer their farmers a greater share of the world price than did the CMB. As Table 4.1 suggests, the combination of higher nominal prices and the currency black market together resulted in a substantial incentive to smugglers.

The neighboring states also ensured that the farmers were expeditiously paid, whereas cocoa farmers in Ghana often came away from the buying centers with chits because there was insufficient cash at hand. The option of seeking higher prices elsewhere was restricted to communities farming in relative proximity to the borders, since the 1970s was a period when the transport network and the roads underwent a marked deterioration. For this reason, Ashanti cocoa farmers may have preferred to substitute food crops for their cocoa.[8] However, it so happened that many of the areas of expanding production, that is, in Brong-Ahafo and the Western Region, were also close to the border with Côte d'Ivoire. In these regions the breakdown of infrastructure had the opposite effect of that witnessed in Ashanti. The difficulties of moving cocoa to the buying centers was an additional reason why many farmers smuggled their crops. Table 4.2 provides a conservative estimate of the tonnage of cocoa that was smuggled annually out of the country.

A third factor contributing to smuggling was the consumption squeeze. Historically, the spread of cocoa in particular had been associated with new patterns of consumption. Commodities that may at one time have been regarded as luxury goods became regular items of consumption and, in that sense, necessities. It was the greater availability of consumer goods in the Gold Coast that had encouraged the smuggling of cocoa into the colony up until the mid-1950s. But two decades later, the shortage of foreign exchange had led to a reduction both in imports and in capacity utilization in Ghanaian

Table 4.1 The Rewards of Cocoa Smuggling into Togo and Côte d'Ivoire, 1970/71–1981/82

| Year | Ghana Price (¢/ton) | Togo Price (CFA/ton) | Togo Price (¢/ton) | Côte d'Ivoire Price (CFA/ton) | Côte d'Ivoire Price (¢/ton) |
|---|---|---|---|---|---|
| 1970/71 | 293.80 | 88,000 | 523.12 | 82,269 | 489.05 |
| 1971/72 | 300.47 | 93,000 | 538.81 | 84,511 | 530.52 |
| 1972/73 | 360.92 | 93,000 | 588.03 | 85,182 | 538.60 |
| 1973/74 | 385.04 | 93,000 | 564.19 | 92,838 | 563.21 |
| 1974/75 | 484.47 | 95,000 | 675.92 | 125,770 | 894.85 |
| 1975/76 | 577.90 | 115,000 | 783.56 | 175,230 | 1,193.94 |
| 1976/77 | 679.15 | 120,000 | 1,055.54 | 176,970 | 1,556.65 |
| 1977/78 | 976.78 | 130,000 | 2,795.70 | 198,110 | 4,620.43 |
| 1978/79 | 1,601.40 | 150,000 | 4,632.04 | 250,340 | 7,730.57 |
| 1979/80 | 3,308.10 | 200,000 | 8,347.46 | 262,890 | 10,972.32 |
| 1980/81 | 3,936.30 | 220,000 | 17,232.23 | 279,160 | 21,866.14 |
| 1981/82 | 5,333.50 | 220,000 | 14,914.72 | 300,000 | 20,338.25 |

*Source*: Ernesto May, *Exchange Controls and Parallel Market Economies in Sub-Saharan Africa: Focus on Ghana* (Washington, D.C.: World Bank, 1985), p. 129.

Table 4.2 Estimated Losses of Cocoa Through Smuggling ('000 tons)

| Year | Production | To Ivory Coast | To Togo | Total | As % of Production |
|---|---|---|---|---|---|
| 1970/71 | 413 | 18 | 16 | 34 | 8.2 |
| 1971/72 | 454 | 21 | 18 | 39 | 8.6 |
| 1972/73 | 407 | 14 | 7 | 21 | 5.2 |
| 1973/74 | 340 | 9 | 5 | 14 | 4.1 |
| 1974/75 | 376 | 16 | 5 | 21 | 5.6 |
| 1975/76 | 396 | 21 | 8 | 29 | 7.3 |
| 1976/77 | 320 | 21 | 5 | 26 | 8.1 |
| 1977/78 | 271 | 38 | 8 | 46 | 17.0 |
| 1978/79 | 265 | 29 | 5 | 34 | 12.8 |
| 1979/80 | 281 | 32 | 8 | 40 | 14.2 |
| 1980/81 | 254 | 31 | 8 | 39 | 15.4 |

*Source*: Ernesto May, *Exchange Controls and Parallel Market Economies in Sub-Saharan Africa* (Washington, D.C.: World Bank, 1985), pp. 69 and 79; D. Bovet and L. Unnevehr, *Agricultural Pricing in Togo* (Washington, D.C.: World Bank Staffing Paper, No. 467, July 1981), pp. 25 and 58; and Paul Nugent, "National Integration and the Vicissitudes of State Power in Ghana: The Political Incorporation of Likpe, a Border Community, 1945–1986," forthcoming thesis.

factories. Moreover, the infrastructural bottlenecks already referred to had begun to disrupt the formal commercial networks of the country, so that the stores of more peripheral towns often stood empty. Most Ghanaians simply had to forego consumption, but border communities also had the option of buying goods outside. However, they needed CFA francs if they were to purchase items such as cloth or medicine, and that meant smuggling produce out. The life cycle of an item like a bar of soap could often be quite complicated. Not uncommonly, the management of a Ghanaian factory would smuggle the item into Togo, where another Ghanaian would buy it and bring it back into the country.

The reaction of successive regimes to the smuggling question was remarkably constant and consisted of two related elements. The first was the use of the media to highlight the damage perpetrated by smugglers. Faced with repeated challenges to its credentials and legitimacy, a regime such as that of Acheampong found in smuggling the one issue on which it could take the moral high ground. Smugglers were repeatedly denounced as "nation-wreckers" and provided a convenient foil for the regime, which could be seen to be safeguarding the national interest.[9] The second element, which followed logically from this, was a rhetorical assertion of state power. That is, the authorities periodically warned that smugglers would be subjected to the full coercive might of the state. This was backed up by very public pronouncements of measures showing that these declarations were being put into effect. The National Redemption Council (NRC) came to power following two successive years of rampant smuggling and swiftly announced its intention to clamp down. Under the Subversion Decree of July 1972, the death penalty was prescribed for certain categories of smuggling.[10] Moreover, the Border Guards were for the first time brought under the umbrella of the armed forces, where they were to receive better training, encounter more rigorous discipline, and benefit from more attractive conditions of service.[11]

The declarations of intent on the part of the NRC and later the Supreme Military Council (SMC) bore little relation to what actually happened. Far from establishing a firmer grip, the center seemed to suffer an even greater loss of control. This had more than a little to do with the behavior of Acheampong and his colleagues. Although members of the SMC publicly condemned smuggling, it was widely believed that they profited from it.[12] It was no accident that Major-General Utuka, a former head of the Border Guards and SMC member, was among those executed by the Armed Forces Revolutionary Council (AFRC) in 1979. This did not mean, however, that the SMC regarded it as open season for everybody else. Hence, one had the apparent anomaly of soldiers confiscating rice from small farmers in the north, while allowing the wealthy farmers to take their crops into Togo and Upper Volta.[13] Nevertheless, the conflicting signals that the Border Guards were receiving no doubt affected their morale. It was the Border Guards who were billed as the agents of state control, and it was they who were blamed for the rampant smuggling from the mid-1970s onward. Given the overwhelming incentive to smuggle, there would not have been enough Border Guards to seal the borders even if they had maintained higher standards of discipline. The reality was that guardsmen were poorly paid and so resorted to taking bribes in exchange for safe passage. During the period of the Third Republic, a member of Parliament complained that guardsmen were forced to seek living quarters with their host communities, which made it impossible for them to carry out their functions impartially.[14] Indeed, guardsmen seemed to become quickly coopted by communities in the places they were posted to. The member for Dormaa in Brong-Ahafo was more specific:

> Now we get a situation in which the farmers and the Border Guards have combined to cheat the nation. For, without the assistance of the Border Guards . . . the farmers alone could not smuggle any significant quantity of cocoa out of the country. Both the smugglers and the guards have found smuggling a very lucrative enterprise. It is alleged that for every bag of cocoa which the guards get across the border, they collect something like ¢200 from the owner of the cocoa, that is the farmer, while the farmer earns not less than ¢1,000 which, of course, is far more than the ¢240 which he gets in Ghana, and which is not paid promptly by the Ghana Cocoa Marketing Board.[15]

## ■ New Departures Under the PNDC

By the time Rawlings returned to power on December 31, 1981, the Limann regime had lost any semblance of control over the economy. According to one World Bank estimate, transactions on the parallel market had mushroomed from 0.27 percent of GDP in 1972 to 32.4 percent in 1982.[16] The incoming regime announced its determination to eradicate a long list of "economic crimes," which had recurred since the housecleaning of 1979. At the top of the list was smuggling, which Rawlings blamed for many of the ailments of the national economy:

> Smuggling has become the number one enemy of our country. Cocoa is smuggled. Rice is smuggled. Maize is smuggled. Imported tractors and bicycles are smuggled. The smuggling does not only reduce our foreign exchange earning, but also increases our import bill. . . . The unpatriotic Ghanaian smuggler has created a situation where Government's ability to provide such essential goods as kerosene, cloth, cutlass, drugs, etc. has been greatly hampered, because we have to import not only for our local population, but also for our neighbors who get it through smuggling. No nation can afford this. And unless we put a decisive stop to it, our efforts at national reconstruction and transformation of the economy will be seriously undermined.[17]

This raised an obvious question: How did the PNDC propose to succeed where previous regimes had failed? The answer lay in the character of the revolution. Smuggling was attributed to a specific social class, embracing large-scale farmers, wealthy traders, and transport owners, who in turn collaborated with politicians and corrupt officials. An attack on smuggling was simultaneously an assault on the economic base of the Ghanaian ruling class. Although there were clear differences of opinion between Rawlings and

Chris Atim (a PNDC member and head of the National Defence Committee) over the direction of the revolution, they spoke as one when it came to the question of smuggling. The borders remained closed for most of 1982, and new penalties were prescribed. Offenders were warned that their farms would be forfeited to the state and that they risked being executed.[18] A more effective judicial machinery was put in place in the major regional centers in the form of the Public Tribunals and there were plans to extend these to every border town. To improve border surveillance, the regular army and the Police Task Force were sent on border duties. They were not only to complement the operations of the Border Guards, but also to maintain an independent check on their activities.

A more significant innovation was the involvement of the newly formed People's Defence Committees in antismuggling operations. An essential point about the PDCs that is often missed is that they were always viewed by the PNDC and the NDC as agents of social control as much as instruments of mass political participation. At a time when the state apparatus had become less manageable, the PDCs were a potentially important substitute. When it came to smuggling, the fact that they were rooted in the communities meant that they had access to local sources of information that were denied to state agencies. It was believed that since the worst offenders were also the most privileged members of the community, the PDCs would have few qualms about exposing smugglers.

By contrast, very little was done during 1982 to ameliorate the conditions that encouraged smuggling. Nothing could be done to rein in the black market as long as the PNDC was unwilling to grasp the nettle of the overvalued currency. Even the foreign secretary, Dr. Obed Asamoah, whom left-wingers had wanted excluded from the government for his conservative views, voiced his opposition to IMF pressure for a devaluation of the cedi.[19] Without a devaluation, it was not possible for the government to raise producer prices, since the tripling of prices by the Limann regime in 1981 had placed the Cocoa Marketing Board in deficit. Yet, the farmers still received only 60 percent of 1970 prices in real terms.[20] Moreover, the high inflation of 1982 quickly eroded the effects of the price rise. When it came to setting a new price for the 1982/83 season, it would have been necessary to raise it significantly in order to keep the real price steady. Rawlings, however, sought to persuade farmers' leaders to accept a reduction. The appeal was rebuffed, although there were reports in the press of farmers voluntarily accepting less for their cocoa. In the event, the decision to maintain the 1981 price for another season was less than a victory for the farmers, especially as the cost of inputs was raised, supposedly to compensate the government for its generosity.[21] Even the introduction of the Akuafo Cheque, which was designed in part to replace the issue of chits, was not a resounding success given the inadequate rural banking facilities. Finally, the supply of essential commodities remained inadequate during 1982. It was not until 1983 that the People's Shops were set up, and they, for the most part, failed for lack of goods.

During 1982, the authorities were able to point to some success in combating smuggling in the Volta Region, which was reflected in improved cocoa purchases. However, the fact that a Ghanaian farmer could receive ¢900 per load in Togo and ¢1,200 in Côte d'Ivoire, as opposed to the ¢360 offered by the CMB, meant that many continued to take the risk.[22] The same was true of communities outside the cocoa belt. The Border Guards were once again accused of assisting smugglers and of sending the soldiers on false trails. The PDCs in a number of areas also complained of harassment from the guards. The failure of the PNDC to equip the PDCs so that they could defend themselves perhaps reflected the sensitivity in military circles about possible competition from the PDCs. Finally, the PDCs often preferred a low profile because of community pressure. Because smuggling was an activity engaged in by a wide range of people, and not just a wealthy minority, the more active PDCs were faced with the embarrassment of having to arrest their kin.

The awareness that something more drastic was required on the economic front pulled members of the regime in different directions, culminating in a purge of the left toward the end of the year. These events have been extensively debated elsewhere, often by people who were closely involved in them.[23] What matters here is the consequences of the split for government policy. Rawlings and his supporters have often claimed that the left had no constructive alternative to the Economic Recovery Program. This is not strictly true, as a document authored by the National Defence Committee would suggest.[24] The alternative would, however, have required a level of state control over economy and society that was probably unrealistic at that time. The essence of the ERP was a return to the logic of the market. The latter was expected to bring about greater productivity but also to cut the ground from beneath the black market. This in turn meant that rather less would be required of state institutions.

Since 1983, the PNDC has been thorough in the implementation of market-oriented policies. Undoubtedly the single most important reform has been the decision to restore the exchange value of the cedi to its real rate. From a rate of ¢2.75 to the dollar in 1982, the official rate of the cedi had fallen to ¢330 by July 1990. Although the foreign exchange auctions were still operative, the PNDC planned to integrate the auction rate with the exchange bureau rate in the course of the year. Already the licensed bureaus have been offering a rate close to that of the black market, taking much of the vitality out of the infamous "Cow Lane" in the process. It is possible that Ghana will once again have a convertible currency in the near future.

Once that happens, a central pillar of the underground economy will have been removed.

Economic liberalization was also expected to alleviate the problem of shortages. The PNDC hoped that the influx of imported goods would eventually slow down, to be replaced by commodities produced inside the country. Although domestic industries have often wilted under the competition of cheap imports, making recovery more difficult, there has been no doubt about the ability of Ghanaians to purchase almost anything since around 1985. The marked improvement in transport and infrastructure has ensured that these essential commodities are to be found in the remotest corners of the country.

Finally, the PNDC has since 1983 embraced a policy of restoring competitive producer prices for cocoa. The Ghanaian state, unlike that of Nigeria, cannot afford to abandon the state monopsony that has been in place since World War II. Nevertheless, the PNDC has been aware of the need to balance the revenue demands of the state against the long-term viability of the cocoa industry. The government has expressed its intention to restore at least half of the world price to the farmers.[25] In 1990, when neighboring countries were cutting producer prices, the PNDC was raising them still further. The hope is that farmers will not only replant cocoa that has died out, but will also market their crops through official channels (see Table 4.3).

These transformations in economic policy tell only half the story. The PNDC also sought to improve its surveillance in border areas. The invasion from Togo that almost toppled the PNDC in 1983 brought home to the leadership the political dangers inherent in having the capital located so close to a boundary that was highly porous. In 1984, the PNDC finally decided to abolish the Border Guards altogether and to make the army responsible for all aspects of border security, including the movement of goods and people. When it came to smuggling, it was hoped that the soldiers would exhibit a more developed sense of the national interest than the Border Guards had. Moreover, since border duties were merely one area of military responsibility, it would be rather easier to rotate the soldiers. That would prevent them from acquiring local attachments. Some lessons were also learned from the experience of the PDCs. A new People's Militia was created using recruits drawn from the villages, much like the PDCs. The difference was that the militia men and women were selected without any particular regard for evidence of political consciousness. It was sufficient that recruits be willing to carry out the tasks required of them. Their loyalties now lay not with the community but with the retired military officers who headed the Civil Defence Organisation (CDO). Unlike the PDCs, they received some weapons training. The fact that the Militia was drawn from an entire district in all probability meant that they would have some access to local intelligence, but

Table 4.3  The Trend in Cocoa Prices, 1981–1987

| Year | Nominal Cocoa Price Index (1977=100) | Real Cocoa Price Index (1977=100) |
|---|---|---|
| 1981 | 900 | 103 |
| 1982 | 900 | 85 |
| 1983 | 1,500 | 64 |
| 1984 | 2,251 | 68 |
| 1985 | 4,246 | 115 |
| 1986 | 6,414 | 141 |
| 1987 | 11,253 | 214 |

*Source*: S. Commander, J. Howell, and Wayo Seini, "Ghana, 1983-7," in S. Commander (ed.), *Structural Adjustment and Agriculture: Theory and Practice in Africa and Latin America* (London: James Currey/ODI, 1989), table 7.2, p. 113.

also that they would not be dealing with direct kin. There is no published material available on the militia. However, my own research in the Hohoe and Jasikan districts revealed that the creation of the militia was something of a master stroke. In the final section I shall explain why.

## ■ The Death of Smuggling?

If we were to confine ourselves to statements of intent alone, the problem of smuggling would have been resolved decades ago. Although there is a clear need to assess the performance of the PNDC, it is notoriously difficult to glean reliable evidence about something that, by definition, does not enter the statistical record. Cocoa poses the fewest complications because COCOBOD does hold the data from which one can make the necessary extrapolations. However, only the figures for national purchases are regularly published. Regional purchases are less accessible, while official secrecy prevents COCOBOD employees from disclosing information about the districts and specific buying centers. This is a severe hindrance, because it is by plotting the fluctuations in purchases at these lower levels and by mapping these against trends in Côte d'Ivoire and Togo that one can most easily gauge the leakage. The alternative approach, which involves calculating the difference between actual production and official purchases, is likely to yield far less accurate results.[26] In the absence of reliable data, I shall rely in this final section upon more qualitative local evidence drawn from the Volta Region in 1985/86 and conclude with some comments on more recent developments.

Fieldwork was carried out over a fifteen-month period in the Hohoe and Jasikan districts and more specifically in Likpe, a small community located alongside the border with Togo. The local economy from Likpe northward has been dominated by cocoa since at least the 1930s. As in other parts of southern Ghana, the spread of cocoa was accompanied by new patterns of trade and consumption. Hohoe stood at the center of a commercial nexus that had its roots in the Gold Coast. Until the 1950s, it was common for cocoa farmers in French Togoland to sell their crops in Likpe so that they could purchase consumer goods that were more freely available there. All this had changed by the 1970s. It became increasingly difficult to acquire basic commodities in Likpe and Hohoe itself. The Togolese had constructed good roads to their border villages, which meant that the markets were always well stocked and the buying stations were easily accessible. In Likpe and neighboring communities, there was an absence of land on which to continue planting cocoa. Although younger members of the community could not replicate the achievements of an earlier generation, there was little to be gained from migrating to the city either. For many young men and women, the most attractive alternative was to engage in petty smuggling. Most simply hired out their services as carriers, although some managed to accumulate sufficient means to recruit the services of others. This type of smuggling was very different from the stock image presented by the official media. Smuggling was less a form of profiteering than a means of survival at a time when many families were being subjected to a reproduction squeeze. For that reason, the PDCs proved much less successful as an instrument of control than the authorities had wished. The PDCs were supposed to appeal to patriotic youth, but in reality it was the youth who were most regularly involved in breaches of the law. Consequently, the PDCs usually opted for the role of spectators in the campaign against smuggling.

From the nadir of 1983, conditions had improved noticeably two years later. Apart from better weather conditions, government economic policies were beginning to take effect at the local level. Hohoe had recovered its position as a bustling commercial town, servicing other centers like Jasikan and Kadjebi as well as a mass of smaller villages. In the case of Likpe, it was once more possible to acquire essential commodities without crossing the frontier, although price differentials often favored that course of action.[27] An inspection of one store in Likpe-Todome in 1986 revealed that seventeen out of twenty items on sale were still of Togolese origin.[28] In some cases, economic recovery actually stimulated new variants on smuggling. In particular, state-subsidized kerosene and petroleum could be sold at a profit in Togo. The rate of return, as shown in Table 4.4, was most respectable when one compares it with the minimum daily wage of ¢90.

Similarly, the PNDC had only partially succeeded in squeezing the profits on cocoa smuggling. Whereas a farmer who sent his beans to Togo in 1980/81 would have earned four times as much as the official price in Ghana, the difference was about double at the start of the 1985/86 season. Similarly, the Ivorian cocoa price was between 1.7 and 1.8 times higher.[29] Of course, the net return was rather lower when overhead costs are taken into account. These included payment to carriers and a standard bribe of CFA1,000 or ¢400

Table 4.4  Profits from Smuggling of Petroleum Products (per 6 gallons), as of August 1986

| Item | Kerosene (¢) | Petrol (¢) |
| --- | --- | --- |
| Purchase price | 600 | 1,100 |
| Transport from Hohoe | — | 100 |
| Bribes to soldiers | 50 | 100 |
| Total overhead | 650 | 1,300 |
| Sale price in Togo converted into cedis | 850 | 1,750 |
| Net profit | 200 | 450 |

*Source*: Interviews in Likpe, 1986.

per load to the soldiers who were on border duty. A smuggler who bought cocoa from other farmers could make a net profit of as little as ¢102 per load, although a person who smuggled his own cocoa stood to earn ¢1,102 per load. The rewards had undoubtedly shrunk by 1986, but they were nevertheless tempting. A more significant shift was that smuggling had ceased to be the only worthwhile activity. It had long been known that there was surplus land in the area roughly between Kpandu and Hohoe. However, the breakdown of the transport system and the lack of spare parts for tractors had discouraged farmers from exploiting its potential. The 1983 drought and the resultant food shortages brought home to the people of Likpe and nearby communities precisely how serious the food deficit had become. The following year, a number of women migrated to the Hohoe area, where they rented land and planted rice. In subsequent years, as cheap transport became more freely available and the government promised easier access to bank loans, the rice migrations attracted increasing numbers of participants. The initial migrants tended to be drawn from the most disadvantaged sections of the community (often widows and divorcees without access to their own land at home), but later participants included older men who perceived rice as a short-term alternative to cocoa, which was now blighted by black pod disease. In between were the landless youth, who found that they could earn almost as much from rice cultivation as from smuggling. Although the authorities probably did not foresee these particular consequences, they could claim some credit for the result.

However, this did not entirely resolve the issue, and it is to the new strategies of control that we must look to account for a widespread local perception that smuggling was no longer worth the effort. The substitution of the Mortar Regiment for the Border Guards did not of itself make an appreciable difference. The process of rotation was so slow that many soldiers were able to bring their families to live with them. Like the former Border Guards, they were allowed the time to build up relations of trust with local smugglers. Indeed, I have evidence that soldiers were paying local youths to headload their own smuggled goods. Instead, it was the People's Militia that tilted the balance of forces in the direction of the authorities. By the end of 1986, the Hohoe District Militia probably consisted of at least 120 recruits, based in Hohoe but drawn mostly from outlying villages.[30] The Militia was composed primarily of the landless and unemployed youth of both sexes, who under other circumstances would probably have been engaged in smuggling. Indeed, the district commander regarded this as their most valuable attribute:

> Since the Militia has been on the scene, smuggling is on the decline. The reason is that some Militiamen are ex-smugglers, so they know the routes and the people involved. Most are operating in their own localities.[31]

The last observation was broadly correct, but most of the militia men and women operating in a specific village at any one time would be strangers. Consequently, they could usually afford to be less responsive to local pressures. Their reason for enlisting in the Militia was that they were guaranteed half the value of any goods they seized. They also received occasional perks from the CDO, although they were expected to supply their own uniforms. The government and the Militia were, therefore, bound together in an unusual relationship of mutual convenience.

By August 1986, the activities of the Militia were creating sufficient discomfort to cause local traders to begin ordering their supplies from Hohoe. People who were accustomed to free access to Togolese markets began to reconsider their options. Some smugglers placed themselves under the protective wing of the soldiers, who were hostile toward the pretensions of the Militia and their interference with trade. By contrast with 1982, when the soldiers clashed with the Militia it was often the latter who received the backing of higher authorities. Other smugglers joined the Militia or switched to rice farming. The Militia did, however, run the risk of putting itself out of business. If cross-border traffic ceased, the Militia would be left without an income. There were signs that this was already beginning to happen by the end of 1986. Many people were intercepted and had their goods seized despite the fact that they were carrying lawful quantities. The explanation was that the Militia were "hungry." There was already resentment at the powers that had been placed in the hands of these so-called small boys. These additional provocations led to at least one clash between the Militia and the villagers. The Militia were often arbitrary and were not above granting favors to people they knew, but as a crude instrument of control they were rather more effective than previous measures had been.

That was how things stood in one locality in 1986. Since that time, the PNDC has made further progress. In his 1990 budget statement, the secretary for Finance and Economic Planning, Dr. Kwesi Botchwey, noted that subsidies on petroleum products continued to reward smuggling.[32] However, for the first time in decades Ghana has been offering a higher cocoa price than its neighbors. As a result, cocoa began to be smuggled into Ghana toward the end of 1989. In his nationwide address on January 2, 1990, Rawlings referred to the inequities of the international cocoa market but was unable to suppress the temptation to contrast the wisdom of PNDC policy with the panic measures of neighboring states:

> As our production has gone up, the world price of our product has gone down. Some cocoa-producing countries have reacted by slashing the price which they pay to the farmers. But we know it would be suicidal to penalize our noble farmers for something which is entirely outside their control, and therefore have managed to maintain a fair producer price. This explains the new, unusual sight of farmers in neighboring countries trying to smuggle their cocoa into Ghana—an ironic reversal of what pertained in the past.[33]

This statement is an indication of the distance Rawlings has traveled since 1982.

## ■ Conclusion

In the wider debate about the economic reforms of the PNDC, it is inevitable and indeed correct that attention be focused on the consequences for social equality and the living conditions of the poorest sections of Ghanaian society. The question of smuggling constitutes only a single angle on this much larger picture. Nonetheless, the conclusions are worth spelling out. Since the 1960s, successive governments have treated smuggling as a law-and-order problem that is best tackled using a firm hand. The results have been disappointing because the conditions that forced ordinary Ghanaians to engage in smuggling were not addressed. However, this failure should not disguise the fact that periodic anti-smuggling drives often took the form of the harassment of ordinary people from border villages, while others with political connections carried on undisturbed. It would be naive to believe that harassment has become a thing of the past under the PNDC. However, what the Rawlings regime has done is to present border communities with options. Indeed, its only real chance of success, given that the smuggling of cocoa and petroleum could not realistically be tolerated, is to arrive at an arrangement that is in the material interests of both the center and the populations living on the frontiers. Rawlings has come closer to achieving this compromise than any of his predecessors.

## ■ Notes

1. I am grateful to the Central Research Fund of the University of London and the Scholarships Committee of the University of Cape Town for funding the fieldwork upon which this article is based. The results will shortly appear in a London University thesis, to be entitled "National Integration and the Vicissitudes of State Power in Ghana: The Political Incorporation of Likpe, a Border Community, 1945-1986."
2. This perhaps explains why so little research has been conducted into smuggling in Africa. However, a recent contribution is that of Janet MacGaffey, *Entrepreneurs and Parasites: The Struggle for Indigenous Capitalism in Zaire* (Cambridge: Cambridge University Press, 1987), esp. ch. 6. A useful continental survey is provided by Robert Barad, "Unrecorded Transborder Trade in Sub-Saharan Africa and Its Implications for Regional Economic Co-operation," a paper prepared for the workshop "Regional Integration and Co-operation in Sub-Saharan Africa," organized by The World Bank, September 1988.
3. Togo has regularly exported diamonds despite the fact that it has no mines of its own. See "Togo: Local 'Wall Street,'" *West Africa* 26 (March 1-April 1990), pp. 505-506.
4. For information on this score, see *Pick's Currency Yearbook*, various editions, and Ernesto May, *Exchange Controls and Parallel Market Economies in Sub-Saharan Africa: Focus on Ghana* (Washington, D.C.: World Bank, 1985), p. 127.
5. Adrian Antoine, "The Politics of Rice Farming in Dagbon, 1972-1979," Ph.D. thesis, London University, 1985, p. 149.
6. Hence the Ghanaian state has been dubbed a "customs post state." See Richard Crook, "Decolonization, the Colonial State, and Chieftaincy in the Gold Coast," *African Affairs* 85, 338 (January 1986), p. 86ff.
7. See D. Bovet and L. Unnevehr, *Agricultural Pricing in Togo* (Washington, D.C.: World Bank Staffing Paper No. 467, July 1981).
8. J. C. De Wilde, *Agriculture, Marketing and Pricing in Sub-Saharan Africa* (University of California, African Studies Center, 1984), p. 86.
9. An attempt was made in 1976 to link smuggling with secessionism in the Volta Region.
10. The decree prescribed a prison sentence of not less than fifteen years and not more than thirty years for the smuggling of cocoa, and the death sentence for the smuggling of timber, diamonds, and gold. Cases arising were henceforth to be tried by military tribunals.
11. The head of the Border Guards was henceforth a senior military officer. When the SMC was established, the head of the Border Guards became a member along with the heads of the army, navy, and air force.
12. Hard evidence is difficult to come by here. Mike Oquaye, who dredged up a lot of other incriminating evidence, states that the "Colonels and Generals were responsible for the very heavy consignments smuggled under the glaring eyes of border guards in huge articulators." See M. Oquaye, *Politics in Ghana, 1972-1979* (Accra: Tornado Publications, 1980), p. 50.
13. Antoine, "Politics of Rice Farming," p. 149.
14. Monica Atenkah, P.N.P. Member for Buem, in *Parliamentary Debates*, December 13, 1979.
15. S. A. Manson, P.F.P. Member for Dormaa, quoted in *Parliamentary Debates*, November 11, 1980.

16. May, *Exchange Controls*, p. 89.
17. A speech made by Rawlings at Tamale on October 14, 1982, in *A Revolutionary Journey: Selected Speeches of Flt.-Lt. Jerry John Rawlings*, vol. 1 (Accra: Ghana Publishing Corp., n.d.), p. 65.
18. Kwame Saarah-Mensah, the Brong-Ahafo regional secretary, quoted in *The Ghanaian Times*, February 9, 1982.
19. *The Ghanaian Times*, March 1, 1982. Like Major-General Utuka, Dr. Asamoah was from Likpe. He had been a member of Parliament for the Biakoye constituency in the Second Republic and failed by the narrowest of margins to retain the seat for the United National Convention in 1979.
20. Interview with Kwesi Botchwey, reported in *West Africa*, January 12, 1987, pp. 63–65.
21. See the speech by Rawlings on the launching of the Akuafo Cheque System in *A Revolutionary Journey*, p. 56.
22. May, *Exchange Controls*, Table B3, p. 129.
23. For example, see Donald Ray, *Ghana: Politics, Economy and Society* (Boulder: Lynne Rienner Publishers; London: Frances Pinter, 1986), Chs. 5–8; Z. Yeebo, "Ghana: Defence Committees and the Class Struggle," *Review of African Political Economy* 32 (1985); E. Hansen, "The State and Popular Struggles in Ghana, 1982–86," in P. Anyang' Nyong'o, *Popular Struggles for Democracy in Africa* (London: Zed Books, 1987).
24. See the unpublished *Report of the Committee of the National Defence Committee and Secretaries on the Economy*.
25. On government agricultural policy and its effects, see S. Commander, J. Howell, and Wayo Seini, "Ghana, 1983–7," in S. Commander (ed.), *Structural Adjustment and Agriculture: Theory and Practice in Africa and Latin America* (London: James Currey/ODI, 1989).
26. Many variables must be taken into account (such as amount of rainfall) when estimating production levels. Even the basic data on the age and acreage of trees is of questionable reliability.
27. This included clothing, blankets, metal pans, beer, sugar, and cigarettes.
28. The Togolese goods included soap, tinned sardines, tinned pilchards, batteries, razor blades, soft drinks, cigarettes, talcum powder, pomade, cocoa butter, sugar cubes, granulated sugar, pens, and tinned tomatoes. The only Ghanaian goods were soap, Cerelac, and Guinness. Personal diary, September 27, 1986.
29. World Bank, *Ghana: Towards Structural Adjustment*, October 1988, p. 46.
30. Although Likpe was still part of the Jasikan District at this time, it was placed under the Hohoe District militia. In July 1986, the second intake, consisting of sixty-eight new recruits and including ten women, passed out. My estimate is a rather conservative one, given that there had been a previous intake and others to follow. See "Militiamen Must Help Combat Economic Crimes," *People's Daily Graphic*, July 29, 1986.
31. Interview with Lawrence Akoto, CDO district commander, Hohoe, October 6, 1986.
32. "The Budget and Highlights of Economic Policy for 1990," *Home Front* 9, 1 (March 1990), p. 10.
33. "Nationwide Radio and Television Broadcast by the Chairman of the PNDC, Flt.-Lt. Jerry John Rawlings," *Home Front* 9, 1 (March 1990), p. 21.

# 5
# Equity Issues in Ghana's Rural Development

*Gwendolyn Mikell*

There is little hope of transforming African rural areas and pursuing rural development without adequately understanding the issue of equity. This appears to be one of the lessons that can be drawn from Ghana's experience with economic collapse during the late 1970s and its gradual economic and political recuperation during the 1980s. Although Ghana's military government has acknowledged its desire to achieve rural economic development, the question is whether competing local and national/global views of the desired development can be reconciled. When the PNDC, under pressure from the IMF, sought to reconstruct the cocoa export sector, diversify the economy,[1] and achieve greater sectoral integration, it appealed to peasant producers for support. With its Economic Recovery Program in place, the government raised producer prices and subsidized inputs for farmers despite serious objections from urbanites in Accra and in other major cities.

Stressing the primacy of rural interests in the government's early policies, the PNDC believed that it could count on the support of farmers and proceeded to reorganize the political system so as to achieve popular participation in local decisionmaking. The 1988–1989 district elections did not allow competitive politics. Nevertheless, during these elections, the issue of equity for the various class, occupational, and gender groups present in the newly reconstructed rural areas rapidly emerged. Both local politics and global economic factors conspired to produce a rural political economy that not only conflicted with the existing philosophical and social systems of the peasants, but one in which they perceived little economic or social equity.

One unforeseen result of structural adjustment in the rural areas has been social and economic diversity. This diversity has been brought about by price adjustments for export crops, the redeployment of civil servants to rural areas, and the creation of local and district assemblies. Structural adjustment has also generated a fear that the "peasant voice" will not be heard, that the whole peasant group will not benefit substantially from the resources it has generated, and that women and children are being impoverished. It will not be possible to understand Ghana's political economy and its emerging problems, such as urban unrest and resurgent local-level activism as well as dissatisfaction, unless an in-depth analysis is made of how rural communities view and are affected by the new economic and political programs.

## ■ Contrasting Rural Versus National Views on Development

Although anthropologists have always emphasized the roles of culture, social structure, and history in the interactions of various internal and external status groups,[2] the concern for power and economic factors has tended to dominate our discussion of African rural producers and the state. Most social scientists agree that the manner in which peasants relate to the state conditions their economic, political, and social well-being, but the necessity of considering other important sociocultural variables is now becoming apparent. The question, as it was phrased earlier, was whether the concern of rural producers with their ethnic or "primordial" identities and parochial socioeconomic interests prevailed over their concern for the national interest.[3] Most discussions of this issue have tended to overlook the complexity of the factors involved and the changes that take place over time. Far from being passive or revolutionary participants in the interaction with their states, peasants have often exhibited surprising flexibility during the precolonial as well as the colonial and independence periods.[4]

Ghanaian experiences during the decolonization and early independence period provide fascinating examples of the clash of nationalist and peasant worldviews about economic development and its political aspects. Although British administrators had initially struggled to develop rural capitalists throughout the southern portion of the Gold Coast (Ghana)[5] who could pioneer the cocoa industry, by the 1930s they were seeking ways to control the intermediaries and chiefs who were viewed as exploiting fluctuations in the economy and thereby forcing indebted farmers to pledge their cocoa farms. Not unconnected with this was the fear that wealthy farmers would agitate for greater involvement in the marketing of cocoa, which had been the province of the European buying firms until that time. The British also moved to develop local agricultural cooperatives that would further encourage production, stabilize producer prices, and allow coordinated local and government influences in the export sector.[6] By this time, however, wealthy farmers were aware of their growing political clout. They joined the emerging African nationalist politicians in the 1950s and often articulated their ethnic and regional interests during the period that followed.[7] The agitation of farmers in the rich cocoa-producing Brong area for regional autonomy from

Asante economic and political control was a major weapon the nationalist leader Kwame Nkrumah could use in combating the challenge of the Asante-based National Liberation Movement for political control of the country.[8]

Nkrumah, as well as others, probably overestimated the extent to which rural culture and rural realities would be obstacles to development. Being Western-educated and sharing Western philosophical notions about traditional "autocracy" versus representative political participation, Nkrumah was determined to combat "tribalism" and the chieftaincy. He felt that modern rural stratification often followed from the advantages provided by traditional status distinctions, so it is not surprising that when he became head of state in 1957, Nkrumah clearly articulated the view that rural stratification was the enemy of Ghana's political future. Nkrumah thought that only with centralized control of export marketing could the wealth of cocoa be freed from the control of chiefs and large-scale farmers. This wealth could then be used in a rational fashion to create the industrial infrastructure that could release Ghana from neocolonialism. Therefore, the cocoa cooperatives, which during this period were composed more of wealthy and stable farmers than poor farmers,[9] were obvious targets for Nkrumah's CCP's wrath. After all, the secessionist Ashanti politicians had advocated "Vote for Cocoa!"

What Nkrumah failed to realize was that behind the broad label of "cooperatives" and of other rural organizations was a complex social and philosophical system. These wealthy cocoa farmers were usually polygynous males. They had large families that helped them manage their farms, and they also hired sizable numbers of farm laborers. Among the cooperative cocoa farmers was a small group of women, many of whom tended to have larger farms or greater economic success than most women farmers.[10] From the local perspective, many of the male cooperative members were the recognized leaders within their communities, and they incurred patron-client and other civic responsibilities that flowed from economic success. In the Sunyani area, the cooperative leaders were a distinct group from the chiefs and other traditional leaders, but over time they tended to have affinal ties to the chiefs and they derived considerable legitimacy from these connections.[11]

When Nkrumah dissolved the peasant cooperatives in 1961 and melded them into the state buying agency, the United Ghana Farmers' Council (UGFC), he generated much rural hostility because he distorted local sociopolitical and economic structures. Sunyani area cooperative society cocoa farmers claimed that CPP domination of their local UGFC committees subsequently prevented them from investing capital in village projects and contributing to local development. This as much as any other of Nkrumah's policies (perhaps even more than the state-controlled cocoa prices) made the farmers perceive themselves as political and socioeconomic pawns, and they were unwilling to cooperate with the CPP government.

There are few indications that most of the governments that arose after

Nkrumah's overthrow in 1966[12] had learned that national economic development was possible only when national plans incorporated, rather than challenged, local socioeconomic and sociopolitical structures and worldviews. During the 1970s, Colonel Ignatius Acheampong's National Redemption Council government developed Operation-Feed-Yourself (OFY), which was designed to utilize local land, local resources, and local coordination to increase agricultural production so that profit from that sector could be used to "feed-our-industries." Although the NRC did encourage chiefs to support their efforts by turning over land for farming, *labor* rather than land had become the most significant variable in rural production in the South. Those who were prepared to take advantage of OFY by requesting agricultural extension loans for labor and inputs to enlarge their farms were mostly large-scale peasants and absentee farmers who were tied into urban social relations. Few small-scale farmers or women farmers could qualify for credit. Therefore, programs such as OFY could scarcely be called serious agricultural initiatives, because they provided virtually no national coordination or additional resources. No "development" linkage was established between the local and national levels. In 1973, when I asked farmers about OFY, they usually responded that it was a great idea, but most asked where they were supposed to obtain the labor or fertilizers and other inputs that were needed to increase production. This general pessimism was even greater among women, whose farms were smaller and who had less available labor. After sporadic local enthusiasm but no significant national response to the needs of small farmers, there was a subsequent decline in OFY productivity in most rural areas.

One should not infer that Ghanaian politicians and soldiers were disinterested in local involvement in development. In fact, during the Acheampong period, the government facilitated some U.S. Agency for International Development (USAID) projects aimed at decentralizing development planning and budgeting.[13] Rather, national-level development models were more heavily grounded in Western individualistic approaches to development than in communal approaches. Movement to the next step—designing development from the bottom up, based on local culture and philosophies—appears to have faltered because of economic collapse and political instability, as well as inadequate cultural and philosophical sensitivity.

### ■ Rawlings: Status/Gender Groups and Rural Development

It is possible that the difficult route that the Rawlings government had to traverse as it proceeded to stabilize the economy and to reconstruct the political process encouraged it to shift the focus away from the importance of rural perspectives in the development process. Rawlings's initial aims were twofold: to reduce the urban/national exploitation of rural producers, thereby making peasants respected participants in the country's economic recuperation; and to establish a "peoples' democracy" within which both rural and urban folk could play equitable roles. Because these goals were focused generally on rewarding rural folk for their contributions, without special emphasis upon the welfare of a particular rural stratum or gender group, there was some ambiguity in the PNDC's development strategies. But perhaps the more important factor is that despite Rawlings's initial aims, his view of development has been proven to be essentially a Western one focused more on outcomes of economic processes than the internal dynamics of the processes themselves. To this extent, the national development approach was in conflict with the indigenous rural one.

The rural ethos or "worldview" stressed the corporate nature of the village and the town despite traditional status differences or even the modern stratification generated by the early cocoa boom. It recognized the responsibility of chiefs to encourage residents to contribute to the development of local buildings, roads, and needs in general. The rural ethos also recognized the important social obligations that leaders had to their clients, employees, and to strangers; and it required participatory processes that would allow some representation for these less powerful groups. This ethos also stressed the complementarity (as opposed to egalitarianism) of male and female roles, whether familial, communal, or economic, and encouraged the display of this complementarity at important communal endeavors.

While twentieth-century events have changed some of the dynamics of the rural worldview, the basic principles still exist and have retained their legitimacy. The development of local government structures since the 1950s has separated chiefs from control over local revenues, but the chiefs retain the moral authority to impose assessments and mobilize efforts for communal needs. Kwame Arhin (1985) has drawn our attention to the fact that the recent crises in political economy, and the rural-urban migrations of the last two decades, have disrupted, but not destroyed, these communal processes.

The local emphasis on corporatism and interdependence has remained a strength within these communities, so much so that Rawlings could utilize it as the basis for the creation of the work groups that helped restore Ghanaian agriculture. However, rural notions of male-female complementarity, which were only vaguely articulated at the level of economic production and community participation,[14] have suffered and have only begun to be integrated into PNDC development plans since 1988. Even the more obvious local strengths such as corporatism have tended to be insufficiently emphasized and have not yet been adequately used as the basis of development strategies.

The national and global factors that continue to affect Ghanaian agriculture and the economy in general have made it difficult for Rawlings to live up to the goal of empowering the ordinary export and food farmer. The key question is whether this is because of extreme external aid requirements or because viable modern agriculture (for export as well as food production) necessitates a different type of rural social structure than that which existed in the earlier phase of cocoa export production when lineage and corporate relationships were of major importance. The PNDC's Economic Recovery Program, which restructured the economy between 1983 and the present, did increase the percentage of the cocoa producer price that was paid to rural producers and stabilize agricultural producer prices, although large-scale farmers and male farmers were the primary beneficiaries.[15] With the development of the concept of "Community Initiated Projects" as part of a PAMSCAD proposal in 1987,[16] the PNDC appeared to give evidence of a desire to make rural viewpoints significant. But, although some PNDC policies improved the relationship of rural areas to the state, others have radically changed the composition of the rural areas and the relationship of various states and gender groups to each other in these areas. As the rural population became more diversified, the peasant voice became submerged beneath the voices of other more powerful strata in rural areas—organized youth farmers, educated bureaucrats, and wealthy absentee farmers.

PNDC policies have increased the differentiation appearing in rural areas, and this has generated considerable peasant concern. In some brilliant initial attempts to utilize the communal ethos in 1983, Rawlings successfully encouraged chiefs to back cooperative work groups (*nnoboa*) so as to regenerate nonproductive cocoa farms. Then, faced with the Nigerian expulsion of Ghanaians, Rawlings also initiated a youth mobilization movement that brought these returning young men (Mobisquads) back into the agricultural development process, first restoring farms and then dramatically heightening rural productivity. These efforts halted and reversed the rural demographic profile in which depressed rural areas were composed primarily of women, children, and elderly or infirm farmers.[17] As temporary mobilization techniques, the new groups were enormously successful— young men were employed in the villages and compensated, and old cocoa farms were replanted with cocoa. Again, both male and female farmers were enthusiastic about this development because it utilized a traditional cooperative principle, although initial control had been exercised by the head of state. Nevertheless, the primarily male Mobisquad groups underwent a rapid transition from voluntary labor to wage compensation to organized youth cooperatives. As they became a force to be reckoned with in the rural areas, the veneer of communal control and responsibility for these groups wore thin, and peasant suspicions rose. The links between the Mobisquads and the PNDC government became more obvious, and cocoa farmers came to view them as organizations that were only slightly less political than the new Committees for the Defence of the Revolution and that had few connections to the rural social structure.

In contrast, the flexibility that was possible in rural attitudes can be seen in the farmers' views of the young male Cocoa Services Division (CSD) workers. This group of literate and educated or semieducated youth (mostly children of absentee farmers or of prosperous peasants) is another stratum enlarged by government policies. These youth were recruited to work with the Cocoa Services Division of the reorganized cocoa marketing board (Cocobod), providing technical assistance to farmers in replanting with new hybrid types of cocoa, promoting crop diversification, and controlling crop diseases. Between 1984 and 1987, these youth were in the most intimate contact with peasant farmers, were perceived as offering real assistance to the farmers, and had become most familiar with and often advocates of the rural worldview. Many of them also took the opportunity to acquire land and start export or food farms for themselves and were a valuable addition to these communities. However, faced with an increasingly difficult national economy, many of the CSD youth technicians are becoming pessimistic about "development" possibilities, and they now face the dilemma of whether to remain in rural work.

New challenges to the volume of the "rural voice" have come with the new local participatory structures that the PNDC established, because these political institutions are increasingly dominated by educated bureaucrats and elites rather than peasants. The collapse of the export economy as well as the 1983 drought triggered a flight of urbanites to the "bush." Moreover, the subsequent government policy of decentralizing government departments and deploying excess civil servants to rural areas further increased the size of the nonpeasant stratum in communities like Sunyani. This has altered the dynamics of the political process that is currently undergirding development processes. Although "decentralization" is intended to simplify economic decisionmaking by letting local districts control revenues generated there, the predominance of elites may ultimately mean that they will control the direction of rural economic development.

With so many new groups present at the local level, the power of traditional representatives and rural peoples has been diluted. In addition, the electoral structure guarantees the predominance of nonproducing strata. For example, the 1988–1989 local and district elections were organized so that PNDC representatives held one-third of the assembly seats, the popularly elected representatives held one-third, and the chiefs held one-third. The PNDC representatives have mostly been bureaucrats, or have come from the CDRs or from the National Mobilisation Programme, which controls the

Mobisquads, or other politically affiliated groups, including the 31st December Women's Movement. In addition, the one-third popularly elected assemblypersons are primarily literate large-scale farmers, schoolteachers, civil and public servants, or local businesspeople, but not the illiterate large-scale farmers, the small-scale peasants, or local queen-mothers. The elected chiefs or chiefly representatives were either from the larger or politically stronger areas or those who best represented traditional legitimacy in the area. Despite urban cynicism about peasant participation, the strongest electoral participation came from regions that were most heavily rural. However, the communal voice is now being submerged beneath the other and stronger two-thirds of the assembly. Farmers are left wondering whose notions of development will be reflected in these assemblies.

Relying on traditional notions of corporate decisionmaking, farmers have thought of decentralized economic planning as a process that would involve their own labor, resources, and decisionmaking, with a reasonable amount of government administrative and financial assistance. The knowledge that agricultural export-generated capital supports the government structure certainly influences the thinking of farmers. In the Sunyani District, cocoa and food farmers began to suspect that it was the Mobisquad members or farmer-bureaucrats who would continue to become economically successful through support from the regional offices of the ministries. To small-scale farmers it appeared that the PNDC was reinforcing certain strata in rural areas so that they could have a dialogue with the economic "bureaucracy" that is being created.

The government's role in providing capital and credit to discrete groups of farmers is significant here. During 1984–1987, the PNDC's plans were to create quasi-cooperatives that would link neighboring cocoa farmers into a center that provided government-subsidized farm inputs to all farmers. However, these plans were shelved because of the new emphasis on privatization called for in World Bank and IMF programs. Therefore, farmers angrily reported that the rising costs of farm inputs made them nonaffordable, while producer prices for cocoa could not keep pace. Even as recently as 1990, the government's financial role in development remained an issue.[18]

In different parts of the country, the clash between rural and national views of who should be involved in local "development" have pointed up the problems with the new diversity in rural areas. In the North, where civil servants bought land for rice farming and became absentee owners during the late 1970s and early 1980s, small and economically vulnerable farmers resented the ability of these migrant elites to obtain loans from the government for agricultural development more easily than they could themselves.[19] In the coastal Ga and Adangbe areas or the Shai areas, farmers resented the "preferential treatment" in subsidized inputs given to cocoa farmers because they brought in export dollars. Their emerging question was "development for whom?—for absentee elite farmers, bureaucrats, and Mobisquad farmers?"

Despite the PNDC's initial rural emphasis, politicians, urbanites, and elites still think of development as a process that would generate resources and political linkages that could benefit the "modern" strata and the state. The PNDC has hastened to warn chiefs that decentralization does not mean that they and their communities can control the disposition of local resources and land in which the government has historically had a stake—for example, they may not control the grants of local contracts for mineral and timber extraction. The new District Councils and the government make these decisions, but rural folk question the viewpoints and loyalties of assembly-persons in these councils.

It is clear that a gap exists between PNDC perceptions of what economic development is and what its dynamics should be on the one hand, and local concepts of equity and legitimacy on the other hand. Although Rawlings has admitted that he is troubled by the deradicalization of his rural policies, he is also clear about the fact that "pragmatism" is necessary to keep global donors and development experts firmly behind Ghana's economic recuperation. From Rawlings's perspective, privatization and the building of agrarian cooperatives must take place to guarantee that production (and therefore foreign exchange from exports) is kept high. His priority is to make sure that the rural strata that emerge as leaders are energetic as well as solidly behind the government's program.

To do this, the PNDC is encouraging the institutionalization of rural groups to make them effective in development. Mobisquads and redeployees in agricultural zones have been urged to transform themselves into formal agricultural cooperatives so that they can obtain credit and loans and play an active role in rural development. Local government in the districts is expanding to incorporate responsibility for new development projects in the villages, while coordination from Accra increases. The control structure over development now consistently runs through government offices, so foreign assistance and PAMSCAD funds are allocated by the ministries in Accra rather than going directly to some independent local-level development groups and projects as they have in the past. Thus, many of the grassroots development initiatives will dissipate unless they can be redirected into government programs. The problem is that it is the educated and well-connected men and women who emerge from the reconfigured rural areas to spearhead "local development," and their efforts often do not have or share truly indigenous viewpoints. These individuals are often the atypical large-scale farmer or farmer-bureaucrat who is not well integrated into local structures and processes. The new development procedures effectively lock out older farmers, stranger farmers, small-scale farmers, and women farmers from equal participation in local development; and they create a young, privileged, and relatively educated farmer group that is tied to the government. Such actions may depress broad production incentives and encourage another version of the rural differentiation that occurred in the period after 1975.

Until recently, there was little attempt to act on the "gender complementarity" present in the rural worldview; and when such actions began to take place, they were part of a program to draw rural women into development by enclosing them within politically identified national organizations such as 31st December. Not only had women already been excluded from the development-related groups such as Mobisquads, cooperatives, and CSD, but there was a pervasive antifemale attitude associated with the notion that women marketers and traders were profiteers who thwarted national development efforts.[20] As the effects of the Economic Recovery Program were felt, as liberalization and privatization proceeded, and as fluctuations in international purchasing of cocoa exports occurred, the repercussions could be seen most clearly in rural areas in the plight of women and children. Few women remain in the cocoa export sector, and women food farmers have also experienced decline. Family cohesion had been affected by the earlier economic crisis and migration, and women sometimes have no husbands or brothers to share the economic burden. Water-related diseases, infant malnutrition, and infant deaths again rose dramatically as "pay-as-you-go" health fees were imposed in rural areas in 1988. As the impoverishment of small farmers, women farmers, and children became national issues, the response was the initiation of a number of controversial Women in Development (WID) programs by the government.[21]

Women in rural towns such as Sunyani tend to have totally different views on how and why they should participate in economic development initiatives than do national bureaucrats and politicians, and this becomes obvious when one tracks women's organizations from the national level down to the local level. Women at the local level have a traditional responsibility to contribute to the maintenance of the family and the lineage, and they generally seek assistance in finding ways to do this that guarantees them some autonomy and control over their proceeds. Local and regional branches of Ghana's National Council on Women in Development (NCWD) actively responded to women's needs between 1975 and 1985, despite the fact that NCWD faced a number of political difficulties vis-à-vis the PNDC.[22] In areas like Sunyani, local WID officials attempted to assess some of the specific cultural constraints facing women and at the same time formed groups and cooperatives for economic development purposes. One of the issues WID had to deal with was whether individual women could be permitted to profit economically if men and extended family members did not also profit through these projects. It was clear to rural WID leaders that to combat resistance to those development projects that extended beyond the

acceptable emphases on women's health, education, an.
to take into consideration local cultural views of wome
responsibilities.²³ WID officials attempted to raise exten.
activities that were "culturally sensitive" and inclusive, bι
frustrated by resistance from the government.

The PNDC was increasingly anxious that economic development be aligned. This was most easily achieved if ι members of PNDC-affiliated organizations such as the 31st ..υer Women's Movement, which is headed by Rawlings's wife, Nana ι .gyeman Rawlings. Therefore, between 1986 and 1990, the 31st December Movement aggressively campaigned in the various regions to recruit local female bureaucrats and civil servants, to convince them to stand for local elections, and finally to open up chapters of the movement in their towns and villages. While initially the orientation was activist and quasi-political ("organizing rural women to become involved"), by 1988 the shift toward a rural development orientation had begun.

Although current government approaches to organizing rural women give the appearance of accepting rural worldviews on how women organize their social and economic lives, they may in fact provide a powerful challenge to these views. For example, the 31st December Movement began to initiate day care centers, to organize the queen-mothers of towns and villages in a region, and, finally, to begin local vegetable cooperatives. Such goals were undoubtedly worthwhile, but local autonomy and initiative was conspicuously absent, since wealthy women farmers or women bureaucrats were the leaders of these local chapters. For the present, women's agricultural and rural income-generating projects located in other branches of government face an uncertain future with very little funding, while national political energy and external funding is channeled into building up rural 31st December chapters and projects. Queen-mothers were often seen as silent appendages of these rural chapters, causing some women to argue that the "cooptation of queen-mothers" may constitute a serious assault on the legitimacy of rural female institutions.

### ■ Lessons for Rural Development Efforts in Ghana

The Ghanaian experience demonstrates the conflicts that may exist between the interests of the state and the party in development plans and the interests of local communities, rural status groups, and gender groups. The PNDC has been forced to shift the national development agenda from a radical quasi-socialist perspective, aimed at eradicating rural inequities and empowering the peasant producer, to a more pragmatic and free-market (but less equitable) development approach. Rawlings, the former "charismatic revolutionary," has forced to rely upon assistance from international donors and, therefore, to reinforce global formulas for development if his country is to achieve economic and political stability. African and Western politicians and development personnel often candidly admit that further social differentiation may be one of the unfortunate costs of stabilizing the rural economy. It was inevitable that adjustment programs such as the ERP address some of the resulting "negative social dimensions" by initiating PAMSCAD projects when pressure built up in rural areas between 1986 and 1988. However, even the implementation of the PAMSCAD has increased national control and centralization in the development planning process and reinforced national notions of how that development should occur. In this process, the possibility of recognizing and incorporating the rural perspectives and viewpoint on development has decreased.

The question is whether African policymakers as well as international donors may be supporting development projects whose inherent philosophical premises are questionable from local perspectives. The consequence may be that small farmers and women farmers will cooperate less and less. Initially, Ghanaian cocoa and food farmers were positive about the PNDC's efforts because local social systems could be mobilized to support common economic objectives. But local enthusiasm has waned as national control over development has increased, as incomes of small farmers have been assaulted, and as emphasis has shifted from the needs of the rural producer and rural community to building a development infrastructure. The national development emphasis is no longer on achieving equity, but on building rural organizations that are structured to support the government. The Mobisquad cooperatives, the "redeployee" cooperatives, the CDRs, and the 31st December Women's Movement currently appear to be having difficulty developing the type of connection to the rural social structure that will make them viable and enduring development organizations. This difficulty exists because the individualistic and/or overtly political principles they embody are not in sync with the rural worldview.

These newly created rural development groups are either transitional in their philosophies and worldviews or they are overtly Western, and this virtually ensures that it will be national/global development perspectives that emerge. Is this what is intended? On the other hand, perhaps the PNDC is making a statement that African export and food production can no longer be entrusted to peasant farmers and locally organized women but must be done by more educated, technically empowered, and large-scale farmers.[24] There is no question that the agricultural transformation in more developed countries such as the United States has involved some of these same experiences. This agricultural transformation excluded most aging, poor, and female farmers and transformed the culture and lifestyles of the U.S. South.

Even if agricultural transformation is the intended scenario in Ghana, the failure to come to grips with existing rural realities and views on development during the transition period cannot be justified. By closing off consciousness regarding the sociocultural contexts that explain and support the actions of rural folk, one blocks the emergence of innovative development approaches from the local level. Community-initiated development projects that do not allow adequate local initiative and control may be counterproductive. Indeed, the PNDC may discover that for many years to come it will be unable to achieve agricultural development in Ghana without the sustained involvement of those persons whose viewpoints have always been vital to rural stability—the autonomous small farmers and female farmers.

■ Notes

1. Cocoa now makes up about 55 percent of Ghana's exports, gold almost 20 percent, and timber approximately 15 percent. See "Is Ghana Turning the Corner Economically?" in *Washington Report on Africa* 7, 13 (July 15, 1989), pp. 50, 52.

2. These concerns are clear, despite the varying ideological concerns with specific rural groups: peasants, classes in rural areas, farmers, etc. See Eric Wolf, *Peasant Wars of the Twentieth Century* (New York: Harper & Row, 1969); L. Fallers, "Are African Cultivators to Be Called Peasants?" *Current Anthropology* 2, 2 (1961); George Foster, "Peasant Society and the Image of Limited Good," *American Anthropologist* 67 (1965), pp. 293–315; Claude Meillassoux, "From Reproduction to Production: A Marxist Approach to Economic Anthropology," *Economy and Society* 1 (1972), pp. 93–104.

3. Goran Hyden's position is that peasants have tended to remain within an "economy of affection" (primarily local and ethnic) in an attempt to prevent the state from controlling or exploiting their actions and resources. See Goran Hyden, "Prospects and Problems of State Coherence in Africa," in Donald Rothchild and Victor Olorunsola (eds.), *State Versus Ethnic Claims: African Policy Dilemmas* (Boulder: Westview Press, 1983).

4. Mudimbe refers to the "europeocentric" and traditional oppositions contained in the Westernizing experience. It is my position, as well as that of the late St. Claire Drake, that many of these eurocentrisms were continued in the notions of development that were imposed upon peasants. See V. Y. Mudimbe, *The Invention of Africa: Gnosis, Philosophy, and the Order of Knowledge* (Bloomington: Indiana University Press, 1988). See also St. Clair Drake, "Traditional Authority and Social Action in Former British West Africa," *Human Organization* 19, 3 (1960), pp. 150–158; and "Prospects for Democracy in the Gold Coast," *Annals of the American Academy of Political and Social Science* 306 (1956).

5. Polly Hill, *The Migrant Cocoa Farmers of Southern Ghana* (Cambridge: Cambridge University Press, 1963). Also see Gwendolyn Mikell, *Cocoa and Chaos in Ghana* (New York: Paragon House, 1989), pp. 58–63.

6. David Kimble, *A Political History of Ghana: The Rise of Gold Coast*

*Nationalism, 1850–1928* (Oxford: Clarendon Press, 1963), pp. 50–51, and Bjorn Beckman, *Organizing the Farmers: Cocoa Politics and National Development in Ghana* (Uppsala: Scandinavian Institute of African Studies, 1976).

7. F. K. Drah, "The Brong Political Movement," in Kwame Arhin (ed.), *Brong Kyempim: Essays on the Society, History and Politics of the Brong People* (Legon: Institute of African Studies, University of Ghana, Legon, 1979), pp. 119–162.

8. See Dennis Austin, *Politics in Ghana, 1946–1960* (London: Oxford University Press, 1970), pp. 250–315, and William Tordoff, "The Brong-Ahafo Region" in *The Economic Bulletin of Ghana* 3, 5 (May 1959), pp. 2–18.

9. Survey data among Ghana Cooperative Society cocoa farmers in the Sunyani District during 1973 revealed that success in cocoa farm ownership and management was often based on advantages conferred by traditional stratification as well as other factors: (1) traditional status—sons of chiefs and elders appeared to be able to work larger farms because they claimed prime land, or had clients who could assist them with farm labor; (2) order of birth—first-born through third-born children tended to inherit farms; and (3) the early education of children of cocoa farmers allowed these persons to maintain farms and hire labor with their income from other occupations. See Mikell, *Cocoa and Chaos in Ghana*, pp. 93–95.

10. The statistics of Birmingham, Neustadt, and Omaboe show that in 1960 women engaged in cocoa growing were approximately one-third of that total economic category in the Ashanti, Brong-Ahafo, and Volta regions; women were one-half of those engaged in cocoa growing in the Eastern Region; and they made up roughly three-eighths of those involved in cocoa growing in the Western Region. However, many of these women worked on farms owned by male relatives or husbands. Of the total number of those listing themselves as cocoa farmers, women were approximately one-third. See Walter Birmingham, I. Neustadt, and E. N. Omaboe, *A Study of Contemporary Ghana, the Economy of Ghana*, vol. 1 (Evanston: Northwestern University Press, 1966), pp. 238–239.

11. Mikell, *Cocoa and Chaos in Ghana*, pp. 98–101. See also Kwame Arhin, *Traditional Rule in Ghana, Past and Present* (Accra: Sedco Publishing, 1985). Despite the fact that the British had initially despaired of the emerging chiefly linkages and attempts to control the cooperative movement as it spread during the postwar period, these status contradictions were losing their explosive potential as local communities adapted to the rural economic prosperity of the 1950s.

12. Robert M. Price, "Neocolonialism and Ghana's Economic Decline: A Critical Assessment," *Canadian Journal of African Studies* 18, 1 (1984), pp. 163–194.

13. Dennis M. Warren, "Anthropology and Rural Development in Ghana," in Michael M. Horowitz and Thomas M. Painter (eds.), *Anthropology and Rural Development in West Africa* (Boulder: Westview Press, 1986), pp. 63–91.

14. This does not mean that male and female roles are vague within Ghanaian (or Akan) culture. On the contrary, they are clear and unambiguous. Nevertheless, the manner in which gender fits into changing work patterns, conjugal work responsibilities, ownership of property and capital, and access to resources has not been overtly elaborated as twentieth-century economic change has occurred. The result is that women's economic roles and needs have, until quite recently, been left out of development discussions. See R. S. Rattray, *Ashanti* (Oxford: Clarendon Press, 1923); Meyer Fortes, "Time and the Social Structure: An Ashanti Case Study," in *Social Structure: Studies Presented to A. R. Radcliffe-Brown* (Oxford: Clarendon Press, 1949); and Meyer Fortes, "The

Submerged Descent Line Within Ashanti," in I. Schapera (ed.), *Studies in Kinship and Marriage* (London: RAIGE, 1963).

15. It has been reported that 32 percent of cocoa farmers received 94 percent of the gross cocoa income, while women and children were among those who did not experience the benefits of economic recovery. See Sayo Seini, John Howell, and Simon Commander, "Agricultural Policy Adjustment in Ghana," Overseas Development Institute, Regent's College, London, September 1987, pp. 35–36, cited in "Structural Adjustment in Africa: Insights from the Experiences of Ghana and Senegal." Report of a Staff Mission to Great Britain, Ghana, Senegal, Côte d'Ivoire, and France, November 29–December 20, 1988. Committee on Foreign Affairs, U.S. House of Representatives, March 1989, pp. 2, 8.

16. *Programme of Actions to Mitigate the Social Costs of Adjustment* (Executive Summary and Project Profiles), Government of Ghana, November 1987, p. 11.

17. Between 1973 and 1978, as the rural economy deteriorated and migrant workers left, women constituted the bulk of the low-paid agricultural workers. See Christine Oppong, Christine Okali, and Beverly Houghton, "Woman Power, Retrograde Steps in Ghana," *African Studies Review* 18, 3 (1975). Studies undertaken during the early 1980s indicate that as a consequence of the earlier deterioration and rural abandonment, children and pregnant mothers were malnourished and infant mortality rose. See *Programme of Actions* (PAMSCAD), p. 3.

18. The new higher prices for agricultural inputs announced by the PNDC in July 1990 threaten to wipe out any gains that small-scale farmers would have made from the new, higher producer prices for cocoa. Agricultural inputs have tripled in price, while producer prices rose by 28 percent. Because of this, CSD employees are now fearful for the welfare of small farmers. See *West Africa*, July 16–22, 1990, p. 2119.

19. Robert Bates, *Essays on the Political Economy of Rural Africa* (Berkeley: University of California Press, 1983), p. 127.

20. Personal interviews with Women in Development leaders in Accra, Ghana, July 1986, and with the Brong-Ahafo regional director of Women in Development, July 28, 1986.

21. There were Women in Development seminars on health and education for mothers, in addition to income-generating activities. The WID involvement has now been replaced by heightened general government emphasis on primary health care, training of traditional birth attendants, and assaults on "the six killer childhood diseases." In addition, the Department of Mass Education and Community Development has begun education and training programs for mothers in the villages.

22. Although the PNDC attempted to draw women into government-affiliated women's organizations such as the 31st December Movement, it was hostile to the continued autonomy of the National Council on Women in Development after the decade ended. By 1986, it had removed the energetic female leadership of this organization, and by 1990 the 31st December Movement had replaced NCWD as the major economic development organization for women.

23. This sensitivity was heightened by the passage of new marital, intestate succession laws that guaranteed wives and children greater access to economic support from the property or estate of husbands. A man's lineage relatives often verbally discouraged women from pursuing these legal guarantees and were hostile to organizations that informed women about the new laws. See Gwendolyn

Mikell, "Socioeconomic Change and Family Roles: The Akan in Urban Ghana," in *TransAfrica Forum* 5, 3 (1988), pp. 31–44.

24. For example, the Kadjebi District Assembly in the Volta Region has just made a decision to review the land tenure system in the area, with the intention of encouraging large-scale farming. See The Economist Intelligence Unit, *Ghana: Country Report No. 1, 1990*, p. 13.

# 6

## The Political Economy of Education Reform in Ghana

*James Cobbe*

Historically, Ghana's education system was of good quality and enrolled a relatively high proportion of at least primary-age children; however, it was also basically elitist, tapering rapidly toward the top of the pyramid, and excessively lengthy. The elite secondary schools and the universities were very good, and they produced graduates of good quality. In the 1950s, 1960s, and early 1970s, the elitist nature of the system was not too problematic politically because wage employment in Ghana expanded quite quickly and many middle school graduates were able to get wage jobs. By the 1980s, however, the situation had changed quite markedly. Education was becoming of very little economic value unless a child got to secondary school; and the congruency between education level (above middle school) and economic inequality was becoming more pronounced. At the same time, although there is no direct evidence since 1974, there is every reason to believe that the tendency for the children of the more successful Ghanaians to be overrepresented at the higher levels of education continued to increase.

Tables 6.1, 6.2, and 6.3 present some evidence on these matters.

Table 6.1 Economically Active Population by Employment Status and Education

| | Employment Status[a] (in percentages) | | | | |
|---|---|---|---|---|---|
| Education Level[b] | Unemployed | Employed Private | Employed Public | Self-employed | N |
| None | 0.6 | 4.3 | 2.6 | 92.4 | 3,024 |
| Primary | 0.8[a] | 8.8 | 3.4 | 87.0 | 625 |
| Secondary | 3.0 | 13.6 | 18.7 | 64.7 | 2,078 |
| University | 0.0 | 17.9[c] | 60.7 | 21.4[c] | 28 |
| All | 1.5 | 8.2 | 8.8 | 81.5 | 5,755 |

Source: Ghana Living Standards Survey, *First Year Report*, April 1989, Table 55.
Notes: a. Employment status is for main or primary occupation.
  b. Education Level refers to "at least some," not necessarily completed.
  c. Cell contains fewer than 10 observations.

Table 6.2 Characteristics of Households by Quintiles

| Characteristic | All Ghana | Quintiles 1 | 2 | 3 | 4 | 5 | Mean per Capita Expenditure |
|---|---|---|---|---|---|---|---|
| | % | % | % | % | % | % | (₵/Year) |
| *Urbanization* | | | | | | | |
| Urban (pop. >5000) | 30.2 | 19.4 | 21.4 | 33.8 | 34.2 | 42.2 | 71,997 |
| Semiurban (pop. 1500–5000) | 19.6 | 15.3 | 23.3 | 25.3 | 21.8 | 12.5 | 53,533 |
| Rural (pop. <1500) | 50.2 | 65.3 | 55.4 | 40.9 | 44.0 | 45.4 | 52,756 |
| *Ecological Zone* | | | | | | | |
| Coastal | 30.3 | 20.1 | 19.4 | 31.1 | 28.1 | 52.8 | 74,836 |
| Forest | 43.1 | 34.6 | 49.7 | 47.2 | 51.0 | 32.9 | 55,613 |
| Savannah | 26.6 | 45.3 | 30.8 | 21.7 | 20.8 | 14.3 | 45,373 |
| *Sex of Head* | | | | | | | |
| Female | 24.9 | 23.9 | 23.6 | 28.7 | 27.5 | 20.6 | 59,042 |
| Male | 75.1 | 76.1 | 76.4 | 71.3 | 72.5 | 79.4 | 58,603 |
| *Employer of Head* | | | | | | | |
| Private | 6.9 | 4.4 | 4.7 | 4.1 | 7.2 | 1.0 | 85,897 |
| Government | 12.1 | 5.9 | 11.1 | 11.5 | 16.4 | 15.4 | 69,091 |
| Parastatal | 2.5 | 1.1 | 3.8 | 2.7 | 2.9 | 2.1 | 64,928 |
| None | 3.9 | 4.0 | 3.5 | 4.3 | 3.6 | 4.0 | 57,963 |
| Self-employed | 74.7 | 84.7 | 77.4 | 77.4 | 69.9 | 64.5 | 54,670 |
| *Occupation of Head* | | | | | | | |
| White collar | 9.1 | 3.7 | 3.0 | 9.9 | 13.2 | 15.6 | 79,428 |
| Sales/services | 10.9 | 3.1 | 9.6 | 14.1 | 13.5 | 14.4 | 76,322 |
| Prod./crafts | 13.3 | 9.9 | 13.2 | 15.3 | 12.0 | 15.9 | 64,853 |
| Unemployed | 2.2 | 1.6 | 2.4 | 3.3 | 0.9 | 2.9 | 61,470 |
| Cocoa farmer | 18.4 | 14.3 | 21.9 | 17.4 | 21.9 | 16.7 | 55,677 |
| Retired | 1.6 | 2.3 | 1.1 | 1.0 | 2.7 | 1.1 | 53,193 |
| Other farmer | 44.5 | 65.1 | 49.1 | 39.0 | 35.9 | 33.4 | 49,843 |
| *Education of Head* | | | | | | | |
| University | 1.2 | 0.0 | 0.0 | 0.6 | 1.6 | 3.7 | 120,015 |
| Postsec. Nonuniv. | 0.4 | 0.5 | 0.0 | 0.0 | 0.7 | 1.1 | 113,294 |
| Sec. sch. A level | 0.3 | 0.0 | 0.0 | 0.3 | 0.5 | 0.7 | 102,059 |
| Sec. sch. O level | 3.0 | 0.0 | 2.0 | 2.3 | 5.7 | 5.1 | 88,482 |
| Middle school | 31.3 | 18.4 | 28.4 | 36.6 | 29.1 | 43.9 | 66,966 |
| Primary | 18.1 | 6.6 | 7.9 | 5.7 | 9.1 | 10.9 | 56,996 |
| Teacher training | 1.8 | 10.4 | 1.5 | 2.9 | 3.2 | 1.0 | 56,581 |
| None | 53.9 | 74.2 | 60.1 | 51.5 | 50.1 | 33.7 | 50,154 |
| Mean per capita expenditures (cedis/year) | 58,713 | 16,538 | 31,890 | 45,592 | 63,988 | 134,198 | |
| Average household size | 4.8 | 6.7 | 5.9 | 5.9 | 4.4 | 2.1 | |
| % Expenditures on food | 68.0 | 71.4 | 70.6 | 70.2 | 67.5 | 63.1 | |

*Sources*: Ghana Living Standards Survey, first six months; average household size and percent of expenditures on food, from first-year report.

*Note*: Quintiles by per capita expenditures

Table 6.3 Education and the Poor (in percentages)

|  | Poorest 10% | Poorest 30% | All Ghana |
| --- | --- | --- | --- |
| Education of household head |  |  |  |
| None | 80.8 | 71.7 | 53.9 |
| Primary | 3.5 | 6.9 | 8.1 |
| Middle | 15.7 | 20.6 | 31.3 |
| Secondary: O Level | 0.0 | 0.0 | 3.0 |
| Secondary: A Level | 0.0 | 0.0 | 0.3 |
| Teacher training | 0.0 | 0.5 | 1.8 |
| Other postsecondary | 0.0 | 0.3 | 0.4 |
| University | 0.0 | 0.0 | 1.2 |
| School attendance by household members |  |  |  |
| Age 6–10 | 43.2 | 57.2 | 66.8 |
| Age 11–15 | 46.0 | 60.5 | 70.8 |

*Source*: Ghana Living Standards Survey.

Table 6.1 shows how self-employment declines with level of education, from 92 percent of those with no education to about 21 percent of those with some university schooling.[1] Tables 6.2 and 6.3 give some information, derived from the Ghana Living Standards Survey (GLSS), on connections between education and income distribution and poverty. The data refer to the period September 1987 to February 1988 and show substantial inequality in mean expenditure per capita by quintile (the ratio of highest quintile to lowest is 8.1 to 1).

Households clearly have higher mean expenditures per capita the higher the education of the head of the household, with one important exception. That exception is teacher training; households where the head has teacher training have slightly lower expenditures per capita than those where the head has primary education. Also relevant is the very small advantage of some primary school education over no education at all (a less than 14 percent advantage), whereas the equivalent advantages for the other levels are 33.5 percent for middle school, 76.4 percent for secondary O level (form 5), 103.5 percent for secondary A level (form 6), 125.9 percent for postsecondary nonuniversity, and 139.3 percent for university. These data suggest, when one considers the combined out-of-pocket and opportunity costs of middle school or teacher training, that it has not been very worthwhile from a narrow economic viewpoint to acquire those levels of education, whereas getting to secondary school or beyond has given a much better return on average.[2]

Finally, Table 6.3 compares the poorest 10 percent and 30 percent of Ghanaian households (by per capita expenditures) with average Ghanaian households, in terms of education of household heads and school attendance by children ages 6 to 10 and 11 to 15. No one with more than middle school education was in the bottom 10 percent of households (more than four out of five of which had no education at all); and no one with secondary education (whether O or A level) or university education was in the bottom 30 percent (more than 70 percent of which had no education at all).[3] With respect to school attendance, substantial numbers of the poor evidently still manage to send their children to school, illustrating the strong faith of Ghanaians in formal education, but at rates considerably below those of Ghanaians as a whole.

## ■ Adjustment and Education Reform

In the education system that had developed in Ghana by the late 1960s, six years of primary school were followed by four years of middle school, five years of secondary school, and a further two years of "sixth form" leading to A-level exams, the university entrance requirement. The normal undergraduate degree program was three years post–A level, modeled on British universities. However, entrance to secondary school was by examination results, and the children of the better-off frequently could bypass entirely the four years of middle school by attending elite private primary schools, which better enabled them to pass the entrance examination for secondary schools. Proposals for the reform of this system (which included abolishing middle schools and recasting secondary schools into a two-stage system of Junior Secondary Schools [JSS] followed by Senior Secondary Schools) [SSS]) were made in April 1974. However, in practice this reform was never implemented.

During the remainder of the 1970s and in the early 1980s, Ghana's economy declined, reaching its low point, by most conventional measures, in 1983. The dimensions of this decline are discussed in other chapters, so here I will note only that by 1983 per capita output and income had been declining for over twenty years and the state had reached a fiscal crisis of severe proportions. In 1982/83, government revenues were less than 6 percent of GDP; although government was running a large fiscal deficit (perhaps as much as 4 percent of GDP), recurrent spending on education, which had averaged about 3.4 percent of GDP in the 1970s, was definitely below 2 percent of GDP and may have been as low as 1 percent. This was below the World Bank's estimate of average spending by governments on *primary* education alone, both in all developing countries and in sub-Saharan Africa.

The education system was in crisis, although enrollment had continued to increase, albeit somewhat slowly at the middle school level. Teachers were underpaid, resulting in losses of qualified teachers and the neglect of duties by many who also had secondary occupations needed for family survival. Nearly half of all primary school teachers were unqualified in 1982/83, as were about a third of the middle school teachers and a fifth of the secondary school teachers. What money was available was spent almost entirely on salaries, so that schools were without textbooks, furniture, chalk, paper, and other nonpersonnel inputs; and maintenance of the physical plant of the system was severely neglected, resulting in some classrooms being totally unusable, particularly in inclement weather.

Not surprisingly, there was a consensus that the quality of the system had declined precipitously and that it was plagued by a number of problems. First, graduates at all levels were widely regarded as ill-educated and inadequately prepared for economic life. Second, the system was grossly inefficient and overly long. And third, the system was at the least perpetuating inequality from generation to generation and quite likely exacerbating it. For some, the system was near collapse; a widespread view was that, except in favored schools, very little of educational value was actually happening in the schools.

When the Rawlings government adopted the Economic Reform Program, later to become the Structural Adjustment Program, it was clear that the education sector's problems had to be addressed. Even at the low point in 1982/83, education was taking around 20 percent of government's total recurrent spending. However, the SAP required (and received) external support; external donors were not likely to be willing to provide additional resources for the education sector without reforms within that sector to address its internal inefficiencies and structural deficiencies as perceived by the external donors. Thus, government could not simply adopt a stance of devoting more resources to an unreformed education system; the attempt to bring quality back into the system had to be coupled with a reform program aimed at remedying the sector's structural deficiencies. The resulting educational reform program, launched in 1986, thus implements the structural reforms proposed back in 1974, but also takes them much further and adds to them some features not included in the 1974 proposals. At least in part, these changes from the proposals of the 1970s can probably be attributed to the influence of outside donors, in particular the World Bank, which has been supporting the educational reforms through its Educational Sector Adjustment Credit (EDSAC). Thus, the reform package extends the structural reforms beyond the replacement of four-year middle schools (and the roughly equivalent so-called continuation schools) by three-year Junior Secondary Schools to include replacement of existing (five- to seven-year) secondary schools by Senior Secondary Schools, also with a shortened three-year program, producing a school system extending only to twelve years instead of seventeen (or thirteen for those able to skip middle schools). This, of course, also implies changes in the curriculum and the examination system; because it will effectively make A levels impossible to achieve, this reform also implies a new entry qualification for the universities and a proposed lengthening of the standard university first degree course from three to four years.

Almost certainly at the Bank's insistence, the reform also includes substantial changes to educational finance, intended (at least according to Bank statements) to make the system more equitable and sustainable from domestic resources after SAP assistance ends. To date, it is these changes in educational finance, involving the reduction of subsidies and enhanced "cost recovery" (i.e., direct contributions by pupils/students, families, and communities toward the explicit costs of education), that have attracted the most controversy and resistance within Ghana. In the early stages of the education reform, these aspects of the package included eliminating (or substantially reducing) feeding and boarding subsidies in secondary schools and the universities; introducing realistic charges for textbooks and individual student supplies at all levels (paid into revolving funds with the intention of indefinite self-supported financing of future supplies, after initial provision of working capital by foreign donors); and encouraging and requiring community and local authority provision of capital and equipment for the Junior Secondary Schools in particular.

One can safely assume that the reform of the education sector in Ghana was seen largely as a necessary prerequisite for arresting the decay of the educational system and beginning to rebuild its quality. The success of the SAP in restoring the fiscal situation of the state, together with the additional resources made available to the education sector by donors, permitted a substantial and fairly rapid increase in the real resources expended by government on education. A very large part of this increase was accounted for by the reform of public sector salaries; rapid inflation had eroded teachers' real salaries (teachers are paid on the same public sector salary scale as all other public servants) to a point in the early 1980s where they were so derisory that it was both essential for the teachers' survival to have some other source of income in addition to their salaries, and also questionable whether it was worth bothering to show up at work other than to collect their salaries. Despite the reforms, teachers' salaries still remain relatively low by the standards of many African countries; however, they are now definitely worth receiving. Similar conditions extending to the inspectorate, together with an almost complete lack of provision of transport for its members during the worst years, also implied that the Ministry of Education had no way of knowing what was actually going on in the schools and little ability to discipline the teaching force even if it had shown the inclination to do so.

## ■ Interpretation

Let us consider the reform of the education sector from the point of view of different interest groups. First, consider the population divided according to income, education, occupation, and location. A useful division is between the educated elite, the high-income private sector groups (entrepreneurs, large-scale farmers), urban wage earners and informal sector persons, and the rural small-scale farmers. One can hypothesize that the first two groups would see advantages in the traditional structure of education, so long as quality is restored: their children will have a good chance of progressing to the higher education levels and should derive economic and social advantages from doing so. The latter two groups see little advantage from the old structures now, because they recognize that their children have little chance of getting to secondary school and that they derived few benefits from primary or middle school in the old system. In addition, the educated elites and the urban working classes have suffered under the PNDC's Structural Adjustment Program, seeing major declines in their real incomes; on the other hand, entrepreneurs and the rural population (or at least cocoa farmers among them) have made gains, at least in a relative sense.

Second, one can think about the groups directly involved in education and education policy. There is, of course, the PNDC itself; the bureaucracy of the Ministry of Education and the Ghana Education Service (GES); the teachers; and the churches, local authorities, and communities. It is probably reasonable to take the PNDC's populism fairly seriously, although circumstances have forced the PNDC to adopt economic policies that have created greater economic inequality in some ways and that have hurt what might be considered some of its natural constituencies. The PNDC appears to wish in the long run to reduce privilege and to increase equality of opportunity, although accepting inequality of outcome as a necessary evil required to reverse economic decline and restore growth. Not surprisingly, the Ministry of Education was, until the PNDC came to power, widely regarded as ineffective and weak. The GES, a relatively autonomous organization nominally under the Ministry of Education, actually employed the teachers, controlled the distribution of public resources made available to schools, and implemented policy. This bureaucracy is alleged to have been affected by corruption in pre-PNDC days as was most of the rest of the public service; a significant subtext of the education reform story in Ghana concerns the efforts of the Ministry of Education to bring the GES under its control and root out its inefficient and corrupt elements.

There are a number of cleavages among the teachers who make up Ghana's educational system. At the level of the universities, there is a tradition of relative autonomy, and the academic staff there have much in common with the professions, which have tended to oppose the PNDC. The

Ghanaian universities' identification with the relatively elitist universities of the United Kingdom (rather than the mass-intake universities of North America) has meant that they also tend to oppose the reduction of entry standards below the A level. In addition, the universities tend to feel that they have already suffered drastic quality declines as a result of resource shortages and staff losses. In the schools, there are definite differences between teachers in secondary schools, who are concerned about quality declines and the implied relative downgrading of their professional status by the JSS/SSS reform, and those in primary schools and JSS. A further and more immediate cleavage is that between qualified and unqualified teachers, since the latter have been informed by the government that if they do not acquire qualifications through in-service training by 1995, they will be retrenched (i.e., lose their jobs), a fate that has already affected some unqualified teachers and nonteaching personnel in schools.

## ■ The First Phase: 1987–1990

The structural reforms undertaken in this phase were relatively uncontroversial; everybody agreed that middle and continuation schools left a great deal to be desired, and if their abolition and replacement by three-year JSS was the price to be paid for extra resources, nobody was likely to be opposed. Similarly, there does not seem to have been much opposition to the new curriculum at the primary and JSS levels, although there is considerable disquiet over the effectiveness of the implementation of the more practical aspects of the JSS curriculum in a resource-scarce context.[4] However, two implicit consequences of this stage of the reform do raise concerns for some groups. First, the implicit, and to some extent explicit, justification for the new JSS curriculum is that JSS graduates will normally make their livelihoods in agriculture, the informal sector, and self-employment, not in wage employment. This is consistent with the actual experiences in recent years of middle school graduates, and there is some indication that the bulk of the population may welcome this attempt to adjust school curriculum to reality. The attitude of elite groups is more questionable, given that the intent of the reform is clearly to provide a more level playing field with respect to entry into SSS (as compared to the old secondary schools). However, government has allowed establishment of private JSS schools, and they will probably be used by the elite to subvert the intentions of the JSS reform, providing overly "academic" treatment (aimed at getting good exam results and raising the success rate for transition to SSS) of the formal curriculum.

The second problem concerns the implications of the JSS curriculum for the SSS curriculum and the implications for SSS of the very much shortened cycle. A-level teaching is doomed, and the SSS curriculum is unlikely to be much like the old O-level curriculum. Secondary school teachers have complained for several years about the decline in the quality of their intake; the JSS reform, and efforts to rebuild the quality of primary and JSS schools, may eventually reverse this perceived quality decline. However, if the curricular reforms are fully implemented the style of the education that SSS entrants will have received will also have changed to something rather different from the traditionally academic O-level curriculum of the old secondary schools. The more traditional and better-qualified teachers in secondary schools, especially elite secondary schools, are almost certainly concerned about the implied change in style of their institutions and professional activities.

In this early part of the reform, however, most controversy has centered on the other parts of the package, those aimed at improving the efficiency of the system and increasing the proportion of the costs borne by students and their families. The key issue, in terms of public awareness, concerns the withdrawal of feeding and housing subsidies for secondary school and university students (which caused some well-publicized difficulties) and the introduction of economic charges for books and supplies. Although the government appears to have won these fights, there are still some ambiguities and the possibility that difficulties will arise again. There are two major potential problems. One is the issue of the relative autonomy of the universities and whether they will in fact do as the government wishes them to. On the food side, they appear to have complied with government wishes; remaining canteen operations at universities are financially separate and self-supporting (students now can get subsidized loans to cover their out-of-pocket costs). The boarding issue, however, is not yet fully settled. The universities do not seem to be happy with the government's desire that they expand their intake of students, have a lower proportion of the students be residential, and convert their boarding facilities into financially independent and self-supporting hostel operations. Part of the difficulty concerns the manner in which the universities are financed; they receive a single block grant from the government, and although the latter çan subtract former subsidies for boarding from its calculation of the grant, the universities could still choose to spend some of their resources on subsidizing student housing.

A further ambiguity arises from the widespread belief that in the recent past the universities have managed, without penalty, to overspend substantially their initial allocations from the Ministry of Education, with the overspending eventually made good (according to rumors, this was done from underspending at basic education levels). Letters to the press and other anecdotal information suggest a good deal of unhappiness with the increases in out-of-pocket costs of school attendance, with only partial acknowledgment that in return at least children are getting books, supplies, and so on. The long-run problem here may concern administration of the processes by which fees are charged to secure student supplies. Fees are set and collected centrally; all monies are supposed to be remitted to single, central revolving funds, out of which the resupply of the physical commodities concerned will be financed (in most cases, the initial supplies were aid-financed). The dangers arise from the weak incentives at the individual school level for enforcing full compliance with the payment of fees when the fees simply disappear into an account in Accra—with only possible administrative consequences for the school of not collecting all it should—and from the potential inadequacy of the revolving funds to finance resupply in a situation where inflation and exchange rate depreciation are both rapid and uncertain.

## ■ What Remains to Be Done

The education reform appears to have made a good start, but in many ways what has been done thus far could be considered the easy part. The future tasks are both inherently more difficult and potentially more politically contentious, at least among the more educated and articulate Ghanaians. The reforms were not scheduled to touch the structure of the old secondary schools until August 1990. The universities face rationalization and consolidation, meaning removal of duplication and loss of some programs at some of the universities; eventually they must totally restructure, abandoning the post-A-level intake, producing new degree programs to deal with the new SSS graduates and bringing them up to degree level in four years. Admittedly, the first post-SSS intake will not appear until 1994, and the complete SSS curriculum is not yet available, but my impression is that the universities have not yet started to think in a serious manner about what this will entail.[5]

Perhaps the biggest problem facing the reform program is that to maintain its momentum it will be vital to continue to increase the relative proportion of resources going into basic education. There are two reasons for this, one overtly political and the other more educational, but also implicitly political. The mass of the population will not have children who go further than JSS. For them to continue to provide support for the educational system, the education their children receive must be worthwhile to them. Thus, basic education must succeed in imparting literacy in English, numeracy, and preferably some skills that are of direct economic value outside the schools; moreover, entrance to SSS (and thereby a chance at postsecondary education) must be seen as being determined on a relatively level playing field. Certainly the masses will be unhappy if it appears that the elite can evade the intent of JSS through private schools and thus gain disproportional access to SSS. It is doubtful that much of the basic education system achieves these objectives at this time, and to improve it will require better-trained and better-supervised teachers and more supplies of nonteacher inputs. This requires money, and, given the enrollments in the various levels and the fiscal stringency facing the state, this implies increased relative expenditure on basic education. In addition, quality during the first nine years must be improved to make it feasible for a further three years of SSS, plus four years of university, to produce university graduates of adequate quality. If the initial intake into SSS is of poor quality, the tendency for the children of the privileged to be more successful in the selection process is likely to become more pronounced, and the incentives for the elite to rely on private schools and/or private tutoring outside the public system will also become stronger. This could well destroy the populist justification for the reform's legitimacy. Already enrollment ratios are falling among poorer groups because of the higher out-of-pocket costs and the low perceived benefits of attendance.

There are a number of reasons for the elite to oppose the remaining stages of the reform program. The abolition of A levels implies the removal of a traditional option for the children of the elite, namely university education in the UK or elsewhere in the Commonwealth. The elites have reasons to be suspicious of the quality of a four-year degree based on only twelve years of school education; they fear a watering down of the quality of the degree and a consequent reduction in the potential mobility internationally of its holders. Teachers in secondary schools and university academic staff suspect a potential degrading of their professions and fear having to teach less well prepared students at a lower standard. There are also concerns about the implied change in status and style of the institutions themselves; schools that have long histories as institutions with seven grades, from form 1 through upper form 6, are to be converted to SSS with but three grades and much larger—and academically less rigorously selected—intakes. Some of these concerns may turn out to be strongly salient politically with sections of the elite who are not supporters of the PNDC regime in general.

Apart from these concerns with the new structure, the reforms also carry economic implications. The shift in the cost of secondary and university education to students and families has not been popular with those who have had to pay for it and is also as yet far from complete. The external donors, especially the World Bank, absolutely insist on it, asserting that it is fully consistent with greater equity in the educational system, provided loans are made available to students at the university level and provided it is accompanied by increased enrollment and equity of access at the lower levels and meritocratic selection at the transition points in the system. Although this argument is often overstated, it has some validity and in Ghana is quite likely correct in the sense that the former system was highly inequitable and the new one may well be less so. But in the short run there are substantial problems. The shift of costs is still not complete (e.g., university student loans are heavily subsidized). Dropout rates in basic education have clearly risen, and it is probably the poor who are opting out. The quality of basic education must be improved to reduce dropout rates and enlarge the fraction of children who attend school, to make attendance at the level of basic education valuable in and of itself for those who go no further, and to equalize to at least some extent the chances of getting into SSS and higher levels of education.

The range of current inequalities and problems is to some extent illustrated by Tables 6.4, 6.5, and 6.6. Table 6.4 gives some basic data on JSS and middle schools, and (old) senior secondary schools for 1988–1989. Both have very low pupil/teacher ratios for Africa (17.6 and 18.1). At the JSS level, this is partly due to the very small size of the average school (only 118 pupils), although the teacher/class ratio of 1.62 also suggests that the schools are, by at least some standards, overstaffed. The secondary schools proper are of decent size, but enrollment is only 32.7 percent female, and the average teacher teaches only 18.9 periods a week. Some instructors in U.S. junior colleges teach more than that. There is a strong suspicion that both JSS and secondary schools are overstaffed, although there are almost certainly real problems of administration and subject coverage in reallocating teachers.

Tables 6.5 and 6.6 give some data on primary schools on a regional basis. I will not discuss them in detail, but they make clear that there are very substantial differences between different parts of the country, with Accra and the South in general performing much better on most indices than the North. The main message of these primary school data for the reform is that if the policy of shifting costs to students and families is consistently applied at the primary level, it is doubtful that it will be possible to reduce inequalities of educational access and attainment between the different regions of the country.

### ■ Prospects and Conclusions

The first stage of the educational reform program has gone relatively well. The currently planned reform will not be complete until 1999–2000, when the final class of three-year first degree students will graduate from the universities. The obvious question is, will the government survive that long; and, whether or not it does, will the education reform endure? The key indicator is likely to be what happens in the next couple of years at the SSS level. If the government succeeds in pushing through the three-year SSS structure, and in abolishing old-style secondary schools with O and A levels, then I think the new system will be locked in, and it will be in almost

Table 6.4  1988–1989 Junior and Senior Secondary School Data, National Average/Totals

|  | JSS/M | Senior Secondary |
|---|---|---|
| Total Enrollment | 608,690 | 154,477 |
| % Enrollment female | 41.3 | 32.7 |
| Enrollment per school | 118 | 631 |
| % Repeaters | 0.69 | 2.72 |
| % Repeaters female/% repeaters | 1.01 | n.a. |
| Total teachers | 34,584 | 8,528 |
| Teachers/class | 1.62 | 2.09 |
| Pupils/teacher | 17.6 | 18.1 |
| Classes/classrooms | 1.15 | n.a. |
| % Teachers untrained | 28.2 | 29.9 |
| Classrooms/school | 3.60 | n.a. |
| Teacher load, periods/week | n.a. | 18.9 |
| % Science stream, forms 4 & 5 | n.a. | 22.4 |
| % Arts stream, forms 4 & 5 | n.a. | 36.7 |
| % Business stream, forms 4 & 5 | n.a. | 40.9 |
| % Science, form 6 | n.a. | 35.4 |
| % Arts, form 6 | n.a. | 37.8 |
| % Business, form 6 | n.a. | 26.8 |

*Source*: Ministry of Education.
*Notes*: JSS/M = Junior Secondary Schools and middle schools
n.a. = not applicable or not available

Table 6.5  Access to Primary School by Region, 1987–1988

| Region | Calculated Radius of Primary School Catchment Area (km) | Private Sector Enrollments as % of Total | Primary 1 Enrollment as % of 6-Year-Olds | Apparent Enrollment Rate |
|---|---|---|---|---|
| Ashanti | 2.20 | 4.5 | 72.3 | 88.4 |
| Brong Ahafo | 3.14 | 1.3 | 79.2 | 86.5 |
| Central | 1.76 | 1.4 | 77.9 | 94.6 |
| Eastern | 1.90 | 1.3 | 79.1 | 93.7 |
| Greater Accra | 1.25 | 18.9 | 56.2 | 77.5 |
| Northern | 4.92 | 0.0 | 56.5 | 49.5 |
| Upper East | 3.10 | 0.0 | 46.2 | 33.5 |
| Upper West | 4.83 | 0.0 | 52.5 | 49.4 |
| Volta | 2.27 | 0.5 | 73.1 | 88.5 |
| Western | 2.65 | 0.5 | 77.0 | 89.6 |
| National | 2.75 | 3.7 | 69.1 | 79.7 |

*Source*: Ministry of Education (Planning, Budget, Monitoring and Evaluation Division), Pandit and Asiamah Report, Table VII.

Table 6.6 Indicators of Regional Disparity in Primary Schools, 1988–1989

| Region | Enrollment per School | Classes per Classroom | Class Size | Pupils per Teacher | % Girls | % Repeaters | % Repeaters Girls/% Girls | % Teachers Untrained |
|---|---|---|---|---|---|---|---|---|
| Ashanti | 195 | 1.06 | 30.6 | 28.5 | 46.2 | 3.6 | 1.05 | 32.9 |
| Brong Ahafo | 145 | 1.10 | 25.2 | 23.0 | 45.4 | 3.7 | 1.09 | 51.8 |
| Central | 184 | 1.05 | 30.6 | 27.7 | 44.7 | 3.1 | 0.98 | 41.9 |
| Eastern | 165 | 0.90 | 27.6 | 23.2 | 44.8 | 4.7 | 0.96 | 33.5 |
| Greater Accra | 320 | 1.29 | 42.3 | 38.1 | 48.9 | 2.7 | 1.10 | 12.0 |
| Northern | 102 | 1.39 | 19.1 | 18.1 | 32.8 | 3.7 | 1.05 | 59.4 |
| Upper East | 157 | 0.99 | 27.2 | 20.2 | 37.5 | 4.4 | 1.08 | 37.7 |
| Upper West | 130 | 1.21 | 25.3 | 24.8 | 39.1 | 5.1 | 0.93 | 29.7 |
| Volta | 161 | 1.00 | 24.9 | 24.2 | 45.2 | 3.3 | 0.98 | 32.0 |
| Western | 170 | 1.05 | 27.7 | 26.5 | 43.9 | 4.9 | 1.11 | 58.3 |
| National | 171 | 1.06 | 28.0 | 25.5 | 44.5 | 3.8 | 1.03 | 39.7 |

*Source*: Ministry of Education.

everybody's interests to improve the quality of JSS and primary schools. This will be difficult to do, though. A fairly safe prediction for the next few years is that there will be a tendency for private secondary schools, catering to O and A levels and elite-financed, to be established. If they are, they will tend to undermine the entire reform program, make the university reform less inevitable, and hold out a possibility for its reversal.

If the PNDC is committed to greater equity, it may well need to strongly discourage, if not forbid, private secondary schools. This would cause the PNDC difficulties, not only with its own elite but potentially with some of its donors. But the logic of economic realities may force it in this direction. Given Ghana's developmental situation, only a tiny fraction of an age group can reach the university level, and not many more can complete a full twelve years of education. Entry to these levels needs to be seen as based mainly on meritocratic grounds. This implies that the rich should not be allowed to buy superior education at the immediately preceding level, which in turn implies that all entry to universities should be from public SSS and all entry to SSS from JSS. This means that if the system is to work, it needs quality improvement at the primary level and, if it is to be affordable, greater efficiency and value for money at all levels. Thus, there is logic to the reform package. The difficulties lie in the interests of the elite in getting the best prospects for their children that they can, in the interests of the educational bureaucracy in maintaining the status quo, and in the interests of existing teachers in not facing more and different tasks. The educational reform program represents a formidable challenge, and carrying it through successfully will be very difficult. One cannot be very confident that it will succeed.

## ■ Notes

I am grateful to participants in the April 1990 conference at SAIS for helpful comments and discussion, and especially to Kwame Ninsin, who corrected some potential errors. My interest in this topic was stimulated by a visit to Ghana in November 1989, on behalf of the USAID project "Improving the Efficiency of Education Systems" of Florida State University's Learning Systems Institute, but all errors and opinions are solely my responsibility.

1. Of course, the nature of self-employment will usually differ markedly between those with no education (mostly farmers) and those with some university education (which will include self-employed professionals such as lawyers, medical practitioners, accountants, and architects).

2. The "on average" qualifier is important; as in all countries, the averages hide wide dispersions, as the table itself makes clear. Although no university-educated heads were in the bottom two quintiles, there were quite a lot in the middle and fourth; whereas in the fifth (highest) quintile, 33.7 percent of heads had no education and 43.9 percent (compared to only 31.3 percent of all Ghanaians) had middle school education. This illustrates the effects of influences other than education (such as assets, occupation, entrepreneurial abilities, and opportunity) on income.

3. At first sight it may seem odd that middle school graduates outnumber primary school graduates in both the poorest 10 percent and the poorest 30 percent. The explanation is simple: transition from the primary school to the middle school level has been high for a long time, so middle school graduates outnumber primary graduates in the population as a whole. From the final column, the ratio of middle school graduates to primary school graduates is 3.86 for all Ghana, 2.98 among the bottom 30 percent, and 4.49 among the bottom 10 percent. It is only in the bottom decile that middle school graduates seem overrepresented compared to primary graduates; the correct explanation is unclear but might be connected with a preference for middle school graduates over primary graduates for wage jobs in the public sector, and the depressed level of real public sector wages compared to private sector wages and agricultural incomes at the time of the survey.

4. For more information on this matter see Helen Scadding, "Junior Secondary Schools—An Education Initiative in Ghana," *Compare* 19, 1 (1989), pp. 43–48.

5. In November 1989, one head of department at Legon assured me that it would never happen; he had no intention of planning for anything other than post-A-level intakes. I was unable to discover exactly what he envisaged as the fate of the educational reform, but he seemed convinced that somehow sixth forms and A levels would survive. The first entrants to SSS should graduate in 1993 but will not enter universities until 1994 because of the requirement of a year's national service between secondary school and university entrance.

# PART 3
# THE CHALLENGE OF POLITICAL AND ECONOMIC REFORM

# 7

# The Political Economy of Stabilization and Structural Adjustment in Ghana

*Jon Kraus*

A critical debate has raged in the 1980s among those concerned with the development and debt crises regarding the nature, value, and impact of the stabilization and structural adjustment programs negotiated by African countries with the IMF, World Bank, and the major capitalist aid donor countries. The extensive conditions required by the IMF, World Bank, and aid donors have involved pervasive efforts to restructure African economies and dictate the key macroeconomic and sectoral policies. Many African and other developing countries were compelled to adopt these conditionalities, with compliance tightly monitored, in exchange for obtaining debt relief and foreign aid.[1] A major debate that preceded this one involved the diagnosis of the critical problems causing low growth in African economies. This unresolved debate focused on the following issues: whether the most critical problems were in origin largely external (world recession, high interest rates, low commodity prices) or largely internal (inefficient statist interventions in production and marketing); the impact of state economic activism; and import-substitution versus export-led development strategies.

The triumphant IMF/World Bank policies require African states to emphasize market mechanisms and prices in allocating scarce resources, reduce or eliminate budget deficits, sell off or sharply rationalize many state enterprises, undertake repeated currency devaluations in order to maximize incentives for exports, and "liberalize" their economies in most other respects. To quiet criticisms, the World Bank sought to justify its policies in a 1989 study. This argued that African countries with strong World Bank reform programs, especially those unaffected by strong "shocks," had much higher performance than countries with weak or no programs in key areas such as GDP growth, agricultural production, export growth, real domestic investment, and per capita consumption.[2] The Economic Commission for Africa, among others, launched a counterattack, accusing the World Bank of manipulating data and largely ignoring explanatory factors other than SAPs.

By its own manipulation of performance data, with different base assumptions, the ECA was able to argue the contrary thesis, that countries with strong SAPs experienced negative GDP growth during 1985–1987 while those with weak SAPs averaged 2 percent growth and those with no SAPs averaged 3 percent growth.[3]

This chapter will pursue several major questions related to these issues. First, what has been the impact of the stabilization and SAP policies upon Ghana's economic growth and development, broadly defined as: (1) increased productive capacities in goods and services; (2) improved living standards or rising individual and institutional capabilities for improving social well-being; and (3) reduced dependency, or an increased ability (in autonomy, knowledge, and leverage) of the state to bargain for resources? Some critics argue that SAP policies seek to reproduce a form of dependent capitalism with no structural change.[4] This study focuses only on medium-term impacts and imagines development as a possible outcome, given Ghana's poor economic performance during 1966–1982 and decline in most capabilities. Second, what has been the impact in terms of the distribution of benefits? Have the benefits systematically tended to favor certain classes? The Rawlings government has always regarded itself as radical and favoring the interests of the poor classes. Third, have the IMF, World Bank, and capitalist aid donor country SAP policies, resources, and leverage altered the political or class coalition of power in Ghana? This question helps in understanding the political dynamics of the regime and how it has sought to create consent for or impose its policies. Finally, can the SAP reform policies be successful over time if broadly positive socioeconomic effects are not felt and if governments cannot develop stable political coalitions of group support for these policies?

## ■ The Impact of Stabilization and Structural Adjustment upon Development

### ☐ The Ghanaian Economy and Feasible Alternatives

One important basis for evaluating the relative success or impact of Ghana's reforms is to ask if, given the economic conditions in 1982 when the PNDC government under Flight Lieutenant Jerry J. Rawlings seized power, there were feasible political and economic alternatives to *some* of the major reforms undertaken. The argument here is that there were *not* feasible alternatives. This does not mean that one must accept as rational or effective all the IMF–World Bank policies that have been pursued. Briefly, feasible alternatives were absent because (1) the collapse of Ghana's economy and infrastructure was extensive and prolonged, leaving no resources for renewed growth; (2) the international political economy was hostile, politically and economically (e.g., sharply falling commodity prices); and (3) the radical populist program had low coherence, few socioeconomic resources, and low, unstable levels of political support. The question of feasible alternatives is important because Rawlings and the government are accused of, first, reversing sharply the PNDC's initial policies (certainly true) and, second, wholly abandoning the radical populist values that had animated these policies, such as populist political participation and affordable prices for the essentials of life.

The PNDC regime confronted in 1982 an economy in an advanced state of collapse. Soaring prices and terrible scarcities had made life desperate for many. Ghana actually had negative per capita growth in the 1960s. Per capita GDP fell more rapidly, by about 3.2 percent per year, during 1970–1981. But the social and economic debilitation and collapse were much greater than this fall in production suggests.[5] From 1970 to 1981 the mineral production index fell by 32 percent, with gold production down 47 percent, diamonds 67 percent, manganese ore 43 percent, and bauxite 46 percent (calculated from Table 7.1). Cocoa production, which averaged 380,000 metric tons in the three crop years 1968/69–1970/71, fell to an average 285,000 metric tons in 1976/77–1978/79 (−25 percent), dropping again to 225,000 tons in 1981/82 (see Table 7.2). In 1982 transport breakdowns prevented export of much of the prior year's crop. Thus, as a result of export declines, Ghana experienced during much of the 1970s and early 1980s a continuous import strangulation, which undermined production and strongly contributed to falling exports through shortages of spare parts, equipment, and transport. The IMF accurately argued that an overvalued exchange rate made production for export increasingly uneconomic for cocoa, gold, diamonds, and timber. But low terms of trade through much of the 1970s and early 1980s (the lowest in thirty years was reached in 1982) made it difficult for Ghanaian governments to increase price incentives for export (see Table 7.2).

Animated by low food growth, droughts, increasingly massive budget deficits during the 1970s and early 1980s, and external oil price shocks, Ghana experienced a debilitating and socially destructive inflation that averaged over 50 percent a year between 1976 and 1981, 116.5 percent in 1981 alone (Table 7.2).[6] Infant mortality rates, which fell from 132 per 1,000 in 1960 to perhaps 86 in the late 1970s, rose to 107–120 per 1,000 during 1980–1983 (helped by the drought and famine). Apart from rising allowances, real minimum wages dropped from an index of 75 in 1975 to 15.4 in 1981, or 80 percent (Table 7.2). Between 1977 and 1983, the real wages of a senior manager in the civil service fell by 90 percent, an accountant's wages by 84 percent.

Ghana's fiscal and institutional capabilities had been devastated in the late 1970s and 1980s, and governmental authority was equally diminished.

Table 7.1 Ghana: Selected Production Indicators

| | 1970 | 1980 | 1981 | 1982 | 1983 | 1984 | 1985 | 1986 | 1987 | 1988 | 1989 |
|---|---|---|---|---|---|---|---|---|---|---|---|
| **Agriculture** | | | | | | | | | | | |
| Cereals ('000 tons) | | | | | | | | | | | |
| Maize | 482 | 382 | 378 | 346 | 172 | 575 | 411 | 559 | 553 | 600 | 700 |
| Rice | 49 | 78 | 79 | 36 | 40 | 64 | 90 | 70 | 88 | 95 | |
| Millet[a] | 141 | 82 | 119 | 76 | 40 | 60 | 53 | 243 | 271 | 300 | |
| Sorghum | 186 | 132 | 131 | 86 | 56 | — | 62 | | | | |
| Starchy staples ('000 tons) | | | | | | | | | | | |
| Cassava | 2,388 | 2,322 | 2,065 | 2,470 | 1,728 | 4,083 | 3,076 | 3,692 | 2,943 | 3,300 | |
| Cocoyam | 1,136 | 643 | 631 | 628 | 720 | 600 | 730 | 650 | n.a. | n.a. | |
| Yam | 909 | 650 | 591 | 588 | 866 | 425 | 880 | 1,098 | 1,001 | 1,200 | |
| Plantain | 1,641 | 734 | 829 | 745 | 342 | 760 | 676 | 677 | n.a. | n.a. | |
| Cocoa ('000 tons)[b] | 413 | 258 | 225 | 178 | 158 | 175 | 219 | 228 | 188 | 305 | 277 |
| **Forestry ('000 m3)** | | | | | | | | | | | |
| Logs | 1,560 | 480 | 550 | 410 | 560 | 578 | 620 | 890 | 951 | | |
| Sawn timber | 360 | 150 | 190 | 189 | 180 | 223 | 232 | 284 | | | |
| **Mining** | | | | | | | | | | | |
| Index-mineral production | 100 | 74 | 68 | 60 | 50 | 58 | 65 | 60 | 65 | | |
| Gold ('000 troy ounces) | 642 | 353 | 341 | 331 | 277 | 287 | 299 | 288 | 329 | 383 | 421 |
| Diamonds ('000 carats) | 2,550 | 1,149 | 836 | 684 | 339 | 346 | 636 | 559 | 442 | 306 | 263 |
| Manganese ore | 392 | 250 | 223 | 160 | 173 | 288 | 316 | 259 | 254 | 282 | 285 |
| Bauxite | 337 | 225 | 181 | 64 | 70 | 49 | 170 | 204 | 195 | 300 | 375 |
| **Electricity** | | | | | | | | | | | |
| Electricity (million Kwh) | 2,920 | 5,306 | 5,382 | 4,973 | 2,569 | 1,815 | 2,996 | 4,435 | 4,676 | | |
| of which: Akosombo Hydroelectricity | 2,882 | 5,276 | 5,341 | 4,103 | 2,080 | 1,469 | 2,461 | 3,678 | 3,881 | | |
| Crudeoil refinery throughput | 1,120 | 1,058 | 1,129 | 1,040 | 481 | 747 | 958 | 985 | 990 | | |

*Sources:* Ghana, *Quarterly Digest of Statistics*, various issues, 1988–1989; World Bank data, 1990.
*Notes:* a. For 1986–1988, includes both millet and sorghum
b. Purchased by COCOBOD during season beginning in year stated

Table 7.2 Cocoa Prices, Inflation Rates, Real Minimum Wages, and Terms of Trade

| Crop Year | Cocoa Producer Price ¢/m ton | Real Producer Price Index (1963=100)[a] | Total Cocoa Production '000 m tons | Year | Rate of Inflation (%) | Local Food Inflation (%) | Real Minimum Wage Index[b] 1963=100 | Terms of Trade | |
|---|---|---|---|---|---|---|---|---|---|
| | | | | 1954–56 | | | | 107 | |
| 1960–61 | 220 | 130 | 432 | 1960 | | | | 100 | |
| 1961–62 | 198 | 114 | 410 | 1961 | | | | 87 | |
| 1962–63 | 198 | 104 | 422 | 1962 | | | | 80 | |
| 1963–64 | 198 | 100 | 428 | 1963 | | | | 81 | |
| 1964–65 | 198 | 83 | 538 | 1964 | | | | 82 | |
| 1965–66 | 145 | 49 | 401 | 1965 | 26.2 | 37.0 | 66.4 | 68 | |
| 1966–67 | 198 | 58 | 368 | 1966 | 13.5 | 15.7 | 58.3 | 68 | |
| 1967–68 | 238 | 77 | 415 | 1967 | –8.5 | –14.8 | 68.6 | 81 | |
| 1968–69 | 256 | 76 | 323 | 1968 | 8.2 | 8.7 | 67.9 | 84 | |
| 1969–70 | 293 | 82 | 403 | 1969 | 7.1 | 8.6 | 63.5 | 100 | |
| 1970–71 | 293 | 79 | 413 | 1970 | 3.7 | 4.4 | 61.2 | 109 | |
| 1971–72 | 293 | 72 | 454 | 1971 | 9.3 | 12.4 | 56.0 | 82 | |
| 1972–73 | 366 | 82 | 407 | 1972 | 10.0 | 9.9 | 68.1 | 72 | |
| 1973–74 | 439 | 83 | 340 | 1973 | 17.5 | 20.8 | 57.1 | 78 | |
| 1974–75 | 549 | 88 | 376 | 1974 | 18.4 | 15.7 | 73.2 | 91 | |
| 1975–76 | 585 | 72 | 396 | 1975 | 29.7 | 30.6 | 75.2 | 95 | |
| 1976–77 | 732 | 58 | 320 | 1976 | 53.3 | 70.1 | 48.1 | 89 | |
| 1977–78 | 1,333 | 49 | 271 | 1977 | 116.3 | 152.5 | 33.4 | 142 | |
| 1978–79 | 2,667 | 56 | 265 | 1978 | 73.7 | 59.4 | 25.6 | 186 | |
| 1979–80 | 4,000 | 55 | 296 | 1979 | 53.9 | 61.7 | 16.7 | 136 | |
| 1980–81 | 4,000 | 37 | 258 | 1980 | 50.1 | 52.3 | 16.6 | 100 | 100 |
| 1981–82 | 12,000 | 51 | 225 | 1981 | 116.5 | 111.2 | 15.4 | 68 | 73 |
| 1982–83 | 12,000 | 41 | 178 | 1982 | 22.3 | 35.8 | 12.6 | 60 | 64 |
| 1983–84 | 20,000 | 31 | 158 | 1983 | 122.8 | 144.8 | 10.2 | | 63 |
| 1984–85 | 30,000 | 33 | 175 | 1984 | 39.6 | 11.0 | 11.5 | | 71 |
| 1985–86 | 56,000 | 56 | 219 | 1985 | 10.4 | –11.1 | 21.4 | | 59 |
| 1986–87 | 85,000 | 68 | 228 | 1986 | 24.6 | 20.3 | 22.0 | | 68 |
| 1987–88 | 140,000 | E94 | 188 | 1987 | 39.8 | 38.5 | 19.7 | | |
| 1988–89 | 165,000 | | 305 | 1988 | 26.6 | 26.5 | 20.5 | | |
| 1989–90 | 174,000 | | 277 | 1989 | 25.0 | | | | |
| 1990–91 | 224,000 | | | 1990 | | | | | |

Sources: Cocoa—World Bank data; Gill and Duffus, "Cocoa Market Report," No. 298 (Nov. 1981), p. 27; Ghana, Central Bureau of Statistics, "Statistical Newsletter," monthly, 1976–1989. Inflation—"Statistical Newsletter," various issues; West Africa, various issues. Terms of trade—UNCTAD data, except 2nd series, 1980–1986, UNCTAD, Handbook of International Trade and Statistics, Supplement 1987 (1988), p. 534.

Notes: a. Cocoa producer price deflated by the rate of inflation and as a percentage of the base year real producer price. This index overstates the price decline to farmers, who produced their own food, the key factor in inflation.

b. From the mid-1970s, trade unions in state enterprises and some private firms often won minimum wages and allowances that were two times the government's, with the biggest differences in the allowances, which were sometimes two times the salary.

Tax revenue fell from 17 percent of GDP in 1973 to only 5 percent of GDP in 1983, this 1983 GDP itself having fallen by over a third in per capita terms. Hence, the government's share of Ghana's economic resources with which it could act in society had diminished by well over two-thirds. The PNDC's capacity to import goods to rehabilitate the economy was slight, with actual imports by volume in 1982 only 43 percent of average 1975/76 levels. The decline in capacity of public institutions was evidenced by the inability of governments to collect revenue, the Cocoa Board's failure to buy and export cocoa, and the deterioration of trunk and feeder roads to the extent that truck drivers declined to ply these routes. Almost a million Ghanaians of some 11 million left Ghana in the late 1970s, including many teachers and professionals, to escape impoverishment.

The radical populism articulated by Rawlings's PNDC regime in 1982–1983 seemed to promise the possibility of an alternative, more equitable, politically accountable, and effective regime. Rawlings argued as late as 1985 that "until every Ghanaian can satisfy his or her basic needs . . . ; until we have rooted out the cheats, the criminals, and the parasites; until participatory democracy is a reality rather than a goal; . . . until there is truth and social justice, the Revolution goes on."[7] But Ghana's early self-reliance and mobilizational policies had no capacity to restore the economic infrastructure and export production. The early months of the PNDC regime involved a wide range of ad hoc measures to increase output and exports (cocoa evacuation, road and transport repair, and antismuggling) and to enforce price controls and reductions. The PNDC mandated the organization of People's Defence Committees for neighborhoods and villages and Workers' Defence Committees for workplaces to mobilize the energies of the popular strata in implementing revolutionary decrees (on prices, rents, cleanups), checking corrupt managers, and supporting the PNDC. The state and capitalist bourgeoisie and petty bourgeoisie were removed from power and their wealth and bank accounts checked by Citizens Vetting Committees for tax evasion. The state media sought to animate class consciousness and conflict. The PDCs and WDCs were coordinated by a National Defence Committee and Regional Coordinating Committees (RCCs), which were staffed by members of Ghana's radical intelligentsia who belonged to a small number of divergent political groups (cliques really), including the June Fourth Movement, to which Rawlings had belonged. The PDCs and WDCs, led by the NDC and RCCs, threatened to challenge the PNDC's power, some acting on their own to dismiss managers, attack judges, and challenge PNDC economic allocations. PNDC leadership and governmental affairs were disorganized and chaotic.

The PNDC's Economic Advisory Committee quickly saw the inadequacy of the early populist mobilization measures and by August 1982 had proposed its own measures to attract the necessary aid from the IMF, World

Bank, and foreign donors. These included: (1) a major devaluation of Ghana's overvalued currency (cedi) in order to provide incentives to export producers; (2) price increases to cocoa producers; (3) containment of government budget deficits to arrest the socially devastating inflation, plus major efforts to collect taxes; (4) gradual decontrol of most controlled prices, which had perversely worked to enrich traders; (5) reduction of some expensive subsidies (on gasoline, electricity) and introduction of charges on some key social services (education, health clinic visits).

The radicals opposed price decontrols, subsidy reductions, and devaluation on the grounds that they would increase consumer prices and that they constituted a sellout to the IMF and imperialism.[8] They proposed further nationalizations of import-export trade and banks and setting up cooperative People's Shops; the latter was tried and briefly supported by the state but involved tiny premises, small informal capital subscriptions, low supplies, no popular accountability, and abuses.[9] These proposals were consumptionist in thrust and offered no new sources of external capital. Rawlings and others strongly opposed new nationalizations. The performance of state enterprises was widely regarded as terrible. Indeed, some radicals, and others, have come to regard many state enterprises as wasteful, socially inequitable, and sources of corruption and inefficiency (an argument also used ideologically).[10] The idea that state workers were unproductive yet demanded wage increases regularly was the source of anti–trade union sentiment among top PNDC leaders, including Rawlings.[11]

Lastly, some aspects of the class antagonism in radical populism, the institutional disruptions (e.g., purges of senior managers), and the frequent violence displayed by undisciplined military, police, and some PDC members had animated a broad and intense opposition to the regime by late 1982 and early 1983. The opposition called upon the PNDC to resign and permit a transitional democratic government. This made a radical project extremely difficult. The PNDC's opponents in late 1982 to early 1983, many of them vociferous, included the very numerous market women, some of them beaten and abused by price control enforcers; many food farmers, reluctant to provide food at controlled prices, especially to armed soldiers; trade union leaders and many rank and file unionists, who liked radical egalitarian views but opposed vigorously the PNDC's takeover of their unions; traditional chiefs; Catholic and Protestant clergy, who repeatedly denounced the military's violence; many senior military officers, who had largely lost control over the other ranks; the merchant-professional bourgeoisie; and consumers angered by hyperinflation.[12]

Profound cleavages also appeared within the ranks of PNDC supporters over what political forces and leadership should control the revolution, the murder of four judges (which led to mutual accusations), and the issue of economic policies and strategies, especially negotiating with the IMF and

World Bank. Many radicals were not interested in economic questions. Rawlings and his economic advisers believed that the economic questions had to be faced to retain state power. These power conflicts and issues led to several abortive coup attempts to weaken or replace Rawlings in October and November 1982. This induced Rawlings to weaken the PDCs and NDC in 1983–1984. And the PNDC's populist support, which the left tends to overstate, was tenuous and premised on increasing consumption, which was impossible in the short run, regardless of strategy.[13]

☐ *Stabilization and Adjustment Goals, Critiques, and Evaluative Criteria*

The major objectives of the stabilization and SAP policies have moved from major macroeconomic policy concerns with Ghana's balance of payments and budget deficits to microlevel sectoral reforms and rehabilitation. The key stabilization goal has been to reduce Ghana's balance of payments deficits and payment crises (arrears) by stimulating exports and restraining demand for imports. Stabilization has involved changing relative prices: foreign exchange by massive devaluations and domestic pricing by ending price controls and subsidies. To reduce domestic inflation and excess import demand, deficits in government spending had to be reduced or ended, credit ceilings set, and money supply growth contained. Slow growth in volume of Ghana's exports and extremely low international prices for them have caused large trade imbalances to persist. This has compelled Ghana to continue highly restrictive IMF stabilization programs. Other key policies have included price decontrol, major allocations for repairing infrastructure (roads, rail, ports) so that market signals would work, abolition of import licensing, tariff reduction (to require Ghanaian firms to compete), market interest rates, and the reform, liquidation, or privatization of state enterprises.[14]

Overall, Ghana's Economic Recovery Program has involved key policy and strategy emphases: (1) the maintenance of price incentives, especially to exporters, which involves continuous devaluations and, implicitly, the idea that Ghana must adjust its economy entirely in terms of world price signals; (2) major efforts to encourage domestic and foreign private capital, which, argue the PNDC and World Bank, will be the sources of Ghana's future growth; (3) reduction of the role of state enterprises in production and marketing, a schedule for which is one major condition of the IMF's 1987 Structural Adjustment Facility loans; and (4) the need to reverse Ghana's deterioration through economic growth, not simply stabilization. This goal has meant that the IMF and World Bank have worked to develop foreign loans and grants for Ghana's ERP, as long as Ghana has remained in compliance with IMF-Bank conditions. An early policy condition was rapid repayment of external loan arrears, with a massive payment of $203 million in 1984, after which payments were smaller and in 1990 (Table 7.3). In exchange, Ghana has benefited from increasingly large foreign grants and loans, most at highly concessional rates (see Table 7.3 for net aid disbursements).

Ghanaian leaders would probably on their own have chosen some stabilization and adjustment policies, and they have managed to moderate and soften some IMF and World Bank conditions in continuous bargaining. But it is overwhelmingly evident that the IMF and World Bank, plus some major donors, have become the most important architects of Ghana's economic policies and strategies. They have been especially important in insisting upon expenditure and credit controls and the scheduled implementation of difficult policies, from higher interest rates to civil service retrenchments to "cost recovery" user fees. Within the government, a small team of economists and managers, led by the finance minister, Kwesi Botchwey, and the cabinet head, P. V. Obeng, has wholly dominated economic policymaking and has the confidence of Rawlings. Its access to major foreign resources and skills enables it to dominate in decisions that are understood only partly by others, including the PNDC chairman, Jerry Rawlings (who is not active in economic policymaking, though his norms cannot be ignored). The IMF and World Bank have massive leverage but neither responsibility nor accountability. Their leverage rests with their large financial resources, their gatekeeping role in disallowing or organizing other aid and debt renegotiations, and their corps of economists, who have undertaken most of the project analyses and proposals in Ghana.

Despite some substantial gains that have been derived from IMF and Bank policies in Ghana, this discussion is informed by broader evidence. Many IMF stabilization programs and Bank SAPs are unsuccessful in ending external payments problems and are highly, and perversely, recessionary. These failures reflect not only developing country incapacities but IMF and Bank definitions of problems and misassumptions. The IMF and Bank manifest a missionary devotion to dismantling state production and marketing firms, while ignoring their structural importance, and to facilitating large capital investment to the detriment of small capital and peasants. The IMF and World Bank concentrate investment on export sectors and ignore those more important in raising living standards, e.g., food crops. And they exhibit spectacular indifference to the income redistributive effects and some of the growth impeding consequences of their policies.[15]

This assessment of the performance of the stabilization and SAP reforms will explicitly use certain criteria: (1) increases in economic output; and (2) the relative equity with which benefits and costs are distributed. The assessment is also based on certain ideas: (1) economic growth and development require investment, or deferred consumption; (2) development should reduce, not increase, poverty, unemployment, and inequality; and (3) major

Table 7.3 Ghana Economic Indicators

|  | 1981 | 1982 | 1983 | 1984 | 1985 | 1986 | 1987 | 1988 | 1989 |
|---|---|---|---|---|---|---|---|---|---|
| *GDP* (% change, constant prices) | -3.5 | -6.9 | -4.6 | 8.7 | 5.1 | 5.2 | 4.8 | 6.2 | 6.1 |
| Agriculture |  |  |  | 9.7 | 0.6 | 3.3 | 0.0 | 3.6 | 5.3 |
| Industry |  |  |  | 8.9 | 17.7 | 7.5 | 11.3 | 10.3 | 8.1 |
| Services |  |  |  | 6.6 | 7.5 | 6.5 | 9.4 | 7.8 | 5.2 |
| *Balance of Payments* ($ millions) |  |  |  |  |  |  |  |  |  |
| Exports of goods + NFS |  |  |  | 605 | 672 | 797 | 906 | 957 | 911 |
| Imports of goods + NFS |  |  |  | 810 | 858 | 968 | 1,199 | 1,264 | 1,347 |
| Trade balance |  |  |  | -114 | -96 | -56 | -198 |  |  |
| Resource balance (incl. NFS) |  |  |  | -205 | -186 | -171 | -293 | -307 | -436 |
| Current account deficit |  |  |  | -214 | -264 | -204 | -224 | -266 | -348 |
| Capital account (net) |  |  |  | 196 | 135 | 185 | 375 | 391 | 438 |
| of which: Net aid disbursements |  |  | 196 | 179 | 334 | 406 | 361 | 370 |  |
| Overall balance |  |  |  | 37 | -118 | -57 | 139 | 125 | 105 |
| Payments of arrears |  |  |  | 208 | 57 | 4 | 72 | 35 | 48 |
| Debt service ratio (%) |  |  |  |  |  |  |  |  |  |
| Excluding IMF |  |  |  | 32.1 | 46.7 | 38.5 | 28.9 | 32.0 |  |
| Including IMF |  |  |  | 36.3 | 53.3 | 48.2 | 53.9 | 65.2 |  |
| Including IMF + arrears |  |  |  | 46.4 | 61.8 | 48.7 | 61.8 | 67.4 | 58.4 |
| *Government Finance* (¢ bn.) |  |  |  |  |  |  |  |  |  |
| Revenues |  | 5.2 | 10.2 | 21.7 | 38.7 | 69.8 | 105. | 142.2 | 193.2[a] |
| % increase |  |  | 96 | 113 | 78 | 80 | 50 | 36 | 36 |
| Expenditure + net lending (¢ b.) | 9.2 | 15.2 | 27.5 | 47.9 | 73.3 | 107.0 | 149.9 | 204.2[a] |  |
| % increase |  |  | 65 | 81 | 74 | 53 | 46 | 40 | 36 |
| Overall deficit/surplus |  | -4.0 | -5.0 | -5.8 | -9.2 | -3.6 | -2.0 | -7.6 | -11[a] |
| Overall deficit/surplus + foreign grants |  | -3.97 | -5.0 | -4.8 | -7.6 | 0.3 | 4.1 | 3.9 | 10.4 |
| Financing: Foreign (net) |  | 0.3 | 0.74 | 2.7 | 5.1 | -1.7 | 4.9 | 13.8 | 26.3 |
| Domestic (net) |  | 3.8 | 4.3 | 3.0 | 4.1 | 5.3 | -3.0 | -6.2 | -15.3 |
| *As % of GDP* |  |  |  |  |  |  |  |  |  |
| Revenues |  | 6.0 | 5.5 | 8.0 | 11.3 | 13.6 | 14.1 | 13.4 | 14.4 |
| Recurrent expenditures |  | 9.3 | 7.4 | 8.6 | 11.2 | 11.9 | 10.8 | 10.5 | 11.0 |
| Development expenditures |  | 0.9 | 0.6 | 1.2 | 2.1 | 1.9 | 2.5 | 2.8 | 2.8 |
| Overall deficit/surplus |  | -4.7 | -2.7 | -2.1 | -2.7 | -0.7 | -0.3 | -0.7 | -0.8 |
| Gross investment |  |  | 3.7 | 6.9 | 9.6 | 9.7 | 13.4 | 14.1 | 15.0 |

*Sources*: Ghana, *Quarterly Digest of Statistics*, various issues, 1987–1988; World Bank Ghana data, 1990; World Bank, *Ghana: Structural Adjustment for Growth* (1989).
*Note*: a. Provisional

dimensions of increased well-being, such as reduced infant mortality and increased life expectancy and literacy, can be increased more quickly by public, collective policies than by awaiting individual income increases.[16]

☐ *Economic Growth*

In mid-1987 Finance Minister Kwesi Botchwey told Ghanaians that "we must jump for joy" because for the three years 1984–1986 Ghana experienced real gains in GDP of over 6 percent per year, compared with 1 percent in sub-Saharan Africa and 3.3 percent in developed countries.[17] Yet, relatively few Ghanaians have jumped for joy despite the persistence of a high average growth rate of 5.7 percent during 1987–1989. Average annual GDP growth was 6.0 percent for six years. This is the longest period of sustained growth that Ghana has experienced. The change in economic conditions since the extraordinarily depressed years of 1982–1983 is palpable to anyone who has been in Ghana. In addition, this growth has not been generated by markedly higher international prices for Ghana's key exports, especially cocoa; Ghana's terms of trade were at a postwar low in 1982–1983, recovered modestly with cocoa prices in 1984 and 1988, but have since deteriorated sharply (see Table 7.3). The renewal of growth is evidenced by the rehabilitation of the truck and vehicle fleet (up to two-thirds of which was off the road in 1981–1982, in the absence of spare parts), a renewal of Ghana's badly deteriorated road and rail networks, strongly revived production in key export industries, sharply higher imports, and sharply higher food production.

However, comparing Ghana's growth during 1984–1989 with baselines of 1982 and 1983 is not useful or honest, since Ghana's economy was devastated by the worst droughts in fifty years, bushfires that destroyed crops, postwar low cocoa prices, and, consequently, plummeting imports. In some senses Ghana's economic recovery has been slow and anemic. Output continues to be relatively low in cocoa, timber, mining, and industry in comparison with 1970 production levels, and this is also true of consumption, minimum wages, and access to social services.

What has been the contribution of some of the major reform policies to growth during 1984–1989? One can argue that the key factors in increased growth have been (1) increased imports made possible by foreign capital inflows; (2) substantially better weather and rainfall during 1984–1989; and (3) some of the stabilization/adjustment reforms, such as fewer inflationary fiscal and monetary policies and market incentives for exports (cocoa, gold, timber), which have induced new investments in these areas and promoted exports. The increased imports financed by the IMF, World Bank, and aid donor grants and loans have made possible the rehabilitation and repair of some key parts of the infrastructure and the supplies of spare parts and inputs for industry, mining, utilities, and agriculture. The good weather and rainfall (slightly less good in 1987) have led to crop production levels that have exceeded the highest prior production levels, which were in the early 1970s (see Table 7.1).[18] In maize, millet (including sorghum), cassava, and yams—major food staples—production in three, four, or (maize) five years of the six was substantially higher than in the highest prior years. Some other crops have persisted in low production, including plantain, most pulses and nuts, many fruits, and most vegetables. Non-cocoa agricultural production in 1984–1986 increased by 19.2 percent (in constant cedis), declined somewhat in 1987, but rose roughly 6 percent in 1988 and an estimated 6 percent in 1989.[19]

Were structural adjustment policies important or not in the agricultural growth? Road rehabilitation and greatly increased availability of spare parts for goods vehicles have been significant in reconnecting farms to markets. There may be higher levels of agricultural inputs, but this is not clear and, if so, they derived from World Bank resources, not policy changes. Has the World Bank induced Ghana to "get prices right" and remove the state from agricultural marketing? This was not a problem in food agriculture. Except for brief periods, no government has attempted to control domestic (as distinct from imported) food prices. The Food Distribution Corporation has primarily sought to provide a floor price for producers as an incentive, by guaranteeing minimum prices and making some purchases (a small percentage).

There are several major reasons for increased non-cocoa agricultural growth. First, good weather and rainfall during 1984–1989 (except 1987) have been crucial. Second, food farmers have continued to enjoy excellent prices and rural-urban terms of trade (as they did throughout the 1970s). The more stable political and social environment since 1984 has encouraged farmers to take advantage of the high food prices. Third, there has been a substantial increase in the percentage of the labor force in agriculture (including forestry and fishing), rising from 57.2 percent in 1970 to 61.1 percent in 1984 to an estimated 66.1 percent in 1987. This was caused by the decay in urban job opportunities and the expulsion of roughly a million Ghanaians from Nigeria in 1983. The government made major efforts to reintegrate these Ghanaians into local agriculture as laborers and producers.[20] There is some evidence, as a result, that acreage planted has increased, e.g., in cereal crops, 11 percent. Fourth, domestic food crops have been emphasized rhetorically and in a number of organizational ways. The Ministry of Agriculture has been more coherent in its modest assistance, rebuilding its extension program, and has been under the aggressive leadership of Commodore Stephen Obimpeh since 1986. Undersecretaries of Agriculture have been appointed in each region to coordinate activities there and with the central government. Roughly 1,000 kilometers. of feeder roads were resurfaced during 1986–1988, a very modest effort that will be more strongly pursued under a World Bank program. Lastly, a number of pre-SAP World Bank regional agricultural projects, with numerous farm service centers making inputs available, and the private, government-adopted Global 2000 small farmer project (providing seeds and fertilizer) are probably having an impact.[21]

In general, the World Bank's structural adjustment programs ignored domestic agriculture as a potentially powerful engine of growth, as the World Bank's representative in Ghana has acknowledged.[22] The overwhelming shift in resources to cocoa rehabilitation and other export sectors (timber, roads, mines) probably denied to food agriculture resources it might otherwise have obtained. Agriculture Ministry budgets as a percentage of the total actually fell from 10+ percent in 1982 and 1983 to 4.2 percent in 1985 and 1986 and 3.5 percent in 1988, excluding foreign aid projects. But agriculture has undoubtedly benefited from other sector expenditures. Food crops contribute much more to Ghana's GDP than does cocoa, but cocoa received 9 percent of capital expenditures in the late 1980s and roughly 67 percent of recurrent agricultural expenditures.[23] Efforts in food agriculture would undoubtedly have far more equitable consequences—for producers because non-cocoa agriculture involves a more equal pattern of producers and land holding than does cocoa, and for consumers by restraining the constant food price increases, the primary factor in depressing living standards.

The most important contributions of the stabilization and SAP policies in the first three to four years were probably in the early devaluations, which permitted the payment of sharply higher cedi prices to cocoa producers as well as gold and timber producers, and the sharp reduction in budget deficits, partly from intensive tax collection. But the relatively meager response in cocoa production, until the 1988/89 crop, to much higher nominal prices since 1983 and greatly improved real prices since 1985 has to be disappointing (see Table 7.2). Since the cocoa crops of 1982 and 1983, the lowest in over twenty-five years, resulted from severe drought, low real producer prices, and a collapse in transport, the "recovery" in 1984–1986 appears to be no more than a rebound given better market, infrastructural, and weather conditions. Production remained low in 1986/87 and 1987/88 despite the highest real prices in twenty-five years (Table 7.2).

The World Bank's strategy has been to increase real prices drastically in the anticipation that farmers would rehabilitate existing farms and undertake new planting of the more productive hybrid cocoa plants. The World Bank's belief, however, that one had only to "get prices right" to induce higher levels of production, in both cocoa and agriculture generally, unduly simplified a complex situation.[24] This is very important because so much of Ghana's recovery strategy has been structured around higher cocoa prices, made possible by devaluations, to induce higher exports to balance external accounts and provide imports. Moreover, the World Bank's belief in price incentives as the most powerful stimulant of behavior has led it to encourage the PNDC government to promise farmers higher and higher minimum food prices rather than work to reduce the major nonprice barriers to production and marketing efficiency (estimates are that up to 25 percent of food crops are spoiled in storage). But food prices are not low. The internal terms of trade have turned massively in favor of food farmers since the early 1970s. The local food price index increased 198 times between 1973 and 1984, overwhelming evidence that prices were not the constraint in food production. During the late 1970s and in 1980–1981, there was evidence that in food-farming villages, even those not on main roads, there was a rising prosperity, while urban Ghana was in profound recession.[25]

The World Bank has made a major case for allocating huge resources to cocoa from foreign loans (soft term IDA) and sharply higher producer prices. This involves important shifts in income from predominantly urban consumers to cocoa producers. Cocoa has been Ghana's major foreign exchange earner. It has an important multiplier effect upon the economy because scarce foreign exchange has been a major constraint on economic growth. Unable to have the Cocoa Board abolished, the World Bank demanded a major reduction in staff and functions so that marketing costs did not exceed 15 percent of the world price; this left at least 50–60 percent for farmers (the rest went to costs and taxes). With these higher prices, Brazilian and Malaysian farmers have cultivated cocoa intensively and obtain yields four times those currently achieved in Ghana. Substantially higher prices have been necessary to induce farmers to harvest and rehabilitate existing farms and plant 12,000–15,000 hectares of new hybrid cocoa per year; and to stop cocoa smuggling to the Ivory Coast, where cocoa could be sold for three times the Ghana price in 1984 and two times Ghana's price in 1987.[26]

This policy strategy can be questioned on grounds of efficiency and equity, even while acknowledging the need to stimulate cocoa production. On efficiency grounds, markedly higher nominal and real cocoa prices were not effective in inducing higher cocoa output in the four postdrought years (1984/85–1987/88) than occurred in the two predrought years (1980/81–1981/82). Second, cocoa has been pushed as the key export sector despite the IMF, World Bank, and other forecasts in the mid-1980s of declining world cocoa prices as greatly increased world supplies glut the market.[27] The income elasticity of demand for cocoa is very low in the short to medium run, leading to sharp price declines in the face of excess supply. Even if Ghana maintains the 300,000 metric tons in production attained in 1988/89 (which it did not in 1989/90), sharp price declines since 1986 mean that increased cocoa exports are not making the anticipated contribution to Ghana's exports.

In equity terms, one of the key reasons that led Ghana to liberalize foreign exchange pricing through weekly auctions has been the commitment to regular, significant increases in prices for cocoa and other exports. The freeing of foreign exchange has led to repeated *real* devaluations in 1986–1990. These have contributed to extremely high rates of inflation (some argue that this is by definition caused by excess demand, not devaluation). This has had the highly inequitable effect of depressing living standards. The

World Bank's devotion to market mechanisms has led it to advocate higher food and agricultural prices to elicit greater supplies from farmers, as if price (not labor, capital, land, knowledge, transport, or custom) were the key or only constraint on production. The Bank has not been disturbed by the devastating impact of higher food prices on much of the population. The World Bank's recent Ghana Living Standards Survey indicates that Ghanaian households, on average, spend 69 percent of their total expenditures on food, including all deciles among the bottom 90 percent of the households by expenditure levels.[28] There is abundant evidence from Ghana and from cross-country surveys that higher food costs contribute to malnutrition, disease, and infant mortality.[29] Devaluation does have an inflationary impact on the consumption items of the poor, in higher transportation charges and higher local food costs through higher fuel, wage, and marketing costs. In addition, the gains from huge increases in cocoa prices go disproportionately to a very small percentage of farmers: older surveys indicate that 20–25 percent of cocoa farmers capture 50–55 percent of income; a 1987 survey of four villages in Ashanti found that 32 percent of the cocoa farmers received 94 percent of gross cocoa income, while the remaining 68 percent received 6 percent.[30]

The forestry industry demonstrates the benefits and shortcomings of SAP policies. Log production collapsed by two-thirds during 1970–1981 and sawn timber by 47 percent (Table 7.1). Exports fell from $130 million in 1973 to $15 million in 1983; four nationalized firms were bankrupted during that period. The World Bank's $157 million in soft loans expanded production and exports very quickly: log production rose 65 percent in 1984–1987 and export revenues rose 665 percent in 1983–1988. But investigations have revealed massive corruption, tax avoidance, capital flight, local firms illegally subletting concessions to foreign firms, little production of higher value-added veneer and plywood, and nonreplanting.[31]

The GDP average annual growth in *industry* during 1984–1986 was 11.4 percent per year; it fell somewhat in 1987–1989 to 9.9 percent. While industry showed higher growth than the other sectors, its key subsectors (mining, manufacturing, electricity and water, and construction) demonstrated different patterns of growth, benefited from SAP policies to different extents, and had distinctive responses in terms of growth and equity. The mining sector is undoubtedly the biggest beneficiary of the stabilization and SAP policies and is now making a major contribution to Ghana's foreign exchange earnings (though how much is retained in Ghana is what is crucial). Renewed growth was slow because of the need for new investment and exploration. Table 7.1 indicates that gold production had risen by 52 percent by 1989 from its 1983 low but was still about 66 percent of 1970 levels; diamond production continued to decline and in 1989 was only 10 percent of its 1970 level; manganese production grew by 63 percent since 1983. And bauxite soared 665 percent from its 1984 low, surpassing the 1970 level. Railway transport is the only barrier to increasing output by 33 percent, to 500,000 metric tons.

The government has made major, somewhat successful attempts to attract foreign capital to gold mining. Ashanti Goldfields Corporation (AGC), 55 percent government-owned, has borrowed abroad to make large new investments and has greatly increased output, 31 percent during 1987–1989 alone. In 1989 it earned 20 percent of Ghana's foreign exchange.[32] Some fifty new gold prospecting licenses have been issued, and new mining companies are investing for the first time since the 1920s. The State Gold Mining Corporation (SGMC), with no capital, is seeking foreign private investment partners. The Ghana government also decided to legalize gold mining by an estimated 150,000 individual Ghanaians. In less than a year it earned tax revenues of ¢2 billion ($6.7 million).[33]

The rehabilitated electric and water sectors grew rapidly after water rates were raised by hundreds of percent in 1986 and later years and electricity rates by lesser amounts. The electrical power grid was to be extended to northern Ghana—its regional capitals and major districts—by 1989–1990. If market rates are charged for power and more efficient water supplies, there will be relatively few customers in the impoverished North.

The two sectors in which private Ghanaian capital is most important are manufacturing and construction. Both sectors were in long-term depression prior to 1984. Manufacturing had an average annual growth of 14.3 percent during 1984–1987, while construction stagnated during 1984–1986 and grew 15.2 percent in 1987. Both sectors in 1987 had, in constant cedis, 36 percent lower production than in 1975 and 26 percent lower than in 1980. Both suffer severe problems. Manufacturers, when they can get credit, have benefited from greater access to foreign exchange and especially from the end of price controls, so they can pass on higher costs. But the extremely high levels of devaluation have made it exceptionally expensive to purchase inputs and difficult to obtain bank credit (because so many more cedis must now be borrowed against the existing value of collateral). In addition, the exceptionally tight monetary policies of the government and the Bank of Ghana have created liquidity crises for manufacturers. At the same time, liberalization of trade has meant that some manufacturers have been faced with competition whose costs they cannot match.

Despite their support for the recovery program, manufacturers and other Ghanaian businesspeople have persistently criticized some major PNDC economic policies. J. V. L. Phillips, vice-president of the Ghana Employers' Association, argued publicly in 1988 that "severe liquidity problems, rapidly rising interest rates, sluggish sales, up-front payments of 100 percent for imports, just to mention a few such matters, have created serious problems" for Ghanaian employers and "in some cases threatened the very existence of their business." Phillips appealed to the government to impose quotas on some imports to save "local industries from extinction," lamented that there was no forum for employers, labor, universities, and other groups to exchange views on the economy and monitor its performance, and wondered why the tripartite National Labor Advisory Committee had not been convened in two years.[34] The National Chamber of Commerce was just one of the business groups that complained about the draconian interest rates; in August 1988, it argued that the increase in interest rates from 21 percent in 1987 to 30 percent in 1988 was excessive and causing great liquidity problems.[35] By September 1988, the *Daily Graphic* reported that almost all the garment factories in Ghana had closed down due to competition from imported garments and secondhand clothing, citing six well-known firms.[36] Rising pressures for limited import controls to permit Ghana's industries to get back on their feet were reflected in the Association of Ghana Industries' (AGI) request in February 1989 that some "measure of meaningful protection" be afforded those sectors severely damaged by imports in the prior year, including firms in the garment, leather-processing, drug, and plastics industries. Finance Minister Botchwey responded toughly that any protection afforded would be exceptional and would require firms to pay for one-third of the effective subsidy, by way of a loan.[37]

High interest rates (to increase savings), tight liquidity (to curtail inflation), liberalization of trade to compel Ghanaian firms to operate more efficiently, and energetic tax collections (to balance the budget) were all part of the stabilization and SAP policies. But they were remarkably inattentive to the problems of industries battered by long recession and hyperinflation: old or out-of-repair equipment; 100 percent advances against imports; weak demand initially; depleted capital; and very tight bank credit. By early 1990, P. V. Obeng, the secretary of the Committee of Secretaries (Cabinet), or effective prime minister since 1982, cited as a major mistake the "over-liberalization of certain economic activities" when industries were not on a "sound footing."[38] Local industries were still closing in 1990. One problem is that the market ideology of the IMF, World Bank, and key donor countries does not admit of the many intractable institutional problems in the Ghanaian and similar economies; they are also simply indifferent to the implementation problems of policies they impose. Tight money is deemed necessary to contain a recalcitrant inflation that might generate excess import demand. However, with capacity utilization in Ghanaian manufacturing estimated at 25 percent in 1985 and no more than 32 percent in 1988, and with unemployment quite high, extending further credit to many manufacturing firms would not generate inflation and might actually ease it. The IMF is itself concerned with unused capacity, and many firms operate at half their potential, largely because of the squeeze on private sector credit set by IMF lending ceilings. Unable to finance auction bids for imports of raw materials or spare parts, they reduce output. Indeed, in late 1989, the IMF was worried about the sharp decline in private investment in all categories: Ghanaian, joint, and foreign equity.[39] Ghana's Central Bank chairman argued: "If there are complaints about tight credit policy, remember that the credit policy is derived from the arithmetic of the economic recovery program; you can't accept the conception [of the ERP] and then fight with its logic."[40] One can, of course, unless one believes that reliance upon market mechanisms always promotes efficiency and socially desirable ends, however imperfect the markets. Reducing some economic distortions can create others. There is apparently substantial monetary liquidity in Ghana in general but little available for manufacturing and agriculture. In part, thus, the problems of manufacturing and construction reflect the internally inconsistent aspects of IMF and Bank conditions and policies and the rigidity of IMF concerns with external imbalances.

Growth in the service sector averaged over 7 percent during 1984–1989, but the "magic of the market" distributed its rewards variously. The major foreign resources made available to the transport sector, especially spare parts, enabled it to grow by roughly 10.7 percent per year during 1983–1987. Thus, there was a far larger percentage of the vehicle fleet on the road in 1985 than previously, even if it had an average estimated vehicle age of 10–15 years. But farmers complained regularly about the difficulty of getting crops to market in the absence of transport, whether in the Eastern Region, near the coast, or in the large, underdeveloped northern regions, where transport is scarce, intermittent, and unpredictable.[41] Roads in many areas of the country are in poor condition, which increases vehicle costs. Market demand and profitability—not social or economic need—ensured that in the July–December 1988 period, 52 percent of all vehicles in Ghana were in Accra, the capital, with 7 percent of the population. Inequality in income determined that only 33 percent of new vehicles were goods and passenger vehicles, which the majority of the population use. Containment of public expenditures meant that one-half of the public buses in Accra were off the road as well as 33 percent of the bus fleet of City Express.[42]

If wholesale and retail trade fell between 1975 and 1980 and each year during 1981–1983, they roared back to life during 1984–1987, with an average growth of 15 percent per year. Unfortunately, as Ghanaians often observe, while goods are now plentiful, they are unaffordable. The number of registered traders in Accra rose from 15,000 in 1986 to 25,000 in 1987, reflecting growing underemployment and school dropouts hawking goods for their families.[43] The service sector that grew the very least during 1983–1987 was government, whose growth was 4.8 percent, less than the economy as a whole. It declined from 15 percent of GDP to 14 percent. The real gains were slight ones in wages, not in the goods and services produced by government.

## ☐ Exports and Devaluation, Imports and Growth

The centerpiece of the ERP/stabilization plan involved massive devaluations in the (by 1983) grossly overvalued cedi so that exports would receive a higher real cedi value for their production and export. Simultaneously, import demand for previously artificially cheap imports would fall. The cedi underwent a draconian series of devaluations, on a continuing basis. (See Table 7.4.)

The IMF pressed the PNDC government to establish a "freer" exchange rate, which is why the "second window," by weekly auction, was established in September 1986. The lesser official rate was retained temporarily for imports of crude oil, essential drug purchases, government debt service, and cocoa revenue, which showed some concern for the inflationary impact of these devaluations in social areas (e.g., transport, drugs/health) and its own debt payments.

Devaluation was imperative in 1983, since overvaluation was destroying Ghana's export capacity, as was government retention of the hard currency. The purpose of continuous devaluations was to maintain or increase incentives to exporters by offsetting internal inflation. If one assumes that the 990 percent devaluation in 1983 reflects the IMF's idea of the extent of cedi overvaluation, one can use 1983 as a base year. By my calculations, in every year since 1983, except 1987, Ghana has had *real* devaluations, that is, devaluations that exceed the prior year's inflation rate. Inflation in the four years 1984–1987 was 160 percent, while devaluation was 486 percent. In 1988–1989 the cedi was devalued by about 72 percent, while inflation was about 58 percent.

Table 7.4 Devaluation of the Cedi, 1983–1990

| Date | Official Rate | Weekly Auction Rate | Private Sale | Cumulative % Change Official Rate |
|---|---|---|---|---|
| March 1983 | $1=¢2.75 | | | |
| April 1983 | $1=¢24.69 | | | |
| Oct. 1983 | $1=¢30 | | | −990 |
| Dec. 1984 | $1=¢50 (in 3 steps) | | | |
| 1985 | $1=¢60 | | | |
| Jan. 1986 | $1=¢90 | | | −3,173 |
| Sept. 1986 | $1=¢90 | $1=¢128 | | |
| Feb. 1987 | | Only rate $1=¢153 | | −5,464 |
| Dec. 1987 | | $1=¢176 | | |
| April 1988 | | | begins | |
| Sept. 1989 | | $1=¢280 | $1=¢360–375 | −10,082 |
| March 1990 | | $1=¢310 | $1=¢345–370 | −11,172 |
| Sept. 1990 | | $1=¢337 | $1=¢355 | −12,809 |

There are several efficiency-based grounds for *not* wholly liberalizing foreign exchange markets and import composition. First, under conditions of scarce foreign exchange and important rehabilitation needs, Ghana has had crucial priorities for imports. The World Bank itself urged the adoption of priorities in exchange allocations under the auction process rather than assume that the market yields efficiency and social desirability.[44] However, since late 1987, restrictions to bidding in foreign exchange auctions ended, whereupon the percentage shares going to industry and agriculture dropped. With the extreme inequalities in income and wealth that obtain in Ghana, rationing foreign exchange through the market simply means that it goes to the most wealthy. (In 1988 the top 20 percent by consumption levels of households in Ghana spent 42.3 percent of consumption—an underestimate, one suspects.)[45] Second, the constant devaluations have made the Ghanaian private sector reluctant to seek foreign exchange for imports because of the constant exposure to losses through new devaluations. This has at times slowed imports and private sector investment.[46] Third, the stabilization/SAP in Ghana has tried to reduce inflation; it simultaneously stimulates it by these devaluations. The massive 990 percent devaluation in 1983 probably did not greatly add to inflation. But during 1984–1987, nonfood items on the consumer price index (CPI)—which have a higher direct and indirect import component—rose three times more rapidly than did local food prices: 43.5 percent versus 14.7 percent in average annual rates.

The devaluations have helped exports, which have increased substantially since their low point in 1983: by 29 percent in 1984, 11 percent in 1985, 18.6 percent in 1986, 13.7 percent in 1987, then more slowly, 5.6 percent, in 1988, followed by an estimated decline of 4.8 percent in 1989 because of falling cocoa prices (Table 7.3). The increase in dollar-denominated exports occurred despite low or declining cocoa and gold prices and the relatively slow responsiveness of several key export commodities until 1988 and 1989. And the PNDC has been able to attract external loans and some investment to the export sectors.

Imports have also increased substantially since the low point of 1983, a poor, because unduly depressed, baseline. However, imports rose in most years less than the percentage increase (by value) of exports, except in the last three years, 1987–1989 (calculated from Table 7.3). The recent higher increases in imports, which have contributed to continued growth, have been financed by rising values in net aid disbursements since 1984 (Table 7.3).

The devaluation and rising exports have not fulfilled a key stabilization goal: both the trade and service deficit and current account deficit have not fallen but increased. Ghana's adjustment had to be one of stabilization through growth, requiring higher imports. But the growing deficits are tolerable only as long as rising aid levels cover them. Net aid disbursements—much of them in soft term loans and grants—increased from

1984 to 1987, to $406 million, dropped slightly in 1988 and 1989 to $361–$370 million, and are estimated at $550 million in 1990 (Table 7.3). Current aid levels will not continue indefinitely. Exports will have to grow greatly to pay for current import levels, which are below those of the early 1970s. The debt service ratio has been exceptionally high (Table 7.3). It averaged 62.5 percent of exports in 1987–1989 but was declining and was estimated at 40 percent in 1990. But debt repayment can be maintained only by the continued flow of aid. Ghanaian economic leaders have been highly successful in obtaining foreign assistance, primarily from multilateral institutions. But Ghana has failed to attract much foreign private investment, only $65 million during 1983–1989. On the basis of this record, domestic and foreign private investment are unlikely to power Ghana's future growth.

☐ *Government Spending, Deficits, and Investment Choices*

The IMF's demand management program has required the PNDC government to reduce the budget deficit, with its inflationary impact, a goal with which Ghanaian leaders agreed. Between 1983 and 1989, revenues and grants increased more rapidly than total expenditures, overall and in every year in percentage terms until 1988/89 (Table 7.3). This led to a small budget surplus (when foreign grants are included) by 1986 and larger ones in 1987–1989. There was a very sharp reduction in the overall deficit in cedi terms and as a percentage of the GDP. Leaving out foreign grants, the government budget deficit as a percentage of the GDP fell from 4.7 percent in 1982 to 2.7 percent in 1983, 0.7 percent in 1986, and 0.3 percent in 1987—a remarkable performance.

The cost of this performance, however, has been high, both because this sharp contraction in government deficits has failed to reduce inflation to tolerable levels and because *real* government spending initially shrank, with grievous effects. Since virtually no layoffs occurred until 1986 (leaving aside shrinkage in the military and in the Cocoa Board), and since real expenditure increases after 1984 tended to go to raising real wages, the decline in real spending occurred in the important goods/services/equipment category. This involved materials for basic government activity, whether in education (books, paper, schoolrooms, chairs), health (drugs, equipment), or various ministries, including agriculture, for which there were no transport funds or gasoline for extension workers. Since expenditures had shrunk in real terms to such a small percentage of the GDP by 1983, as Reginald Green observes, it was clearly counterproductive to growth and well-being to shrink government expenditures still further. "The initial reduction of government spending is now perceived as an error and has been reversed but its costs in nearly destroying government health services and gravely undermining education, transport, and works and agriculture remain."[47]

The PNDC government has increased its economic capacities in society as it has raised government expenditures (recurrent and development) as a percentage of the GDP from 8 percent and 9.8 percent in 1983 and 1984 to 13.3-13.8 percent in 1985–1989 (Table 7.3). The recurrent expenditure level has been reduced since 1985 as a percentage of the GDP so that development expenditures could be increased (Table 7.3). Expenditure control has been imposed rigidly to meet IMF goals. In 1986, when it appeared that the budget deficit would widen because of revenue shortfalls and an inability to cut wages and benefits in the face of trade union protests, all expenditures in the last half of the year, especially development, were cut drastically to meet IMF targets. The exercise was unnecessarily brutal, as a budget surplus was attained. Many government ministries and institutions (schools, hospitals) remain unable to conduct their activities because of scarcities of essential materials and equipment. Without paper and printing ink, government ministries publish a tiny fraction of the information they routinely made available to the public twenty-five years ago.

The government has been under strong pressure from the IMF and World Bank to contain expenditures relative to revenues in ways that increase the efficiency of government services. Budgetary transfers to state corporations were huge—over 1 percent of GDP in 1983 and 1984—and had been reduced to 0.7 percent by 1987. Many of the state corporations were heavily overstaffed during the Acheampong regime (1972–1978), rarely rendered financial accounts to the government, and were remarkably unproductive, though they were often without adequate capital budgets, working capital, and imports. State corporations that will remain as such, including the Cocoa Board, have undergone major budgetary and managerial reforms. Some thirty-two major state companies are being readied for sale. This involves a significant redefinition of the role of the state, an erosion in the idea that industrial restructuring requires a strong state role, and faith in the interest of foreign and domestic capital in manufacturing in Ghana that prior experience does not justify.

The PNDC also has come under strong IMF–World Bank pressure to reduce the size of generally overstaffed civil service ministries and state corporations. This has been to permit a higher percentage of government expenditures to be devoted to equipment and services versus salaries and to permit remaining workers to be paid a higher real wage. The government was slow to move on dismissals, started in late 1986, and was regularly below its target of 15,000 workers per year during 1987–1989. Equity concerns are real but have been somewhat diminished by large termination benefits, in many cases, and by a public and PNDC perception that taxpayers have sustained an overlarge public service; the idleness of some civil servants is visible.

Revenue collection has been vigorously pursued and has retained some of the populist overtones it possessed in 1982–1984, when the Citizens Vetting Committees investigated the unpaid taxes of the rich and self-employed; it is now the Office of Revenue Collection. The tax net has been broadened to include a much wider range of the untaxed and underassessed self-employed. Effectiveness and equity of revenue collection have increased as have institutional capacities. However, even minimum wage workers are currently taxed and would be more heavily taxed except for the persistent protests of trade unions.

Development (capital) spending not directly tied to foreign assistance projects grew slowly as a percentage of the budget because of spending constraints. However, the government is raising capital investment at the expense of increased current consumption to permit future growth. Capital expenditures rose from 8.9 percent of the budget in 1983 to 12.5 percent in 1984, 15.2 percent in 1985, 17.3 percent in 1987, 19.9 percent in 1988, and 18.7 percent in 1989 (calculated from Table 7.3). In both the three-year public investment programs of 1984–1986 and 1986–1988, the productive sectors have received roughly 33 percent (especially the export and supportive sectors), physical infrastructure 62 percent, and the social sectors (health, education, welfare) only 4.7–5 percent. In addition, most loans and all foreign investment are going to the productive and physical infrastructure sectors. By 1989, agriculture's share of the development budget had risen rapidly and was the second highest.[48]

The relatively low levels of budgetary investment in education and health may be criticized on grounds of effectiveness (in increasing growth), equity, and development (increasing human and institutional capacities). Real expenditures in health and education fell drastically in the 1970s, before the PNDC's advent. The health budget as a percentage of GDP was 1.2 percent in 1970 and 0.26 percent in the 1980–1983 period, versus 0.95 percent of the GDP in other low-income countries in Africa in 1982. The education budget as a percentage of the GDP was 3.9 percent in 1970 and 0.85 percent in 1980–1983, versus 2.81 percent in low-income Africa.[49] Facilities deteriorated, health and education standards fell, worker productivity suffered, and teachers, nurses, and doctors fled abroad (or, in the case of doctors, also to private practice). As of 1980–1983, average caloric intake as a percentage of requirements had fallen from about 97 percent in 1970 to roughly 68 percent. Malnutrition estimates and the percentage of the urban and rural population below the poverty line had all increased dramatically.[50] In both health and education, the PNDC and prior governments found themselves in a major financial squeeze, particularly with the sharply rising costs of secondary and university education. Rising local food costs greatly increased the budgets of residential secondary schools (now being phased out) and universities. Students have rioted and demonstrated over rotten and inadequate food.

In the areas of health, education, and water, the PNDC government has developed, at World Bank insistence, schemes of user charges or "cost recovery," which provide services that would not be possible on existing budgets. Finance Minister Kwesi Botchwey argues persuasively that schools were free in 1982, but there were no textbooks, desks, pens, or pencils. The PNDC was accused of being "counterrevolutionary" and "antisocialist" for asking parents to pay a small fee. The PNDC, argues Botchwey, could have "continued the deceit, sending workers' children to schools which had nothing, and saved ourselves the criticisms." Hospitals and clinics, he noted, were lacking basic drugs, dressings, linens, and other essentials. With the introduction of a small fee, "we were accused of attacking 'free health,' but health was free and non-existent."[51]

In 1985, the PNDC government introduced a range of fees for hospitals and clinic consultations and laboratory tests. The basic fee for an adult to consult with a doctor was from two-thirds to a full day's minimum wage (₵50–₵75 in 1985, excluding a minimum 56 percent additional in allowances). There was an immediate 25 percent drop in the number of visits to the Korle-Bu hospital by children outpatients between June and August (Korle-Bu being Accra's main hospital) and a 50 percent decline in the much more heavily used polyclinic of Korle-Bu.[52] People are chronically ill in Ghana. A major survey found that 35 percent of Ghanaians indicated that they had been ill in the last four weeks, for an average of 7.6 days, during 3.8 days of which they had been rendered inactive. When ill, 52 percent of all Ghanaians saw no health personnel (73 percent of the poorest 10 percent, 64 percent of the poorest 30 percent), while 26 percent saw a doctor (10.5 percent of the poorest 10 percent), 4.6 percent saw a nurse, and 11 percent saw a medical assistant.[53] The user fees in clinics and hospitals have become very important to them in acquiring drugs, dressings, and other supplies, and such fees now constitute 12 percent of the Ministry of Health's budget, though the clinics and hospitals are permitted to keep what they collect. In some areas (for example, Ashanti), 75 percent of the fees collected are for drugs (which might not be available in the absence of fees).[54] After an initial decline in the use of health facilities following the start of the higher fees, there has apparently been some increase again in use. But clinic use in the poor areas of Accra, for instance, remains lower than before.[55] Moreover, the real cost to workers and others of these hospital/clinic fees in reduced real wages is not adequately reflected in the percentage of the Consumer Price Index noted for medicines and health (1.8 percent). The clearly destitute supposedly do not have to pay fees, but fee collection efforts are insistent. Initial consultation fees by 1987 were ₵200, almost two days of minimum wage. An inpatient is required to make a ₵1,500 initial deposit against costs, about ten days of a minimum wage worker's earnings.[56] Some patients have absconded to avoid payments.

Only a constant 25 percent of the Ministry of Health's budget has gone to primary health care over the 1983–1988 period; the rest goes to doctor-delivered curative services, which affect a very small percentage of the population. While the number of doctors in the public sector grew from 1,075 to 1,700 between 1975 and 1982, falling real salaries and equipment scarcities reduced the number of public doctors to a scant 665 in 1987; another 3,000 are in private practice.[57] Health is a low government priority. In 1986 the government allocated to the Health Ministry for drug procurement no more than $13.6 million, a mere 18 percent of the requested sum and less than in any of the previous seven years.[58]

The PNDC government has undoubtedly confronted some major dilemmas in allocating scarce funds. But regime leaders appear not to be serious about such a fundamental matter as childhood immunization, and wildly different numbers are offered in ritualistic exercises of public concern. Jerry Rawlings announced with fanfare at June 4 celebrations in 1989 that the government had exceeded its target of 80 percent for immunization of all children under two years against the major childhood diseases. Two months earlier, the secretary for Health noted that less than 50 percent of the children were immunized against the six childhood killer diseases, which account for 70 percent of preventable deaths among children.[59] In 1988, a health specialist reported a figure of 20 percent, while in early 1989 the UNICEF health team noted that only 5 percent of the children in all the North have been fully vaccinated against the six killer diseases.[60] The urban poor suffer, too. Greater Accra had the highest proportion of clinics with very high levels of child malnutrition (fourteen of seventeen, or 83 percent, compared with 27 percent in the rest of the country).[61]

User costs have directly increased disease and reduced economic output. During 1988 and 1989 there were widespread reports from all over Ghana of outbreaks of guinea worm infection (partly reflecting the fact that World Health Organization teams were studying the problem). Guinea worm is an infection that comes from drinking pond water with the worm larvae, which then breed inside the body, grow to two or three feet in length, and then emerge slowly and painfully from the skin to the outside. In the Upper West Region, a coordinator of the guinea worm campaign reported that many villages had had boreholes drilled and fitted with hand pumps so that they could obtain clean water; the incidence of the disease had subsided. But when in 1986 the Ghana Water and Sewerage Corporation imposed a fee of ¢19,000 per borehole annually, many rural communities abandoned use of the boreholes and returned to drinking pond water. As a result, thousands of local farmers were wholly debilitated by pain and unable to work their fields.[62] Clearly, the user fees per se are not responsible for the widespread prevalence of guinea worm disease. It is, argued Rawlings, "a disease of underdevelopment," as many villagers refuse to believe that the larvae are ingested through pond water.[63] But the low priority given to maintenance of clean water supplies leads to their regular disruption, as in Tamale, when a large part of the student population at the Tamale Secondary School got guinea worm infection when they used well water because the Tamale municipal water system provided inadequate supplies. The PNDC government has mounted a five-year campaign to eradicate guinea worm disease. And it has made substantial strides in increasing urban health care in a few areas where there has been little—for example, in the urban slum of Nima, in Accra.[64]

The decision to charge new or increased fees in elementary schools (book-user fees) and, in 1988, in residential secondary schools and universities (housing and feeding costs) has raised major protests about equity. The costs are quite large for Ghanaian incomes: secondary school costs in 1988 were estimated at ¢12,000 per year ($46–$53 at 1988 or 1989 exchange rates) and university costs at ¢42,000, if all subsidies were removed; they have not been. University students demonstrated vigorously during 1987–1989 against these fees and for larger food allowances, with the result that the universities have been closed down repeatedly.[65]

The PNDC has made great strides in repairing the desolated state in which it found the educational system in 1982. It has (1) greatly increased its budget as a percentage of the total (from about 20 percent to 32 percent of recurrent costs) and of the GDP, (2) raised in real terms the teachers' pathetic salaries, (3) restocked the schools with materials, and (4) implemented a major reform in educational structure and curriculum. The fees at primary school level are very modest: ¢120 per year in book fees and ¢100 in other fees (together, a day's minimum wage in 1990). However, between 1973/74 and 1982/83, total and primary enrollment and the total number of teachers increased by 3.6 percent, 3.9 percent, and 4.6 percent, respectively. In contrast, between 1983/84 and 1986/87, primary enrollment *fell* by 3.4 percent. Between 1982/83 and 1988/89, total and primary enrollment grew by 1.7 percent and 1.9 percent per year, less than population growth rate. And the dropout rates at the primary, middle, and secondary levels have all increased dramatically, probably most among the poorest.[66] Ghanaians have become alarmed at dropout rates and the degree to which child labor is becoming prevalent, as farmworkers in northern Ghana and as hawkers and peddlers in the markets in urban Ghana.[67] It is not clear to what extent reduced school attendance reflects school fees, or whether, as some evidence suggests, increased urban and rural poverty is inducing children to seek wage and sales work to supplement family income.

## ■ Impact on Real Wages and Other Measures of Living Standards and Well-being

There have been dramatic changes in relative prices under the PNDC government, and this has occasioned some significant benefits to certain groups in the socioeconomic order. In the Acheampong regime of 1972–1978 and its short-lived military and civilian successors, the hyperinflation and unraveling of the fabric of the economy and society drastically reduced the beneficiaries of the economic order to traders, importers, food farmers, smugglers, and those in senior government and parastatal positions who could sell state resources on the black market. Under the PNDC government, the changes in relative prices brought about by devaluation and the ending of price controls and subsidies have tended to benefit cocoa farmers, food farmers, export businesses, business firms with access to credit, and traders. Those on fixed incomes were hurt badly by the hyperinflation of the 1970s and early 1980s. They have also been hurt by continuing inflation and spiraling prices to consumers in the 1980s.

The stabilization and SAP policies have not reduced the real wages of the working class, blue and white collar, if one accepts estimates based on the CPI. But the CPI fails to convey adequately the impact of many increased costs. Informal sectors have undoubtedly suffered declining real wages in the face of a large reserve army of unemployed. The real wages of minimum-wage workers fell from 1975 on, and in 1982 were worth only 12.6 percent of what they had been in 1963. They fell by about 84 percent from 1975 to 1982 (see Table 7.2). With allowances added, the government minimum wage worker's real wage was perhaps 18.5 percent of the 1963 level rather than 12.6 percent (tax-free allowances were about 56 percent of base income). Those who worked for the private sector firms or parastatals, of which there were over 150, were in trade unions and often had larger minimum and other wages and allowances than civil servants. In a few parastatals (e.g., the Cocoa Board and Social Security and National Insurance Trust, or SSNIT), wages and allowances were very high; at SSNIT in 1986, minimum-wage laborers had allowances over three times their salary, stenographers and messengers 151 percent of their salary, and the managing director 427 percent of his salary.[68] However, in most parastatals, wages and allowances were only double the civil servant norms.

The horrendous drought and famine and 145 percent food inflation in 1983 reduced real wages by another 20 percent. Since then, however, the PNDC government has, except for 1987, been able to increase minimum and other wages more than the level of inflation and to gradually lift real wages. Constant union pressure has been required for this effort, however. That real minimum wages were roughly doubled from the 1983 low to 1985, and have stayed at about this level, has occasioned no joy among wage and salary workers, however (see Table 7.2). Wages are still so low that they have kept most members of the working force impoverished. During 1983–1985, the PNDC did try to focus on the interests of the poorest workers and tended to increase their wages disproportionately to those of middle- and senior-level workers in the public and private sectors. Senior and middle ranks of the civil service and parastatals were more hurt by the hyperinflation in 1975–1983 than minimum-wage workers. Between 1977 and 1983, senior civil service managers lost 90 percent of their salaries, accountants 84 percent, and clerks 74 percent. During 1983–1985, the PNDC increased the wages of lower-level workers disproportionately (72 percent versus 30 percent for senior managers). This pattern drastically compressed differentials between the highest and lowest wages in the civil service (and to a lesser degree parastatals) by 1985 to 2.3 to 1 (2.3:1) before taxes and only 1.8:1 after taxes.[69] All workers were impoverished and demoralized. In 1986, the government gave higher-percentage increases to middle and upper ranks, increasing the differentials to 4:1 after taxes, a move opposed by the Trade Union Congress (TUC).

What do these real wages mean, in practice? In 1970 and 1982, a gallon of kerosene (used for cooking) was about 42 percent of a day's minimum wage (allowances excluded), in 1983 it was 80 percent, in 1984 100 percent, in 1985 79 percent—one measure of the impact of eliminating oil subsidies. In the early 1970s, principal secretaries (PSs)—the PS is the top civil servant in each ministry—and deputy principal secretaries had multiroom government bungalows, at 7–10 percent of their salaries. In the mid-1980s the deputy principal secretaries and deputy assistants rented a room or two for their family in a house with an outside latrine. A first-class postage stamp in Ghana in 1988 cost one-seventh of a day's wage, an overseas stamp 40 percent. A local phone call cost 14 percent of a minimum-wage worker's daily pay; to call up to 20 miles away cost 28 percent. Travel by bus was cheaper: the fare from Accra to Ho in the Volta Region in 1988 was roughly two days' minimum wage, or half a day's wage for a top civil servant. In 1987, a kilogram of rice cost two-thirds of a minimum-wage worker's daily pay, a kilogram of bread a day's pay, a kilogram of fresh cassava one-third of a day's pay, a kilogram of cassava-gari 90 percent of a day's pay, a kilogram of shelled peanuts (previously a favorite snack) one and a third days' minimum wage. Small bananas were cheap, a kilogram for one-quarter of a day's pay, but a kilogram of medium-sized tomatoes for a stew cost 1.6 days' minimum wage. One tin of evaporated milk was a day's minimum wage. The consequences were that 30.6 percent of preschool children under five showed chronic (past) malnutrition in 1988 and 7.8 percent acute (present) malnutrition. This was an improvement on higher malnutrition levels in 1982–1984 but higher than or equal to many of the country's poorer neighbors and much higher than 1961–1962 indicators of malnutrition in Ghana. Among adults in 1987–1988, 16.7 percent of men and 9.4 percent of women were malnourished, and another 23.9 percent of men and 9.4 percent of women were significantly underweight.[70]

One sixty-page schoolbook for one's child cost 42 percent of the minimum-wage worker's daily wage. In 1987, one bar of Guardian soap cost only 22 percent of an unskilled worker's daily wage, but by 1989 it consumed 175 percent of a day's wage. Most women petty traders make substantially more than a skilled worker's wage, often three to four times the minimum wage. A secretary with a middle school education takes home only 40 percent of what a petty trader who retails tomatoes makes.

As a consequence of such minuscule purchasing power, many workers at all levels are poorly motivated to work and are probably extremely hungry as well. Moreover, since about 1985, PNDC Finance Secretary Botchwey has been arguing that wages must be set on "the ability to pay" norm, so that some private sector firms have been refusing to give pay hikes equal to the public sector's.

The SAP policies of "rationalization" of state-owned enterprises (SOEs) or their liquidation or full or partial privatization have raised the issue of retrenchment since 1986. The state has been required to examine the massive subsidies it pays to SOEs, which for years have operated at a loss or, as with the State Fishing Corporation (SFC), are inoperative but still maintain a large staff. The government has interests in 235 companies, in 181 a majority interest; in 93 SOEs it is the sole owner, while in another 88 SOEs the state is co-owner with another state SOE.[71] In 1982, the PNDC spent 10 percent of its budget on subsidies for SOEs; in 1986 it was still spending 8 percent, while many SOEs fail to pay their taxes and debts to the state and to each other. The government has selected thirty enterprises for the first phase of divestiture, some for sale, others for liquidation. Few sales had been announced by mid-1990; the slow pace is one indication of internal opposition. Retrenchments have been undertaken to prepare some SOEs for sale. But the state itself faces a financial crisis in paying large severance and termination benefits to workers.[72] Attempts to avoid these have created conflicts with unions.

By August 1989, the PNDC government had laid off 29,052 public sector employees, to whom full benefits had been paid. This was substantially lower than the initial target of 45,000 for 1987–1989. At least another 34,500 workers have been dismissed from the Cocoa Board. The PNDC is committed to laying off or "redeploying" another 5 percent of the public service in each of the next three years, 1990–1992, or 45,000 workers. Many SOE workers are scheduled for dismissal. Retrenchments and low-wage sector hiring in recent years have shifted the structure of the labor force. Agricultural employment rose from 57.2 percent of the labor force in 1970 to 61 percent in 1984 to 66 percent in 1987. Although the government insists that actual unemployment is low, there is massive unemployment and underemployment in all urban areas. Some people have been without jobs for years.

There is no direct evidence of changes in the real income of peasant food farmers. But returns to food production are partly reflected in food inflation, which has ranged from 20 percent to 38 percent in 1987–1989 after two years of lower inflation.

The World Bank and PNDC government have been relatively insensitive to the pain associated with structural adjustment. However, PNDC leaders have not believed entirely in the market, aware as they are of its imperfections. Urban bus costs are controlled and low. Rent control laws continue in effect, making rent a small part of most workers' budget. But in 1987–1990 landlords were again ignoring the laws, charging several years of rent in advance for empty premises. The PNDC ensures regional distribution of some essential commodities, knowing otherwise that market forces would divert them largely to the urban centers. But it was only when confronted with insistent UNICEF studies on the levels of poverty, malnutrition, and disease, and the added pain of structural adjustment, that the World Bank started to support UNICEF's "Programme of Actions to Mitigate the Social Costs of Adjustment" (PAMSCAD). The PAMSCAD now promises to create 40,000 mostly unskilled jobs in the next several years, and to stress nutrition, job training, and basic needs programs.[73] Its valuable components, however, were only belatedly getting started in 1989.

## ■ The Impact of Structural Adjustment on Political and Class Coalitions and the Structure of Power

The stabilization and SAP policies animated a substantial change in the political and class coalitions of support for the regime and also in the structure of power. Importantly, the pursuit of these policies provided the state with major resources to rebuild state capabilities and to attempt to develop some relative autonomy from major contending class and other group forces in Ghanaian society. However, it explicitly gave up some autonomy from international forces (the IMF, World Bank, major Western donors) and served the class interests of domestic and, to a lesser extent (because it is less significant), foreign capital. On the other hand, in postcolonial political life in Ghana, no class or coherent class coalition, or alliance with ethnic/regional groups, has been able to establish political hegemony for its interests and values for any length of time. That remains true today.

Because Ghana's political life is closed, some of the coalitional shifts that have occurred have been partial, tentative, and implicit rather than active and committed. They are important, nonetheless, in the regime's assessment of the relative weight of its support and opposition and important also to the groups that attempt to trade their support for rewards. The Rawlings regime has used a number of resources to mobilize or demobilize support: material goods, directly or indirectly; public offices; social status; access to power; and coercion.

The practical demands of recreating a workable administration and economy in Ghana induced Rawlings to back away, gradually, from groups whose disorderly challenges to existing institutions he had initially encouraged and championed. He sought out some pillars of stability and order and the partial demobilization or control of populist groups. Early support had included the military's other ranks and NCOs, the small left-wing intelligentsia and students, and portions of the working class and the urban artisanal and bazaar community that joined the PDCs. In 1983–1984, Rawlings made repeated overtures to technocrats and managers among the professionals whose bourgeois lifestyles and values he had recently attacked. Ex–private sector managers and public sector ones who had escaped corruption charges were given control over, and the freedom to manage, important state corporations, as with the Ghana National Trading Corporation. Many of the cabinet secretaries since 1983 have been professionals or state managers. However, the previously most prominent portion of the commercial-professional-managerial bourgeoisie, the lawyers, remained open, adamant opponents of the regime. The other two major groups offered public offices and status were the younger and more energetic senior bureaucrats and, increasingly, the officer corps of the military (and to a lesser degree the police). The PNDC needed the officers increasingly to help contain coup threats and reestablish order (though Rawlings did not much trust the army). It has also turned more and more to officers for cabinet jobs, state corporate leadership, and regional administrative heads.

In the political community, the PNDC made substantial efforts to recruit to its support some established, prominent members of Ghana's bourgeoisie, as with Justice D. F. Annan, a judge who was made a PNDC member. But it has been largely unsuccessful in this effort. Second, the PNDC solicited the support of many of the prominent chiefs, some of whom had suffered ignominiously at the hands of local PDC groups. The chiefs were often happy to make peace and use this recognition to curb local agitation (as occurred in Ashanti). Third, Rawlings sought to maintain the PDCs under more direct control, and with less autonomy, and with a new name (Committees for the Defence of the Revolution) to lessen the stigma the PDCs had acquired among some sectors. In the rural areas they were encouraged as a community organizing group among the young men and women. In the key urban areas, CDRs essentially became inactive or were used ritualistically. The PNDC's open encouragement of cocoa and food farmers, and the much higher price for cocoa, plus road and vehicle repair, have induced many farmers to support PNDC policies. The PNDC's setting up of District Assemblies in 1988, the first new mostly elective body of representation, has given it a new capacity to tap and mobilize rural support. Farmers and teachers were the largest occupational groups among those elected to the DAs.

Crucial to the PNDC's economic success, it thought, was soliciting the economic participation and support of Ghana's domestic and foreign commercial, construction, and (less numerous) industrial bourgeoisie. The regime offered these economic actors major access to material resources and capital and fewer regulations but provides them with little access to power and consults with them rarely.

Of these, only the senior managers, bureaucrats, and officers were actively part of the regime. The prior opposition of the others in the 1982–1983 period was partly neutralized. With the renewal of economic growth came grudging consent from some. But the persistence of extremely harsh living standards has consistently tempered any enthusiasm for the regime. The agents of the IMF and World Bank have become major participants in policymaking and have provided the regime with major resources that have helped it to manage political and economic life.

The PNDC, however, has also had major opponents. If the most open have been the lawyers and the Ghana Bar Association, the most important has been the Trade Union Congress and its seventeen-member unions with roughly 650,000 members. If the regime excited the union members with populist rhetoric and deeds early on, it enraged them by ousting the union leaders and temporarily suspending their collective bargaining rights. Resistance from lower union ranks compelled the PNDC government to permit the unions to elect their own leaders in 1983. The new general secretaries were united in behalf of a number of demands that created continuous conflict with the regime: their own autonomy; collective bargaining rights; the need to increase the minimum and other wages drastically (the most persistent source of conflict); and strong opposition to the PNDC's core macroeconomic stabilization and adjustment policies, especially devaluation and retrenchments. Union leaders have also demanded repeatedly a return to civilian, democratic rule. The PNDC has minimized consultation with union leaders, sought to curtail worker benefits, and threatened and used coercion if unions demonstrated against PNDC policies or went on strike. Coercion has kept strikes lower in the 1982–1989 period than in any other eight-year period since 1945.

From mid-1990 on, public opposition has increased, with two new major movements announcing their organization, opposition to PNDC rule, and demand for multiparty democratic rule: the Movement for Freedom and Justice and the Front for National Unity, Democracy, and Development.

## ■ Conclusion

The stabilization-SAP policies have renewed economic growth and institutional capabilities on a sustained basis for almost seven years (1984–

1990). Economic growth has been high. Ghana's totally eroded infrastructure has been renewed, exports revived, inflation curbed (but not tamed), incentives for production reestablished, rational public financial policies reimposed, and investments made for continuing growth and development. But the beneficiaries of the growth have been largely rural and too few, and the distributive impact of the policies often inequitable. Urban unemployment and inequality have increased and are highly visible. The key institutions fostering human development—education and health—have been revitalized but in ways that are inequitable to the poor majority of Ghanaians.

In the highly authoritarian political life of Ghana, the state and the leaders of its key allied groups—officers, managers, senior bureaucrats—have been able to exercise substantial power while forestalling direct public pressure. The capitalist sector is clearly increasing its resources and economic capabilities, but it is denied direct access to influence in making policies (and IMF and World Bank power is no substitute). Despite six years of high real growth, the PNDC has been unable to benefit from this to substantially increase its legitimacy. Its implicit coalition of support remains tentative and could give way, quickly, to massive public pressures. The major reason is that the economic gains attained have not made a significant difference in the living standards of most Ghanaians. This is not simply because of the depth of Ghana's economic depression in 1977–1983, but largely because the architects of the reform program have been relatively indifferent to core sources of growth and well-being in Ghana.

# ■ Notes

1. See Sidney Dell, "Stabilization: the Political Economy of Overkill," in Charles Wilber (ed.), *The Political Economy of Development and Underdevelopment*, 3d ed. (New York: Random House, 1984), pp. 146–168; Richard Feinberg and Edmar Bacha, "When Supply and Demand Don't Intersect: Latin America and the Bretton Woods Institutions in the 1980s," *Development and Change* 19, 3 (July 1988), pp. 371–400; "External Finance and Policy Adjustment in Africa," special issue, *Development and Change* 17, 3 (July 1986), containing case studies on adjustment generally (and in Zaire, Sudan, Malawi, and Mozambique); Paul Mosley, "Agricultural Performance in Kenya Since 1970: Has the World Bank Got It Right?" pp. 513–530; Laurence Harris, "Conceptions of the IMF's Role in Africa," in Peter Laurence (ed.), *World Recession and the Food Crisis in Africa* (London: James Currey; Boulder: Westview Press, 1986), pp. 83–95; Gerald Helleiner, "The Question of Conditionality," in Carol Lancaster and John Williams (eds.), *African Debt and Financing* (Washington, D.C.: Institute of International Economics, 1986), pp. 63–91; Tony Killick et al., *The IMF and Stabilization* (London: Heinemann, 1984); John Loxley, "The IMF and World Bank Conditionality and Sub-Saharan Africa," in Laurence (ed.), *World Recession*, pp. 96–103.

2. World Bank, *Africa's Adjustment and Growth in the 1980s* (Washington, D.C.: World Bank, 1989).

3. *West Africa*, March 27, 1989, pp. 478–479; May 15, 1989, p. 791; July 17, 1989, pp. 1160–1161.

4. See Harris, "Conceptions of the IMF's Role in Africa," and Loxley, "The IMF and World Bank Conditionality," in Laurence (ed.), *World Recession*.

5. World Bank, *World Development Report*, 1983 (Washington, D.C.: World Bank, 1983), p. 150; Jon Kraus, "The Political Economy of Agrarian Regression in Ghana," in Stephen Commins, Michael Lofchie, and Rhys Payne (eds.), *Africa's Agrarian Crisis* (Boulder: Lynne Rienner Publishers, 1986), pp. 103–108.

6. Andrew Shepherd, "Agrarian Change in Northern Ghana: Public Investment, Capitalist Farming, and Famine," in Judith Heyer et al. (eds.), *Rural Development in Tropical Africa* (New York: St. Martin's Press, 1981), pp. 169–172; Jon Kraus, "The Political Economy of Food in Ghana," in Naomi Chazan and Tim Shaw (eds.), *Coping with Africa's Food Crisis* (Boulder: Lynne Rienner Publishers, 1988), pp. 90–96; UNICEF/Ghana, "Ghana: Adjustment Policies and Programmes to Protect Children and Other Vulnerable Groups," typescript, 1988, pp. 6–24, revised version of chapter in C. A. Nornia, R. Jolly, and F. Stewart (eds.), *Adjustment with a Human Face*, vol. 2 (New York: Oxford University Press, 1987).

7. *People's Daily Graphic* (Ghana), July 11, 1987, p. 1.

8. Adotey Bing, "Popular Participation Versus People's Power: Notes on Politics and Power Struggles in Ghana," *Review of African Political Economy*, 31 (December 1984), pp. 100–101.

9. Interviews with neighborhood leaders and inspection of store sites in three neighborhoods of Accra, July 1985.

10. See Tom Callaghy, "Lost Between State and Market: The Politics of Economic Adjustment in Ghana, Zambia, and Nigeria," in Joan M. Nelson (ed.), *Economic Crisis and Policy Choice: The Politics of Adjustment in the Third World* (Princeton: Princeton University Press, 1990), pp. 258–260.

11. Interviews with leaders of the Maritime and Dockworkers Union (MDU), July 1985, several of whom had been branch leaders in Sekondi-Takoradi in April 1982. Rawlings and some soldiers who accompanied him to Takoradi in 1982 showed great hostility toward workers and union leaders.

12. *West Africa*, July 11, 1983, pp. 1596–1597.

13. The accounts by Emmanuel Hansen and Zaya Yeebo tend to overestimate the meaningful base of PNDC support, underestimate or simply ignore the character and level of opposition (e.g., to military violence), and also ignore Ghana's incredible economic crises; other radical participants do not leave out the economic crisis (e.g., Yaw Graham) but often also make little effort to discern just how much support the radicals could muster. See Emmanuel Hansen, "The State and Popular Struggles in Ghana, 1982–86," in Peter Anyang' Nyong'o (ed.), *Popular Struggles for Democracy in Africa* (London: Zed Press, 1987), pp. 173–192; Zaya Yeebo, "Ghana: Defence Committees and the Class Struggle," *Review of African Political Economy* 32 (April 1985), pp. 64–72. These writers all ignore the strong opposition among rank-and-file trade unionists in many unions to the forced ouster of their leaders and the imposition of new ones and to the efforts of often nondemocratically chosen WDCs to displace the role of the local unions.

14. World Bank, *World Development Report*, 1983 (Washington, D.C.: World Bank, 1983); John R. Nellis, *Public Enterprises in Sub-Saharan Africa*

(Washington, D.C.: World Bank, 1986); Daniel Swanson and Taferra Wolde-Semait, *Africa's Public Enterprise Sector and Evidence of Reform*, World Bank Technical Paper No. 95, 1989.

15. Loxley, "IMF and World Bank Conditionality," in Laurence (ed.), *World Recession*; Killick et al., *The IMF and Stabilization*; Robert Pastor, "Latin America, the Debt Crisis, and the International Monetary Fund," *Latin American Perspectives* 16, 1 (Winter 1989), pp. 79–110; Helleiner, "The Question of Conditionality"; Cheryl Payer, *The World Bank* (New York: Monthly Review Press, 1982).

16. Amartya Sen, "Development: Which Way Now?" in Charles Wilber (ed.), *The Political Economy of Development and Underdevelopment*, 4th ed. (New York: Random House, 1984), pp. 37–58.

17. *West Africa*, June 15, 1987, p. 1173; February 1, 1988, p. 164.

18. Kraus, "Political Economy of Food," p. 109, Table 4.3.

19. *West Africa*, January 9, 1989, p. 19.

20. Gwendolyn Mikell, in "The State, Local Resources, and Political Participation in Ghana," paper presented at the African Studies Association meeting, 1989, pp. 3–6, discusses the role of *nnoboa* cooperative work groups and of the Mobisquads, composed of young men who returned from Nigeria. Ben Ephson, "Mobilization for Farmers," *West Africa*, February 23, 1987, pp. 364–365.

21. Margaret Novicki, "Going for a Green Revolution," *Africa Report* (September–October, 1988), pp. 22–23; Kraus, "Political Economy of Food," pp. 101–102.

22. *West Africa*, January 9, 1989, p. 19.

23. Kojo Vieta, "The Food Horizon," *West Africa*, January 9, 1989, pp. 20–21.

24. World Bank, *Accelerated Development in Sub-Saharan Africa* (Washington, D.C.: World Bank, 1981).

25. Merrick Posnansky, "How Ghana's Crisis Affects a Village," *West Africa*, August 15, 1980, pp. 2418–2420.

26. Nonpublic World Bank memoranda on the economy of Ghana, 1987.

27. International Monetary Fund, *Primary Commodities: Market Developments and Outlook* (May 1987); Overseas Development Institute (London), "Commodity Prices: Investing in Decline?" briefing paper, March 1988.

28. Paul Glewwe and Kwaku Twum-Baah, "Ghana Living Standards Survey," preliminary data, 1989. Mimeo.

29. UNICEF/Ghana, "Ghana: Adjustment Policies and Programmes"; Sue Horton, Tom Kerr, and D. Diakosavvas, "The Social Costs of Higher Food Prices: Some Cross-Country Evidence," *World Development* 16, 7 (July 1988), pp. 847–856.

30. Steve Weissman, "Structural Adjustment in Africa: Insights from the Experiences of Ghana and Senegal: Report of Staff Study Mission," Committee on Foreign Relations, U.S. House of Representatives, March 1989, p. 8; Kraus, "Political Economy of Food," pp. 7–8.

31. Nii Bentsi-Enchill, "Timber Scandals," *West Africa*, March 3, 1989, p. 344; *West Africa*, January 23, 1989, p. 123; September 18, 1989, p. 1577; November 13, 1989, p. 1908.

32. *West Africa*, February 5, 1990, p. 190; Nii Bentsi-Enchill, "Ghana's New Gold Boom," *West Africa*, April 11, 1986, pp. 628–629.

33. See Ben Ephson, "'Galamsey' Goes Legal" and "Golden Potential," *West*

*Africa*, May 1, 1989, p. 680; May 8, 1989, p. 720; December 11, 1989, p. 2076.

34. *West Africa*, June 6, 1988, pp. 1012–1013.
35. *West Africa*, August 8, 1988, p. 1460.
36. *West Africa*, September 12, 1988, p. 1684.
37. Ben Ephson, "Call for Import Controls," *West Africa*, March 6, 1989, pp. 348, 372.
38. "Managing a Revolution," *West Africa*, March 5, 1990, p. 359.
39. *West Africa*, December 25, 1989, p. 2165.
40. *West Africa*, January 11, 1988, p. 23.
41. Ben Ephson, "Northern Journey," *West Africa*, June 19, 1989, p. 1005; Novicki, "Going for a Green Revolution," p. 20.
42. Kojo T. Vieta, "Congestion Menace," *West Africa*, August 21, 1989, p. 1366.
43. *West Africa*, January 11, 1988, p. 21.
44. Reginald Herbold Green, "Stabilisation and Adjustment Policies and Programmes: Country Study 1, Ghana," research paper, World Institute for Development Economics Research, Helsinki, Finland, 1987, p. 35.
45. Glewwe and Twum-Baah, "Ghana Living Standards Survey."
46. *West Africa*, January 11, 1988, pp. 23–24; June 6, 1988, p. 1012.
47. Green, "Stabilisation and Adjustment," p. 44.
48. *West Africa*, January 9, 1989, p. 19.
49. UNICEF/Ghana, "Ghana: Adjustment Policies and Programmes," p. 14.
50. Kodwo Ewusi, *Economic Inequality in Ghana* (Legon, Ghana: Institute of Statistical, Social, and Economic Research, 1977); and note 70.
51. *West Africa*, June 15, 1987, p. 1173.
52. Ben Ephson, "The Price of Health-1," *West Africa*, October 7, 1985, p. 2086; "The Price of Health-2," *West Africa*, October 14, 1985, p. 2156.
53. Paul Glewwe and K. Twum-Barima, "The Distribution of Welfare in Ghana" (World Bank, Ghana Living Standards Survey, draft, 1989), p. 42f.
54. Ronald Vogel, *Cost Recovery in the Health Care Sector: Selected Country Studies in West Africa*, Technical Paper No. 82 (Washington, D.C.: World Bank, 1988), p. 140.
55. Weissman, "Structural Adjustment," p. 12.
56. Vogel, *Cost Recovery*, p. 144.
57. Weissman, "Structural Adjustment," p. 11; *West Africa*, March 28, 1988, p. 574.
58. Vogel, *Cost Recovery*, p. 132.
59. *West Africa*, May 19, 1989, p. 573; June 12, 1989, p. 952.
60. Weissman, "Structural Adjustment," p. 11; *West Africa*, May 1, 1989, p. 704.
61. UNICEF/Ghana, "Ghana: Adjustment Policies and Programmes," p. 23.
62. *West Africa*, August 22, 1988, p. 1550; September 12, 1988, pp. 1672–1673; August 7, 1989, p. 1308; March 26, 1990, p. 514.
63. *West Africa*, June 27, 1988, p. 1180; *New York Times*, January 24, 1989, p. C3.
64. *Financial Times*, June 6, 1988.
65. *West Africa*, February 2, 1987, pp. 192–194; June 22, 1987, pp. 1191–1192; July 11, 1988, pp. 1252–1253.
66. Ghana, Ministry of Education, "Data on Primary and Secondary School Enrollment," 1989, mimeo provided to author; chapter by James Cobbe, ch. 6, this book.

67. Nick van Hear, "Child Labor and the Development of Capitalist Agriculture in Ghana," *Development and Change* 13, 4 (October 1982), pp. 499–514; *West Africa*, August 22, 1988, p. 1550.

68. Ben Ephson, "Margins for Manoeuvre," *West Africa*, May 12, 1986, pp. 990–991.

69. World Bank data.

70. Harold Alderman, *Nutritional Status in Ghana and Its Determinants* (Washington, D.C.: World Bank, 1990), pp. 3–5, 12–13. Alternative measures of child malnutrition indicate two-thirds of the levels noted.

71. William Adda, "Privatization in Ghana," in V. V. Ramanadham (ed.), *Privatization in Developing Countries* (London and New York: Routledge, Chapman and Hall, 1989), pp. 303–321.

72. C. L. Morena, "Ghana: the Privatization Drive," *Africa Report* (November–December 1989), pp. 60–62; Adda, "Privatization in Ghana," pp. 320–321.

73. Ghana, *Programme of Actions to Mitigate the Social Costs of Adjustment* (Washington, D.C.: World Bank, 1987).

# 8

# Leadership Commitment and Political Opposition to Structural Adjustment in Ghana

*Richard Jeffries*

Few would have guessed, when the young radical Jerry Rawlings came to power in Ghana in January 1982, that his government would shortly adopt an IMF- and World Bank–supported stabilization and adjustment program. Fewer still would have guessed that if he were to adopt such a program he would still be in power eight years later. A notable feature of this program in Ghana, moreover, has been the remarkably high degree of commitment and thoroughness, and the relatively low degree of "slippage,"[1] with which it has been implemented.

In this chapter I seek to explain the political whys and hows of these three superficially rather surprising facts. In doing so, I make use of some of the analytical framework and several of the concrete suggestions supplied by Joan Nelson in her excellent piece "The Political Economy of Stabilization: Commitment, Capacity, and Public Response."[2] By doing so, I hoped to situate the Ghanaian experience more clearly in a comparative perspective, though it may have the disadvantage for Ghana specialists of at times stating what might seem fairly obvious.

Nelson emphasizes that her study focuses on the effects of politics on stabilization, rather than the impact of stabilization on politics. Although the former is the focus of this discussion also, it becomes increasingly difficult over time in the Ghanaian case to preserve the distinction. One of the themes, indeed, of the second half of this chapter will be the way in which the Rawlings regime's overriding commitment to economic reform helps explain, in part though not entirely, an approach to politics that has made the reform process itself progressively more difficult to sustain, or at least (and which is probably the same thing) has made it progressively more difficult for the regime to sustain itself in power.

In the interests of expository clarity, I have divided the chapter into two halves. The first deals with the period from 1982 to 1984 and considers why the Structural Adjustment Program came to be adopted, the extent of initial opposition to it, and how this opposition was overcome or defeated. The second deals with the period from 1985 to the present and considers the main political problems that have arisen in sustaining the program.

## ■ Leadership Commitment and Political Opposition, 1982–1984

Shortly after the coup d'état of December 31, 1981, I wrote:

> It is at the time of writing impossible to predict, with any degree of confidence or precision, just what economic policies the PNDC will adopt. The composition of the recently announced Cabinet suggests that it is concerned at least not to alienate foreign capital or international financial institutions completely. The eventual acceptance of an IMF package therefore remains a possible, if somewhat unlikely, scenario. As has been argued, the adoption of such a radical liberalization strategy would be to the long-term benefit of the majority of Ghanaians. The problem, of course, is that such measures would be likely to encounter intense resistance not only from vested urban economic interests but from the neo-Marxist preconceptions of many of the students, intelligentsia and radicalized soldiers to whom Rawlings looks for political and moral support. . . . A certain statist brand of economic nationalism, combined with romantic anticapitalism, is a highly powerful if somewhat unthinking force in Ghanaian politics and one to which Rawlings himself seems unfortunately prone.[3]

Over the next few months, my fears seemed to be in the process of being realized. Neo-Marxists—or "leftists" as I shall more commonly term them—came to dominate the Interim National Coordinating Committee, later retitled the National Defence Committee, charged with coordinating the activities of the local People's Defence Committees and with directing the course of the revolution. Their ideas were expressed in the Policy Guidelines of the PNDC, which attacked "the continued domination of our economy by foreign financial interests" and asserted the need for a fundamental break from "the existing neo-colonial relations."[4] The government solicited economic and military assistance from Libya and sought to develop closer relations with socialist countries.

By early 1983, this policy orientation had been overturned. An agreement had been reached with the IMF on a short-term "stabilization" program, soon to be supplemented by an Economic Recovery Program. In accordance with this, a series of fundamental economic reforms was announced in the April budget. What accounted for this turnaround? And what factors might have persuaded Rawlings and other PNDC leaders that such a program would prove politically practicable when many were predicting that it would be politically suicidal?

The beginning of an understanding lies in an appreciation that the central fact of Ghana's political and economic experience since 1982, in a sense even since 1979, has been that of Rawlings's personal political domination.[5] This is not to say that he has been an actively autocratic ruler, personally dominating decisionmaking or supervising day-to-day administration. Nor is it to suggest that this domination has always been very assured or, in reality, single-handed—he seems to have relied especially heavily on (retired) Captain Kojo Tsikata to preempt or put down the several coup attempts against him. Nor is it, finally, to suggest that his personal charisma, such as it was, in the eyes of the populace in January 1982 weathered the experience of the next few years in anything like its pristine condition. It is to say, however, that, notwithstanding the idea of the leftist radicals, and doubtless of some other groups, that he could be used as a figurehead to lend legitimacy to their own rule, he alone enjoyed sufficient popular support in both the civilian population and the army to be able to provide stability in a potentially highly unstable and very bloody situation. He was the linchpin on whom the new experiment—any new experiment—crucially depended. The widespread domestic recognition of this fact was one of the factors that provided him with more freedom of maneuver than most outside observers seemed to realize. He was also far more open minded about the best economic strategy to pursue than seemed to be generally appreciated.

It seems fair to say that Rawlings had been welcomed back to power in January 1982 on a wave of popular enthusiasm. And it is important to emphasize here that he, not the leftist radicals who surrounded him, had been welcomed back to power. His personal popularity derived, of course, from the role that he had played in the AFRC uprising and interregnum of June-September 1979. He had developed a very real and inspiring rapport with the urban masses on the basis of a rhetoric that conveyed his transparent moral sincerity and a widely shared sense of justice. His heroic image had been augmented rather than reduced by the actions of the elected civilian government of President Hilla Limann. The Limann administration had, first, failed to continue the process of "house-cleaning" that Rawlings had initiated or to address itself in any serious way to Ghana's economic problems. Second, it had sought to dispose of the AFRC problem by bribing most of the leaders to leave the country and, when this failed with Rawlings, by harassing him and his associates. The urban populace had shown what they thought of this when, at the second anniversary celebrations of the Limann government, Limann entered the Black Star Stadium to silence and Rawlings subsequently entered to rapturous applause.

Rawlings's return to power signaled the final discrediting of the old party networks and of the old muddling-through approach to the economy. Some sort of radical departure in economic policy was obviously required and was widely expected. It cannot be said that most Ghanaians evinced much faith in Rawlings's own ability to hit on the right solutions. The AFRC intervention had not indicated any more sophisticated a grasp of the problems than a kind of looting populism. At the time, Rawlings had been the first to admit to his limited education and his especially limited understanding of economics. It was one thing, people realized, to lead a campaign of moral reform from the top of an armored car or the shade of a tree, quite another to run a modern government so as to engineer economic salvation in a decidedly uncharitable international environment. Nevertheless, it was felt, the young man deserved to be given a chance. At least he was honest. Who else, after all, was there?

It seems that, initially, Rawlings had little idea what he was going to do; or, to put it in another, more positive way, he had an open mind. The view held by some academic and journalistic observers at this time, and by the U.S. government (among others), that he was some sort of Castro-ite neo-Marxist never seemed to have much substance. He certainly had not been in 1979, when the whole shape of his thought and tenor of his speeches had been decidedly liberal and moderate for a revolutionary.[6] The neo-Marxist students and other intellectuals of the June Fourth Movement and the New Democratic Movement had attempted to surround and cultivate him over the intervening period. But if one looks closely at his speeches on resuming power, or more specifically at those for which he was clearly responsible (as distinct from policy statements decided jointly with leftist members of the INDC), there is really no evidence that they had succeeded in converting him intellectually.[7] They were the speeches of a populist patriot, determinedly nonideological, even anti-ideological in their perspective on Ghana's economic plight.

Rawlings also enjoyed far more freedom of maneuver in relation to domestic political forces than was commonly the case in other African countries. It was not just that his was a new and popularly welcomed regime, enjoying the usual honeymoon period of charitable acquiescence. The groups that, following Robert Bates's analysis,[8] might normally be expected to mount opposition to proposals for economic liberalization were numerically small and/or politically weak in Ghana by this time. Very few businesspeople, import oriented or otherwise, had benefited from the policies of the Acheampong and Limann regimes. Many, finding it impossible to operate or to live reasonably comfortably under prevailing conditions, had left the country altogether. The same was true of Ghana's professional middle classes, including many civil servants. By way of an indication of the scale of the exodus, some 14,000 trained teachers left the Ghana education service between 1975 and 1981, of whom approximately 3,000 were university graduates.[9] It is important to recognize the paradox by which policies that might initially have been intended, in part at least, to favor such urban elites had ended up virtually decimating them. When the PNDC came to power, many more fled the country and those remaining fell politically silent, feeling themselves under threat from the new, revolutionary organs of popular power, more especially the Public Tribunals.

Unionized workers were disunited and demoralized. The TUC leadership of Secretary-General Issifu had collaborated with successive regimes (Acheampong, Akuffo, Limann) even while their policies reduced the real value of a lower-paid worker's wage to approximately one-sixth of its 1971 level. Issifu resigned shortly after Rawlings's return to power, to be replaced by Richard Baiden, a highly experienced trade unionist who had led the movement of opposition to Issifu within the TUC. But he had trod on many toes, including those of the railway workers, in the course of his career; and many workers, mindful of the principle of union independence, were wary of his ties with the liberal wing of the old political class. In any case, a sizable group of workers in Accra-Tema had shifted their support to an alternative, radical trade union center, the Association of Local Unions (ALU), whose leaders advocated overthrowing the TUC bureaucracy altogether and were linked with the June Fourth Movement. In April 1982, the existing TUC leadership was indeed deposed and the Congress placed under the control of an appointed Interim Management Committee composed predominantly of radical supporters of the PNDC. This obviously goes a long way to explaining why the labor movement leadership did not instigate strike action in protest at the April 1983 budget measures, despite the fact that these undoubtedly made for a deterioration in workers' real incomes. Even when, in December 1983, the interim committee was voted out and replaced by pretakeover union leaders, including Ambrose Yankey as secretary-general, these leaders were, initially at least, very unsure of themselves and of their room for maneuver in opposing government policies.

Unofficial protests by workers nevertheless seemed likely and constituted, potentially, the single most serious obstacle to initial implementation of the adjustment program. Several factors must be taken into account in understanding why these did not occur on any significant scale.[10] First, the deterioration in real incomes was not nearly so severe as a devaluation of almost 1,000 percent and the removal of price controls might at first sight seem to indicate. Most workers had already been obliged to adjust to paying black market prices as high as the new prices for most imported goods. Second, many workers were sufficiently impressed by Rawlings's seriousness to be prepared to give his economic efforts a chance. But, third, they were probably also afraid of repression. The first year of PNDC rule was marked by many instances of detention and molestation, and even some instances of murder, of suspected opponents of the regime, including quite ordinary people. The fact that most of these seemed not to be centrally directed, but rather to be wanton acts of unruly soldiers and self-proclaimed supporters of the revolution, did little to allay workers' fears of what might happen to them if they openly protested the economic reforms.

If the weakness of the former, major socioeconomic groupings, together with the distinctly nebulous character of Ghanaian civil society by this time, permitted the new Rawlings regime exceptional policy latitude, and was later to facilitate the adoption of a stabilization program, it also, initially, placed the leaders of the leftist, "progressive" organizations in a seemingly powerful position. But this position also depended on their personal closeness to Rawlings. The first uprising of junior ranks in 1979 had produced a flowering of radical movements or factions—the June Fourth Movement, the New Democratic Movement, the Kwame Nkrumah Revolutionary Guards, the People's Revolutionary League of Ghana, and others.[11] One must obviously beware of overgeneralizing about their beliefs. It nevertheless seems not unfair to say that, as Douglas Rimmer has put it, "neocolonialism was the bugaboo of these groups."[12] For them, the main cause of the impoverishment of the Ghanaian masses lay, beyond the depredations of corrupt government leaders and officials, in the alleged repatriation of extortionate profits by multinational corporations as well as in the neocolonial structure of the economy more generally. They accordingly believed salvation to lie in excusively national and state-directed control of economic affairs.

There was an important difference, however, between the two main groups—the JFM and the NDM—regarding the questions of timing and class alliances. The JFM hoped to move quite rapidly to socialism, attacking the rich and breaking all ties with "imperialism." The NDM was influenced, as its name suggests, by Mao's strategy of "new democracy" as an intermediate stage on the path to a fuller form of socialism. They were ready to make alliances with other classes, including patriotic professionals and businesspeople, in order to rebuild Ghana's wasted economy.

The majority of active members of the JFM and the NDM were students, ex-students, or lecturers from the University of Ghana, where the "dependency" school of political economy had been very popular since the mid-70s. Their numbers were really very small, and their beliefs regarding neocolonialism did not enjoy much currency among the populace at large. But it was part of their strategy, and for some also a matter of conviction, to emphasize the democratic element in their program, the need to mobilize the "popular forces"; and this enabled them to attract sympathizers and allies among the junior officers and in the rank and file of the army, in the trade unions, and among the youth more generally. Members of these organizations played a leading role in establishing the PDCs and the WDCs that rapidly sprang up in the wake of the coup, more especially in the urban areas, and that were intended to provide the organizational base of the new regime. Still, these were not terribly popular in the wider community, many of their activists were opportunists rather than ideologically committed or loyal protégés, and so one should not imagine that they provided the leftists with much of a mass base.[13]

The main key to the leftists' temporarily ascendant influence within the PNDC lay in their personal closeness to Rawlings. Several deserve mention as being especially close: the two Tsikata brothers, law lecturers at the University of Legon and founders of the NDM; Chris Atim, ex-NUGS vice-president and chairman of the JFM; and Sergeant Alolga Akata-Pore, a member of the JFM and generally credited with organizing and leading the actual coup d'état. Rawlings the populist shared their enthusiasm, initially at least, for enhancing popular political consciousness and participation. They were, like Rawlings himself, unquestionably sincere if a little youthfully naive in their consuming concern for the welfare of the masses. It was not an irrelevant matter that they were extremely nice people. The difference that was increasingly to emerge between Rawlings and some of them (more especially, the JFM leaders) was not exactly that their "leftism" was more extreme. It seems to have been Rawlings himself, for example, who was responsible for the Libyan initiative. It was rather that they were more intellectual and theoretical in orientation, whereas Rawlings was both more passionate and more pragmatic.

The first and main reason Rawlings increasingly turned away from them was simply that they proved unable to articulate any practical strategy either for dealing with Ghana's immediate economic crisis or for reviving the country's productive potential in the longer term. The PNDC inherited a situation of acute economic insolvency in which a very considerable injection of capital was required if rehabilitation of the transport infrastructure and other prerequisites of any form of economic recovery were to be effected. Despite their making friendly noises and gestures, neither Libya nor the Soviet Union nor any other socialist country proved willing to provide assistance on anything like the necessary scale. The Soviet response is said to have been that Ghana should go to the IMF.[14]

It was not simply over the question of immediate financial assistance, however, that Rawlings and the JFM leaders came to differ, even if this was to provide the immediate catalyst of the rupture between them. When given the opportunity to outline concrete plans for restructuring the economy, they could come up with little more than, first, a proposal to renegotiate the terms on which hydroelectricity was provided to Valco—a just and desirable move but hardly one that would dramatically improve the government's financial situation—and, second, a series of proposals to extend public control of banking and to establish state monopolies of the import and distributive trades. Nothing, of course, could have been better calculated to extend the sway of the corruption that so concerned Rawlings. And there was nothing here to suggest how to revive production. This was not just an unfortunate failure of particular individuals. It is a more general failure of dependency theory that it commonly does not distinguish between relatively large economies with abundant resources, at one extreme, and small economies with few resources, like Ghana's, at the other. Self-reliance might be a practicable option, even if not a developmentally optimal one, in the former case. It remains to be shown what alternative there is to international trade if one wants to raise living standards much above subsistence level in the latter case.

One indicator of Rawlings's skepticism toward the leftists' economic views, from the very beginning of the PNDC regime, was his refusal to appoint from among their ranks a minister/secretary in charge of the economy. In June 1982, he eventually appointed Kwesi Botchwey as secretary for Finance and Economic Planning. This was a very shrewd move. Botchwey was a university lecturer in law, politically acceptable to the leaders of the NDM, with which he had been associated, as well as highly intelligent and hardheaded. Despite some initial reservations, Botchwey gradually became convinced of the necessity and even desirability of an IMF agreement and restructuring program. Together with a small group of "patriotic professionals"—senior civil servants and bank officials—who had approached him, he succeeded in communicating the logic of this conviction to Rawlings himself.

As Nelson notes, one of the major obstacles to the adoption of stabilization measures has frequently been the fact that political leaders with limited economic training have difficulty understanding their logic.[15] This group of "patriotic professionals" played an extremely important role in this regard. Particularly crucial was their presentation of this logic to Rawlings in terms of the "urban bias" of past policies and the contribution of stabilization to providing a more just return to rural producers. This seems to have induced a genuine intellectual conversion on the part of this highly moralistic young man. As Rawlings himself was later to put it: "We are acknowledging the historic debt of the whole nation to the farmer and have thus repudiated the monstrous injustice of a past in which we virtually ran the machinery of the state on the tired backs of rural producers and provided little for their basic needs."[16] Henceforth the ERP was to be pursued with a consistency, even fervor, that reflected its having been taken on board as a moral issue.

## ■ Managing Political Opposition

Rawlings returned to power seemingly committed both to improving the economic welfare of the masses and to establishing new, democratic forms of political participation. His commitment to the latter seems, over time, to have faded or at least to have taken a much lower position in the order of priorities. The PDCs and WDCs, originally intended to provide the organizational base of the new democracy, were abolished in December 1984 after Rawlings had criticized them for attempting to create "parallel structures of authority";[17] their supposed replacements, the CDRs, notably were not accorded any politically representative functions. They were instructed instead to focus their energies on improving discipline and productivity in Ghanaian society.

Increasingly, the PNDC has become an authoritarian administrative regime, resorting to harrassment and arrests to cow its opponents and silence its critics, leavened by the occasional speech by Rawlings attempting to persuade and exhort. Relations with the TUC leadership, which has done its best to walk the tightrope between confrontation with the government on the one side and loss of credibility in its members' eyes on the other, have deteriorated sharply, largely as a result of the uncompromising stance of the government and the arrest of two senior unionists. The holding in 1988 of elections for new District Assemblies, which are to exercise greatly extended responsibilities under a decentralized system of administration, seems generally to have been regarded as a diversion from the ever more insistent (urban) demand for popular representation where it really matters, at the center. The PNDC government now gives the appearance of being suspended in midair, lacking any institutionalized social roots. It survives, as of today, not through popular support nor through lack of enemies. Its sources of strength lie in the loyalty of (much of) the armed forces, the command structure of which was rebuilt, with senior officers joining the PNDC in 1985; the efficiency of the state security service under the direction of Kojo Tsikata; and, rather more questionably, as we shall see, the monopolization of opinion in the newspapers and broadcasting, the effect of which was to create by 1988 a "culture of silence" in national affairs.

All this is by way of observation, not criticism. Criticisms of this process that attribute it to alleged personal failings of Rawlings—his lack of genuine democratizing enthusiasm and his increasingly authoritarian temper—are surely missing the point. Although this may be a part of the matter, the basic dynamic has lain in the logic of the economic recovery program itself, taken together with certain characteristic features of Ghanaian popular participation in politics. It really is difficult to see how, given the overriding commitment to implementing the ERP, things could have been very different. This is not to say that they could not have been different at all. But it is important that criticisms be realistic in their assessment of difficulties and alternatives if they are not to be simply glib.

Rawlings turned against the PDCs for several reasons. First, many of their activists were ideologically and personally close to the June Fourth Movement leaders, some of whom had been implicated in an attempted putsch in October and November 1982, others of whom stayed on in the NDC but with their loyalty highly questionable and ever more severely tested. Rawlings obviously feared that the PDCs might be used to build up a movement of leftist opposition. Even if they were not, he felt the utmost distaste for what he termed their "ideological slogan-shouting."[18] In addition, and notwithstanding their claim to represent the "popular forces," they clearly did not, on balance, enhance the popularity of the regime. One should be wary of overgeneralization here, since their operation seems to have been highly uneven. But their leaders were almost always unelected and often exercised their powers in an overweening, bullying, and opportunistic manner, seeking to channel imported food aid and other government-distributed benefits to their own members. Attempts to justify their composition and mode of operation in terms of an arbitrary division and phony class war between the "people" and other "bourgeois" citizens obviously antagonized many ordinary poor people.[19] In the rural areas, they often appeared as disgruntled elements attacking chiefs without real justification or majority support.[20] In the industrial workplace, the WDCs' attacks on managerial incompetence and high-handedness, while initially appreciated, came to be seen as an obstacle to getting back down to work and reviving production. It was admittedly a condition of further assistance from the international agencies that the disruptive tactics of the WDCs be curbed. But there is no evidence that their passing was greatly mourned by the majority of workers themselves.

If these were good reasons for abolishing the PDCs, it might nevertheless be asked why they were not replaced by fresh organizations for the more authentic representation of popular opinion. In view of the nature of the ERP and the popular reactions it was bound to arouse—at least in the short to medium term—it was surely simply a matter of pragmatic good sense not to replace them. Any such organizations were likely to function most vigorously and most vocally in the urban areas, and there it was readily predictable that, if they were to be authentically representative, they would become vehicles of opposition to the government and its policies.

The government, we have seen, had weathered the first year of the ERP's implementation through a combination of popular respect for Rawlings, efficient military intelligence, and decentralized repression. However, Rawlings's personal powers of persuasion were bound with frequent use to wane, while the ERP was calculated to impose continuing austerity, for at least another three or four years, on the urban population.[21] Workers would find their real wages falling rather than improving in the short term, and some would lose their jobs entirely. Notwithstanding the understandable protests from the TUC leadership, these measures have actually been implemented in an admirably caring and judicious way, far less severely than some economists would have preferred. Even so, it was inconceivable that they should not arouse resentment.

It was also evident, as of 1984, that there were not going to be many jobs available in the public sector for school leavers or university graduates. Current and prospective university students were inevitably going to be antagonized by the introduction of a more economic (and arguably more equitable) system of financing higher education, with a reduction in public subsidy of students' living expenses. Informal sector employees and the underemployed were likely to find survival increasingly difficult and arduous as their ranks were, temporarily at least, swelled even further. All these and other aggrieved groups would likely have played a leading role in any organs of popular representation.

One gains the impression from the drift of government statements over time that Rawlings hoped to introduce institutional arrangements for the election of popular representatives to the central government as the economic benefits of the ERP materialized and hopefully converted urban opposition into a more supportive mood. The original projections of the ERP formulators gave reason to believe that, granted reasonably favorable terms of trade and other circumstances, this situation would be emerging toward the end of the 1980s. In fact, of course, falling world market prices for cocoa and other export commodities have meant that it has been impossible to pass on the anticipated benefits. This has no doubt been as galling to Rawlings as to anyone. It is largely for reasons quite outside its control that the government has been obliged to delay the introduction of representative political arrangements (with the exception, that is, of the elected District Councils) and to resort to authoritarian methods of containing mounting economic and political dissatisfaction. It deserves sympathy in its dilemma, rather than unrealistic liberal carping, at least from those who acknowledge the desirability of the ERP for Ghana's economic future.

Some left-wing critics of the regime appear to believe that there need not and should not be any conflict between the working masses and a government that is genuinely attempting to improve their economic welfare.[22] This is, of course, utopian nonsense. Others take the rather more sophisticated view that it ought to have been possible to develop popular organizations as two-way channels of communication and control between the government and the masses, providing education in the government's aims and thereby serving overall as agencies for building popular support. The model is that of the Leninist single party as idealized and ideologically neutralized by Samuel Huntington.[23] The short response here is that the PNDC has lacked reliable cadres in anything like sufficient numbers to implement and supervise such a structure. But it is important, in any case, to recognize that the actual operation of such organizations rarely if ever matches the democratic rhetoric of their proponents. Leninist parties have in practice always been downward vehicles of political control rather than genuine vehicles of popular representation and have needed to be supplemented by an extensive apparatus of popular repression and terror.[24] Rawlings, to his credit, has displayed no taste for such fascism.

To the extent that African single-party regimes have managed to develop and maintain a political following, this has been largely through the distribution of patronage. To say that the PNDC regime gives the appearance of being suspended in midair is to say, in part and under present economic conditions, that it does not operate much in the way of a clientelist system. It chooses not to do so because it believes—and the experience of the past thirty years surely confirms this—that, if Ghana is to recover and to proceed to develop economically, it cannot afford (at least on anything like the same scale) the clientelist politics of the past. Central government must begin to operate more efficiently and economically, less as a distributor of patronage. This is ultimately what structural adjustment is about.

A move away from clientelist politics is unlikely to be realized in any very permanent fashion, once representative politics is reintroduced at the national level, unless there is a radical change in popular attitudes toward the state's proper economic role and responsibilities. The first step here must be to link more firmly the procedures for taxation and representation. This, of course, is the rationale for the new system of District Councils and for introducing elections at this level prior to doing so at the national level. With their extended responsibilities for both formulating and financing (from local taxation) development projects, and with their revised procedures to facilitate the full participation of all sections of the citizenry, including illiterates, they are designed to provide education in the economic realities of responsible self-government. Hopefully, lessons learned there will subsequently inform attitudes toward representation in central government. The rationale is a sound one and sincerely intentioned. But there has not been much chance of its being regarded as such in the developing climate of public resentment. There is too much of a discrepancy between the exhortation to participate and debate at the local level and the attempt to silence all criticism at the national level. By turning increasingly, from approximately 1986 onward, to suppressing debate in the newspapers and broadcasting and arresting its critics simply for criticizing, the PNDC government has arguably lost the moral authority it once possessed and consequently its capacity to initiate effectively in such matters.

I have argued until now that the PNDC's refusal to institute regular arrangements for political representation—its operation as an administrative regime—has been perfectly rational and a practical prerequisite for implementing the recovery and adjustment program. It has been justified on the same grounds in dealing severely with those who have attempted to subvert it or to incite public disorder. I am not so sure, however, that the same applies to its increasingly intolerant attitude toward criticism. The dividing line between criticism and incitement to disorder can, of course, be a narrow one. But acting as though there isn't one has arguably been, even by the most Machiavellian criteria, counterproductive. It has been, psychologically, an understandable reaction, not just to the numerous coup attempts and the mood of urban popular dissatisfaction but to the very experience of being in power so long, one's best efforts seeming to go unappreciated. Such intolerance of criticism is perhaps also encouraged by the difficulty of communicating successfully to an economically unsophisticated public the counterintuitive logic of many structural adjustment measures. But it has not been, I think—and I hasten to add that this is very much a personal judgment made without a great deal of confidence—the wisest reaction.

One of the great strengths of the regime in the early years was its willingness to try to persuade, coupled with the particularly persuasive quality of Rawlings's distinctive political voice. The move toward monopolization of the mass media, though doubtless conceived as a means of mass suasion, has probably had the opposite effect, rendering the regime indistinguishable in this respect from that of, say, Acheampong. In a relatively liberal political culture such as that of Ghana, the harassment of public critics does little to stem quieter criticism in the bars or the markets, while itself becoming a source of resentment. Professor Boahen's critique of the PNDC in his 1988 Danquah lectures implies that it might in fact have prevented protests and riots:

> We have not protested or staged riots not because we trust the PNDC but because we fear the PNDC! We are afraid of being detained, liquidated or dragged before the CVC or the NIC or being subjected to all sorts of molestation.[25]

I nevertheless suspect that the costs have outweighed the benefits as regards the regime's image both at home and abroad. Several of its erstwhile closest friends have recently deserted it, at least in part over this issue, some becoming involved in the attempted coup d'état of September 1989.

The attempt to silence public criticism has been particularly resented because it has been accompanied by what most observers agree to have been an increase in the incidence of corruption. In such a context, the former is obviously likely to be construed as an attempt to cover up the latter; and it can all too easily become precisely that. Nothing could be more damaging to what residual legitimacy the regime enjoys, or to public acceptance of the need for continuing economic austerity. In a recent radio and television broadcast to mark the eighth anniversary of PNDC rule, Rawlings acknowledged that many government appointees have over time "extended those privileges into lifestyles which are not compatible with revolutionary humility," and promised that such people "will be made to disembark before the train gets into full gear." There is a clear analogy here with Nkrumah's Dawn Broadcast. According to one reporter at least, Rawlings's "frank and incisive speech has to a large extent diffused the latent tension which had been building up in Ghanaian society."[26] It is to be hoped that, unlike Nkrumah, he will act on it.

### ■ Notes

1. To borrow a term from Paul Mosley, "On Persuading a Leopard to Change His Spots: Optimal Strategies for Donors and Recipients of Conditional Development Aid," in Robert H. Bates (ed.), *Toward a Political Economy of Development* (Berkeley: University of California Press, 1988), pp. 47–79.
2. Joan M. Nelson, "The Political Economy of Stabilization: Commitment, Capacity and Public Response," in Bates, ibid., pp. 80–130.
3. Richard Jeffries, "Rawlings and the Political Economy of Underdevelopment in Ghana," *African Affairs* 81, 324 (July 1982), pp. 307–317.
4. Quoted by Donald Rothchild and E. Gyimah-Boadi, "Ghana's Economic Decline and Development Strategies," in John Ravenhill (ed.), *Africa in Economic Crisis* (New York: Columbia University Press, 1986), p. 269.
5. For a fuller account, see Richard Jeffries, "Ghana: The Political Economy of Personal Rule," in Donald B. Cruise O'Brien, John Dunn, and Richard Rathbone (eds.), *Contemporary West African States* (Cambridge: Cambridge University Press, 1989), pp. 75–98.
6. See, for example, the speeches quoted in Barbara E. Okeke, *4 June: A Revolution Betrayed* (Enugu, Nigeria: Ikenga Publishers, 1982).
7. See, for example, Jerry John Rawlings, *A Revolutionary Journey: Selected Speeches of Flt. Lt. Jerry John Rawlings*, vol. 1 (Accra: Ghana Publishing Corporation, n.d.).
8. Robert H. Bates, *Markets and States in Tropical Africa: The Political Basis of Agricultural Policies* (Berkeley: University of California Press, 1981).
9. *West Africa*, September 6, 1982.
10. For a fuller account and explanation, see Jeffrey Herbst's Chapter 9 in this book, to which I am greatly indebted.
11. For details, see Donald I. Ray, *Ghana: Politics, Economy and Society* (Boulder: Lynne Rienner Publishers; London: Frances Pinter, 1986), pp. 35–64.
12. Douglas Rimmer, untitled draft paper.
13. Jeffrey Haynes, "Rawlings and the Politics of Development Policy in Ghana, 1979–86," Staffordshire Polytechnic CNNA Ph.D. thesis, 1988.
14. *West Africa*, February 25, 1985.
15. Nelson, "The Political Economy," pp. 91–93.
16. *West Africa*, January 12, 1987.
17. *West Africa*, September 17, 1984.
18. *West Africa*, December 24, 1984.
19. Jeffrey Haynes, "Rawlings."
20. See, for example, Paul Nugent, "National Integration and the Vicissitudes of State Power in Ghana: The Political Incorporation of Likpe, a Border Community, 1945–1986," University of London Ph.D. thesis, near completion.

21. World Bank, Ghana—Policies and Program for Adjustment (Washington, D.C., World Bank 1984).
22. See, for example, Chris B. Atim and Ahmed S. Gariba, "Ghana: Revolution or Counter-Revolution?" *Journal of African Marxists*, no. 10 (June 1987), pp. 90–105.
23. Samuel Huntington, *Political Order in Changing Societies* (New Haven: Yale University Press, 1968).
24. Alexander J. Groth, "The Institutional Myth: Huntington's Order Revisited," *The Review of Politics* 41, 2 (April 1979), pp. 203–234.
25. *West Africa*, March 28, 1988.
26. *West Africa*, January 15, 1990.

# 9
# Labor in Ghana Under Structural Adjustment: The Politics of Acquiescence

*Jeffrey Herbst*

One of the most contentious issues in the implementation of economic reform in Africa has been the ability of states to impose programs that noticeably discriminate against urban populations, especially labor. Indeed, the "IMF riots" that occurred in countries such as Sudan and Zambia have led some to conclude that African states are simply too weak to implement the policies biased against urbanized labor that are inevitably part of a structural reform program. This chapter examines why the PNDC in Ghana has been able to implement a series of policies that apparently have resulted in significant income losses on the part of workers while suffering almost no popular unrest. Ghana is a particularly interesting example in this regard because at least some writers had claimed that trade unions in the country were relatively politicized and that it would be very difficult for any government to carry out reforms that were noticeably antilabor. In this chapter I will also examine an issue that has received far less attention in the general debate concerning structural adjustment: how the government's initial implementation of stabilization measures will affect its long-term efforts to develop significant political support for itself and its economic policies.

## ■ Labor Power in Africa

Observers of African workers and trade unions have long recognized the weaknesses of organized labor in Africa. In their important early article, Elliot Berg and Jeffrey Butler argued that African labor unions were not noticeably political during the terminal colonial period.[1] However, within the context of African societies, where all groups that seek to organize for political power suffer from grave organizational deficiencies, some have suggested that labor is among the more powerful political organizations. First, simply because it is somewhat concentrated, labor has the advantage over many other groups, notably the peasantry, which are atomistically dispersed over the countryside. Second, irrespective of the amount of organization they have, workers are usually located in the cities in Africa and therefore have at least the potential to threaten the government through organized or spontaneous demonstrations. The potential for urban labor to threaten governments in the cities, especially the capital, is particularly important, because in a significant number of African countries the political power of the state rests solely on its ability to control the cities. Robert Bates notes, "The contemporary histories of many of the independent African nations might credibly be recorded by focusing on major periods of strike action and worker protest."[2] Indeed, Bates argues that it is precisely because workers can exercise power through both organized and unorganized means that African governments find it particularly difficult to suppress them.

> Direct attacks on labor movements are open to reprisals; in moments of economic stress, labor movements can join with their urban constituents, paralyze cities, and create the conditions under which ambitious rivals can displace those in power. And attempts at co-optation still leave open the chance for wildcat actions; during moments of economic crisis in the cities, workers can and have acted on their own."[3]

The potential power of workers is actually higher than is suggested by their numbers or their organizations because their actions may quickly combine with the simmering discontent found in all African cities to cause an avalanche of popular protest.[4]

Activism among workers in Ghana has been especially noticeable because, while they share all the weaknesses traditionally attributed to labor in Africa, they have at certain moments organized to present a real threat to the government in power. St. Clair Drake and Leslie Alexander Lacy were moved, perhaps somewhat overenthusiastically, to claim in the 1960s that "the main threat to national stability will no longer be tribalism, but the wildcat strike."[5] Similarly, Richard Jeffries, in his thorough study of the railway workers of Sekondi-Takoradi, noted:

> The Sekondi-Takoradi railway strikes of 1950, 1961 and 1971 were all highly political in conception. That is to say, they were consciously directed against the government rather than the management, and were expressions of protest at general policies and characteristics of the regimes in question rather than narrowly occupational grievances.[6]

Some of the railway workers' actions, notably the strike in 1961, resulted in the mobilization of the entire community. The market women and unemployed who joined the protests were motivated not only by their own financial dependence on the railway workers, but also by the desire to add their grievances against Nkrumah's government to that of the striking workers.[7] There is little evidence that these other groups would have acted had the striking workers not provided the spark. More generally, it is claimed that Ghanaian workers may ignite social unrest because labor's own interests are not fundamentally different from those of the larger society. Jon Kraus has noted that workers' strikes between 1968 and 1971 tended to "articulate the interests of the broadest stratum of labour, the lower-paid and minimum wage earners."[8]

There is thus the belief among many scholars in Ghana that labor unions can exercise at least some political power there. For instance, Bill Freund observes, "A sensitive analysis of developments in a country such as Ghana also shows that the unions are conduits at times for shocks that can present difficulties for regimes."[9] Similarly, Jeff Crisp notes, "The history of Ghana in colonial and post-colonial periods is a testament to the susceptibility of the Ghanaian state to the threat of popular unrest and protest."[10] However, Crisp makes clear that for a number of reasons, including internal organizational and ideological reasons, the mine workers have not been able to go beyond being an episodic political force in the country.[11] Although not able to be a consistent political force in the country, organized labor may therefore have the ability to mobilize significant portions of the society in order to protest specific policies and thereby sabotage any effort at economic reform. For instance, Jim Silver argues that should Ghana sign an economic reform program with the International Monetary Fund that demands a freeze in wages, the mine workers will inevitably resist. He suggests that they will either strike, with the result that the country's foreign exchange reserves will be depleted, or that the workers will rebel while staying on the job, with the result that the country's flow of minerals will be severely reduced.[12]

## ■ Structural Adjustment and Labor

Precisely because they are able to exercise at least some political power, workers, especially in the urban areas, have been able to receive a disproportionate number of political goods from African governments across the continent. A central theme in Bates's book is that fear of unrest on the part of urban workers has been a consistent factor in the drive by African governments to keep food prices as low as possible. Thus, peasants have usually been taxed in order to buy the political acquiescence of workers. In addition, many African governments have found it politically convenient to try to coopt the urban population by padding state-owned enterprises with as many surplus workers as possible. Also, the urban population has traditionally benefited from subsidies on fuel and government services that usually are not available to the rural population. Finally, the urban population has often been the beneficiary of artificially cheap imported goods, especially food but also clothes and other consumer goods, brought into the country when the currency has been overvalued.

Not surprisingly, therefore, urban workers are one of the chief targets of structural adjustment programs that hope to bring about fundamental reforms of economies in Africa. These economic reform programs seek to reduce subsidies on crucial commodities such as food, fuel, and transport that the urban population benefits from disproportionately. Also, all economic reform programs hope to eliminate overvaluation of exchange rates and thereby increase the price of many goods that the urban population consumes. Finally, many reform programs demand sharp reductions in the staffing of public sector enterprises, which will inevitably increase unemployment among the urban working class.

It is true that, in the medium term, parts of the working class will benefit if industries start to export more, and, presumably, a great many workers will eventually benefit if there is a long-term improvement in their economy. However, it could take years for any African economy to adjust so that it can actually begin to export nontraditional exports and potentially much longer until the economy improves enough so that growth makes up for the specific benefits that the urban population lost out on. In the short run, the urban population is almost certain to face nothing but income losses, and there will be great temptations for labor to attempt to mobilize to block economic reform programs. The fact that so much of the cost of structural adjustment will be visible immediately thus plays to the urban working class's political strength, because the potential for strikes and labor unrest igniting more general popular protest will clearly be greatest during a drastic program that suddenly causes a sharp deterioration in the standard of urban living. Thus, especially in the first few years of any structural adjustment program, one of the central questions for any government is whether it can contain labor protests until the benefits of the reforms become obvious to workers.

In Ghana, which has adopted the most ambitious structural adjustment program on the continent, much of the reform program was ostensibly directed against the urban population. For instance, the country embarked in 1983 on a radical reform of the cedi, which overnight lowered the value of the currency from ¢2.54 to the dollar to ¢25 to the dollar. Since then, the government has instituted a series of devaluations, auctions, and liberalizations of the foreign exchange market so that there has been a real devaluation of 1,500 percent since the beginning of the program.[13] Inevitably, the inflationary impact of this devaluation will have a particularly strong impact on workers. The link between devaluation and inflation was made particularly clear to the workers because, especially between 1983 and 1986, every time the government announced a devaluation, the prices of all the major commodities would increase the same day.[14] There were also some reports of petrol stations hoarding supplies until the next devaluation was announced so that they could sell the fuel at the higher price.[15] Thus, it was no wonder that the Trades Union Congress noted "with grave dissatisfaction and disapproval, the government's announcement of another devaluation of the cedi" in 1986.[16]

Beginning in the 1983 budget, the government also embarked on a radical reform of prices. Subsidies for many government services were eliminated, with the result that the urban population was faced with sudden price increases for basic goods. For instance, hospital fees were introduced in 1983 and increased in 1985, water fees rose by 150 percent, postal tariffs increased by 365 percent, and electricity rates by 1,000 percent.[17] There was also a dramatic effort to reform price controls. Previous governments had established a byzantine system of regulating close to 6,000 prices on nearly 700 producer groups. The PNDC government quickly abolished almost all of these price controls, and by the late 1980s, only a handful still existed, and these regulations had only a minimal effect on the pricing decisions of companies.[18]

Since 1983, the government of Ghana has also embarked on a wide-ranging program to reform state-owned enterprises that has as its central mission the reduction of surplus workers. For instance, in the mid-1980s, the government undertook an evaluation and redeployment exercise that reduced the size of the Cocoa Board's payroll from 100,000 employees to 50,000.[19] Other state enterprises are undergoing similar programs, although none could claim quite the extravagance of waste that the Cocoa Board achieved. The government is also hoping to reduce its own work force, and the structural adjustment program plans to eliminate approximately 36,000 positions from a total civil service of approximately 540,000.

Finally, the government has made it clear through its intervention in the wage process that it is not going to allow significant wage increases for workers in the near future for fear of reigniting inflation. Although Ghana has retained its Prices and Incomes Board (PIB), this body now only regulates wages. In 1988, for instance, when some companies agreed to raise the incomes of their workers by 30 to 50 percent, the PIB decreed that no raises of greater than 25 percent would be allowed.[20] In addition, if employers promise workers a wage increase but have not paid their taxes, social security contributions, and put aside money for terminal benefits, the Board will make employers reduce the size of the wage increase in order to meet these other commitments.[21]

Thus, workers in Ghana, at least some of whom have been portrayed as having a history of antistate activity, have been hit by what appears to be a large number of blows over the last few years. As the Trades Union Congress noted:

> Although the various statistical indicators are moving in the desired directions under the nation's Economic Recovery Programme, the going is still hard for the working people. . . . The sum effect of the IMF and World Bank sponsored economic policies are the cheapening of the local currency through the foreign exchange auction system, the high rates of unemployment and a rising cost of living brought about by the decontrolling of prices, removal and subsidies on essential goods and services and the partial freeze on wages and salaries of the working people.[22]

Certainly, the structural adjustment program has instituted more far-reaching changes in the economy than either the 1961 or 1971 budgets, which activated a large amount of worker unrest. Indeed, the Ghanaian reforms are at least near the magnitude of the price increases in Zambia that caused large-scale rioting and the eventual abandonment of that reform program in 1987.

However, Ghana has not experienced significant popular unrest ignited by organized or unorganized labor (or anyone else for that matter) since the massive Structural Adjustment Program was first announced in 1983. As Figure 9.1 shows, while there have been some strikes, labor unrest is nowhere as high as it was in the 1970s; indeed, strikes are currently about as low as they have ever been in Ghana. Both government and union leaders are agreed that despite the government's economic policies there has not been a significant number of protests.

The question that immediately poses itself is why there has been this amount of labor acquiescence to structural adjustment programs, especially given Ghana's labor history. The explanation given by many Ghanaians, both within government and the Trades Union Congress, derives from a belief that Ghanaians have a desire to avoid conflict and that they will stand for almost anything that a government does. As one Ministry of Finance official noted in an interview, "The Ghanaian has his own personality. If this would have been Nigeria, heads would have rolled."[23] However, this explanation seems particularly unsatisfactory given that Ghana has had, if anything, a more active labor movement than many other African countries over the last twenty-five years. Certainly, very few, if any, of the scholars who studied Ghanaian labor movements in the 1960s and 1970s pictured Ghanaian workers as particularly acquiescent, and the mobilization of workers during 1982 makes this nonfalsifiable argument unpersuasive.[24]

## ■ Explaining Political Acquiescence

The PNDC, led by Flight Lieutenant Jerry Rawlings, came to power on December 31, 1981, promising "nothing less than a revolution."[25] With a flourish of populist and socialist rhetoric, the government sought to mobilize

**Figure 9.1 Work Days Lost Due to Strikes**

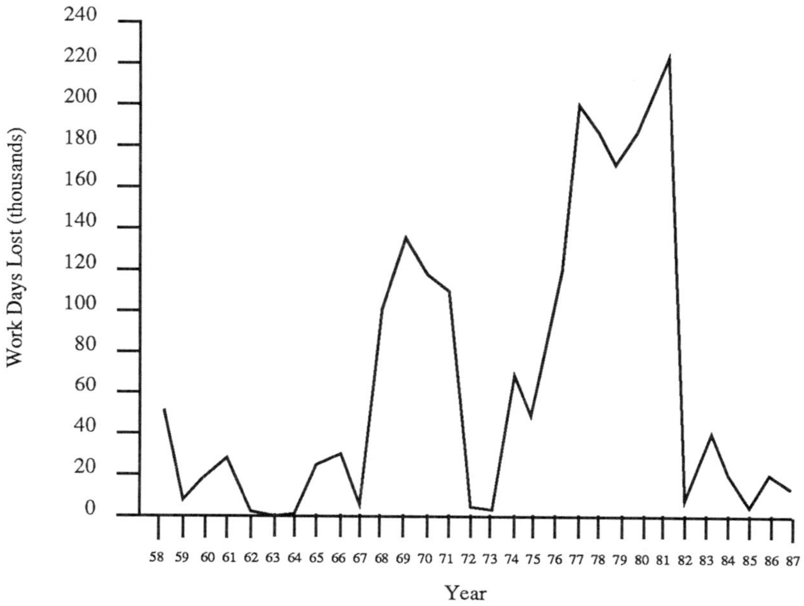

*Source*: International Labour Office, *Yearbook of Labour Statistics*, Geneva, various years.

workers, students, and the rest of the urban population in order, through unspecified policy measures, to bring about radical change in the economy. Workers' Defence Committees and People's Defence Committees were established to mobilize the population, and quite a bit of organization was done on the shop floor.

However, while the PNDC certainly counted workers among its constituency in its first years of rule, the Rawlings regime was notably antagonistic toward the trade union leadership. The new regime viewed the existing trade union leadership as part of the problem that had to be overcome rather than as part of the solution. As Rawlings noted in a speech in 1987, "The traditional union movement, like other institutions . . . has had its own history of power being exercised by a few who do not always express the real interests of that constituency."[26] Beginning shortly after the 31st December coup, the previously elected TUC officials were subject to continual harassment. For instance, sixteen general-secretaries of various unions were "reported to have gone into hiding for fear of molestation by the workers, some of whom cursed and cried for their blood."[27] In April 1982, the existing union leadership was deposed and the TUC was placed under the control of an appointed Interim Management Committee made up of radical supporters of the new regime.[28]

The Workers' Defence Committees, especially as they operated during 1982, can be seen as a profound challenge to the organized union structures that were supposed to represent workers' interests on the shop floor. Certainly, other Ghanaian governments had attempted to coopt the labor movement.[29] However, this was the first time in the nation's history that a regime had gone as far as to try and supplant actual union organization on the shop floor. As Emmanuel Hansen noted, "The WDC's became the main centres for the expression of shop-floor militancy and struggle within the labour process, first for the control of the labour movement and secondly for the control of the labour process itself."[30]

The PNDC was therefore able to mobilize a significant number of workers outside normal union channels. For instance, when the Ghana Textile Products Company threatened in February 1982 to lay off one-half of its workers because of the country's grave economic condition, the workers took over the factory. The government did nothing until the police attacked a WDC march in Tema in March 1983. It then intervened and supported the workers, condemned the police action, and deported the expatriate manager.[31] More generally, there were large turnouts of workers at the near-constant rallies that the PNDC had during 1982.

However, it soon became apparent that the regime could not continue its economic policies if it hoped to deal with the crisis that was confronting Ghana. First, the Soviet Union and Eastern European countries, which the PNDC had hoped would come to the aid of its revolution, told Ghana that they had no money and that the Rawlings regime should negotiate a program with the IMF. Second, soon after Rawlings took power there was an increasing realization, among at least some members of the regime, that the socialist/populist slogans they were mouthing did not really add up to anything approaching a coherent economic program. Finally, 1982 was an absolutely disastrous year. The country suffered from a severe drought, with the result that agricultural production decreased and bushfires damaged a substantial portion of the countryside. Further, Nigeria, experiencing its own problems, expelled approximately a million Ghanaians who had been working in the country illegally. Thus, almost overnight and during the worst economic crisis the country had ever faced, the government had to cope with the prospect of an additional 10 percent of its population looking desperately for work. Therefore, the Rawlings government began to negotiate with the World Bank and IMF and finally announced its radical program of economic change in April 1983.

## ☐ Surviving the Budget Announcement

Despite the PNDC's previous efforts at mobilizing the workers, the devaluation and increases in prices that the government announced in April, as well as the firm indication that more costly reforms were on the way, led to immediate protests by unions. One division of the General Transport and Chemical Workers Union summed up the immediate response of the workers to the budget by calling the program, "anti-people, a killer, callous and inhuman."[32] Similarly, E. K. Aboagye, chairman of the TUC interim committee, proclaimed that "the 1983 budget has come to add more petrol to the steadily burning fire of the peoples' anger."[33] Many workers went beyond these statements and publicly protested the budget. For instance, Finance Secretary Kwesi Botchwey was not allowed to speak in Kumasi in May 1983 due to worker protests.[34]

However, in the crucial period immediately after the budget announcement, the government was able to survive with little difficulty. After considerable bluster, there was not much concentrated worker action in the streets. Similarly, as Figure 9.1 indicates, although there was an upsurge in strikes in 1983, it was not a significant increase compared to past labor activism in Ghana. Indeed, there are some indications that in the period immediately after the budget announcement, the PNDC retained the support of at least some of the workers. For instance, Hansen notes that when the regime faced its most severe coup threat on June 19, 1983, the WDCs mounted roadblocks and rallied to support the regime.[35]

There are probably several reasons why workers did not organize in the days immediately after the coup and present a significant challenge to the government. The first factor, usually ignored in political studies, is simply chance. Large mob actions of the type that African governments fear most usually form spontaneously, and it may just have been that the mob did not come together in the right manner. Once a few days had elapsed, the moment for mass popular protest had passed. Second, the PNDC itself had destroyed much of the unions' traditional leadership and replaced it with people who owed their political survival to Rawlings. These new leaders were then fatally compromised when the PNDC announced its economic reform package. There was therefore no core of leaders around whom workers could coalesce in a concentrated wave of antiregime protests. In fact, the only leaders the workers had "appealed to workers to exercise utmost restraint whilst the leaders engage in consultation with the government in order not to jeopardize the long-term goals of the workers' struggles."[36] Third, Rawlings, after an exciting year of political mobilization, probably did retain the support of at least some workers, or at least had enough legitimacy for them not to want to rush out immediately into the streets. Fourth, some of the economic measures, notably retrenchment, would not be implemented for some time, and other price increases had not been fully passed through yet. Also, it was not clear in the first part of 1983 just how far-reaching the regime's program of economic reform was going to be. Therefore, the workers may not have protested more because they simply did not realize how bad off they were going to be.

Finally, the role of government repression must be made clear. Rawlings had a universal reputation for being tough after ordering the execution of three former heads of state when he briefly seized power in 1979. In addition, the first year of PNDC rule was replete with violent acts against those who even appeared to be in opposition to the regime, notably the kidnapping and brutal murder of three high court judges on June 30, 1982. The Catholic bishops of Ghana stated:

> In the wake of the "revolution" atrocities of all sorts have been committed against innocent civilians by some members of the armed forces and various groups purporting to support the revolution. The wanton killings, senseless beatings, merciless molestation and general harassment continue without the Government showing any willingness or ability to do anything about them.[37]

It must have been very easy for the workers to imagine that the regime was more than willing to turn its violence on them should they publicly oppose the new reforms. Indeed, Finance Secretary Botchwey immediately made clear that criticism of the budget would be seen as a disloyal act:

> The sudden alliance between certain negative elements in society and workers following the release of the 1983 budget is an attempt by such elements to hide behind legitimate workers grievances and subvert an economic programme meant to put the economy right.[38]

Officials certainly indicate that fear of repression had to be an important factor in the relative ease the government had in imposing its program. As one government official said,

> This government was prepared to take action. It also had a strong constituency among those who hold the gun. The population knows that if you complain, you will be silenced. If you did misbehave you would be taken care of.[39]

Or as another official said, "The message gets down that if you do something against the regime do not expect a lawyer to get you out of jail. The regime will only try you when they get around to it."[40]

Bates and others have noted that repression often does not work against trade unions because, especially in Africa, threats to the government usually come in the form of wildcat strikes rather than organized actions that can be prevented by locking up leaders. However, the particular type of repression so evident in 1982, when violence was directed in a highly decentralized manner against many members of society, may have inadvertently deterred workers from engaging in any kind of antiregime activity because it was clear that even the ordinary person was susceptible to repression. Of course, the central role that repression played suggests that arguments about the political nature of Ghanaians have relatively little relevance in understanding the unfolding of post-1983 developments.

☐ *Government Survival and Political Acquiescence in the Medium Term*

Simply because the government survived the immediate period after the budget did not mean that it would be able to implement its reform program without hindrance. Workers and the rest of the urban population could still be extremely hostile to the regime, and the potential for popular protest would not be eliminated. However, it is difficult to assess the degree of popular hostility toward the PNDC because it is not altogether clear just how badly urban workers were hurt by the structural adjustment program. In particular, the effect of the government lifting almost all price controls is ambiguous because, especially by 1982, most of these price controls were not being enforced and the vast majority of workers were paying black market prices that were probably at least as high as the shadow prices for most basic commodities. As early as 1970, Tony Killick had found that only 17 percent of items in stores were priced according to government controls and that 72 percent of the goods actually cost more than they should have. In the urban areas, where most of the workers were concentrated, there was a 30 percent observance rate.[41] Given the decay that Ghanaian administrative structures underwent after 1970, it is highly likely that even fewer of the controlled prices were being observed by the early 1980s. Similarly, given that the black market rate of the cedi was roughly twenty times higher than the declared rate, there were very few goods on the shelves of stores (and nothing in the markets) that were priced according to the official rate. Indeed, government officials are quite confident that more worker protest against the budget announcement and subsequent reforms did not emerge because most of the society was already paying shadow prices for the goods. Finally, because of the economic crisis, most urban workers were forced to take second jobs or otherwise supplement their income, so a decrease in wages or even outright loss of their jobs may not have been quite as significant as it appeared.[42]

However, the structural adjustment program undoubtedly imposed some costs on workers, even if it was less than initially suggested by government proclamations. Once the government survived the initial budget announcement, it still faced an extremely difficult task of surviving possible threats as workers realized that their plight was not going to improve in the near future.

One of the factors that was particularly important in allowing the government to survive without significant labor unrest was calculations by the unions concerning the amount of political space they had to operate in. In December 1983, the interim committee of the TUC was voted out and many pretakeover leaders of the TUC were returned to power. The new leadership continued to attack the evolving economic reform program of the government. A. K. Yankey, the new head of the TUC, said, "The plain truth is that the ordinary Ghanaian, the poor worker, is suffering. And the government must know that there is a limit to human endurance."[43] Similarly, a resolution adopted by the TUC executive board in 1984 noted that

> as a result of these IMF and World Bank conditions, the working people of Ghana now face unbearable conditions of life expressed in poor nutrition, high prices of goods and services, inadequate housing, continuing deterioration of social services and growing unemployment above all. . . . We caution government that the above conditions pose serious implications for the sharpening of class conflict in the society.[44]

In addition, there were sporadic worker protests that were embarrassing to the regime. For instance, in January 1986, after a minimum wage announcement, workers in Tema marched through the streets while the local labor coordinator said that the increase in the minimum wage represented nothing more than "a slave-wage which is not our choice."[45]

However, while they continued to agitate about the reforms, union leaders clearly recognized that, given the nature and history of the PNDC regime, there were real limits to the regime's patience in confronting actual protests. For instance, when the TUC sought to protest the Cocoa Board's retrenchments and the matter of paying out terminal benefits, the PNDC surrounded the labor movement's building with armored cars.[46] Accordingly, trade union officials have adjusted their tactics. As one senior TUC official said to me,

> The TUC knows that if it had a militant policy with strikes it might end with the dissolution of the TUC. Then we would have the double task of trying to get reinstated and to help protect the workers' movement. We are working toward the survival of the workers' movement. Therefore, we use these methods [talks with government] rather than violence.[47]

In addition, the TUC was also handicapped by the fact that it did not have the analytic and organizational ability to develop an alternative to the government's programs. Thus, protests against the government could only be viewed as a negative action that did not actually lead the country anywhere.

Despite the workers' timidity, the regime was, by 1986, becoming increasingly insecure about popular reaction to its policies because of sporadic worker actions and increasing resistance to its economic policies among its cadres. In particular, senior government officials were beginning to voice, in public, serious concerns about the political implications of continued exchange rate reform. In a bold challenge to government policy, Lieutenant Colonel (ret.) J. Y. Assasie, who was at that time political counsellor for economic development of the Committees for the Defence of the Revolution (as the WDCs and PDCs had been renamed), said,

> We are of the view, that the burdens that tend to flow from currency adjustments fall disproportionately heavily on the deprived and poorer sections of community without adequate and corresponding compensatory benefits. This sector of our society is the constituency of the Revolution which must not be unnecessarily burdened in the pursuit of growth.[48]

Similarly, one Finance Ministry official said, "Exchange rate announcements became more and more difficult with each successive announcement of devaluation. The government began to look bad. Revolutionaries asked if the government was for the workers. Every devaluation brought an increase in prices."[49] By this time, government officials admitted that they faced too much popular pressure to simply continue the practice of administrative announcements of devaluations.

In a crucial move, instead of forcing further reforms down the throats of workers and the rest of society, the PNDC resorted to finesse. The government decided to institute a foreign exchange auction, which constituted a "second window" for foreign exchange allocation. As Dr. Botchwey noted, the auction tended to "depoliticize" currency adjustments because the government could plausibly deny that it was responsible for further devaluations and just blame it on the market.[50] Similarly, an editorial in a local newspaper noted how the auction deflected blame away from the government:

> Each and every Ghanaian, therefore, must be aware that the way he or she goes about the tasks and responsibilities of daily life will be reflected in the weekly auction results. We can no longer hide from the truth or blame it on international financial institutions or economists who talk a language which we don't understand . . . it is our efforts which will determine the weekly economic temperature.[51]

The government soon confirmed its commitment to the auction by closing the first foreign exchange window so that the auction became the sole means of foreign exchange allocation in the country. Labor protests did in fact seem to decrease once the exchange rate was no longer driven by government announcements. Thus, labor acquiescence in Ghana is based not only on repression but also on the government's at least occasional ability to adopt strategies that avoid outright political conflict.

The PNDC government has also occasionally capitulated to labor demands to avoid conflict. For instance, the government in 1987 announced that it was eliminating end-of-service benefits to employees. There was a huge uproar throughout the country, and the TUC, under severe pressure from workers, asked government to review the announcement, which it eventually did.[52]

Finally, as the structural adjustment program progressed, some workers probably began to do better economically. Unfortunately, the data that Ghana Statistical Services provides on wages is so erratic that the figures cannot be used for any type of serious analysis. Therefore, it is unclear how workers' salaries have evolved over the last few years. It is, however, clear to everyone in Ghana that the overall economic situation is improving and that the regime's policies are bringing benefits, even if these benefits are not immediately concentrated among the working class. As Figure 9.2 shows, Ghana has experienced a real increase in per capita income of approximately 2 to 3 percent each year. This is a spectacular performance given that the rest of the continent had, at best, no real per capita growth in income.[53] Of course, Ghana is still well below where it was even in the late 1970s, but there has been enough progress to dissuade some from opposing the government. Some workers, notably those in gold mines, also were probably beginning to benefit from the upturn in their export-oriented industries by 1986 and 1987 due to the devaluation. As the incomes of some workers increase, the potential popular coalition against the government weakens, making any kind of action against the government more unlikely.

Thus, due to a combination of luck, repression, and political skill, the government was able to survive worker anger and implement a far-reaching structural adjustment program. This analysis accords with the developing conventional wisdom on structural adjustment that finds that the coalition that develops to oppose cuts in subsidies and price increases during structural adjustment is often far less threatening than is usually imagined. For instance, Henry Bienen and Mark Gersovitz noted that "urban food prices in African countries have in fact risen in recent years without endemic instabilities."[54] Given the structural weaknesses in Ghana and the fact that the PNDC will probably not look more kindly on worker protests in the near future, it is unlikely that, however they feel about the structural adjustment program, workers will rise up in protest in the near future.

The primary lesson of Ghana for the rest of Africa is that urban unrest cannot be predicted primarily on the basis of the severity of the structural

Figure 9.2 Real Per Capita Income

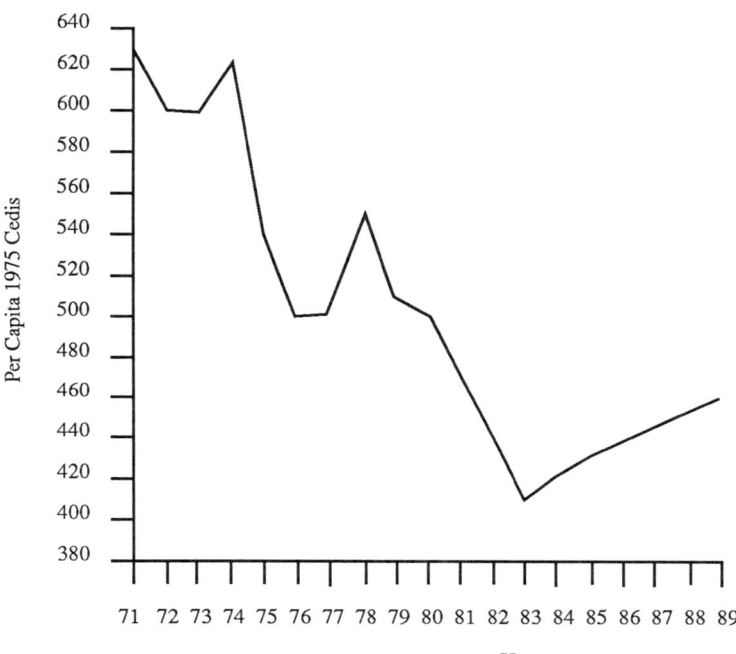

*Sources*: Kodwo Ewusi, *Statistical Tables on the Economy of Ghana, 1950–1985* (Legon: Institute of Statistical, Social and Economic Research, 1986); Statistical Service, *Quarterly Digest of Statistics*, December 1988; Ghana, *Towards a New Dynamism* (Accra: Ghana, 1989).

adjustment program. For instance, the fact that so few were benefiting from price controls and the overvalued exchange rate meant that the actual effect of the structural adjustment program on workers has probably been far less than the announcements themselves would indicate. In view of the fact that the program hurt less than it appeared and that opposing the regime publicly could entail large costs, popular unrest was not an attractive option.

■ **Building a Coalition for Structural Adjustment**

Arguably, a much more interesting question than why urban labor has not been able to protest against the PNDC is whether the structural adjustment program will actually ever allow the Rawlings regime to develop a political constituency among the workers. It can be argued that rural dwellers are the obvious constituency for the PNDC regime because so much of the structural adjustment program is devoted to promoting agriculture. However, previous

Ghanaian governments sought to marginalize the rural areas, and it will obviously be very difficult to effect any kind of political mobilization among this atomized population. In addition, the high proportion of Ewes in the national leadership has made it particularly difficult for the PNDC to establish support in Ashanti Region, despite the fact that cocoa farmers there have clearly benefited from the regime's policies.

It is one of the great ironies of present-day Ghana that precisely those factors that allowed the PNDC to impose such a drastic program of economic reform in the short run now pose substantial obstacles to creating any constituency, much less one based on the support of workers. The PNDC during the early days of the structural adjustment program, when it was unclear if it could survive the popular uproar caused by the reforms, was small, not dependent on the support of any particular group, and willing and able to use a large amount of force against opponents. To build constituencies, however, the PNDC must be able to consult and build support among other groups and must appear to have put aside any recourse to violence. This may be too great a transition for the regime to make.

For instance, one way that the PNDC could at least begin efforts to establish a constituency among workers would be to develop closer ties with the unions. However, in direct contrast to previous governments that sought to coopt the trade unions, the PNDC has not yet made any effort to make the TUC more closely associated with economic programs. As one senior TUC official noted in an interview, "The impression given is that the TUC is part of the planning process but it is not. Since 1983 the TUC has not been consulted. We are not in a position to participate."[55] The government is clearly still wary of the TUC after its muted protests against the structural adjustment program, and tolerance of criticism is not one of the personality traits of senior government officials. This attitude may change in the future but, given the amount of mistrust that has developed between the PNDC and official trade union structures, it will be a very long time before the government can develop a constituency among workers through the TUC.

In addition, structural adjustment programs create problems for regimes trying to build constituencies, as opposed to simply trying to repress groups, because there are so few popular symbols around which to rally the population. The PNDC did have some success in 1982 in mobilizing workers around pledges to bring about a "revolution." However, the visible symbols of the revolution are not at all obvious these days when the government is collaborating so closely with the IMF and the World Bank. As Justice D. F. Annan freely admits, the "blood and thunder politics" of the early years of the PNDC are gone.[56] Indeed, the obvious income disparities that have appeared as at least some have become rich under structural adjustment makes it clear to all Ghanaians that, whatever else, the euphoric populist rhetoric of 1982 has now been abandoned. Indeed, Rawlings, in his

1990 New Year's speech, was put in what must have been for him the highly difficult position of defending the well-to-do:

> We need not condemn or resent all people merely for their affluence. We must acknowledge the fact that a great many people have taken full advantage of the economic conditions which the government has deliberately created to encourage individual initiative.[57]

Clearly, there is not much for the workers to rally around.

The PNDC has in the last few years made a concentrated effort to resurrect Nkrumah as a nationalist symbol, and there has been at least some energy devoted to portraying Rawlings as Nkrumah's natural successor. However, this effort is extremely difficult because, just as the regime is promoting Nkrumah's legacy, it is systematically dismantling the economic measures so closely associated with Ghana's first ruler. Thus, the state enterprises that Nkrumah established to control the commanding heights of the economy are being dismantled, and price controls that were portrayed as helping the poor have been eliminated. When taking these actions, the regime implicitly (and correctly) ties Ghana's economic decline directly to its first leader. Therefore, Nkrumah probably cannot serve as an important symbol for workers and others to rally around.

Another avenue open to the PNDC to build a constituency among workers is through the recently created local political structures. In 1988 and 1989, voters throughout Ghana went to the polls to elect citizens to 110 newly created District Assemblies. In addition to those elected, the PNDC appointed a certain number of people to serve on each District Assembly. These elections were done on an individual basis, without political parties. The PNDC hopes that the District Assemblies will be the beginning of a decentralized political power structure that will not revert back to the political abuses of the past. Whether it will actually succeed is unclear, and it would not be unreasonable for it to take years for any kind of local government system in Ghana to be created.

The implications of the PNDC being unable even to develop an approach whereby it gains a constituency among workers has important ramifications for the structural adjustment program. Clearly, the political logic of structural adjustment programs is that if a government is able to get through the immediate crisis posed by devaluation and the elimination of subsidies and price controls, it will be able to garner increased political support in the long term as the economy improves. However, given how reluctant the PNDC has been to consult with the TUC or develop viable symbols around which workers could rally, even if workers' incomes do begin to improve, it is hard to see how those gains will translate into political support for the Rawlings regime. Thus, even if the economy should improve, the regime will remain isolated from the urban population and with the unnerving habit of occasionally lashing out and trying to impose behaviors that might have been volunteered by the unions had they been properly consulted.

## ■ Conclusion

The Ghanaian experience suggests that earlier examinations of the political implications of structural adjustment programs fundamentally misunderstood the dynamics of economic reform. It has not been the case in Ghana, or many other countries, that the short-term shocks imposed by stabilization programs have ignited wide-scale popular protests threatening to the regime. In Ghana and elsewhere in Africa, the chances of wildcat strikes igniting urban popular protest are low and can be further decreased by skillful government policies. However, the Rawlings regime has not been able to develop noticeable support for its policies despite an exceptional economic performance over the last few years. Indeed, the very factors that enabled the regime to impose such a tough reform program initially now hinder its ability to reach out and develop new constituencies. Since there is no popular basis for the PNDC's reforms, the regime will continue to have to impose them by force, and there is a good chance that the economic recovery program will not survive beyond the life of the current government.

## ■ Notes

1. Elliot J. Berg and Jeffrey Butler, "Trade Unions," in James S. Coleman and Carl G. Rosberg (eds.), *Political Parties and National Integration in Tropical Africa* (Berkeley: University of California Press, 1966), p. 348.

2. Robert H. Bates, *Markets and States in Tropical Africa: The Political Basis of Agricultural Policies* (Berkeley: University of California Press, 1981), p. 31.

3. Ibid., p. 33.

4. Richard Sandbrook, "The Political Potential of African Urban Workers," *Canadian Journal of African Studies* 11, no. 3 (1977), p. 425.

5. St. Clair Drake and Leslie Alexander Lacy, "Government Versus the Unions: The Sekondi-Takoradi Strike, 1961," in Gwendolen M. Carter (ed.), *Politics in Africa: Seven Cases* (New York: Harcourt, Brace and World, 1966), p. 110.

6. Richard Jeffries, *Class Power and Ideology in Ghana: The Railwaymen of Sekondi* (Cambridge: Cambridge University Press, 1978), p. 197.

7. Richard Jeffries, "The Labour Aristocracy? Ghana Case Study," *Review of African Political Economy*, no. 3 (May–October 1985), pp. 68–69.

8. Jon Kraus, "Strikes and Labour Power in Ghana," *Development and Change* 10, no. 2 (April 1979), p. 281.

9. Bill Freund, *The African Worker* (Cambridge: Cambridge University Press, 1988), p. 108.
10. Jeff Crisp, *The Story of an African Working Class: Ghanaian Miners' Struggles, 1870-1980* (London: Zed Books, 1984), p. 183.
11. Ibid., pp. 183-184.
12. Jim Silver, "Class Struggles in Ghana's Mining Industry," *Review of African Political Economy*, no. 12 (May-August 1978), p. 86.
13. Jeffrey Herbst, "How 'Soft' Is the State in Africa: The Case of Exchange Rate Reform in Ghana," 1989. Mimeo.
14. For instance, on December 5, 1984, the *People's Daily Graphic* reported a devaluation, and the accompanying story on the page concerns an announcement from the Ministry of Fuel and Power that fuel prices were increasing because of the new exchange rate.
15. *People's Daily Graphic*, January 14, 1986.
16. *The Pioneer*, January 16, 1986.
17. *West Africa*, January 13, 1986, p. 78.
18. World Bank Staff, "Removing Price Controls in Ghana," in Gerald M. Meier and William F. Steel (eds.), *Industrial Adjustment in Sub-Saharan Africa* (Washington, D.C.: Oxford University Press, 1989), pp. 180-182.
19. World Bank, *Ghana: Policies and Program for Adjustment* (Washington, D.C.: World Bank, 1984), pp. 12-13.
20. H. T. Mbiah, "Towards a National Wages Policy in Ghana," Tema, October 10, 1989, p. 3. Mimeo.
21. Interview, Accra, September 26, 1989.
22. Trades Union Congress, "Economic Survey of Ghana, 1980-1987," Accra, 1988, p. 32. Mimeo.
23. Interview, Accra, July 19, 1989.
24. See, for instance, Silver, "Class Struggles," p. 86.
25. Radio Broadcast to the Nation, December 31, 1981, reprinted in *A Revolutionary Journey: Selected Speeches of Flt. Lt. Jerry John Rawlings*, vol. 1 (Accra: Ghana Publishing Corporation, n.d.), p. 1.
26. *People's Daily Graphic*, January 8, 1987.
27. *The Echo*, January 31, 1982.
28. U.S. Department of Labor, *Foreign Labor Trends: Ghana* (Washington, D.C.: U.S. Department of Labor, 1989), p. 4.
29. See Ukandi Godwin Damachi, *The Role of Trade Unions in the Development Process with a Case Study of Ghana* (New York: Praeger, 1974), pp. 47-56.
30. E. Hansen, "The State and Popular Struggles in Ghana, 1982-86," in Peter Anyang' Nyong'o (ed.), *Popular Struggles for Democracy in Africa* (London: Zed Books, 1987), p. 179.
31. S. K. Kwakyi, "A Study of Social and Political Struggles in Ghana Since 31st December 1981: A Case Study of TUC/Government Relations," honors thesis, Department of Political Science, University of Ghana, Legon, 1988, p. 30.
32. *People's Daily Graphic*, April 30, 1983.
33. *People's Daily Graphic*, May 3, 1983.
34. *People's Daily Graphic*, May 13, 1983.
35. Hansen, "The State," p. 181.
36. *People's Daily Graphic*, April 25, 1983.
37. Catholic Bishops' Conference of Ghana, *Statement on the State of the Nation* (Accra: Catholic Bishops' Conference, 1982), p. 2.

38. *People's Daily Graphic*, April 27, 1983.
39. Interview, Accra, September 26, 1989.
40. Interview, Accra, July 14, 1989.
41. Tony Killick, *Development Economics in Action* (New York: St. Martin's Press, 1978), p. 288.
42. Reginald Herbold Green, *Ghana* (Helsinki: World Institute for Development Economics Research, 1987), p. 23.
43. *The Pioneer*, September 21, 1984.
44. *The Pioneer*, November 5, 1984.
45. *The Pioneer*, January 22, 1986.
46. *West Africa*, January 13, 1986, p. 78.
47. Interview, Accra, September 27, 1989.
48. J. Y. Assasie, "CDRs and the National Economy," *The CDR Eagle Flies* 1, no. 1 (December 1986), p. 16.
49. Interview, Accra, July 25, 1989.
50. Quoted in Baffour Agyeman-Duah, "Ghana, 1982–1986: The Politics of the P.N.D.C.," *Journal of Modern African Studies* 25, no. 4 (December 1987), p. 635.
51. *People's Daily Graphic*, September 15, 1986.
52. Kodwo Ewusi, "Social Welfare Theory, Structural Adjustment Policies and Labour Responses in Africa," paper presented at the International Conference on Planning for Growth and Development, Legon, March 1989, p. 13.
53. World Bank, *Sub-Saharan Africa: From Crisis to Sustainable Growth* (Washington, D.C.: The World Bank, 1989), p. 222.
54. Henry Bienen and Mark Gersovitz, "International Debt and Political Stability," *International Organization* 39, no. 4 (Autumn 1985), p. 753.
55. Interview, Accra, September 27, 1989.
56. *West Africa*, February 25, 1985, p. 347.
57. Quoted in *People's Daily Graphic*, January 4, 1990.

# 10
# State Enterprises Divestiture: Recent Ghanaian Experiences

*E. Gyimah-Boadi*

This chapter reviews the progress of Ghana's divestiture program by the end of 1989, some five years after its inception. The divestiture of state-owned enterprises is a key component of the poststabilization phase of Ghana's Economic Recovery Program and Structural Adjustment Program (SAP II). Divestiture is consistent with the privatization thrust of the World Bank and IMF, and it accords with the prevailing ideological positions of leading Western European and North American governments. Divestiture has also been presented as a budgetary and managerial necessity in view of the manifest failures of SOEs. In addition, it is seen as a major means of promoting private local and foreign investment or, at least, demonstrating a retreat from statism and socialism. SOE divestiture is considered to be a crucial step if a government is serious about "rolling back the frontiers of the state."[1]

In this chapter I seek to highlight the impediments, especially the political and administrative ones, standing in the way of the successful implementation of this important program. I look at the history of SOEs in Ghana and the road toward divestiture, the process of divestiture and its achievements, and problems and prospects. In doing so I show that countervailing forces in the Ghanaian political economy (especially political and administrative ones) have acted to impede the divestiture program. This continues to be the case despite the presence of a relatively favorable climate for private investment (i.e., macroeconomic improvements brought about by the ERP/SAP, liberalization of currency and imports, and so forth) and the government's apparent new determination to court private investment.

## The History of SOEs in Ghana

Ghana's involvement with SOEs began during the colonial period, when the colonial government established a number of public utilities such as water, electricity, postal and telegraphic services, rail and road networks, and motor bus services on a rather limited basis and in what were mainly urban centers. However, the most significant developments in the establishment of SOEs in Ghana were to take place in the late colonial and post–World War II period, when the wartime West African Produce Marketing Board was replaced in 1947 by the colony-specific Cocoa Marketing Board, which was charged with the export marketing of cocoa, and, in 1949, by the Agricultural Produce Marketing Board, which was to handle the export marketing of palm kernels and coffee.

In the late colonial period, a number of public corporations came to be established for the purposes of promoting economic and social development. The Industrial Development Corporation (IDC) was established by Gold Coast Ordinance No. 38 in 1947 and charged with the duties of "securing the development of industry on the Gold Coast and for matters connected herewith." The Agricultural Development Corporation (ADC) was formed in 1951 (as a successor to the Gonja Development Company of 1949) to promote large-scale agricultural development in the country.

The 1950s and the early 1960s saw rapid expansion in the number of SOEs. The Nkrumah CPP nationalist government came to rely heavily on SOEs as instruments for the achievement of "socialist" goals. During this period, the government established state enterprises in various sectors of the economy, including commerce, agriculture, transport, construction, manufacturing, services, mining, finance, mass communications, and the Volta River Authority, a multipurpose agency. Under the National Liberation Council (NLC), the military junta that replaced the Nkrumah-CPP regime in the February 24, 1966 coup, there was a marked reduction in the emphasis on the use of the SOEs as instruments of rapid social and economic development. However, under the civilian-constitutional government of Kofi Busia and his Progress party, a few more SOEs were established. They included the Bast Fibres Board in 1970 and the Food Distribution Corporation in 1972.

There was a return to emphasis on SOEs under the second military administration of the National Redemption Council/Supreme Military Council headed by I. K. Acheampong. As part of its bid to "capture the commanding heights" of the economy, the Acheampong government undertook a partial nationalization of the Lonrho-owned Ashanti Goldfields Corporation, the Consolidated African Selection Trust (diamond mining), and the Ghana Bauxite Company; took complete control over foreign-owned companies such as the Loyalty Group of Companies (textile and garment manufacturers, farms, etc.), Fattal Brothers (auto and retail auto parts), and R. T. Briscoe (auto parts); established new SOEs such as the Meat Marketing Board and the Ghana National Procurement Agency; revived and expanded the activities of existing SOEs such as the Food Distribution Corporation; entered into joint ventures with local and foreign companies—the Kwahu Dairy Farms, Ghana Oil Palm Development Corporation (with the World Bank); and created multipurpose development agencies known as Regional Development Corporations for each of the regions of the country (nine at the time).

The roster of Ghana's SOEs was further extended in 1979 during the six-month interregnum and "house cleaning exercise" of Jerry Rawlings and the AFRC. The companies confiscated by the state during this period were A. S. Electrical Clips, Darkmak Farms, Darkmak Houses Properties, Ghanaian General Establishment, Ghanaian Marine and Industrial Maduries, Ghanaian Wood Industries, Kool Bottling Factory, Trans Africa Engineering and Motors, Tarek Trading Company, United Soaps Industries (Ghana), Whab Incandescent Lamps Enterprises, and West African Chemical and Metal Industries.

## ■ SOE Problems and Attempted Reforms in the Pre-PNDC Era

With very few exceptions, Ghana's SOEs initially have been plagued by poor feasibility studies and project planning and, after their establishment, by shortages of critical staff, overstaffing, inadequate capitalization, undue political interference, mismanagement, corruption, and inefficiency. As a result of such problems, and contrary to all expectations, the SOEs have constituted a drain on national budgets and have failed to contribute to the country's rapid social and economic development.[2]

Both the IDC and the ADC, on which much of Ghana's hopes for industrial development and agricultural modernization, respectively, were pinned in the 1950s, proved to be dismal failures and were to be liquidated in the early 1960s. The reports of various commissions of enquiry in the 1950s (e.g., Jibowu Committee,[3] Abraham Report[4]) and during the NLC period (de Graft Johnson Report,[5] etc.), as well as work done by various researchers such as Marvin Miracle and Ann Seidman[6] and Tony Killick,[7] present a sorry picture of poor performance, corruption, and mismanagement of government agencies in general and SOEs in particular.

To deal with the many problems facing the burgeoning SOE sector and to improve its performance, Ghanaian governments have initiated a variety of reforms. SOE reform before the ERP/SAP took three main forms: liquidation, divestiture, and, most commonly, reorganization.

Liquidations of problematic and nonperforming SOEs took place during the 1950s and the Nkrumah-CPP era. The unsuccessful Gonja Development Company was liquidated; so also were the ADC and the IDC. However, it is important to note that after liquidation, the functions of such companies were likely to be transferred to another government agency. The functions of the ADC, for example, were transferred to the State Farms Corporation.

As part of the NLC's ideological and economic program of retrenchment and liberalization, it initiated a program of SOE divestiture. Nonstrategic SOEs such as the State Metal Works, State Bakery, State Furniture and Joinery Corporation, State Tyre Services Corporation, and State Laundry Service were fully sold off to private investors, and the State Textile Manufacturing Company, State Match Factory, Tema Cement Works, and State Tobacco Products Corporation were partially sold. Foreign management was brought in to run the Sugar Estates and Units, and the rubber estates were transferred to joint ownership with the U.S. Firestone Corporation.

The NLC's program of divestiture (as well as other measures in the retrenchment and liberalization policies) ran into heavy public opposition, particularly from the Ghanaian press and sections of the intelligentsia. The NLC's attempt to sell off the state pharmaceutical company to Abbott Laboratories of the United States was especially opposed by the attentive public.[8] In the face of strong opposition to outright sale and joint ownership, especially with foreign investors, the NLC limited itself to reorganizational measures. All manufacturing SOEs were brought together under a corporate outfit called the Ghana Industrial Holding Corporation (GIHOC), established by NLC decree 207. GIHOC was charged with bringing order and rationalization in the utilization of scarce resources at the disposal of its divisions, which initially numbered twenty-four divisions but later were pared down to sixteen.

In general, Ghanaian governments in the period under discussion have tended to choose reorganization as the key instrument of SOE reform. Disappointed over the performance of the relatively infant SOEs of the "socialist-state-in-transition" period, the Nkrumah-CPP government established the State Enterprises Secretariat (SES) in April 1964 to exercise general supervision over state corporations, to ensure their efficient and profitable operations, and to look after government's interests in joint or mixed ventures (see Legislative Instrument No. 457). All nonmanufacturing state corporations in the sectors of mining, agriculture, trade, works, communications, etc., were put in the hands of the various sector ministries.

The proliferation of SOEs outside the umbrella of GIHOC in the 1970s (the Acheampong era) increased the need to create an outfit to exercise general monitoring and supervisory control over their operations and to advise government on appropriate ways to ensure profitability. The State Enterprises Commission (SEC), created by SMC decree 10 in 1976, was bestowed with both executive and advisory powers over all statutory boards and corporations. This included profit-oriented service organizations. In 1979, further reorganization occurred when the National Industrial Companies (NIC) was established. The NIC brought together a total of eighteen companies confiscated during the SMC (Acheampong) and AFRC (Rawlings) regimes. They included a vehicle assembly plant and workshop, an electrical fittings and accessories factory, estates, farms, etc.

## ■ SOE Reforms Under the PNDC

Like most previous Ghanaian governments, the PNDC has been concerned with the poor record of SOE performance and resentful of the heavy burdens they impose on the national budget. In the 1980s, most SOEs, including those that were commercially oriented, were not able to break even, let alone turn a profit.

SOE dependence on government subventions has been persistent, reaching 10 percent and 8 percent of government expenditures in 1982 and 1986, respectively. The SOEs have been unable to meet their tax obligations and pay social security contributions on behalf of their employees; nor have they been able to service government-guaranteed loans, on which virtually no interest or principal was being paid. In addition, SOEs are heavily indebted not only to the government but also to themselves. Some eighteen SOEs were said to be indebted to the government to an amount of ¢40 billion and ¢5.2 billion between themselves. Such a situation was declared untenable under the ERP/SAP's program of economic retrenchment and rationalization.

The PNDC has sought to reform SOEs through reorganization, as did previous governments. Managements have been reshuffled, performance contracts have been signed between the government and management in SOEs such as COCOBOD, foreign management consultants have been contracted for key SOEs such as the Electricity Corporation of Ghana, and the government has been more insistent on applying the principles of profitability and break-even to SOEs, including service-oriented ones and public utilities.[9] The SEC has been reorganized, better provisioned, and given legal backing in PNDC law 170.[10]

By far the greatest emphasis has been placed on divestiture, though. Preparations for divestiture got under way in late 1984 when consultants from the Management and Productivity Institute (MDPI) and the Ghana Institute of Management Development and Public Administration (GIMPA) were given the task of collecting data on some 100 SOEs. This was followed in 1985 by the World Bank/United Nations Development Program (UNDP) sponsorship of the Dutch firm Borenschot-Moret-Bosboom (BMB) to do a diagnostic study of Ghana's SOEs.

In November 1985, the government set up an SOE "Task Force," which compiled a package of reform measures to be embodied in the second phase of SAP 1980–1988.[11] This task force, drawn from the SEC, MDPI, GIMPA, etc., reclassified SOEs into seven categories as follows:

1. SOEs to remain wholly state-owned
2. Wholly State-owned enterprises to be turned into joint ventures
3. Wholly state-owned enterprises to be sold
4. Wholly state-owned enterprises to be liquidated
5. Joint ventures to remain joint ventures
6. Joint ventures to be divested of state participation
7. Mergers (seven groups)

The Divestiture Implementation Committee (DIC) was appointed to manage the program. It was composed of the following personalities and institutions: William Adda, PNDC secretary, executive chairman of the SEC, as chairman; K. G. Erbynn, executive secretary, Ghana Investment Centre, as vice-chairman; K. B. Amissah-Arthur, PNDC deputy secretary, Ministry of Finance and Economic Planning; D. S. Boateng, PNDC deputy secretary, Ministry of Mobilization and Social Welfare; Dan Abodakpi, PNDC deputy secretary, Committees for the Defence of the Revolution; Pandit Adu, acting PNDC secretary, SEC; Shirley Ababio, PNDC secretariat, Castle; E. K. Gakakuma, executive secretary, Land Valuation Board; Henry Dei, chief administrator, Social Security and National Insurance Trust; E. J. A. Aryee, managing director, National Trust Holding Company; and representatives from the State Enterprises Commission, the Ministry of Industries and Technology, the Trades Union Congress of Ghana, the Bank of Ghana, and the attorney general's department. In addition, four foreign consultants from the firm of Price Waterhouse and two local consultants served the committee. (It is instructive to note that the private sector had no representation on this committee.)

The DIC's Technical Sub-Committee (TSC) collects and analyzes data, undertakes a valuation of the assets of enterprises, and prepares dossiers and briefing documents on enterprises earmarked for divestiture. The Negotiating Sub-Committee (NSC)—whose membership includes a DIC project coordinator, representatives of the relevant sector ministry, and the TUC—negotiates with prospective investors and informs the DIC of the offer made. The DIC then reviews the offer and submits its recommendations to the Committee of Secretaries for approval. The Committee of Secretaries then sends its decision to the PNDC for ratification. Thus, in theory at least, each sale must be approved and ratified by the Committee of Secretaries and the PNDC, respectively, before transfer documents can be prepared. (The

Committee of Secretaries or the PNDC may refer memoranda back to the DIC for clarification and adjustment.) This process is summarized in Figure 10.1.

Figure 10.1 The Organizational Structure of the Divestiture Program

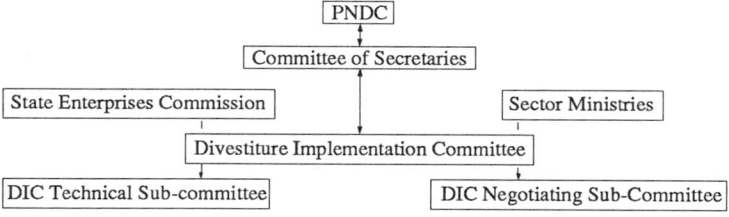

## ■ Scope of PNDC Divestiture Program

The PNDC's divestiture program is far more ambitious than the one attempted by the NLC in the 1960s. In addition to the forty-two Cocoa Board coffee and cocoa plantations whose sale was advertised in August 1987, the DIC advertised the sale of thirty-two SOEs in mid-1988. The list of SOEs under divestiture was expanded by the addition of another forty-six on the instructions of P. V. Obeng, chairman of the Committee of Secretaries, in July 1989; the field was left wide open, with the provision that applications for the purchase of SOEs not yet listed would be considered. The first list contained mainly moribund and loss-making state-established SOEs such as the State Fishing Corporation, Food Production Corporation, State Farms Corporation, and some ailing divisions of GIHOC. Most of the remainder of the SOEs belonged to the category of companies confiscated by the state from private owners in the NRC/SMC (Acheampong) and the AFRC (Rawlings) regimes: e.g., Famekwa Trading Company, DL Steel Company, and G. E. Amoah and Associates.[12] It is important to note that the second list included SOEs previously classified as "strategic" and thus not subject to divestiture, such as GIHOC steel, cannery, paints, bottling, and paper conversion divisions, as well as profitable SOEs such as the Achimota Brewery Company (formerly Tata Brewery, confiscated from Ghanaian owner J. K. Siaw in 1979 by the AFRC) and the Tema and Juapong Textile Printing companies, whose takeover from their multinational owners by militant workers in 1982 had been endorsed by the PNDC.[13] (The scope of the divestiture program is larger when one considers the fact that some of the companies listed have many subsidiaries and units. For instance, the State Farms and Food Production corporations have over 125 farm units that are to be sold separately.)

## ■ Achievements

The record of achievement reported by the DIC at the end of 1989 could only be described as meager. A total of thirty sales were reported to be "substantially completed," six of which—DL Steel Ghana, Metalico Ghana, Overseas Knitwear Fabrics, Two Worlds Manufacturing Company, National Industrial Companies Farms, and Nkwakubew Animal Husbandry—had reached the stage at which the approval of the Committee of Secretaries had been secured, and nineteen companies—including GEA and Associates, Victory Industries, GEA Packaging Gava Farms, Kwahu Dairy Farms, Ghamot Enterprises, Ghamot Textiles, Ghamot Motor Engineering, and GEA General Chemicals—were in various stages of liquidation, though assets had not been realized on any of them. Negotiations at the DIC level were reported to be complete for four companies, the DIC was in correspondence with investors on eleven others, and work was in progress on another twenty-nine (i.e., valuation reports and other TSC information packages were being prepared). Work had not started at all on twenty-two other companies on the list. In addition, investors had been given an interim right-of-entry to ten of the COCOBOD farms upon payment of a deposit of 10 percent of estimated value, pending the final valuation. (Only about ¢3.765 million has been realized so far from these interim sales.)

## ■ Key Problems Impeding the Implementation of Divestiture

Many technical problems, typical of sub-Saharan African countries, have bedeviled the effective and speedy implementation of Ghana's divestiture. These problems include the general weakness of the private sector,[14] the absence of stock markets and/or facilities for the routine trading of shares, and organized financial markets from which investment funds could be raised.

Among the specific technical problems facing the divestiture program is a shortage of technical expertise. The divestiture program was under way when a recruitment campaign was mounted to fill the critical vacancies on both the SEC and the DIC. Only one out of the many candidates interviewed opted to take up an appointment with the DIC. Poor conditions of service and lack of proper compensation explain the DIC's and SEC's inability to attract high-level technical personnel. In the event, the DIC and SEC have been forced to rely on "cheap labor," which consists of young, inexperienced, though enthusiastic, recruits from the National Service Secretariat, and expensive (and somehow impolitic) foreign consultants. The SEC and DIC continued to face personnel shortages in the critical areas of accounting, auditing, financial analysis, legal economics, and industry-specific specializations by the end of 1989. And Chairman William Adda was perhaps the busiest PNDC official, as chairman of SEC with cabinet status, head of the Monitoring Unit of the PNDC, and chairman of the board of Ghana Airways.

The program also faces a serious problem of data deficiency. Many SOEs are several years behind in preparing their statements of accounts and balance sheets (Loyalty Industries was said to be unable to prepare any statement of account for six years). Assets of some SOEs, especially the ones hastily acquired by the state through confiscations, have not been fully identified, nor have their legal titles been fully regularized. Assets of the State Fishing Corporation, one of the largest companies affected by the divestiture exercise, could not be fully identified for some time because they were spread all over the country, and there were fears that there could be some assets that remain unidentified.[15] Indeed, the last complete audited accounts of the State Fishing Corporation available to the DIC were from 1985. A DIC team that visited twenty-three agricultural SOEs earmarked for divestiture discovered that twenty-two of the units had no title deed whatsoever and that the lease on the remaining one had expired in 1980. By 1989, the DIC was still cataloging the farms of the Food Production and the State Farm corporations by size.

In some cases, the DIC knows only the size of the shares owned by the government and not the specific state organization that holds the shares on behalf of the government. The DIC had to conduct an investigation to discover that it was the parastatals—Bank for Housing and Construction and the National Investment Bank, as well as the United Africa Company (in which the government is minority owner)—that hold the government's share. In the case of those SOEs acquired through confiscation (often by radio announcement), no legal steps had been taken or instruments made to back the confiscations. In such instances, the DIC can only transfer ownership after the pertinent legal issues have been resolved.

Similarly, the DIC's information on the liabilities of the SOEs has not always been adequate and up-to-date. An earlier valuation of the assets of the State Fishing Corporation had taken place before the DIC discovered that the corporation had taken a Danish International Development Agency (DANIDA) grant of 3.2 million Danish kroner for rehabilitation. Some original landowners have suddenly appeared and demanded compensation and unpaid ground rents from the DIC and threatened to reenter the lands. In the case of Famekwa Trading Company, negotiations for its divestiture were in progress when it was discovered that the building that houses the company was not company property and that its lease was about to expire.

The divestiture program is faced with grave valuation problems, given the absence of a stock market and the prevalence of nonperforming assets in the numerous moribund SOEs. The DIC has been faced with the problem of choosing a consistent and rational basis for computing its values, in the face of the wide discrepancies between book and market values, as well as acquired acreages and cultivated acreages. These problems are compounded by the acute shortage of valuation resources. Despite the membership of the executive secretary of the Land Valuation Board (LVB) on the DIC, the board has been slow in preparing the valuation reports and/or vetting reports submitted by private valuers. The responsibility for bearing the cost valuations has been the subject of contention between the DIC and the Ministry of Finance and Economic Planning. Although the Land Economy Department of the University of Science and Technology was subcontracted to undertake the valuation of the forty-two COCOBOD plantations in 1988, no report has been submitted.

Delays in submitting valuation reports and identifying assets and liabilities have held up the preparation by the TSC of briefing documents and other information on SOEs that can form the basis for meaningful negotiations between the SNC and prospective investors. The DIC has therefore often been faced with the difficult choice of either proceeding with the negotiations with prospective investors on the basis of draft valuation reports (to keep investor interest alive) or waiting for vetted reports (and risk losing investor interest). The problem of delayed valuation reports is apparently the reason behind the granting of right-of-entry to the agricultural SOEs upon the payment of a 10 percent deposit of estimated value—a concession bound to raise questions of fairness and equity in the minds of skeptics.

The political factors impeding the quick and successful implementation of Ghana's divestiture program can be roughly subdivided into two specific political factors—general and PNDC regime. The general political factors include the following:

1. The legacy of history that has been passed down—i.e., the anticolonial struggle, with strong elements of economic nationalism, fostered by Kwame Nkrumah and his band of radical populists.[16]

2. The transcendental association of SOEs with economic independence, national sovereignty, and rapid industrial development is a positive association that appears to outlive the reality of chronic SOE failures.

3. The largely ineffectual divestiture of the NLC period (discussed above) and the strong opposition it aroused among sections of the Ghanaian intelligentsia have left bitter memories about the idea and practice of divestiture.[17] This is well summed up in an editorial in the *Daily Graphic*, which said: "'Privatisation' is a loaded word. It conjures up in some minds past experience where state owned businesses were disposed of cheaply behind closed doors to favoured cronies. It also raises issues of exploitative rich

businessmen taking over and kicking helpless workers into the street to face unemployment."[18]

4. SOE divestiture also has been persistently presented by radical Ghanaian and foreign scholars as an antinationalist, unpatriotic, proimperialist maneuver usually undertaken by compradorial and authoritarian ruling classes and regimes.[19] While the theoretical and empirical validity of such conspirational claims may be questioned, their impact on the thinking of policymakers and opinion leaders may be considerable.

Ghana's SOEs, moribund or active, are referred to in nationalist terms as "our patrimony" and "national heritage."[20] In this perspective, Acheampong's reckless brand of statism in the 1970s was more nationalist than the NLC's divestiture. It has taken extraordinary political courage on the part of the PNDC to broach the subject of divestiture; and the caution with which it has gone about tackling the implementation of the program reflects the government's deep sensitivity to nationalist opinion. Perhaps the desire to assuage nationalist feelings against denationalization explains why the government was careful to select only clearly moribund SOEs for divestiture on the first list. Only clearly "dead" or/and ailing SOEs could be parted with.

Group interests also count heavily among the factors arrayed against the divestiture program. Organized labor has fears that mass layoffs will come along with divestiture and that end-of-service benefits and other expensive items enshrined in various collective agreements may not be honored by the government or new owners of the companies. The TUC secretary-general's comments regarding divestiture in his May Day 1989 press statement are instructive. He only grudgingly conceded the necessity for SOE divestiture, saying:

> Organised labor has no quarrel with the divestiture of some selected SOEs, if the only way to resuscitate them is to seek partnership with private capital. After all a "dead" enterprise is of no benefit to any one.

He went on to state:

> Our concern with the enterprises earmarked for divestiture is the fate of our workers. . . . Such workers if they are declared redundant would want their benefits paid to them according to the provisions of their collective agreements.[21]

Sensitivity to the feelings and concerns of organized labor explains the heavy presence of the TUC on the DIC (three representatives, until the recent reconstitutions). The government has also sought to appease labor by suggesting that some government shares would be sold to workers in exchange for social security pension and other end-of-service benefits. It is not clear, however, whether workers are willing to sacrifice such benefits in exchange for shares in enterprises with uncertain prospects.

SOEs appear to have staunch defenders from among the ranks of an unlikely quarter—Ghana's middle class. Some members of Ghana's managerial and professional class (particularly those located in strategic places in the various SOEs who benefit from loose accounting systems and the siphoning off of parastatal resources) and participants in private business interests (some of them former employees of SOEs who enjoy "sweetheart" relations with these entities) may be found opposing divestiture. Many of Ghana's private businesspeople who support privatization in principle do strongly oppose the sense in which the program favors the well-capitalized, better-organized, and better-networked foreign investor. It has been difficult to combine Ghana's divestiture program adequately with the promotion of business indigenization goals, given the many problems that face the local private sector. The social and political base on which the divestiture program rests is rather weak. While the program poses an immediate threat to many established interests (labor, SOE managers and professionals, private suppliers and contractors, etc.), its potential benefits are indefinite and amorphous.

A significant number of divestiture-inhibiting political factors are rather specific to the PNDC regime. If the scope of the PNDC divestiture program is wide, it is partly because so many companies were added to the list of SOEs during the confiscation-happy days of the AFRC (1979) and, to a lesser degree, early 1982.

The populist beginnings of the Rawlings era—the anticapitalist sentiments, the threat to nationalize foreign private concerns, the endorsement of the takeover of the Ghana Textile Printing Company (Tema) and Juapong Textiles by militant workers in 1982, etc.—have created an initial credibility problem for the PNDC as it seeks to pursue neoorthodox conservative economic policies, including divestiture. This gap has been wide and the government has been compelled to bend over backward to win the confidence of business. The need to dip into "strategic" and previously reserved SOEs may have been suggested by the realization that the program lacked investor confidence.[22]

The contradictions of the past and the present PNDC are reflected in the schizoid tendencies of the government. A populist and oftentimes strident nationalist tendency, which seeks to cling to the coattails of Kwame Nkrumah and his political and economic legacy, exists side by side with a technocratic/pragmatic, sometimes conservative tendency, which is determined to do whatever is necessary to resuscitate the economy. Ebo Tawiah, member of the PNDC and chairman of the reconstituted DIC,[23] and Dan Abodakpi, PNDC deputy secretary and member of DIC, may be said to belong to the first camp, while Kwesi Botchwey, PNDC secretary for

Finance and Economic Planning (a former radical and member of the reconstituted DIC), and Tsatsu Tsikata, an influential PNDC adviser and operative (also a former radical), may be said to belong to the second camp. The combination of these sharply conflicting tendencies creates great ambivalence over a program whose implementation is normally extra complex. Thus, unanimity of voice and purpose eludes the program.

Fear of offending nationalist sensibilities and arousing worker opposition, as well as the desire to refrain from disturbing the shaky political status quo, may partly explain the lack of transparency surrounding the program. The addition of forty-six SOEs to the initial DIC list of thirty-two SOEs under divestiture was never publicized. Instead, investors interested in SOEs not listed are advised to contact the DIC or the sector ministry concerned. Underadvertisement certainly has detracted from the attractiveness of the divestiture program.

Nationalist sensibilities may partly explain the wishful preference that Ghanaian investors buy SOEs under divestiture. The DIC has expressed a preference for Ghanaians and organized bodies like the District Assemblies, cooperatives, and Mobisquads to buy COCOBOD plantations. The secretary for Local Government and other leading government spokespersons have been advising District Assemblies and unions to buy some of the companies earmarked for divestiture—without much regard for the DIC's other technical criteria of ability to buy and run such enterprises. There has also been talk of offering the government's share in various SOEs to the public—in order to cater to equity concerns and secure public goodwill. But it has not been easy to find sufficiently attractive (i.e., profitable and trouble-free) enterprises for such purposes.

On the other hand, it has been difficult for the government to resist the political use of the divestiture program. There have been reports that the sale of the State Hotels might be speeded up to enable new owners to undertake the necessary rehabilitation in time for the conference of Non-Aligned Nations scheduled to be held in Accra in 1991.

The high incidence of institutional disruption in the PNDC era has also taken its toll on the divestiture program. An important member of the DIC, Mr. Gakakuma, was lost to the DIC when he was summarily sacked from his post as executive secretary of LVB in December 1989. More disruptions were to come in early 1990 with the reconstitution of the DIC, the replacement of the "technocratic" William Adda by "populist" Ebo Tawiah as chairman of the DIC, and the dismissal of Pandit M. Adu, PNDC deputy secretary and member of the DIC, who had been very active in the Special Negotiating Sub-Committee of the DIC. Though the new membership is politically high-powered, its relative lack of experience in divestiture matters could have a negative effect on the DIC. In any case, the departing DIC membership carries away considerable accumulated divestiture experience.

Lack of coordination among the various agencies involved in the divestiture program has also impeded the implementation of divestiture. Even though many of the relevant government agencies have been represented on the DIC, they have not necessarily been forthcoming with specific information to guide DIC decisions. The information on foreign loans contracted on behalf of SOEs by the government has not always been revealed to the DIC on time; the attorney general's department could not always provide the DIC with information on the exact legal status of SOEs and their assets, etc.

The poorly defined structure of the PNDC government may also be causing the delays in approving and ratifying DIC decisions at the levels of the Committee of Secretaries and the PNDC. The DIC decision to sell off government interests in some twenty SOEs in mid-1989 was still waiting for final government approval by the end of the year. It is indicative of the political fluidity and unclear demarcation of authority that by the end of 1989 the DIC was still unsure about the political backing and status of the directive from P. V. Obeng/Committee of Secretaries adding forty-six SOEs to the list of enterprises subject to divestiture.

## ■ Conclusion

Divestiture is normally a technically difficult program. In Ghana, strong forces of a political, institutional, and administrative nature prevalent in the environment are exerting additional pressures on the program. The need to be mindful of the "political impediments to economic rationality"[24] in Ghana cannot be overstated. Political and administrative problems must be frontally addressed if Ghana's divestiture program is to make significant headway in the coming months and years.

## ■ Notes

1. For an overview of the privatization (divestiture) thrust of contemporary development ideology see Paul Cook and Colin Kirkpatrick, *Privatisation in Less Developed Countries* (Brighton, Sussex: Wheatsheaf Books, 1988). Also see Tony Killick, "State Divestiture as a Policy Instrument in Developing Countries," *World Development* 16, 2 (December 1988). An earlier statement is found in *Accelerated Development in Sub-Saharan Africa* (Washington, D.C.: World Bank, 1981), also known as the Berg Report.

2. For a discussion of the checkered record of Ghana's SOEs in the late 1950s and throughout the 1960s, see Tony Killick, *Development Economics in Action: A Study of Economic Policies in Ghana* (London: Heinemann, 1978), ch. 9. For a more recent assessment of SOE performance in Ghana and other African countries, see John R. Nellis, *Public Enterprises in Sub-Saharan Africa* (Washington, D.C.: World Bank, 1986).

3. *Report of the Commission of Enquiry into the Affairs of the Cocoa Purchasing Company* (Jibowu Commission), 1956.

4. *Report of the Commission of Enquiry into Trade Malpractices in Ghana* (Abraham Commission), 1964.

5. *Report of the Commission of Enquiry on the Purchase of Cocoa* (de Graft Johnson Commission), 1966. Also relevant are the following: *Report of the Commission of Enquiry into the State Furniture and Joinery Corporation* (Tsegah Committee), 1967; Report of the Investigation Team that probed the Star Publishing Company and the Guinea Press Limited (Quist Report), 1969; *Report of the Commission Appointed to Enquire into the Function, Operations and Administration of the Workers Brigade* (Kom Report), 1967.

6. Marvin Miracle and Ann Seidman, *State Farms in Ghana*, Paper No. 43, Land Tenure Center, University of Wisconsin, 1968.

7. Killick, *Development Economics in Action*.

8. Ibid., p. 313.

9. The *Daily Graphic* of April 12, 1989, reported that SOEs have signed such contracts with the State Enterprises Commission. Also see Daniel Swanson and Teferra Wolde-Semait, *Africa's Public Enterprise Sector and Evidence of Reforms* (Washington, D.C.: World Bank, 1989).

10. Details of the PNDC's managerial reforms and reorganization are reported in the opening address by E. A. Sai, member of the Committee of Secretaries and head of Civil Service at the Workshop on Public Enterprises and Privatization in Africa at the Ghana Institute of Management and Public Administration, Greenhill, May 1–7, 1989.

11. See *Progress of the Economic Recovery Program, 1984–1986 and Policy Framework 1986–1988*, prepared by the Government of Ghana for the Third Meeting of the Consultative Group for Ghana, Paris, November 1985, pp. 23–24.

12. The three main criteria used in this reclassification were (1) strategic importance, (2) profitability, and (3) net–foreign exchange earner/saver. A fourth criterion—the economic performance of the SOE—was not used due to "data and time limitations."

13. The GTP and Juapong Textile takeover is discussed in detail by Yao Graham in "From GTP to Assene: Aspects of Industrial Working Class Struggles, 1982–1987," in E. Hansen and K. A. Ninsin (eds.), *The State, Development and Politics in Ghana* (London: Codesria Book Series, 1989).

14. For a comprehensive overview of some of the historical, economic, and sociological obstacles to private sector development in Africa, see Paul Kennedy, *African Capitalism: The Struggle for Ascendancy* (Cambridge: Cambridge University Press, 1988).

15. The paucity of data on the State Fishing Corporation was possibly aggravated by the fact that its administration block was ravaged by fire in the early 1980s.

16. For details of economic nationalism in Ghana during this period (and after), see Roger Genoud, *Nationalism and Economic Development in Ghana* (New York: Praeger, 1969).

17. See Killick, *Development Economics in Action*, p. 313.

18. *Daily Graphic*, Editorial, June 2, 1988, p. 2.

19. The views expressed about NLC policies in Eboe Hutchful, "A Tale of Two Regimes: Imperialism, the Military and Class in Ghana," *Review of African Political Economy*, no. 11 (January–April 1980), reflect such sentiments. For a summary and critique of such views, see Robert M. Price, "Neocolonialism and

Ghana's Economic Decline: A Critical Assessment," in *Canadian Journal of African Studies* 18, 1 (1984); also see James C. W. Ahiakpor, "The Success and Failure of Dependency Theory: The Experience of Ghana," in *International Organization* 39, 3 (Summer 1985).

20. The latter phrase is actually used in a letter from the Interim Management Committee of the State Fishing Corporation protesting over the process of the company's imminent divestiture and signed by Dr. Morrison, chairman of the committee, dated July 19, 1989.

21. Statement by Brother A. K. Yankey, secretary-general of the TUC of Ghana at a press conference in Ho held to herald the celebration of May Day, April 26, 1989 (mimeo). The end-of-service liabilities for the State Fishing Corporation alone stand at ¢2 billion for a company worth roughly ¢8 billion. Also see P. B. Arthiabah, "Public Enterprises and Privatization in Africa: A Ghanaian Trade Union Viewpoint," presented at the workshop on Public Enterprises and Privatization at GIMPA, May 1–7, 1988 (mimeo).

22. This cue might have been picked up from a Tuesday, July 11, 1989, *Financial Times* (London) supplement on Ghana.

23. The new membership of the DIC is as follows: Ebo Tawiah, PNDC member as chairman; Kwesi Botchwey, secretary for Finance and Economic Planning; Tsatsu Tsikata, chief executive and chairman of the board of directors of the National Petroleum Corporation; K. G. Erbynn, chief executive of the Ghana Investment Centre; D. S. Boateng, secretary for Mobilisation and Social Welfare; Martin Amidu, deputy secretary for Justice; Dan Abodakpi, deputy secretary for CDRs; a representative of the armed forces; and a floating membership consisting of the relevant PNDC secretary and the general-secretary of the national union under which a particular enterprise falls. J. K. A. Wiredu of the Management Development and Productivity Institute heads the DIC secretariat. The absence of private sector representation in the reconstituted DIC is worthy of note.

24. This phrase is taken from the title of Jeffrey Herbst's paper "Political Impediments to Economic Rationality: Explaining Zimbabwe's Failure to Reform its Public Sector" (mimeo).

# 11

# Export Diversification Under the Economic Recovery Program

*Kwasi Anyemedu*

The promotion of exports is an important component of the Economic Recovery Program launched by the PNDC government of Jerry Rawlings in 1983. Elements of the macroeconomic program as well as of the structural and sectoral measures have been aimed at achieving a rapid expansion of foreign exchange earnings. This emphasis on exports reflects in part the current conventional wisdom about an appropriate development strategy. The dominant policy conclusion that emerges from mainstream development economics as well as from the IMF and the World Bank is that an export-oriented or outward-looking development strategy is more likely to generate rapid growth for developing countries. Yung Whee Rhee has observed that "three major empirical studies on the effects of foreign trade regimes on the economic growth of developing countries more or less reach the same conclusion; economies with outward-looking strategies have had better export performance and better economic growth than economies with inward-looking strategies."[1] The promotion of exports is consequently a fixture in all the structural adjustment programs being implemented by Ghana and other countries in Africa.

In Ghana, the case for export-orientation can also be made by reference to the heavy dependence of the Ghanaian economy on imports. Major sectors of the economy—manufacturing, mining, transportation, and energy—depend heavily on imported equipment and supplies. Agriculture is less dependent on imported equipment and supplies, but there is a growing dependence on imported fertilizer and pesticides. Consequently, there has been historically a very strong relationship between the growth of the economy and the availability of foreign exchange. There is universal agreement, for instance, that one of the key elements of the economic crisis that engulfed Ghana in the 1970s and early 1980s was a severe shortage of foreign exchange that led to what has been called the "import strangulation" of the economy. In view of this, an improvement in the capacity to earn foreign exchange has been seen to be an indispensable condition for economic recovery.

Though dominant, the policy conclusion that export-orientation is good for growth and development is not universally accepted. In the African context, the ECA has cautioned against, in particular, "indiscriminate promotion of traditional exports," citing among its possible dangers an oversupply that could lead to a fall in prices.[2] The current very depressed levels of commodity prices show that such dangers cannot be ignored. But even those who point out the dangers of enthroning exports as the prime mover of development recognize that for a small country such as Ghana the continued expansion of exports is an unavoidable necessity. Thus, Adebayo Adedeji approvingly quotes Paul Baran to the effect that "the costs of development in a small country, poorly endowed with energy and material resources, will be increased and growth held back unless it is prepared to take full advantage of the international division of labor."[3] Similarly, Lance Taylor, while recommending that poor countries concentrate on internally oriented development, concedes that in a small country more openness is inevitable. He suggests that the constraint of small size, which makes openness unavoidable, "may bind at a population of (say) 20 million—surely no less."[4]

Even if export promotion is accepted as an appropriate development strategy for Ghana, the dependence on one crop—cocoa—for such a high proportion (60–70 percent) of Ghana's foreign exchange earnings has long been recognized as undesirable. In 1919, Governor Gordon Guggisberg told the Legislative Council of the Gold Coast, "We have put all our eggs in one basket. The cocoa baskets are full. What about the other baskets if anything gets wrong with the cocoa crop or the cocoa market?"[5]

Although monocrop export dependence has long been known to be undesirable, and governments of Ghana since colonial times have favored a policy of "export diversification," there has been no precision about the meaning of the phrase. Tony Killick observed that "the precise meaning of diversification is rarely stated. . . . At a minimum it involves a reduction in the share of cocoa revenue to the total. More ambitiously, it could mean a declining share in total exports of primary products, implying the processing of raw materials before export and creating entirely new levels of manufactured exports."[6] Others would go even further and require not only diversity in commodity composition but also in the direction of trade, in the markets to which the exports are consigned. Thus, the ECA sees export diversification for African countries not only in terms of increasing shares of processed and manufactured goods in exports but also in the "refocusing" of these exports on African markets.[7]

However it is defined, the policy of export diversification in Ghana up to the launching of the ERP had been unsuccessful. In 1983, cocoa accounted for more than 60 percent of total foreign exchange earnings, and primary commodities (cocoa, timber, gold, diamonds, and manganese) accounted for about 90 percent of total export receipts.

In the rest of this chapter, I will review the policies and institutional arrangements that have been employed to increase non-cocoa export earnings during the ERP. Two subsectors of the non-cocoa export sector—gold and "nontraditional exports"[8]—will be emphasized. The performance of these subsectors as well as future prospects will be analyzed. The definition of export diversification used in this discussion is the "minimum" one, i.e., a reduction in the share of cocoa earnings in total export earnings; but performance in relation to diversifying commodity composition and market destination will also be analyzed. I will show that the export promotion and diversification program under the ERP has been modestly successful.

## ■ Policies and Institutional Arrangements in Support of Exports Under the ERP

### ☐ Improved Economic Incentives

When the ERP was introduced in 1983, Ghana had an exchange rate that was grossly overvalued and acted as a disincentive to all types of exports. The World Bank estimated in 1984 that the real effective exchange rate had appreciated by 816 percent by 1981, if 1973 is used as a base.[9] This problem of exchange rate overvaluation has been addressed during the course of the ERP. Beginning in April 1983, there were many devaluations of the cedi, and since September 1986, Ghana has been operating a system of market-determined exchange rates. Initially, there was a two-tier foreign exchange market consisting of an administratively determined rate (window I) and an auction-determined rate (window II). Under this two-tier system, the window I rate applied to earnings from cocoa and residual oil and import payments on government debt contracted before January 1, 1986. All other external transactions channeled through the official banking system were settled at the window II rate. The two markets were unified in February 1987.

Effective February 1, 1988, foreign exchange bureaus have been established with the approval of the Bank of Ghana. These bureaus are authorized to deal in eight major currencies: the U.S. dollar, the pound sterling, the deutsche mark, the CFA franc, the Japanese yen, the Swiss franc, and the Canadian dollar, though there is an effective market for only the first four. Each bureau fixes its own rates according to demand and supply conditions. Currently (June 1990) the auction rate is about ₵328/US$1, and the Forex Bureaux rate about ₵345/US$1. The exchange rate in April 1983 was ₵2.75/US$1, and the massive depreciation brought about by these developments has greatly increased the attractiveness of exports.

Exporters are also permitted to retain part of their export proceeds in external accounts to defray foreign exchange costs associated with their business. The rates of export retention are 5 percent for log exports, 20 percent for other traditional exports, and 35 percent for nontraditional exports. Rates of retention outside these rates are permitted in specific cases (e.g., to meet repayment obligations arising from foreign loans). The retention scheme has been received favorably by exporters and constitutes a major inducement to export production.

☐ *Specific Export Promotion Measures*

*Nontraditional Exports*
In addition to instituting an exchange rate policy that gives incentives to exporters, the government has taken other measures to promote nontraditional exports. Among these measures is the reinvigoration of the Ghana Export Promotion Council. Under new and energetic leadership, the council has stepped up publicity to increase awareness of export prospects among the Ghanaian business community and the public at large. It has organized schools and seminars on various issues related to exports and organized trade fairs to link Ghanaian exporters with prospective importers of Ghanaian products. Under its auspices, technical assistance from international organizations is given to various groups of export producers such as furniture makers and pineapple producers.

The government offers fiscal concessions to nontraditional exporters. There is a system of duty drawbacks under which up to 95 percent of duty aid on imported inputs used to fill export orders can be refunded. In addition, there is no sales tax on manufactured goods destined for export markets. (The current standard sales tax rate is 22.5 percent.) With respect to corporate taxes, there is a graduated rebate on tax liability ranging from 20 percent to 50 percent, depending on the proportion of total production exported. As was already indicated, nontraditional exports are given a preferred rate with respect to the retention of export proceeds.

*Gold*
*Fiscal concessions.* In 1986, the PNDC promulgated the Minerals and Mining Law (PNDC law 153), which offered enhanced fiscal incentives and benefits to the mining industry. Mining operators pay income tax at the rate of 45 percent, as compared to 55 percent previously. That law also provided quite generous capital allowances. Holders of mining leases are entitled to (1) depreciate a capital allowance of 75 percent of the capital expenditure incurred

in the year of investment and 50 percent in subsequent years, (2) carry forward losses in each financial year not exceeding the value of the capital allowances for the year, (3) take investment allowances of 5 percent, and (4) capitalize all expenditure on approved reconnaissance and prospecting when the holder of a mining lease starts development of a commercial find. Other benefits conferred by the law are as follows:

1. Exemption from payment of customs duties on plant machinery, equipment, and accessories imported specifically and exclusively for the commencement of the mineral operations. Additional relief from the payment of customs and excise duties may also be received after establishment.
2. Personal remittance quota for expatriate personnel free from any tax applicable to transfer of external currency out of Ghana.
3. Retention of not less than 25 percent of exchange earnings by mining operations for the acquisition of machinery and equipment, spare parts and raw materials; debt servicing; and dividend payment and remittance in respect of quota for expatriate personnel. The Minerals Law also provides for the free transferability in foreign currency for (a) dividends or net profits attributable to the investment of such convertible currency; (b) payment of loan servicing where a foreign loan has been obtained by the holder for mining operations; and (c) remittance of foreign capital in the event of the sale or liquidation of the mining operations of any interest attributable to foreign investment.

The law fixes royalties on minerals produced at the rate of not more than 12 percent or less than 3 percent of the total value of mineral produced, but the secretary of Finance, on the advice of the Minerals Commission, may defer wholly or in part royalty payable on any mineral for as long as the secretary is satisfied that it is in the national interest and in the interest of the production of such a mineral to do so.

*"Regularization" of small-scale gold mining.* Indigenous Ghanaians (Gold Coasters) were from the beginning (about 1860) quite actively involved in gold mining in the country. David Kimble reports that the pioneer of the modern mining industry was a Thomas Hughes of Cape Coast, who imported some heavy machinery and commenced working in Western Wassaw but who in 1861 was forbidden by the chief to exploit a rich vein he had discovered.[10] The rich and famous Obuasi mines were originally discovered by a group of indigenous concessionaires, including J. P. Brown, J. E. Ellis, and J. E. Biney, who subsequently transferred their rights to E. A. Cade, the founder of Ashanti Goldfields Corporation.

From the beginning of the twentieth century, however, modern gold mining became an exclusively European preserve. In addition to difficulties that the indigenous operators faced in mobilizing the substantial capital resources required for modern mining, these operators were hampered by legislation enacted in the colonial era that remained on the books right up to the PNDC era. Thus, under the Mercury Ordinance (Cap. 184) of 1935, it was illegal for any person to attempt to import any mercury into the country, possess, buy, sell, or transfer any mercury except under license. As T. E. Anin has pointed out, such licenses were rarely if ever granted to the natives of the Gold Coast.[11] Possession of gold was illegal. There was no institution of licenses for small-scale gold operators such as existed for diamond miners. Thus, although small-scale gold mining was carried on for years, it was effectively illegal.

On April 19, 1989, the PNDC promulgated the Mercury Law (PNDCL 217), which repealed the Mercury Ordinance (Cap. 184). While PNDCL 217 maintained the requirement of a license for importation of mercury, it made provision for licensed small-scale gold miners to purchase from licensed mercury dealers such reasonable quantities of mercury as may be shown to be necessary for the purpose of their mining operations.

The Small-Scale Gold Mining Law (PNDCL 218), also of April 19, 1989, provides that licenses may be granted to Ghanaian citizens of eighteen years and above to undertake small-scale gold mining. Such small-scale gold miners are to be exempted from the payment of income tax and royalties for a period of three years. The law provides for licensed dealers to buy and deal in gold and provides further that "a person shall be presumed to be lawfully in possession of gold until the contrary is proved." PNDC laws 217 and 218 thus legalized or "regularized" small-scale gold mining that Ghanaians had carried on illegally for many years.

By PNDC law 219 of April 19, 1989, the Diamond Marketing Corporation established in 1963 was converted into the Precious Minerals Marketing Corporation and charged with the responsibility for purchasing and marketing precious minerals (gold and diamonds) from small-scale operators in Ghana and promoting the precious minerals in Ghana. The Precious Minerals Marketing Corporation has registered buying agents who purchase gold and diamonds from the small-scale operators on its behalf.

## ■ Response to the PNDC's Policies and Initiatives

### ☐ Nontraditional Exports

The improved incentives and the promotional efforts of the Export Promotion Council have generated considerable response from a large number of small exporters engaged in a wide array of export products. In 1988, for example, there were 727 exporters dealing in 123 export items. Although the value of nontraditional exports is still not very significant, as Table 11.1

Table 11.1 Value of Nontraditional Exports (1978–1988) in US$ Million

| Year | Unprocessed Agricultural Products | Processed and Semiprocessed Products | Total | % of Total Exports |
|---|---|---|---|---|
| 1978 | 2.25 | 28.05 | 30.30 | 2.97 |
| 1979 | 5.55 | 15.43 | 20.98 | 1.86 |
| 1980 | 3.58 | 52.48 | 56.06 | 4.45 |
| 1981 | 4.90 | 8.07 | 12.97 | 1.57 |
| 1982 | 5.72 | 22.67 | 26.39 | 3.27 |
| 1983 | — | — | 5.45 | 1.19 |
| 1984 | — | — | 6.65 | 1.11 |
| 1985 | — | — | 19.70 | 3.36 |
| 1986 | 13.03 | 1.36 | 14.39 | 1.98 |
| 1987 | 17.82 | 10.14 | 27.96 | 3.40 |
| 1988 | 27.10 | 15.24 | 42.34 | 5.00 |

*Sources*: 1978–1985, from the Foreign Operations Department, Bank of Ghana; 1986–1988, from Ghana Export Promotion Council.

indicates, there have been quite impressive increases in value over the last few years.

## Product Composition

Exports of nontraditional products are categorized into three broad groups: agricultural, processed and semiprocessed, and handicrafts. The relative percentages of these categories of exports in recent years have been as follows:

|  | 1986 | 1987 | 1988 | Jan.–Sept. 1989 |
|---|---|---|---|---|
| Agricultural | 74.9 | 67.2 | 63.4 | 61.3 |
| Processed and Semiprocessed | 24.9 | 32.6 | 36.0 | 38.1 |
| Handicrafts | 0.2 | 0.2 | 0.6 | 0.6 |

Agricultural products constitute the biggest item of nontraditional exports, but their relative importance has been declining gradually with a corresponding increase in the relative weight of processed and semiprocessed products in total nontraditional exports. The most important agricultural exports are tuna fish, cocoa waste, kola nuts, and pineapples. Important processed and semiprocessed exports are furniture and parts, salt, rubber, canned tuna, and aluminum products.

## Market Destination

The advanced industrialized countries of Europe and North America take the bulk of Ghana's nontraditional exports, as they do the traditional exports. In terms of the value of these exports, the United States appears as the single most important destination of Ghana's nontraditional exports, but its imports are limited to frozen tuna fish. The United Kingdom serves as a market for virtually all of Ghana's nontraditional exports and is dominant in a number of items. It takes over 50 percent of pineapple exports, over 97 percent of yam exports, and about 90 percent of furniture exports.

Ghana's neighbors in the West African subregion constitute an important market for nontraditional exports. Among the more significant exports that go to this market are aluminum products (utensils, sheets, and coils), salt, and fresh kola. The subregion also served as a market for a wide range of miscellaneous manufactured products such as electrical cables and fittings, footwear, soap, watch straps, egg trays, ice cream, napkins, toilet rolls, and food-processing machines. African countries outside West Africa are noticeably absent as markets for Ghana's nontraditional exports, although Libya has emerged as a significant destination for pineapple exports in the last two years.

## ☐ Gold

The improved incentives to the mineral sector, the regularization of small-scale gold mining, and a general improvement in the investment climate in Ghana have produced increased activity in gold mining at three levels: new mines, small-scale mines, and existing mines.

### New Mines

Numerous private Ghanaian and foreign investors have since the promulgation of the Minerals Law applied for reconnaissance and prospecting licenses. As of December 1989, five new companies had actually been granted mining leases, signifying that these companies had established the existence of gold in commercial quantities in the areas in which they had been prospecting and had been given permission to commence exploitation. (Approval had been given for the issue of leases to two others.) In mid-1988, one of these companies, Southern Cross Mining, opened the first new mine in Ghana in over forty years. Southern Cross is currently producing about 34,000 ounces per year, and its production is projected to reach 100,000 ounces by 1994. Two other companies, Terberebie Goldfields and Canadian Bogosu Resources, are expected to start production by 1991. The other two companies with mining leases are expected to be in operation by 1993.

### Small-Scale Mining

Small-scale mining operators have responded to the regularization of small-scale mining with considerable enthusiasm. As of October 1989, eighty-four individuals, twenty-seven companies, twenty-six cooperatives, and twenty groups (other than cooperatives) had been granted mining licenses. The

Precious Minerals Marketing Corporation had purchased in the period between April and December about 9,000 ounces from the small-scale operators. The estimated production of small-scale gold miners is about 50,000 ounces per year, and the majority of operators have apparently not been reached by the new arrangements. It is expected that with time more miners will register more buying agents so that a greater proportion of the small-scale miners' output will be sold through legal channels.

*Rehabilitation and Expansion of Existing Mines*
Rehabilitation projects financed, in part, by the World Bank have taken place in the two mines in existence at the time of the launching of the Economic Recovery Program. The State Gold Mining Corporation began its rehabilitation in 1986 with funding from the International Development Association. It also benefited from the Export Rehabilitation Technical Assistance Project, which enabled it to engage the services of a Canadian management contractor. The rehabilitation program managed to stop the decline in production, which bottomed at 35,000 ounces in 1985; current production is around 50,000 ounces.

A major rehabilitation program was also started at the Ashanti Goldfields Corporation, owned jointly by the Ghana Government (55 percent) and Lonrho (45 percent). The program, which began in 1985, had the objective of increasing production from an output of 243,000 ounces in 1985 to 400,000 ounces in 1991. In 1989, the company produced 337,000 ounces, and the output of 400,000 ounces was expected to be reached in 1990, ahead of schedule. The rehabilitation and expansion program cost about $160 million, with $45 million provided by the International Finance Corporation (IFC) and the rest from internal cash flow.

In 1987, the company embarked on another project to mine low-grade oxide deposits through a surface mining operation and recovery through heap leaching. The project is expected to cost $93 million, with the IFC providing $60 million and the AGC providing the remainder. It is a reflection of the confidence with which the IFC views the prospects at AGC that it is not only producing two-thirds of the project's financing, but is providing the funding solely on the strength of the AGC's balance sheet and without a government guarantee. The expectation is that AGC's output will reach the level of 700,000 ounces by 1994.

■ Has Export Diversification
Under the ERP Been a Success?

In 1988, exports of cocoa beans and products accounted for about 51 percent of total export earnings, down from the 1983 figure of about 60 percent. There are reasons to believe that the share of cocoa in export earnings will decline further in the coming years. There are good prospects for gold output to reach about 1,000,000 ounces by 1995. The Ghana Minerals Commission projects output at about 1.5 million ounces by 1995. Cocoa output in the medium term may average around 300,000 tons per annum. At current (June 1990) prices, gold output of 1,000,000 ounces will yield about $350 million and cocoa output of 300,000 tons about $390 million. The prices of both commodities are currently at historically low levels, and forecasts of future prices with respect to both commodities are notoriously difficult.[12] Given the projected outputs of the two commodities and that of timber products (which, under ERP, has shown export earnings increases from about $15 million in 1983 to an estimated $105 million in 1988, and are projected to reach $140 million by 1991), it seems likely that the share of cocoa earnings in total foreign earnings will be substantially below 50 percent by 1995. This is roughly consistent with the World Bank's "base case scenario" under which cocoa's share of total export earnings is expected to fall from 60 percent in 1987 to 40 percent in 1991 (and through 1995). As the Bank points out, "this reflects both the impact of poor prospects for cocoa prices and the structural adjustment of the economy which would lower Ghana's dependence on this commodity in spite of the recovery in output."[13] It is worth emphasizing that the projected decline in the share of cocoa in total earnings is not due to a neglect of cocoa in the course of the ERP. The output of 300,000 tons assumed for the key projects is double the output of 150,000 tons achieved in 1983.

Therefore, with respect to the definition of export diversification used in this discussion, there is a real prospect that ten years from the launching of the ERP, the structure of exports will have been sufficiently altered to reduce the share of cocoa substantially from the 80 percent of earnings in Guggisberg's time (1919–1927), and also from the share of the average of 60 percent over the past thirty years.

How has the export diversification drive done with respect to the more ambitious objective of increasing the share of processed export earnings and refocusing export trade on Africa? Processed and semiprocessed export products account for only about 2 percent of total export earnings, and Africa provides a market for only about 4–5 percent of Ghana's exports. It is unlikely that this picture will change dramatically over the next five years, although the situation can be expected to improve gradually. Quite vigorous efforts are being made to attract foreign direct investment into processing for exports. Current efforts are being concentrated in agroprocessing, especially of cocoa and fruits, fish processing, and furniture manufacturing. The Ghana Investment Centre and the Multilateral Investment Guarantee Agency (MIGA) of the World Bank have recently organized jointly a conference in

Accra on the promotion of foreign private investment, with emphasis on investment in the above-mentioned areas.

There are also many initiatives to increase the share of exports going to other African countries, especially countries of the West African subregion. Some of these initiatives are within the program of economic cooperation being implemented by the members of the Economic Community of West African States (ECOWAS). Beginning in January 1990, ECOWAS members are implementing a program of trade liberalization under which tariffs on trade in processed goods from member countries are to be phased out over the next four to six years.

In the past, poor transport and telecommunication facilities have hindered trade within the subregion. In the course of the ERP, Ghana's roads leading to its neighbors to the east and west have been greatly improved, and part of the road to its northern neighbors has similarly been rehabilitated. Microwave radio links have been established with all Ghana's neighbors, thus doing away with the anomaly whereby telephone and other telecommunications links with neighbors had to transit through London and Paris.

There have, of course, been problems and setbacks. In particular, the credit squeeze, which has been part of the macroeconomic policies of the ERP, has hit very hard the small-scale export sector, and exporters of some processed products such as furniture have not been able to fulfill export orders because of their inability to obtain the necessary working capital to produce the requisite volume of output. Lack of technical knowledge, especially in such areas as styling and packaging, have also prevented processed exports from reaching the levels that they might otherwise have attained. For instance, although Ghana-made chocolates are of very high quality, it has been difficult to break into the major markets because of the poor quality of the wrappers.

All in all, export promotion and export diversification have to be counted as part of the modest successes of Ghana's structural adjustment efforts. Total export earnings have almost doubled since 1983, and there is a good prospect that the share of cocoa in total export earnings will be significantly reduced in the next few years.

## ■ Notes

1. Yung Whee Rhee, *Instruments for Export Policy and Administration: Lessons from the East Asian Experience* (Washington, D.C.: World Bank, 1985), p. 9. The empirical studies that Yung Whee Rhee cites are the following: (a) For the World Bank—Bela Balassa and Associates, *The Structures of Protection in Developing Countries* (Baltimore: Johns Hopkins University Press, 1971), and Bela Balassa, *Development Strategies in Semi-Industrial Economies* (Baltimore: Johns Hopkins University Press, 1982); (b) For the OECD—I. Little, T.

Scitovsky, and M. Scott, *Industry and Trade in Some Developing Countries: A Comparative Study* (London: Oxford University Press for the OECD, 1970); (c) For the National Bureau of Economic Research (NBER)—Jagdish Bhagwati, *Anatomy and Consequences of Exchange Control Regimes* (New York: NBER, 1978), and Anne O. Krueger, *Foreign Trade Regimes and Economic Development: Liberalization Attempts and Consequences* (New York: Columbia University Press for the NBER, 1978).

2. Economic Commission for Africa, *African Alternative to Structural Adjustment Programmes* (AA-SAP), 1989.

3. Paul Baran, quoted in Adebayo Adedeji, "Special Measures for the Least Developed and Other Low-Income Countries," in Ernest H. Preeg (ed.), *Hard Bargaining Ahead: U.S. Trade Policy and Developing Countries* (New Brunswick: Transaction Books, 1985), pp. 152–153.

4. Lance Taylor, *Economic Openness—Problems to the Century's End* (WIDER Working Papers, 1988), p. 67.

5. Quoted in Walter B. Birmingham (ed.), *A Study of Contemporary Ghana* (Evanston, Ill.: Northwestern University Press, 1966), p. 33.

6. Tony Killick, "External Trade," in Birmingham, *A Study of Contemporary Ghana*.

7. Economic Commission for Africa, *African Alternative to Structural Adjustment Programmes* (AA-SAP), 1989.

8. Nontraditional exports in Ghana are defined as exports other than cocoa, timber, and minerals (which include gold, diamonds, bauxite, and manganese) in their raw forms. They thus include non-cocoa agricultural exports as well as processed and semiprocessed exports. In a comment on an unpublished paper of mine, Tony Killick pointed out that this definition appeared to distinguish between minor and major exports rather than between traditional and nontraditional (new?) exports. The definition for Ghana is based on a distinction between exports for which Ghana has been known and other exports, even if these exports are not new. This definition appears quite adequate to me.

9. World Bank, *Ghana: Policies and Programs for Adjustment* (Washington, D.C.: World Bank, April 1984), p. 4.

10. David Kimble, *A Political History of Ghana* (Oxford: Oxford University Press, 1967), p. 15.

11. T. E. Anin, Gold in Ghana (Accra: Selwyn Publishers, 1987), p. 15.

12. Some forecasts have nevertheless been made. The World Bank's *Price Prospects for Primary Commodities, 1988* forecast gold prices at $380/ounce in 1990, at $360/ounce in 1991, and at $420/ounce in 1995. In the case of cocoa, price forecasts were for $1,600/ton in 1990 and $1,900/ton in 1995.

13. World Bank, *Ghana: Structural Adjustment for Growth*, Report No. 7515-GH (Washington, D.C.: World Bank, 1989), p. 65.

# 12

## Reviving Cocoa: Policies and Perspectives on Structural Adjustment in Ghana's Key Agricultural Sector

*Cord Jacobeit*

Adam Smith once said, "when you are tempted to speculate in cocoa, lie down until the feeling goes away." While this may still be good advice for today's bargain hunters at futures markets in New York or London, African producers—loaded with hundreds of thousands of metric tons of quality beans—find it hard to follow. When a country depends on cocoa exports as one of the few reliable and substantial sources of badly needed foreign exchange, there is no short-run alternative to the sale of the crop on the world market and the hope for remunerative prices.

With the International Cocoa Organization's (ICO) buffer stock practically full and world market prices falling for the fifth consecutive year, however, most producers find themselves facing a situation in which they are exporting more cocoa for less revenue. Since their last peak in the mid-1980s, cocoa prices have lost more than 50 percent of their former level. The end of the 1980s saw nominal prices as low as those at the beginning of the 1970s. After a 30 percent rise in cocoa prices during the spring of 1990, hope was high that the worst was over in a cycle that takes about a decade to get from one peak to the next. In addition, much is expected from the changes in Eastern Europe, where the introduction of significant economic reforms could translate into higher standards of living, thereby increasing substantially the demand for goods not much seen before, such as cocoa.[1] However, some observers believe that structural change in the cocoa-producing countries and developments in the major consuming countries will translate into world market prices likely to be very low for much longer than has been observed in the past.

How does the story detailed above affect one major African producer who managed to double cocoa production within half a decade since the mid-1980s? For Ghana, cocoa has been and will be the key sector in agriculture, if not the economy in general. The commodity was introduced at the end of the last century and quickly became the engine of growth in the southern half of the colony. For some sixty-six years—between 1911 and 1978—Ghana was the world's leading cocoa producer, capturing a market share of close to 40 percent and setting the widely accepted quality standard for the product. Today, cocoa still contributes some 50–60 percent of the country's export revenue, nearly 20 percent of government revenue, and approximately 7 percent of Ghana's GNP. By providing income and jobs for some 265,000 cocoa farmers and their families in the southern half of the country, cocoa has an important multiplier effect for the economy. Nevertheless, cocoa production has experienced tremendous ups and downs. After having reached a total production of more than 500,000 metric tons by the mid-1960s, an absolute low of 159,000 tons was reached in the 1983/84 season.

The story of the decline in Ghana's cocoa economy provided both the impetus and the empirical data for much creative work on how government policies in Africa's agricultural sectors ought not to be tailored. Detrimental policies included overvalued exchange rates, price policies designed only to extract surplus from the sector for the benefit of the urban bureaucracy and nonagricultural sectors, and parastatal intervention in the marketing and handling of the crop. As a result of these adverse conditions, tens of thousands of tons of Ghana's cocoa were smuggled annually to neighboring Côte d'Ivoire by the end of the 1970s. After 1983, however, these policies were significantly changed, and—judging by the results—they have turned the depleted cocoa sector around.

This leads us to our two major questions: How was the upsurge in cocoa production achieved after 1983, and what are the prospects for this key sector, given that world market prices are now not sufficiently high to support the cocoa economy? It is to be hoped that an examination of these questions will not only produce some interesting insights into structural reform in Ghana's cocoa sector, but will also be of interest to other African cocoa producers, if not to African agricultural development in a much wider context.

To answer these questions, I will examine the cocoa sector in three parts. In the first part of the chapter, I will deal with structural adjustment for the economy in general and the policy reforms in the sector introduced by the Rawlings administration after 1983. I will examine the impact on cocoa and the social and political implications of these policies in rural areas. In the last two parts of the chapter, I will look at the current situation and the perspectives arising from a depressed world market. What will determine the future price trend: cyclical or structural factors, and—depending on our answer—what steps should be taken by an African cocoa producer?

## ■ Policy Reforms in the Cocoa Sector After 1983

The Rawlings administration, like many of its predecessors, made a variety of promises to cocoa farmers: "It is with your agricultural products that we buy cars, lorries, petrol, kerosene, matches, soap, sugar, etc., and yet how many of you really have access to these things? We intend to reverse this trend and bring back the wealth of the country to where it belongs, in the rural area."[2] This administration differed from some of its predecessors in that it started to keep its promises, at least in the cocoa sector. A different pricing policy and other supportive measures reversed a downward spiral that, in the decades after independence, had slowly squeezed the life out of the economic backbone of rural areas in the southern half of the country.

Looking at the policy reforms after 1983, one would have to distinguish between those benefiting the economy in general and those specifically slanted toward the cocoa sector. The initial phase of the Economic Recovery Program launched in 1983 with the support of the World Bank and the IMF provided urgently needed imports for the rehabilitation of the shattered infrastructure. Improving, rebuilding, and rehabilitating trucks, roads, railways, and ports benefited the economy in general and the export sector, including cocoa, in particular. Prior to 1983, the lack of spare parts, the gradual destruction of transport capacity and the transport system in general, and deteriorating conditions in the storage facilities had led to a situation where cocoa had started to rot on every step of the marketing chain. With the massive investment in infrastructure and rehabilitation, one necessary precondition for the revival of the cocoa sector was met: farmers were once again connected with the world market. The same holds true for the macroeconomic reforms embarked upon after 1983 along the lines of the standard IMF remedy. The devaluation of the grossly overvalued cedi, the policy of fighting inflation, and that of maintaining budget austerity helped to shift the internal terms of trade back in favor of the tradable sectors of the economy, such as cocoa.

Although these reforms were a precondition for a revival of the cocoa sector, other policy measures were directly aimed at cocoa. As Table 12.1 illustrates, between 1981 and 1988 significant nominal producer price increases translated into a trebling of real producer prices for the first time in decades. After a time lag due to the nature of the crop, the supply response began to be felt from 1988 onward.[3] Cocoa output increased from the low of 159,000 metric tons in the 1983/84 crop year to 305,000 metric tons in 1988/89.

Ghana's share in the world market for cocoa rose by some 2 percent to 12.5 percent. While one can certainly attribute part of this increase to the benign climatic conditions experienced after the devastating drought and

Table 12.1 Cocoa Producer Prices and the Development of Real Income, 1957–1988

| Year | Nominal Producer Prices ¢/ton | Barter-Terms of Trade of Cocoa Farmers (1975=100) | Income-Terms of Trade of Cocoa Farmers (1975=100) | Producer Prices US$/ton Exchange Rate | |
|---|---|---|---|---|---|
| | | | | Official | Black Market |
| 1957 | 276 | 231 | 164 | 386 | |
| 1958 | 264 | 221 | 123 | 370 | |
| 1959 | 236 | 192 | 132 | 330 | |
| 1960 | 220 | 177 | 151 | 308 | 308 |
| 1961 | 220 | 167 | 195 | 308 | 308 |
| 1962 | 220 | 153 | 169 | 308 | 308 |
| 1963 | 216 | 144 | 164 | 302 | 387 |
| 1964 | 198 | 117 | 138 | 277 | 341 |
| 1965 | 182 | 85 | 128 | 255 | 278 |
| 1966 | 152 | 63 | 70 | 213 | 71 |
| 1967 | 198 | 89 | 90 | 235 | 119 |
| 1968 | 247 | 103 | 115 | 242 | 113 |
| 1969 | 279 | 108 | 97 | 274 | 159 |
| 1970 | 294 | 111 | 122 | 288 | 170 |
| 1971 | 293 | 101 | 105 | 285 | 194 |
| 1972 | 338 | 106 | 130 | 256 | 201 |
| 1973 | 387 | 103 | 114 | 332 | 258 |
| 1974 | 487 | 109 | 101 | 423 | 181 |
| 1975 | 578 | 100 | 100 | 502 | 290 |
| 1976 | 679 | 75 | 79 | 590 | 210 |
| 1977 | 976 | 50 | 42 | 848 | 106 |
| 1978 | 1,599 | 47 | 33 | 1,056 | 178 |
| 1979 | 3,314 | 64 | 42 | 1,205 | 212 |
| 1980 | 3,941 | 50 | 36 | 1,433 | 270 |
| 1981 | 5,333 | 31 | 21 | 1,939 | 203 |
| 1982 | 12,000 | 58 | 35 | 4,363 | 194 |
| 1983 | 16,667 | 36 | 17 | 4,832 | 218 |
| 1984 | 25,417 | 39 | 16 | 719 | 212 |
| 1985 | 45,073 | 63 | 29 | 834 | 300 |
| 1986 | 70,800 | 80 | 46 | 787 | 373 |
| 1987 | 112,500 | 91 | 38 | 732 | |
| 1988 | 152,500 | 94 | 62 | 757 | |

*Sources*: Calculated on the basis of *Ghana Quarterly Bulletin of Statistics*; IMF, *International Financial Statistics*; ICO, *Quarterly Bulletin of Statistics*; and *Pick's World Currency Yearbook*.

bushfires of the early 1980s, and to the higher availability of rural labor after the exodus from Nigeria, the effects of the aforementioned economic and direct financial reforms should not be underestimated. The Rawlings administration made a deliberate decision after 1983 to shift incentives and investments to the export sector, where cocoa was a major beneficiary. The production increase in the second half of the 1980s and the new plantings are ample evidence that cocoa farming has once again become worthwhile.

The economic and financial reforms were backed by institutional and managerial reforms in the state-run handling of the crop. In September 1979, the abuses listed in the investigative report of the Archer Committee led to the dissolution of the Ghana Cocoa Marketing Board. Grossly overstaffed, extremely corrupt, inefficient, and lacking motivated personnel, the Board was increasingly unable to perform its basic functions. Renamed the Ghana Cocoa Board (COCOBOD) and given a new legal basis in 1984, the Board underwent institutional reform (although it stopped far short of the radical reforms applied in neighboring Nigeria) aimed at putting cocoa marketing on a more commercial footing.[4] The key features of the reform included a greater role for private transport of the crop and COCOBOD's release of some 40 percent of its staff. The number of produce-buying stations was reduced from 4,279 (1981) to 3,118 (1984), and fifty-two of Cocobod's state-owned large-scale cocoa plantations were sold off. On every level of the marketing chain, efforts are being made to raise COCOBOD's performance and managerial efficiency.

The Akuafo Cheque System, which replaced the old cash system in 1982, was introduced at the point of purchase of the dried beans. In the past, the produce buying clerks had often held back cash payments, abused funds, and paid farmers with phony checks, thereby completely discrediting the old system. Under the new system, farmers are given a check signed by the produce clerk and the treasurer, which they can cash at a bank of their choice. As a result, the amount of money necessary for the entire operation and the possibilities for fraud have been reduced. Farmers are also now more closely linked to the rural banking system. This move coincides with the intention to drop all the state-run programs that provide farmers with credit facilities.

For cocoa, in particular, the new-found availability of imports that was brought about by the economic reforms translated into new chances to fight cocoa pests and diseases that bore heavily on overall production. Estimates put the annual loss due to diseases and insects in the 1970s and 1980s at as many as 130,000 tons. While there has been a general increase in the availability of cocoa-related inputs in the rural areas in recent years, cocoa farmers will soon have to become accustomed to paying for a hitherto subsidized service. Government subsidies on fertilizer and insecticides—which in the past were subsidized up to 90 percent of cost—will be phased out altogether. Farmers will also be charged for new cocoa pods for planting. However, since these subsidies existed only on paper for most farmers during the 1970s and much of the 1980s because the inputs were simply not there, the new cost-oriented policy will initially not make much of a difference.

What have been the social and political implications stemming from the reforms in the cocoa sector since 1983? At first sight, compared with neighboring Côte d'Ivoire, Ghana seems to have a more equal distribution in the size of its cocoa farms. Average cocoa farm size in Côte d'Ivoire is 6 hectares, and in Ghana is 2.6. However, a number of studies have found that the national average disguises a relatively high concentration in Ghana's cocoa sector, where a few farmers capture a disproportionate share of the total income, notably in Ashanti, Brong-Ahafo, and in the Western Region. In the course of the reforms, the larger farmers also found it easier to have access to newly available and subsidized inputs. Even after the phasing out of subsidies on inputs, larger farmers will be better able to afford the much-needed sprayers and insecticides. In sum, the reforms have disproportionately benefited the larger farmers. It can be argued, however, that this was intended by the Rawlings administration and certainly by the international donors. The World Bank pursues agricultural policies and projects everywhere in the developing world under which the larger and better farmers tend to do better. This is considered to be a normal part of structural change in the agricultural sector; whether it is justified in equity terms is a different issue altogether. Nevertheless, the marked increase in real producer prices after 1983 reached small farmers as well. Larger farmers whose economic and social centers of activities still lie in their local areas tend to spend additional income within the country, if not in cocoa then in other rural economic endeavors. With these reservations in mind, the reform package introduced at the beginning of the 1980s left cocoa farmers as a group the main beneficiaries, while leaving previously courted groups in society with a rebalanced burden to carry.

Was the administration able to capture a political reward from the cocoa farming community for these advantageous reforms? It is certainly no mere coincidence that the PNDC started the political drive for legitimized political bodies at the district level. The setting up of the District Assemblies in 1988 provided an opportunity to channel rural support into the ranks of the PNDC. As witnessed by the results of the election, farmers now play an important part in the new assemblies. However, when compared to two groups largely antagonized by the reforms—students and organized labor—cocoa farmers cannot be expected to provide a reliable basis of support for the PNDC when it comes to mobilization in times of need. General difficulties of organization and communication in rural areas persist; the often fatalistic attitude toward political influence in general will not be altered overnight by the District Assemblies; and the often hard and exhausting labor on the cocoa plantations will exclude a majority of cocoa farmers from active political participation. In addition, an inevitable reverse, or at least a break in the cocoa pricing policy because of the dictates of the depressed world market, might easily lead cocoa farmers to reconsider their political alliance.

## ■ The Current Situation:
### Near the Optimum Cocoa Production Level?

The second phase of reform in the cocoa sector started with the new five-year, $128-million cocoa rehabilitation project in November 1988. The project is cofinanced at concessionary aid rates by the World Bank and other donors. It will focus mainly on the Western Region—the area with the youngest and hence most productive trees and also the area closest to neighboring Côte d'Ivoire. While the price incentive to smuggle cocoa across the border has been substantially reduced—and might even be reversed with the cutting in half of the Ivorian producer price for the 1989/90 season—the road system in the Western Region is still hopelessly inadequate. For many cocoa farmers it is easier to sell to Lebanese traders from Côte d'Ivoire than to rely on the Ghanaian collection and transportation routes. Therefore, the bulk of the project's money will be spent to upgrade long-neglected routes already built and to construct 3,000 kilometers of new feeder roads.

The other focus of the project—besides the support for COCOBOD's drive for better management, cutback of subsidies, and higher efficiency—will be on increasing Ghana's productivity. With a production of some 300 kilograms per hectare (kg/ha), Ghana is far behind the results achieved on some plantations in Malaysia: 1,000 kg/ha is not the exception but the rule for the Southeast Asian newcomers on the world cocoa market. The logic behind this focus of the project is that increased yields can compensate for falling prices.

The increase in yields is expected to follow from the new emphasis on extension services, the research in and provision of drought- and disease-resistant, high-yielding cocoa varieties, and the training in more timely and more accurate application of inputs such as fertilizers and insecticides. The initial project proposals from the middle of the 1980s set an optimum target of 300,000 metric tons produced by 1991 under the five-year life span of the project. However, the expected target was achieved in the 1988/89 season, thereby adding to the glut on the world market. This leaves the new project and the cocoa sector in general with a number of unanswered and difficult questions that must be addressed in the second phase of structural adjustment: How can one achieve the optimum production level? Is further rural stratification acceptable and, if so, how much? If the objective of the pricing policy is to increase farmers' share above 60 percent of the cocoa world market price and reduce the share of the government, how are the loans from abroad—though largely on concessional terms—ever to be repaid? How can private interests be motivated to invest in marketing of the crop and in input supply services? How much government intervention in the sector is deemed necessary? What will be the future of the small processing sector of the cocoa industry, which operates today under great strain and has thus far been excluded from the project's attention? What happens if the price collapse on the world market assumes even more dramatic proportions?

Table 12.2 shows that until the middle of the 1980s the reform program in the cocoa sector provided additional stimulus for the strained government budget. This was, in fact, the economic rationale of the whole reform drive.

Table 12.2   Development of Cocoa Revenue for the Government, 1954-1986

| Year | 1<br>Cocoa Revenue in ₡ Millions | 2<br>Total Government Revenue in ₡ Millions | 3<br>Share of 1/2 (%) | | 4<br>Index of Real Cocoa Revenue (1975=100) | | 5<br>Index of Real Government Revenue (1975=100) | |
|---|---|---|---|---|---|---|---|---|
| 1954/55 | 81.2 | 161.8 | 50 | | 147 | | 101 | |
| 1955/56 | 33.9 | 128.8 | 26 | | 59 | | 78 | |
| 1956/57 | 29.5 | 98.8 | 30 | (39) | 51 | (89) | 59 | (77) |
| 1957/58 | 58.5 | 119.7 | 49 | | 101 | | 71 | |
| 1958/59 | 52.7 | 133.2 | 40 | | 88 | | 77 | |
| 1959/60 | 54.2 | 140.3 | 39 | | 90 | | 81 | |
| 1960/61 | 64.9 | 166.5 | 39 | | 102 | | 90 | |
| 1961/62 | 68.0 | 150.0 | 45 | (35) | 98 | (84) | 74 | (86) |
| 1962/63 | 55.2 | 165.0 | 33 | | 76 | | 79 | |
| 1963/64 | 43.4 | 245.0 | 18 | | 53 | | 104 | |
| 1965 | 21.4 | 284.0 | 8 | | 21 | | 95 | |
| 1966 | 9.5 | 115.7 | 8 | | 8 | | 34 | |
| 1966/67 | 34.6 | 235.3 | 15 | (17) | 32 | (38) | 75 | (74) |
| 1967/68 | 77.6 | 293.1 | 26 | | 67 | | 87 | |
| 1968/69 | 79.9 | 283.6 | 28 | | 64 | | 78 | |
| 1969/70 | 124.7 | 360.6 | 35 | | 97 | | 97 | |
| 1970/71 | 196.5 | 486.2 | 40 | | 139 | | 119 | |
| 1971/72 | 122.4 | 421.9 | 29 | (32) | 79 | (90) | 94 | (95) |
| 1972/73 | 96.4 | 391.7 | 25 | | 53 | | 74 | |
| 1973/74 | 173.0 | 583.0 | 30 | | 80 | | 93 | |
| 1974/75 | 279.7 | 810.5 | 35 | | 100 | | 100 | |
| 1975/76 | 179.8 | 869.8 | 21 | | 41 | | 69 | |
| 1976/77 | 269.0 | 1,151.6 | 23 | (29) | 28 | (47) | 42 | (55) |
| 1977/78 | 287.2 | 1,392.1 | 21 | | 18 | | 29 | |
| 1978/79 | 1,220.0 | 2,578.4 | 47 | | 48 | | 35 | |
| 1979/80 | 1,492.0 | 2,949.9 | 51 | | 39 | | 27 | |
| 1980/81 | 560.3 | 3,279.3 | 17 | | 7 | | 14 | |
| 1982 | — | 4,855.3 | — | (23) | — | (15) | 17 | (20) |
| 1983 | 2,800.0 | 10,240.9 | 27 | | 13 | | 16 | |
| 1984 | 4,509.0 | 22,641.0 | 20 | | 14 | | 25 | |
| 1985 | 8,861.0 | 40,311.0 | 22 | | 26 | | 40 | |
| 1986 | 14,000.0 | 73,600.0 | 19 | (21) | 33 | (30) | 60 | (50) |

Sources: A. Bequele, "Stagnation and Inequality in Ghana," in D. Chai and S. Radwan (eds.), *Agrarian Policies and Rural Poverty in Africa* (Geneva: ILO 1980); S. M. N. Dodoo, *The Tax of Cocoa Income in Ghana*, Thesis (Legon: University of Ghana, 1974); The World Bank, *Ghana: Policies and Programme for Adjustment* (Washington, D.C.: The World Bank, 1984); Republic of Ghana, *The PNDC Budget Statement and Economic Policy for 1986* (Accra, Ghana, 1986).

Note: The figures in parentheses in columns 3, 4, and 5 are averages for the preceding five years.

Huge resources and foreign loans devoted to the export sector were to provide additional much-needed foreign exchange for the economy and the treasury. Cocoa had to play this role because of the already-existing knowledge, multiplier potential, and—although heavily shattered—infrastructure that the traditional export was able to offer. However, the shortfall in projected revenue as a result of falling prices had already reached $180 million by

1989, thereby calling the entire reform endeavor into question. While at the beginning of the 1980s a revival of cocoa was one of the prerequisites for an overall revival of the economy, the situation a decade later clearly drives home the vulnerability of this strategy.

It is clear that prolonged success in the revival of Ghana's cocoa sector depends upon more favorable world market prices for the crop. While in the long run there appears to be a need to diversify into other nontraditional exports, a short-run alternative to cocoa is not available. Every attempt to start anything else in the immediate future would be met by almost equal uncertainties and would also require substantial initial funding to get started. Flowers, tropical fruits, and fresh vegetables for the markets in the European Community, for example, require an infrastructure—reliable communication networks, cold-storage depots, constant airlinks, etc.—that might attract transnational corporations. However, African producers, with their relatively high investment costs, find it hard to compete with producers from Southern Europe or from the Mediterranean.[5] Besides, everyone else in the cocoa- and coffee-producing world is thinking about nontraditional exports. Even after the initial efforts of the early 1980s, Ghana's infrastructure is still a long way from attracting significant direct foreign investment.

## ■ Perspectives: Cyclical or Structural Factors Determining Cocoa World Market Prices?

What are, after all, the chances that cocoa prices will rebound? As with most simple questions, there is no easy answer. Commodity forecasts by the IMF and the World Bank predict continuously depressed prices until the middle of the 1990s, when the seven- to ten-year cyclical pattern of cocoa production will have created a decline in world cocoa stocks. At the beginning of 1990, there appears to be some hope for producers: cocoa prices have risen by more than 30 percent from their previous fourteen-year low. The key question is whether we are already witnessing an end to the depressed prices or whether this is only a technical reaction, after which the market will rapidly come back to the underlying fact of supply surpassing demand. World cocoa stocks are now up to a record level of 7.6 months of annual consumption. At a level of £800/metric ton, cocoa production is a worthwhile and remunerative activity for the low-cost, highly productive competitors from Southeast Asia, but for most African producers this price level is still too low to survive for long.

What leads us to be cautious about any predictions of an early end to the cyclical drop to very low price levels? One consequence of the debt crisis has been that most LDCs short of funds have tried to increase production of their traditional exports. In addition to cocoa, coffee prices collapsed in July 1989, increasing pressure on some African producers already struck by the cocoa decline—Côte d'Ivoire and Cameroon, among others. On the supply side, this policy was clearly supported by the IMF and the World Bank, as illustrated in Table 12.3. In fact, Ghana's cocoa rehabilitation project was only one of many others in Africa funded by the international donor community. Funding ranged from cocoa monoeconomies (such as São Tomé and Equatorial Guinea) to countries like Cameroon and Togo, where cocoa is only one export crop among others.

The logic of this project policy is hard to follow,[6] given that in the early 1980s the Bank's own commodity forecast division announced depressed cocoa world market prices due to overcapacities in producing countries for much of the 1980s. In a situation where most producer countries have no alternative but to accept an offered project, the international donor community must make a stronger effort to coordinate and set priorities for products and places. Under present international economic conditions, only the more productive producer countries ought to receive support for continued output. Alternatives ought to be given more thought and support. Project policies do not operate in a vacuum; they exert an influence on the world market price level, no matter how small the expected incremental production increase might be. The only reaction the World Bank has shown thus far is to tailor more recent cocoa projects toward increased productivity. In addition, these projects no longer contain any massive replanting elements. Nevertheless, the apparent paradox of encouraging cocoa production in today's world market situation remains.

What are the factors on the consumption (demand) side that lead us to be cautious in our predictions about an early end to the cyclical dip toward low price levels? Technological progress has increased the use made of one unit of a raw material; changes in inventory management techniques have reduced the previously high necessity for larger stocks; health concerns increasingly suggest a lowered consumption of tropical beverages; the progress in bio- and genetic technologies has provided industry with a high number of substitutes that are constantly improved, such as vegetable fats in the production of chocolate. In sum, while we are not neglecting the arguments put forward to support the cyclical explanation for the price trend on the world cocoa market, there seem to be indicators suggesting that the pattern of the cycle may well have changed. If producers are forced to behave in line with this cycle and consumers are reducing their demand even beyond the existing low price elasticities, then it seems prudent not to anticipate a quick end to the depressed prices.

This leaves us with a less optimistic outlook not only for Ghana but for other African agricultural producers as well. Although the current situation does not provide major short-run alternatives unless the international donor community starts to reconsider its strategy and priorities, the widely

Table 12.3 Cocoa Projects by the World Bank and Other Donors Since 1980, in Millions of US$

| Year of Acceptance by World Bank/IDA | Country | Project Sum | Of Which World Bank |
|---|---|---|---|
| 1988 | Ghana | 128.0 | 40.0 |
| 1988 | Cameroon | 285.4 | 103.0 |
| 1987 | São Tomé and Principe | 21.8 | 7.9 |
| 1987 | Togo[a] | 33.2 | 17.9 |
| 1986 | Papua New Guinea[a] | 68.3 | 27.6 |
| 1985 | Equatorial Guinea | 16.2 | 9.3 |
| 1984 | Indonesia[a] | 369.8 | 154.6 |
| 1982 | Liberia[a] | 28.0 | 15.5 |
| 1981 | Dominican Republic[a] | 40.0 | 24.0 |
| 1981 | Malaysia[a] | 200.0 | 50.0 |
| 1981 | Indonesia[a] | 322.0 | 161.0 |
| 1980 | Western Samoa[a] | 20.6 | 8.0 |

*Source*: The World Bank, *Annual Report* (various issues).
*Note*: a. Projects supporting other tree crops (coffee, palm oil, etc.) besides cocoa

acclaimed blessings of structural reform in the traditional export sector probably will not lead to economic progress as soon as was initially expected.

# ■ Notes

The author wishes to thank Rodger Wegner, who worked on the chapter for Ghana in the forthcoming book *Der Kakaoweltmarkt* (The Cocoa World Market), edited by Rolf Hanisch and Cord Jakobeit (Hamburg: Institut für Überseeforschung, 1990). The general reference for data is the aforementioned book, unless otherwise indicated. The views expressed in this paper are the sole responsibility of the author.

1. Kenneth Dadzie, head of UNCTAD, recently suggested that the current cocoa consumption in Eastern Europe—some 300,000 metric tons per annum—may double over three years.

2. Jerry Rawlings, in his address to the Ghana Federation of Agricultural Cooperatives on February 2, 1983, reprinted in J. J. Rawlings, *Forging Ahead— Selected Speeches of Flt. Lt. J. J. Rawlings, January 1st, 1983–December 31st, 1983*, vol. 2, Tema, 1984, p. 43.

3. As a perennial crop with a three- to five-year gestation period, cocoa's short-term supply response is significantly lower than that of most food crops. The long-term response was found to be significant, even in Africa. For a summary of output changes to price changes in Africa, see World Bank, *World Development Report 1986* (New York and London: Oxford University Press for The World Bank, 1986), p. 68. However, it is also widely believed that nonprice factors are important explanatory factors, especially in the African context.

4. The Nigerian government decided to abolish the Nigerian Cocoa Marketing Board in June 1986, leaving the handling of the entire crop to private cocoa trading houses.

5. This is not to say that such a strategy does not work in the African context at all, as illustrated by the relative success Kenya was able to achieve in this field.

6. One is tempted, however, to locate one reason in the fact that most West African World Bank cocoa projects are handled by the same British consulting company that provides the expertise during the evaluation of the projects and runs the same projects during their life span.

# PART 4
# THE CHALLENGE OF INTERNATIONAL NEGOTIATIONS

# 13

# Negotiating Adjustment and External Finance: Ghana and the International Community, 1982-1989

*Matthew Martin*

The PNDC's negotiations with the international financial community have been—and still are—a key component in the political economy of Jerry Rawlings's Ghana. They have dominated economic policymaking since 1982 and will continue to do so in the 1990s. However, they have also been secret. In this chapter I use sources from behind the scenes to give a more detailed and accurate picture of the talks than appears in many previously published works.[1] I examine how the PNDC and the international financial community have overcome domestic political, administrative, and economic barriers to adjustment; faults in the design of programs; and foreign exchange shortage in order to implement adjustment. I ask what the negotiations tell us about the political economy of Ghana in the 1980s and its future in the 1990s.

## ■ How Adjustment Was Negotiated

Table 13.1 shows Ghana's principal adjustment loans in 1983–1989. The PNDC agreed to five IMF (Fund) programs: three standby loans in 1983–1986, simultaneous Extended Fund Facility (EFF) and Structural Adjustment Facility (SAF) loans in 1987, and an Enhanced SAF (ESAF) loan in 1988. The PNDC also signed more than twenty policy-based "program" loans with the World Bank covering economic sectors (agriculture, industry, finance, education, public enterprises, health), and many Bank loans for projects included policy conditions. How were these loans prepared and negotiated, and were they implemented?'

### □ Preparing Adjustment

Although the PNDC ostensibly designed its own economic recovery programs in 1983 and 1986, in reality their preparation was very different. In

Table 13.1 Ghana's Policy-Based Loans, 1983–1989

| IMF | Year | Amount (SDRm)[a] |
|---|---|---|
| Standby | 1983–84 | 238.50 |
| Standby | 1984–86 | 180.00[b] |
| Standby | 1986–87 | 81.80[b] |
| Extended Fund Facility (EFF) | 1987–90 | 245.40[b] |
| Structural Adjustment Facility (SAF) | 1987–90 | 129.86[b] |
| Enhanced SAF (ESAF) | 1988–90 | 368.10 |
| Total Committed 1983–1988 | | (SDRm)[a] 1204.06 |
| *World Bank* | | (US$m) |
| Reconstruction Import 1 | 1983 | 40.00 |
| Export Rehabilitation 1 | 1984 | 35.88 |
| Export Rehabilitation 2 | 1984 | 40.12 |
| ER 3 (Technical Assistance) | 1984 | 17.10 |
| Reconstruction Import 2 | 1985 | 60.00 |
| Health and Education | 1986 | 15.00 |
| Industrial Sector 1 | 1986 | 24.95 |
| Industrial Sector 2 | 1986 | 28.50 |
| Structural Adjustment | 1987 | 80.90 |
| Education Sector | 1987 | 34.50 |
| Structural Adjustment | 1987 | 14.66 |
| Agricultural Services | 1987 | 17.02 |
| Structural Adjustment | 1987 | 34.00 |
| Institutional Support | 1987 | 10.80 |
| PAMSCAD | 1988 | 10.60 |
| Financial Sector | 1988 | 100.00 |
| Public Enterprise Assistance | 1988 | 10.50 |
| Cocoa Rehabilitation | 1988 | 40.00 |
| Total Amount Committed 1983–1988 | | (US$m) 654.12 |

*Sources*: IMF and World Bank Annual Reports, 1983–89; Matthew Martin, *The Crumbling Facade of Africa's Debt Negotiations: No Winners* (London: Macmillan Press, 1991); John Toye, "Ghana's Economic Reforms and World Bank Policy-Conditioned Lending, 1983–88" (University of Sussex: Institute of Development Studies, March 1989, mimeo, draft).

*Notes*: a. It has not been possible to convert SDR loans into US$ because the date of loan disbursement was unknwn.
b. Loan partly canceled before end of program

1983, the PNDC had several highly qualified and committed economic staff to draft measures but also needed some World Bank advice. PNDC staff members spent a great deal of time compiling data requested by the Fund, which left little time to draft arguments about the political, administrative, or economic feasibility of measures. The Bank's more gradual, sensitive approach allowed more time to prepare arguments. Yet, the PNDC was so overworked in 1983–1984 that it prepared thoroughly on only the more controversial issues—notably devaluation, where it designed the multiple exchange rate system adopted in 1983. However, by 1985–1986, PNDC preparation was much improved, due to staff continuity and experience and to simpler government structures that allowed the preparatory team to report directly to Finance Secretary Kwesi Botchwey, the PNDC, and Rawlings.

This helped it draft a complete program, negotiate more assertively (notably on the foreign exchange auction), and gain several concessions from the IMF.

Meanwhile, the IMF prepared a complete draft program or "letter of intent," containing precise measures and targets. This tended to constrain the negotiations until 1986, with the PNDC having to argue for movement from the draft. In 1982–1983, the Fund regarded PNDC inflation, fiscal, and balance of payments data as faulty and estimated its own. Some Ghanaian policymakers were astonished by the estimates and resulting policy suggestions, which they saw as bearing no relation to the economy; this led to some disputes, with the IMF overruling PNDC figures. However, the drafts varied considerably: some IMF staff listened to PNDC and World Bank ideas and softened drafts, especially in 1983 and 1986–1987. The Bank also prepared draft programs. Though these defined broad negotiating topics, their less detailed conditions and less specific timetables left more room for flexibility. There were occasional disputes on the quality or meaning of data, notably price changes, but most were resolved amicably by joint Bank-PNDC teams.

The Fund, Bank, and PNDC concentrated on targets, dates, and wording of measures rather than on how to implement them. They had too little staff time to assess domestic political support for measures or how appropriate they were to Ghana's administrative or economic circumstances. This omission created problems for implementation. Nor did the three bodies prepare accurate data on how much foreign exchange would be available. This caused problems in talks on finance.

☐ *Negotiating Adjustment*

Many in the PNDC agreed with most principles of IMF conditions, including fiscal and monetary austerity and devaluation. They also agreed increasingly with Bank principles such as increasing the producer price of agricultural products, slimming down parastatals and the civil service, devaluing, and reforming the budgetary process. It was the scale, speed, and sequencing of measures that caused disputes.

The PNDC, IMF, and World Bank disagreed on the following issues:

1. *Price increases or decontrol* (notably on fertilizer, gasoline, and basic consumer goods). In 1981–1982, the PNDC fixed prices, burned down the main market in Accra to curb high prices, and controlled rents for workers' housing; the 1983 program introduced gradual price rises.

2. *Exchange rate.* The PNDC and Bank insisted on a multiple exchange rate as a transition to devaluation, aware that past devaluations had caused coups. Later they insisted on a foreign exchange auction mechanism for devaluation, to avoid government allocation of foreign exchange and to

remove the political problem of negotiating devaluation. The PNDC also achieved a semimanaged auction, partly because the IMF recognized that unmanaged auctions had failed in Uganda and Zambia.[2]

3. *Trade liberalization.* This was so sensitive that until 1986 the Fund and Bank concentrated on areas of agreement, such as simplifying tariffs and reorganizing import licensing to reduce delays. However, due partly to Bank sensitivity and gradualism, the PNDC agreed in 1986 to liberalize imports.

4. *Privatization.* This was initially highly controversial, and the Bank agreed to limit it to reforming parastatals in key export industries; but by 1987, with parastatals still draining the budget, the PNDC saw privatization as necessary and feasible. It agreed to sell thirty parastatals—though not COCOBOD.

5. *Monetary policy.* Although the PNDC agreed with tight monetary policy to fight inflation, by 1986–1987 it and the Bank felt that IMF credit ceilings were too tight and interest rates too high, reducing private sector investment. The Fund argued that stagnant investment reflected commercial banks' reluctance to lend because they had huge bad debts. It relaxed monetary targets only marginally; instead, the PNDC and Bank designed a financial sector reform program to improve bank accounting and solvency and to start a stock exchange to diversify investment channels.

6. *Fiscal policy.* The PNDC and Bank wanted to protect investment and some other budget expenditures, but the Fund insisted on lower budget deficits to reduce inflation. The availability of sufficient foreign exchange to raise budget spending and enable a budget surplus proved satisfactory to both sides.

7. *Import levels.* The PNDC and Bank saw higher imports as necessary for growth, while the Fund saw room to cut imports if their composition and the allocation of foreign exchange was rationalized, and insisted on cutting the current account deficit. Again, large foreign exchange inflows allowed both aims to be fulfilled.

Three factors decided the IMF and World Bank positions:

1. *Negotiations Within the Fund and Bank.* These were resolved by the strength and views of staff (missions, desk officers, and resident representatives in Accra) and departments and the backing they received from top management. IMF and especially Bank staff in Ghana, notably resident representatives and African department staff in 1982–1983 and 1986–1987, were generally flexible—in IMF parlance, "pragmatists" rather than "theologians." However, individual IMF staff members had a major impact because of the IMF's overwhelming power. "Theologians" exacerbated the 1985–1986 disagreements by presenting draft letters of intent as the only possible program. Even PNDC officials committed to reform resented such

actions.[3] In the Bank, the regional department had greater influence, producing more flexibility.

2. *Fund and Bank "institutional memory" of Ghanaian compliance with programs.* Before 1983, the IMF memory was negative; however, this allowed the government to gain some concessions by arguing that drastic measures would lead to political instability. PNDC fulfillment of programs improved its image, and in the 1986 disputes, IMF theologians could not convince senior management that the PNDC lacked the "political will" to implement reform. The Bank had no firm negative memory and therefore was consistently more open-minded about the PNDC's "will" to implement reform measures.

3. *Views of major Organization for Economic Cooperation and Development (OECD) governments* on the IMF and World Bank executive boards changed dramatically during the period 1983–1990. In 1983, the PNDC had few supporters. By 1986, Canada and the United Kingdom argued vociferously for concessions because of the PNDC's adjustment record and their trade and investment interests, and even U.S. and West German hostility waned (for more on OECD government views, see my later discussion on financing). Because of its adjustment record, Ghana became *the* "test case" for economic reform by 1985–1986, and the Bank board was especially anxious to sustain its adjustment by showing more flexibility. On the IMF board, this was largely offset by a harder attitude toward sub-Saharan Africa until 1986, due to program breakdowns and growing arrears to the IMF, which minimized concessions.

The Bank's limited influence on IMF programs during 1983–1986 partly reflected the procedure for Fund-Bank coordination. Fund and Bank increasingly decided upon an informal division of labor. The Fund negotiated monetary, fiscal, exchange rate, and external debt policy. The Bank discussed sectoral reform, trade liberalization, incentive policies, public expenditure details, public sector management, privatization, poverty, and social welfare. Yet, when there were Fund-Bank disputes, the IMF prevailed until 1986, due to three main factors: OECD governments and commercial lenders regarded the Fund as senior; the PNDC regarded IMF agreement as the priority; and Bank staff were often more divided than Fund staff.

Without access to PNDC preparatory documents, it is extremely difficult to judge which side "got what it wanted" in talks. However, a comparison of IMF draft letters of intent with final programs shows that until 1986, the IMF got 80–85 percent of what it wanted on its core monetary, fiscal, and exchange rate targets, against a norm in many sub-Saharan programs of 90–95 percent. Yet, this proportion varied: in 1983, and again in 1986–1987, it was only 70–75 percent, though the Fund had already given ground in preparation. The Bank settled for less of what it originally wanted (in this instance, measurement is less easy because many reforms were not precise targets).

### ☐ Implementing Adjustment

On the whole, the PNDC achieved an astonishing degree of compliance with Fund and Bank conditions for a period of six years.[4] In each IMF program, it fulfilled most fiscal, monetary, and exchange rate conditions. However, it missed some monetary targets and inflation and current account objectives. There were also problems during programs. In the 1983/84 and 1986/87 programs, midyear budget expenditure and monetary growth were well over target. In 1986, this largely reflected the PNDC decision, after popular protest, to reverse civil service wages and allowances cuts and reduce gasoline prices. There were few problems implementing World Bank conditions, because most were part of the government's own agenda. The fertilizer subsidy was not removed, though it was kept down by frequent price rises. The PNDC did not enforce user charges on drugs, and privatization and COCOBOD rationalization fell behind schedule.

Four main factors complicated implementation: domestic political problems, misdesign and misimplementation of programs, economic and administrative barriers to adjustment, and foreign exchange shortfalls. Conversely, the absence of these problems—or measures taken to overcome them—explain the PNDC's remarkable degree of implementation.

## ■ Overcoming Domestic Political Problems: Consultation Doesn't Pay

Adjustment programs interacted with the domestic political economy in two ways: (1) by affecting the composition, unity, and stability of the PNDC; and (2) by changing the relationship between government and the wider society. The programs' likelihood of success depended on whether they were appropriate to Ghana's political, economic, or administrative circumstances and on whether they had the intended effects on the economy.[5]

In 1981–1990, Ghana was governed by an unelected military government, headed by the PNDC under President Jerry Rawlings. Its public ideology was neo-Marxist revolutionary. How did such a government agree to a program with the IMF? The answer is that pragmatism prevailed—PNDC objectives changed over time, in response to economic and political pressures.[6] The most powerful motivation was the long-standing economic decline, to which there was no end in sight. In 1983, GDP had been falling for ten years, real wages were 80 percent lower than in 1975, and real imports were 80 percent below the 1981 peak. This was exacerbated by a sudden collapse in 1981–1982, partly due to a drought that brought severe food shortage (increasing the import bill), power shortage (reducing manufacturing capacity utilization), and fires (cutting timber and cocoa exports). The foreign exchange available for imports, including vital food and petroleum products, was drying up, and a million migrant workers were expelled by Nigeria and returned seeking jobs.

The PNDC had no initial intent to sign Fund or Bank programs. In fact, most members of the PNDC opposed IMF-style policies. The government took drastic alternative measures in early 1982, but these were powerless in the face of the dramatic collapse and extreme foreign exchange shortage. The government pursued a three-track strategy to mobilize extra foreign exchange, less as a result of a conscious policy decision than of conflicts within the PNDC. One group sought funds from non-OECD countries, but they provided only token loans and several advised the PNDC to go to the IMF. A second group initially sought loans from OECD countries without a formal IMF agreement, but even potential allies such as the Canadians and Standard Chartered Bank referred the PNDC to the IMF. The third group favored many IMF-style policies, partly because they saw no other option, and began to negotiate with the IMF in April 1982, when the impotence of independent measures was becoming clear.

The first two groups delayed agreement by approximately six months. When those most opposed to the Fund tried coups in 1982–1983, Rawlings had an excuse to purge almost all anti-IMF government members by the end of 1983. Several backed unsuccessful coup attempts in 1983–1985 but had no influence on economic policy. Most remaining senior politicians and officials saw no alternative to the IMF: they feared for government stability unless they produced some economic recovery.[7]

Once the PNDC agreed to a Fund program, several factors inside the government contributed to its ability to implement required measures. Internal divisions diminished in 1984–1986 and were unpublicized due to restraint by policymakers and government control of the media. Fund and Bank salesmanship convinced many officials and PNDC members that adjustment would allow rapid recovery and huge net flows of aid, bank loans, and foreign investment. A clear, simple policymaking structure also helped. The negotiating team was small, cohesive, and highly competent. It advised united pragmatic military leaders in the PNDC, who made decisions led by Rawlings. The military in turn supported the negotiators, giving them a broad mandate and retaining them during 1983–1986. Continuity enabled them to develop experience and the ability to negotiate and implement. Rawlings remained at the top, able to resolve or override division by making rapid decisions after consulting a few army officers. He exhibited great political shrewdness, cared about Ghana's economic future (though without formal economic training), and was not personally corrupt. He was highly pragmatic, seeing adjustment as the only way to raise extra foreign exchange. He was also prepared to be ruthless when he believed it was necessary, by detaining trade unionists, academics, or students, or overruling or sacking anti-IMF politicians or officials. For all these reasons, after 1984–1985 the PNDC largely avoided disputes inside the government (which were common in other sub-Saharan countries) over approving measures, and later their specific timetables, exact details, and implementation methods.

There were also countervailing negative factors. The team faced strain and overwork from talks within the government and with the Fund, Bank, and creditors, as well as from day-to-day economic management. They were acutely short of support staff and financial and technological resources, and these constraints were only marginally eased by the end of the decade. In addition, the team received few concessions from the Fund to assuage potential domestic political opposition to measures. Many IMF, Bank, and OECD government staff tried to convince a limited group composed of Rawlings, some members of the PNDC, and a core team of professionals about the efficacy of structural adjustment. Other politicians were often simplistically pigeonholed as "opponents" of reform, to be bypassed or replaced, or as "proponents," who could be relied on to implement reform without any concessions. The proven implementation ability of the PNDC encouraged some donor and IMF staff to dismiss domestic political opposition until 1986.[8] This behavior was something to which even proreform PNDC officials reacted negatively.

Opposition inside government accounted for the main implementation problems. The armed forces, politicians, and government officials had the most power to prevent or delay implementation—though coup attempts by some lower army ranks found little support in the face of army wage and benefit increases and new equipment. These individuals' interests were jobs, living standards, political stability, "rent" from existing policy (for example by selling import licenses), and government or armed forces prestige. But many also genuinely believed that IMF policies would not work. This applied particularly to reform or privatization of parastatals, including the COCOBOD, and to civil service wage or benefit cuts or redundancies.[9] The reversal of the civil service benefit cuts in 1986 reflected intragovernmental division. In turn, this was due partly to extragovernmental pressure and foreign exchange shortfalls, which made many in government begin to believe that adjustment's political problems outweighed its economic benefits.

The PNDC was able to implement conditions partly because it had little need to renege on them to pacify extragovernmental opinion. Many groups in Ghana backed or opposed adjustment (and especially the IMF) because of their interests and their belief in adjustment measures or the lack of an alternative, though no group was unanimous or favored or opposed all IMF conditions.[10] These groups were largely disorganized and disunited, and the many changes of government during the 1970s had disrupted their lobbying channels.

Multinationals, white and expatriate businesspeople, and large-scale farmers tended to support adjustment, from which most of them gained more access to foreign exchange. However, many local businesspeople gradually became disillusioned after 1985 as inflation and devaluation continued, tight monetary policy and the burden of bad debts on commercial banks constrained borrowing, and import liberalization subjected them to foreign competition. The other supporters were large- or middle-sized commercial farmers, who saw major income increases. Their power led agricultural reform initially to concentrate on providing foreign exchange and raising producer prices, rather than improving inputs, infrastructure, or storage. Smallholders were unorganized, had less influence on policy, and received less dramatic gains.[11]

Opposition came from trade unions, students, academics, the urban poor, and many in the middle class. Only in 1986, when they were joined by civil servants, lower army ranks, and students, did trade unions have a major effect, making political stability a major issue in Fund-Bank-PNDC talks and gaining a substantial increase in the minimum wage and the restoration of allowances. However, they were sufficiently vociferous in their protests to induce marginal minimum wage increases in other years and to lead the government to detain or deport union leaders.[12] Student and academic protests were quashed by closing the universities as often as the government believed necessary, trade unionists were detained, harassed, or deported, and the urban poor and middle class were unorganized.

Adjustment programs discouraged political participation and consultation. The PNDC launched campaigns to mobilize support for reform as the only viable and "revolutionary" route to recovery and to proclaim that it had designed the program, which mobilized mass support by urban workers and some students and academics in 1983-1984. It also had a "honeymoon period" during which it could blame past governments for the economic disaster, admit its seriousness, dismiss alternatives, and exhort people to tighten their belts. This was also a period during which the country was sick of coups and instability. During 1983-1986, these factors and the powerlessness or repression of dissent created a political "culture of silence" in Ghana. Although protests grew in 1986-1988 as many groups blamed the PNDC for their failure to reap the benefits of higher GDP, these had little effect on policy. Many other groups did not protest the PNDC's adjustment measures because they were benefiting from higher growth and real wages.

The government's one major attempt to consult and to mobilize rural support was the 1987-1988 local government election. Even a slower pace of adjustment and higher social spending could not guarantee a result favorable to the PNDC, because adjustment policies were not satisfying voter economic expectations. The PNDC resorted to banning political parties, appointing one-third of local government members, and emasculating their powers. The elections became centrally directed rather than participatory. If one assumes that most countries are divided over whether to follow IMF programs, and that many governments are reluctant to risk losing power by consultation or election, the unwelcome conclusion from Ghana's experience is that the less consultation a government allows, the better it will negotiate and implement adjustment as presently designed.

## ■ Overcoming Design, Economic, and Administrative Problems

An equally important conclusion is that Ghana's programs also produced economic "carrots" that reduced popular protest. As shown in Table 13.2, the adjustment programs (and associated external finance) helped to achieve major positive trends in Ghana's economy. Per capita GDP rose substantially and per capita consumption marginally. Exports and imports grew in real terms and as a percentage of GDP, and the current account deficit fell. Real wages and (as a percentage of GDP) gross fixed capital formation, savings, and investment all rose (though falling in 1987–1988). Budget revenue improved dramatically, producing a surplus in spite of higher spending.

These developments occurred because the programs were to some extent appropriate to Ghana's economic and administrative capacity for reform, and flexible implementation overcame inappropriate or misdesigned conditions. Such capacity was not a major issue in the international talks and, because of limited data and research, could not be identified by the IMF, World Bank, and PNDC until 1986. Even after that, nobody knew which exact policies would produce "adjustment with growth." Thus, adjustment measures had ample scope to be misdesigned or misimplemented, and this did occur in three main ways:

1. *Experimentation.* In several respects, programs "learned by doing," implementing measures that had never been tried in Ghana—such as user charges for health—with the negative effects described above.
2. *Incorrect sequencing.* Cutting budget spending on agriculture and subsidies on inputs and petroleum, in combination with higher imported input and consumer goods prices because of devaluation, reduced the use of inputs (especially fertilizer) and the profitability of food production, before farmers could respond to higher producer prices.[13] Similarly, tight credit ceilings and trade liberalization reduced capacity utilization before Bank measures to increase it could take effect.[14]
3. *Conflicting conditions* (either within IMF programs or between Fund

Table 13.2 Ghana—Main Economic Indicators, 1983–1989

|  | 1983 | 1984 | 1985 | 1986 | 1987 | 1988 | 1989[d] |
|---|---|---|---|---|---|---|---|
| Real GDP (% change) | –4.6 | 8.6 | 5.1 | 5.2 | 4.8 | 6.2 | 6.0 |
| Real per capita GDP (% change) | –7.0 | 5.9 | 2.3 | 2.6 | 2.1 | 3.5 | 3.0 |
| Real per capita consumption (% change) | –1.8 | 5.1 | 2.2 | 0.5 | 4.0 | 3.9 | 3.5 |
| Savings/GDP (%) [a] | 2.4 | 5.3 | 6.0 | 4.0 | 5.0 | 5.0 | 4.6 |
| Investment/GDP (%) | 7.8 | 6.9 | 9.6 | 9.7 | 10.8 | 12.3 | 14.1 |
| Inflation (CPI, %) | 122.0 | 40.2 | 10.4 | 24.6 | 39.8 | 31.4 | 29.6 |
| Money supply (M2, %) | 38.1 | 40.9 | 60.7 | 53.7 | 53.0 | 43.4 | 32.6 |
| *Budget*[b] | | | | | | | |
| Revenue/GDP (%) | 5.5 | 8.0 | 11.3 | 13.6 | 14.1 | 13.4 | 14.3 |
| Expenditure/GDP (%) | 8.2 | 10.1 | 14.0 | 14.3 | 14.3 | 14.2 | 15.2 |
| Deficit or surplus (%) | –2.7 | –2.1 | –2.7 | –0.7 | –0.2 | –0.8 | –0.9 |
| *Balance of Payments* (% change) | | | | | | | |
| Export value | –46.0 | 28.9 | 11.7 | 18.5 | 10.1 | 6.9 | –5.8 |
| Import value | –14.6 | 26.3 | 7.0 | 9.3 | 27.3 | 6.1 | 9.2 |
| Export volume | –27.9 | 2.0 | 21.1 | 10.8 | 7.7 | 12.3 | 16.1 |
| Import volume | –9.7 | 27.0 | 11.2 | 14.3 | 12.9 | 4.7 | 7.3 |
| Terms of trade | 6.2 | 30.3 | –5.9 | 12.5 | –8.3 | –3.9 | –22.2 |
| Current account deficit (% GDP)[c] | –3.4 | –2.8 | –4.2 | –3.9 | –5.0 | –5.1 | –7.0 |

*Sources*: World Bank 1989 Country Economic Memorandum and Consultative Group documents; Government of Ghana Ministry of Finance and Economic Planning; Bank of Ghana; and *Quarterly Digest of Statistics*.

*Notes*: a. Domestically generated savings (i.e., excluding aid grants)
b. Budget figures are narrow coverage, i.e., they exclude foreign aid tied to projects.
c. Excluding aid grants
d. Estimated data

and Bank). Devaluation pushed up the cost of debt service and other foreign exchange payments in the budget, causing lower rises in domestic spending. It also reintroduced petroleum and fertilizer price subsidies compared to world prices, breaching IMF conditions and making the IMF insist on more price rises. Small farmers and businesses were supposed to lead growth, but devaluation and tight domestic credit (including high interest rates) made them unable to find or borrow enough local currency to purchase in the auction foreign currency needed to import capital goods and inputs to raise productivity.[15]

In addition, Fund staff and many in the Bank wanted to build on previous reforms, leading to four other trends:

1. *Proliferating conditions.* IMF conditions rose from less than twenty

in 1983 to between forty and fifty in 1988–89, partly because SAF and ESAF programs incorporated World Bank issues. The PNDC also had to implement more Bank policy-based loans.

2. *"Tighter" conditions.* Especially in the 1984 standby, many conditions required sharper or more rapid adjustment than in 1983.

3. *"Deeper" conditions.* Conditions became much more specific as broader targets produced unexpected results or were not implemented, and as the Bank used more detailed sectoral conditions. For example, the civil service benefit cuts in 1986 were specified by the Fund, and health service charges were listed in a Bank health loan.

4. *Preconditions.* Though the PNDC had an excellent implementation record, conditions that had to be implemented before the Fund or Bank would begin to disburse a new loan proliferated, tightened, and deepened. These included devaluation, interest rate rises, budget cuts, and arrears clearance.

These trends increased political and administrative problems for the government, constraining its freedom to implement reform as it chose. Some of the proliferation and deepening was encouraged by the PNDC, as more specific targets gave its administrators ways of measuring progress toward meeting overall program targets. However, they meant that even committed proadjustment officials were overworked by preparing for, negotiating, and implementing programs and finance and running the economy. They also stretched Fund and Bank staff time to tailor conditions to Ghana's circumstances, avoid or reduce the faults discussed above, or monitor compliance. Monetary and fiscal targets caused the gravest administrative problems, though the foreign exchange auction was initially a "nightmare" (according to PNDC staff) because of its complex documentation and monitoring procedures and reports that donors insisted on before disbursing more aid. The wide range of new measures all needed new organization, coordination, delegation, and monitoring systems and staff training in technical details. According to one World Bank official, almost all had "teething problems, and it was only through the dedication and skill of senior officials that these gradually disappeared." With technical assistance of variable quality, the PNDC vastly improved fiscal and monetary monitoring and aid processing by 1988.

Other administrative problems caused the main breaches of World Bank conditions. The PNDC had no permanent institutional mechanism for calculating and introducing periodic increases in agricultural producer prices or for keeping fertilizer or fuel prices in line with international prices; thus, these prices had to be recalculated and renegotiated each year, delaying implementation. Similar institutional weaknesses delayed reforms in public expenditure programming and necessitated large-scale technical assistance.[16] In addition, the Bank and PNDC leadership took four years to translate general intentions to cut the size of the COCOBOD into specific feasible measures. Technical difficulties with insufficient funds for staff redundancy payments and disentangling the web of interparastatal debt have delayed privatization.[17]

Ghana also suffered from low economic capacity to adjust. Contributing factors included major imperfections in capital, product, and factor markets—many private and public sector monopolies or monopsonies; poor communications and incomplete or delayed information flows; an inadequate transport system; declining education, training, and health provision; and low social and labor mobility. Protracted recession and import shortages had exacerbated all but the last of these. They caused "lags" and shortfalls and unexpected results from reform policies. By cutting the availability of capital goods, they prompted decay of capital equipment and capacity underutilization in industry, which reduced manufacturing supply response to reform. Recession and shortages also contributed to collapsing storage and rural transport facilities, which cut agricultural supply response. Huge repressed demand for foreign exchange caused rapid devaluation in the auction. Falling living standards and employment cut the tax base and propensity to save.

However, Ghana had an economic capacity greater than many sub-Saharan nations:

1. A better-educated and better-trained labor force increased the availability of skills in all sectors of the economy.

2. An influx of highly mobile labor (expelled from Nigeria) in 1983–1984 provided relatively cheap labor for cocoa farms and timber companies.

3. There was room for a major supply response in export commodities. Ghana's large cocoa plantations could respond to sizable producer price increases in the short term (by cutting smuggling through neighboring countries and increasing officially marketed production) and to rehabilitation in the long term. Substantial underexploited natural resources—notably gold, other minerals, and timber—were relatively accessible (and also being smuggled) and could be exported given price incentives and transport improvements.

4. The notoriously large informal sector determined true prices for most goods and for foreign currency and imports, well above official levels. The high official inflation rate in 1983–1984 did not represent the prices people paid—even for food—and devaluation did not weaken purchasing power. Formal sector workers could also compensate for real wage falls (or add to rises) by holding second and third jobs in the informal sector, or switch to informal jobs if laid off.

5. After drought in 1982–1984, which delayed agricultural growth and prompted food-price inflation, better weather helped to improve conditions in 1984, with food prices accounting for 50 percent of the fall in the official

inflation rate. The better weather also contributed to increased GDP growth in 1984 by raising non-cocoa agricultural output.[18]

All of these characteristics led the PNDC, Fund, and Bank to have high expectations of output and export supply response in Ghana and (partly because of greater import capacity) to design a more growth-oriented program after 1984. This design enhanced economic capacity through a number of measures that raised supply instead of compressing demand:

1. After sharp real expenditure cuts in 1983, the budget deficit was turned into a surplus by increasing revenue, especially tax receipts from rising imports and exports, and aid grants. The expenditure/GDP ratio rose from 6 percent in 1982 to average 15 percent in 1987–1988, and especially during years of budget surplus, development/capital expenditure increased in spite of high interest payments and exchange losses from devaluation.

2. Fiscal stability reduced the government's share of borrowing, freeing more resources for private sector investment, producing "crowding in" in 1984, 1986, and 1988. The private sector share of fiscal deficit financing fell to single digits in 1984 and has remained there since.[19] Both government development expenditure and higher private sector investment boosted gross fixed capital formation and savings/GDP and investment/GDP ratios.

3. Nominal wages were allowed to rise relatively quickly, partly because recurrent budget expenditure was protected. Real minimum wages rose by 120 percent during 1983–1987, helping to reduce urban and trade union protest.

4. Imports rose substantially. In addition, PNDC management of the foreign exchange auction made good use of available currency to boost supply. It used a preferential exchange rate for items excluded from the auction, notably debt service, oil/fertilizer, and pharmaceutical imports, thereby respectively reducing the proportion of government expenditure going to debt service and protecting against shortages of essential imports. Finally, it excluded consumer goods imports from the auction in 1986–1987, to concentrate officially scrutinized foreign currency on priority capital or intermediate goods.

In addition, the PNDC showed a remarkable ability to fine-tune measures by flexible implementation and, by sustaining adjustment, to convince the Fund and Bank to react flexibly. Though pushed to the limit by the growing demands of conditionality, the simple policymaking structure, the quality of senior staff, and the economic recovery (which reduced the atmosphere of collapse) allowed for flexible responses. For example, in 1984, the PNDC overcame midyear budget overruns by sweeping spending cuts. The best example of flexible implementation was the PNDC ability (with World Bank support) to convince the IMF to allow it to "manage" the foreign exchange auction by changing auction rules. It limited speculative bidding and controlled the pace of devaluation by reducing demand for foreign currency. It introduced "Dutch" bidding (whereby the successful bidder paid the rate it bid), 100 percent prior deposit of local currency used to bid, and strict and changing eligibility and documentation requirements. All of these measures reduced the number of bids made or accepted, especially in crucial periods of foreign exchange shortage. In addition, flexible implementation also included finding bridging loans from Standard Chartered Bank to increase the supply of currency to the auction. In 1987–1988, measures switched to improving the supply of foreign exchange to the auction and narrowing the gap between the parallel market and official exchange rates.[20]

Many other conditions were redesigned or delayed as they proved inappropriate. For example, the Bank and PNDC saw that constant large fertilizer price increases were damaging forward planning by farmers and reducing agricultural supply response. PNDC and Bank social sector staff learned by mid-1986 that cost recovery was reducing use of health facilities, and many (including UNICEF, nongovernmental organizations, and government officials) were seeing falls in health indicators that led them to begin to doubt the utility of cost recovery. The Bank ignored nonimplementation of charges for drugs and in 1987 agreed to a much more gradual package of educational reform. The World Bank also slimmed down the privatization program. Such flexible responses to nonimplementation were vital to enabling programs to produce their desired results.

The exception to fine-tuning and flexibility came in April 1986. The pressure of popular protest left the PNDC no time to assess the effects of restoring wages and benefits on IMF fiscal, monetary, and wage targets. The Fund reacted inflexibly and suspended lending, which forced the Bank to delay disbursements on program loans for ninety days. During talks, the Bank and PNDC united in arguing that the minimum wage had to be raised and differentials in public sector pay increased to restore incentives and reduce political pressure. The IMF first refused and then insisted on compensating cuts in other expenditures and rises in revenue. This IMF inflexibility, added to IMF dominance in talks, almost led a government wholly committed to adjustment, with remarkable administrative capacity and relatively little political instability, to reconsider talks. Growing exasperation within the PNDC culminated in severe "adjustment fatigue" in 1986.[21] The 1986 negotiations were at times acrimonious. Several interviewees suggested that a breach with the IMF was close in June–July. They regretted the delay in agreement and the IMF's inattention to the political, administrative, or economic feasibility of measures, or to the amount or terms of supporting finance. However, by September the Fund's board saw that the PNDC was having major political problems and softened the program. In particular, the

Fund moved a long way on gasoline prices and budget targets. These concessions reflected general trends in IMF talks: more effort to tailor conditions to national circumstances, more influence for Africa department staff and resident representatives, and growing Bank influence. Yet, above all, IMF flexibility reflected pressure from OECD governments, the collapse of other sub-Saharan programs, and a desire to reward Ghana's adjustment efforts and to maintain the program.

## ■ Overcoming Foreign Exchange Shortage: Talks on Financing

The Bank and Fund played a major role in talks on external financing to support adjustment.[22] However, they often disagreed over how much financing Ghana needed, partly because they used different calculation methods. The World Bank calculated a requirements-based "financing gap," consisting of the amount of financing needed to provide a target annual import growth, which was assumed to produce a target GDP growth. The IMF calculated an availability-based "adjustment gap," which was equivalent to how much financing donors were thought likely to provide. Especially in 1983–1984, they made these calculations in the last stages of negotiations. Because their power to mobilize additional last-minute funds was limited, both institutions had to increase their loans or adjust projections to the finance they thought likely: indeed, they often recalculated financial needs after the program had been agreed upon. To "close the financing gap," export prices or production therefore often had to be overprojected, or import or reserve levels allowed in the program had to be cut. This sometimes caused acrimonious disputes among Fund, Bank, and PNDC representatives, with most officials in the Bank and PNDC wanting higher imports to boost growth and higher reserves to protect against foreign exchange shortfalls. Projections were therefore not objective but negotiated.[23] These changes in projections allowed the meetings that promised external financing to appear to close the financing gap. For Ghana, the only formal forum was a Consultative Group, attended by most government and multilateral institution aid donors. This became the meeting at which Ghana's financing gap was closed.

Multilateral institutions provided 75 percent of new lending in 1983–1984, and 60–65 percent in 1985–1988. The Fund lent $200 million a year in 1983–1986, but then huge projected net repayments to the Fund became a major issue in talks in 1985–1987. The PNDC and Bank argued that Ghana required net new loans on softer terms, but the Fund board took until November 1987 to agree. Then Ghana received SDR 143 million from the SAF and SDR 245 million from the EFF, followed by SDR 368 million from the ESAF in November 1988. These loans were not huge; they were disbursed over three years and the ESAF included SDR 250 million of the SAF and EFF loans. They did not prevent net payments to the IMF in 1987–1989; however, the softer repayment terms of SAF reduced net payments enough to revitalize the PNDC's commitment to Ghana's Structural Adjustment Program.

Since 1983–1984, the World Bank has played the major role in financing adjustment. Large new loans on soft terms have enabled the Bank to make net payments to Ghana averaging $200 million a year. These have risen rapidly in 1989–1990, under the Special Program of Assistance (SPA), which has also mobilized large bilateral aid. Bank exhortation and persuasion of OECD governments were vital to disbursing more aid. In addition, in 1988–1989 the Bank relieved US$7 million of interest payments due on International Bank for Reconstruction and Development (IBRD) loans borrowed when Ghana was a middle-income country.

Negotiations for bilateral aid centered on Consultative Group meetings. However, most bilateral donors—with the notable exception of Canada—responded slowly and with only small aid increases. This stemmed from a mixture of antagonism toward the PNDC, engendered by its anti-Western foreign policy statements, and uncertainty over whether adjustment would continue. The former motivation was paramount for the United States and West Germany, and the latter for most other donors. At these meetings, donors made nonbinding "indications" of aid, which were later signed as commitments and then disbursed to the PNDC. Until 1986, indications were disappointing: in 1983 and 1984 they fell short both of overall amounts requested by the Fund, Bank, and PNDC, and of the fast-disbursing aid needed to fill financing gaps. However, they met both targets in 1985–1986, when they reached $600 million. They rose sharply in 1987–1989, when donors were encouraged by large Fund and Bank loans and less radical foreign policy rhetoric and tried to compensate for cocoa price falls and to sustain adjustment by allowing more imports. Bilateral donors pledged $800 million in 1987 and 1988 and $900 million in 1989, meeting (and in 1989 exceeding) targets. This demonstrated donor support for adjustment and reinforced that of the PNDC. It was also due to better preparation for the meetings by the PNDC and the Bank, and to the SPA, which enabled the Bank to increase its lobbying for aid.

Indications also more often became commitments, and after 1985 individual governments frequently increased commitments in follow-up meetings. Yet, until 1986, disbursements lagged well behind donor commitments, creating a pipeline of aid waiting to be disbursed. More important, they lagged behind projections in programs, reopening the "financing gap" and pushing the Bank and Fund to lend more or the PNDC to cut imports. Such lags were due to problems with project or technical assistance implementation; falls in food import needs and therefore in food aid; tying, procurement restrictions, or complex documentation; recipient or donor delay in processing aid; and tight monetary policy under IMF programs, which cut private sector demand for aid-funded imports. By 1987–1988, PNDC and donors had overcome some hurdles. In the SPA, the Bank monitored disbursements and simplified processing by channeling bilateral aid into its own programs, reducing demands on Ghanaian and donor staff. Disbursements reached $250 million a year but were still 10–15 percent behind schedule.

In addition, Ghanaian officials had many meetings to negotiate debt relief, arrears clearance, new bridging and trade finance loans, and foreign investment. Table 13.3 shows Ghana's debt and debt service for 1983–1988, broken down by creditor type. Total debt (including arrears) rose dramatically, from $1.91 billion in 1983 to $3.39 billion in 1988. After Ghana rescheduled all of its debt to OECD governments in 1974, only aid agencies would lend to it; thus, the terms of its debt were relatively "soft," and debt service was an average of "only" 48 percent of export earnings in 1982–1984. As most new bilateral aid was in grants, the huge new loans from the IMF and World Bank made multilateral debt dominate the total. IMF loans had short repayment periods, earlier World Bank loans fell due, and multilateral debt was by tradition not rescheduled. Thus, the percentage of debt service to multilateral creditors rose sharply. By 1987–1988, 47 percent of debt service was to the IMF—an amount equal to 10–20 percent of exports. All multilateral creditors were expected to lend amounts equal to service but only the Bank did so, as described above. Multilateral service was responsible for a rapid rise of service, to average 66 percent of exports in 1986–1988.

The most important creditor governments were the United States, West Germany, the United Kingdom, and Canada. Together they accounted for 75 percent of bilateral debt. They refused to "re-reschedule" payments due under the 1974 agreement (which were a major burden throughout 1983–1989) and argued that the PNDC should pay to restore loans from their export credit agencies. The PNDC accepted this but received few new loans until 1986–1987. In 1985–1988, OECD governments made new efforts to cancel Ghana's aid debt as it fell due. Canada, France, Germany, the United Kingdom, and the United States canceled US$412 million, but because aid loans had soft terms, this saved under U.S.$15 million per annum of service in 1988–1990. Because it did not "re-reschedule," Ghana did not benefit from the Paris Club Toronto menu, which partly canceled or cut interest on export credit debt.

In 1983, the PNDC had $439 million of *arrears* on debt inherited from the civilian government. The IMF program made clearing these a priority to improve access to new goods and services. The arrears were largely short-term debt to commercial suppliers of goods and services. Standard Chartered and

Table 13.3 Ghana—Debt and External Finance, 1983–1988 (All Figures US$ Million)

|  | 1983 | 1984 | 1985 | 1986 | 1987 | 1988 |
|---|---|---|---|---|---|---|
| *Total Debt* | 1,908 | 2,255 | 2,555 | 2,910 | 3,408 | 3,392 |
| Medium- and long-term | 1,793 | 2,017 | 2,372 | 2,645 | 3,209 | 3,216 |
| Multilateral | 754 | 964 | 1,286 | 1,676 | 2,098 | 2,155 |
| IMF | 331 | 515 | 701 | 786 | 867 | 762 |
| World Bank | 269 | 299 | 377 | 580 | 851 | 1,004 |
| Other | 154 | 150 | 208 | 310 | 380 | 389 |
| OECD governments | 702 | 611 | 640 | 699 | 881 | 861 |
| Export credits | 216 | 159 | 124 | 125 | 198 | 196 |
| Aid | 486 | 452 | 516 | 574 | 683 | 665 |
| Other governments | 170 | 147 | 160 | 140 | 125 | 107 |
| Commercial banks | 166 | 294 | 286 | 130 | 105 | 93 |
| Short-term | 115 | 238 | 183 | 265 | 199 | 176 |
| *Total Debt Service* | 232 | 295 | 415 | 388 | 561 | 628 |
| Medium- and long-term | 218 | 268 | 335 | 381 | 541 | 610 |
| Multilateral | 51 | 51 | 81 | 122 | 284 | 377 |
| IMF | 20 | 27 | 51 | 85 | 238 | 324 |
| World Bank | 22 | 17 | 21 | 22 | 29 | 32 |
| Other | 9 | 7 | 12 | 15 | 17 | 21 |
| OECD governments | 48 | 46 | 64 | 70 | 89 | 105 |
| Export credits | 22 | 23 | 24 | 46 | 56 | 69 |
| Aid | 26 | 23 | 27 | 34 | 33 | 36 |
| Other governments | 22 | 27 | 29 | 33 | 27 | 20 |
| Oil loans | 62 | 61 | 49 | 116 | 59 | 64 |
| Commercial banks | 15 | 23 | 54 | 26 | 14 | 14 |
| Arrears reduction | 20 | 60 | 57 | 4 | 72 | 30 |
| Short-term | 14 | 27 | 78 | 17 | 20 | 18 |
| *External Financial Flows* | | | | | | |
| Gross disbursements | 472 | 519 | 602 | 632 | 714 | 797 |
| Net transfers | 238 | 252 | 217 | 199 | 210 | 227 |

*Sources*: World Bank 1989 Country Economic Memorandum and Consultative Group documents; World Bank Debtor Reporting System; OECD Financing and External Debt of Developing Countries; Bank of Ghana; confidential IMF and World Bank documents; and author's own estimates based on interviews with debt data compilers.

Nigeria rescheduled $250 million owed for oil imports, reducing the annual debt service ratio by 6–8 percent, but other creditors did not reschedule. Reducing arrears cost an average of $60 million a year in 1983–1989 because they were larger than initially thought, and there were foreign exchange shortfalls during IMF programs. The PNDC successfully negotiated a slower and more realistic timetable for clearing arrears; it was now set at seven years (four more than planned in 1983). Yet, it is unclear whether clearance increased access to new loans, for neither OECD export credit agencies nor commercial banks would lend medium-term until 1986. When most OECD governments were slow to increase aid in 1983–1984, and when the financing gap "reopened" in 1986, the PNDC had to turn to bridging loans of $20 to $150 million from Standard Chartered Bank. In 1983–1984, they paid for oil imports, and in 1986 they supported the foreign exchange auction and prevented arrears to the IMF or World Bank. As such, they were a vital stabilizing force for adjustment, making up for delays in other foreign exchange receipts.

The PNDC made strenuous efforts to attract foreign investment after 1985. It introduced new incentives; replaced bureaucratic multiagency approval with one fast-moving agency, the Ghana Investment Center; and joined the World Bank's Multilateral Investment Guarantee Agency, which guarantees profit and dividend remittance for investors. The Bank and Fund expected $15 million a year in their "financing gap" projections for 1983–1986; however, investment fell to $4 million by 1987, before rising to $12 million a year in 1988–1989. Most of these funds continued to go to commodity exports, notably gold and timber, with virtually none to manufacturing. This reflected the small domestic market and low demand in West Africa, as well as the side effects of adjustment: potential manufacturing investors saw that cheap imports might undercut them; interest rates made local currency borrowing expensive; and devaluation increased local currency costs of imported inputs.[24] In March 1990, MIGA's first African investment promotion conference in Accra produced $65 million, including two commodity-based manufacturing projects. But IMF, Bank, and government officials remain worried by the poor response and are considering the provision of more incentives for investors.

Overall, gross inflows of foreign exchange rose from $472 million in 1983 to $740 million in 1988. The key period was 1984–1985, when they rose by 13 percent each year, showing strong support from the international community. A rise of only 5 percent in 1986 coincided with adjustment problems, as the PNDC felt it was being let down, but rises of 9.5 percent a year in 1987–1988 reassured it. Because debt service rose faster, net inflows fell from $232 million in 1983 to $191 million in 1988. The sharpest falls were in 1985 and 1986 (16 percent and 9 percent, respectively), which was also the most problematic time for adjustment.

Yet, trends in export earnings and terms of trade meant that lower net inflows did not produce import cuts. Exports grew by 89 percent between 1983 and 1988, due largely to local currency price incentives for cocoa and other agricultural products, new foreign investment in minerals and timber, and transport rehabilitation. In the key period 1984–1986, the terms of trade rose by 37 percent, explaining 60 percent of the rise in exports. In 1987–1989, cocoa prices fell sharply, but higher cocoa production and gold, timber, electricity, and nontraditional exports and low oil import costs offset this. As a result, imports grew by 99 percent (91 percent in volume) in 1983–1988.

The large gross foreign exchange inflows Ghana received in return for reform, and rising imports, cemented PNDC determination to implement almost all IMF conditions. Higher gross financial inflows and export earnings also enabled Ghana to pay most debt service on time. These PNDC actions increased donor confidence in the future of the program. They raised net inflows, allowing higher imports, budget spending, GDP, and per capita consumption. These reduced domestic political opposition and kept PNDC commitment firm. In contrast, adjustment problems in 1985–1986 coincided with lower gross and net inflows and import growth, and the level of imports to be allowed in 1987 became a major issue in talks.

Ultimately, program "financing gap" projections often proved inaccurate. This was due partly to faulty debt data, especially on short-term debt, arrears, IMF credits, and bridging loans. Yet, it also reflected overoptimism about exports—prices fell short for cocoa in 1986–1988 and gold in 1988—and the rate of aid disbursement, partly because otherwise the gap could not be closed. As a result, import levels were on average 13 percent lower in each program year than projected. This led financing gap targets and aid requirements to double by 1989. As the PNDC was efficient enough to calculate its own "gaps" and trends in aid disbursement, it was aware of World Bank and IMF optimism. By 1985–1986, it became increasingly exasperated at aid shortfalls and saw cocoa price falls and large payments to the IMF looming. When the Fund and Bank suspended disbursements on adjustment loans, thus increasing the foreign exchange shortage, Finance Secretary Botchwey, expressing the disillusionment felt by the PNDC, declared that the economy was "dead in the water" and adjustment was "in danger."[25] In 1986–1988 the PNDC insisted on lower export projections to allow for possible cocoa price falls, and a more flexible IMF agreed. However, the terms of trade turned out to be worse in 1987–1988, and only large export production increases enabled Ghana to meet its current account deficit targets. Inadequate negotiating procedure on external finance was still undermining adjustment.

For all of these reasons, the Ghanaian adjustment programs in 1983–1989 cannot be said to have suffered "external shocks"—those foreign exchange shortfalls (compared to targets) that were external to the program and could not be predicted or guarded against. Ghana's shortfalls (which were minor compared to those of many other African countries) could well have been guarded against; it was, rather, negotiating procedure that made adjustment vulnerable to shortfalls.

The issue of the amount of external finance provided by the international community was not prominent in Ghana's domestic political economy. In part this was because the PNDC criticized shortfalls publicly only once, in

1986, and because figures were largely secret. Yet, it also reflected the effectiveness of PNDC negotiations for external finance and the rise in export production, which brought import rises and removed one potential focus of discontent. Compared to many other sub-Saharan countries, the PNDC negotiated relatively effectively with its creditors. However, the results of talks, especially the need to clear arrears and not re-reschedule Paris Club debt, reflected the conflicting interests and perceptions of bilateral creditors and the Fund and Bank. Such results indicated the superior power of Ghana's "creditors," as well as the Ghanaian economy's desperate need for foreign exchange and its lack of alternative foreign exchange sources.

## ■ Conclusion: Democracy and Growth in the 1990s?

On balance, particularly compared to many other sub-Saharan nations, the PNDC negotiated remarkably well with the international community. That it did not achieve more of what it wanted was due to the superior power of the international community. Yet, the PNDC succeeded in some ways in reconciling the demands of domestic and international politics and economics in order to agree upon and implement adjustment measures. This reflected positive political characteristics such as governmental unity, and less positive characteristics, including the lack or repression of opposition, and the absence of domestic political consultation. Administrative capacity to adjust was remarkable, and incapacity was overcome by flexible implementation. Above all, relatively growth-oriented adjustment programs took account of Ghana's economic capacity and reduced opposition by providing positive economic results for many. The international community also softened its attitude in 1986 when the PNDC needed concessions to overcome mounting political problems. The IMF, World Bank, and OECD governments, prompted partly by the fall of several other African programs, realized that the negotiating procedures and terms did not fulfill their interests and began to change them. Having persisted with adjustment, Ghana gained from the reforms in 1986–1989.[26]

Yet, the international community responded inadequately in providing both external finance and appropriate adjustment measures (though it was more flexible than for many other sub-Saharan countries). This largely reflected inadequate negotiating procedures for agreeing to and implementing adjustment and external finance. In turn, this was due to the conflicting short-term interests and perceptions of creditors, to their power over the PNDC because it needed foreign exchange, and to time pressures and uncertainty. Although the international community's response improved considerably in 1986–1990 (as OECD governments realized their longer-term shared interests in sustaining sub-Saharan adjustment), major problems remain. Among these are several important aims that have not been fulfilled, partly because of the same developments that sustained adjustment, and partly because of basic economic incapacity. The strong expansion in domestic demand and output since 1983 has not been matched by agricultural and manufacturing supply response. Food production has not risen as hoped, due largely to drought. Devaluation has increased the domestic currency cost of tradable goods. Rising real wages have raised wage costs. Rising foreign reserves have contributed to higher money supply. All of these factors have kept inflation high. The recovery is also vulnerable in the long term. Budget expenditure, investment, and import levels are dependent on large amounts of aid. There is a narrow range of exports, in which three commodities—cocoa, gold, and timber—account for 85–90 percent of exports. The program is taking measures to overcome these problems by putting more emphasis on supply response and food production, diversifying and increasing exports, and raising domestic investment.

The political support base for reform remains narrow and, whether or not extremely gradual redemocratization proceeds, future government commitment to adjustment may be uncertain. The present procedure for negotiating adjustment provides a disincentive to consultation, participation, and democracy. Social and environmental problems also remain. Stagnant or declining social welfare and growing levels of income concentration have prompted the PNDC, World Bank, and UNICEF to design a Programme of Actions to Mitigate the Social Costs of Adjustment, which consists of social sector projects to be funded separately by aid donors. This is the first program of its kind in Africa, but it is small (U.S.$88.4 million over three years) and has lacked coordination among ministries or donors, which delayed disbursement of funds. By December 1990, less than U.S.$45 million had been spent. The Bank, the UNDP, and the African Development Bank have carried out studies on living standards and on incorporating antipoverty measures into adjustment under their Social Dimensions of Adjustment (SDA) program, but this has so far produced few concrete measures. The environmental risk of drought undermining food availability has led recent World Bank agricultural loans to include measures to increase food security and has led the Fund program to include an environmental action plan to reduce the danger of soil degradation by soaring timber exports.[27]

Looking forward to the 1990s, it is not possible to forecast the impact of continued adjustment on domestic political and economic stability. The PNDC may be able to sustain a continuing debt service burden of 25–30 percent of export earnings. It may be able to continue implementing adjustment, by combining carrots and sticks. It may even be able to find the route to longer-term self-sustaining development, overcome social and environmental problems, and move back to democracy. This path will be much more likely if the international community increases its response by improving negotiating procedure and financing and creating a genuine policy dialogue that involves all sections of society. There are several priorities for improving negotiating procedures.[28]

☐ *Economic Policy*

Preparation should involve a systematic and comprehensive assessment of political, economic, and administrative constraints on future adjustment in Ghana by an independent team examining past adjustment. This team would aim to maximize domestic political support and democratic participation, increase economic capacity to reform while enabling broad-based self-sustaining development, and enhance Ghanaian administrative capacity to design and implement policy. The team could also resolve Fund-Bank-PNDC disputes on policies by suggesting compromises. IMF, Bank, PNDC, and independent experts should prepare impartial and accurate data jointly to remove them from the negotiating arena. Fund, Bank, and PNDC staff should draft separate programs, focusing on implementation details and methods but leaving room for concessions in talks by suggesting broad ranges, instead of precise targets, and several methods of achieving them. The Bank should have more influence and equal representation in SAF and ESAF talks, because it has more expertise and experience than the Fund on the longer-term, structural issues that are the key to self-sustaining growth in Ghana. If the Bank assumed program leadership, this would demonstrate the focus on longer-term issues; but the World Bank should also draw on expertise from other specialist international organizations and nongovernmental environmental and social organizations.

Priorities for preparation and negotiation should include diversifying exports; cutting budgetary and import dependence on aid; reducing debt stock and debt service; resolving food production, social welfare, income distribution, and environmental issues; rehabilitating communications and transport infrastructure; improving supply response, notably in manufacturing; and increasing domestic savings and investment. In addition, the political coalition behind reform must be widened. It is not enough to give the PNDC a greater say in adjustment design. During preparation, negotiation, and implementation, PNDC and IMF-Bank staff should consult all parts of government and interest groups (especially civil service, parastatals, trade unions, business, farmers, and local economic experts) and consider the interests of the unorganized (notably women, rural smallholders, and urban poor). The program should incorporate the views of these groups, concentrating on measures that have caused political problems such as wage and benefit changes, education and health charges, gasoline and fertilizer price rises, and privatization. The staff should aim to mobilize support for measures that combine maximum short-term economic gains (rising GDP, imports, budget expenditure, real wages, and benefits) with maximum long-term development.

Negotiations must allow more flexible *implementation* and reaction to problems. The Fund, Bank, and PNDC must continue political analysis and must consult affected interest groups about implementation, where this is possible without encouraging speculation. They should ensure that thorough staff training and appropriate administrative structures are given as much priority as actual measures.

Furthermore, the IMF, Bank, PNDC, and donors need to change *internal procedures*. The Africa vice-presidency of the Bank, the Africa department of the IMF, and the offices of the two institutions in Accra should have more staff, access to and support from top management, and a greater voice in adjustment measures. They should have the resources to prepare regular comprehensive reports on domestic political opinion and reaction to programs; on administrative, environmental, and social issues; and on the causes of implementation problems. The PNDC needs more training and expansion of staff to support the negotiating team and a mechanism for the team to consult other government agencies and extragovernmental groups. Donors need more resources for their staff in Accra to allow them to warn of political, economic, or administrative problems.

☐ *External Finance*

Several bilateral donors are suggesting that large amounts of aid may be unsustainable in the 1990s, especially in the light of Eastern European developments. If continual increases in aid disbursements are thought unsustainable, it becomes vital to maximize the effectiveness of future finance and minimize the amount needed. The faults of financing gap calculations and the talks that fill them must be remedied. The amount of debt reduction and new money should be based on a true "financing gap" calculation, to sustain 2–3 percent annual per capita growth, using worst case projections of the balance of payments. Once the gap is filled, constant monitoring should enable foreign exchange shortfalls to be compensated immediately by contingency loans on very soft terms.[29] Filling such a gap implies debt relief and new finance from all creditors. As most financing decisions center on Consultative Groups, it would be sensible to make these the forum for negotiating all of Ghana's external finance to save time for Ghana's creditors and its policymakers to design and implement economic policy. The first major issue at these meetings should be how to decrease debt stock and increase net financial flows. The key task is to reduce or refinance debt service to multilateral institutions, which will exceed $200 million each year in 1990–1995, thus totaling 75 percent of all debt service. The Fund and Bank should provide net inflows, on softer terms, implying faster disbursement of new ESAF and IDA loans, not least because large repayments to the IMF will fall due in 1992–1997. In turn, this requires expanding ESAF loans and extending their repayment period to forty years to match IDA loans, as well as real increases in IDA funds. Such measures need not mean additional costs for OECD taxpayers; it would suffice to sell a part of IMF gold reserves (or use their invested income), undertake a special issue of SDRs, or use 100 percent of IDA repayments due in 1990–1995.

All creditors, including COMECON, Arab, and other developing countries, should implement a number of measures, including canceling all aid debt, which would reduce annual service by $30–40 million in 1990–1995; canceling 100 percent of export credit debt or agreeing to interest rates of 0.5 percent (each 10 percent cancellation would save $8 million a year and each 1 percent interest cut $7 million); and re-rescheduling the remaining service due in 1990–1993 to give Ghana the benefits that other sub-Saharan nations are receiving. Instead of canceling or cutting interest rates, they could refinance debt service with additional grants, accept payment in local currency, or agree to long-term moratoria on service (without charging interest on arrears); or donate the debt to social development or conservation funds. They should also provide new money as grants or very soft loans—hard export credits will merely create additional debt service for the 1990s.

Ghana is also now eligible for World Bank money to reduce commercial debt or service. It may wish not to use this money, to avoid losing its access to small new commercial loans. These loans—especially short-term bridging loans—are expensive. However, commercial creditors are unlikely to agree to reduce the debt, because Ghana is paying on schedule and had cleared all its arrears by the end of 1990. Instead, the PNDC and donors should find cheaper ways to finance trade and bridging loans.

There is no guarantee that such measures will be undertaken or that if they are they will encourage the PNDC to return to democracy. Many participants in the negotiations believe that the PNDC did not redemocratize in 1986–1990 because it feared that it would be undermined, returning Ghana to political instability and old-style economic policymaking. To the extent that the PNDC is able to offer the people more carrot and has less need to use the stick, its fears may evaporate, making it more willing to encourage popular participation. Even those who see the PNDC as a "predatory regime" that wishes to maintain itself in power must admit that a change in negotiating procedures and terms offers some hope of finding the route to long-term self-sustaining development and of overcoming the political, social, and environmental problems of Ghana as it enters the 1990s.

# Notes

1. Some facts in what follows in this chapter are not fully sourced because they are based on IMF and World Bank documents and interviews with all sides in the talks. For an earlier comparison of Ghana with the unsuccessful adjustment program in Zambia, see Matthew Martin, "Neither Phoenix nor Icarus: Negotiating IMF Programmes in Ghana and Zambia, 1983–1989," in Thomas M. Callaghy and John Ravenhill (eds.), *Hemmed In: Responses to Africa's Economic Dilemma* (New York: Columbia University Press, 1991). I am grateful for invaluable help from many experts on and participants in Ghana's negotiations with the international community and United Kingdom Economic and Social Research Council funding for the book on sub-Saharan Africa's debt talks on which this paper is based. Yet, responsibility for the views expressed is mine alone.

2. For similar views, see John Toye, "Ghana's Economic Reforms and World Bank Policy-Conditioned Lending, 1983–88" (University of Sussex: Institute of Development Studies, March 1989, mimeo, draft), and Reginald Herbold Green, "Ghana: Progress, Problematics and Limitations of the Success Story," *IDS Bulletin* 19, 1 (January 1988), pp. 7–15.

3. The terms "theologians" and "pragmatists" were used in interviews with three IMF staff. Thomas M. Callaghy, "Lost Between State and Market: The Politics of Economic Adjustment in Ghana, Zambia and Nigeria," in Joan M. Nelson (ed.), *The Politics of Economic Adjustment in Developing Nations* (Princeton: Princeton University Press, 1989), p. 39, says some Ghanaian officials believed some IMF staff were acting tough to try to get promotion. This was also suggested in my interviews with PNDC and IMF officials—as was unquestioning belief in IMF conditions or overwork—but none of these can be verified.

4. For more details of IMF noncompliance by other African countries, see Matthew Martin, *The Crumbling Facade of Africa's Debt Negotiations: No Winners* (London: Macmillan, 1991), ch. 2. For more details of World Bank noncompliance, see Paul Mosley, Jane Harrigan, and John Toye, *Aid and Power* (London: Routledge, 1990).

5. The best published sources on post-1983 Ghanaian politics are Kwame A. Ninsin, "Ghanaian Politics After 1981: Revolution or Evolution?" *Canadian Journal of African Studies* 21, 1 (1987), pp. 17–37; Donald I. Ray, *Ghana: Politics, Economics and Society* (Boulder: Lynne Rienner Publishers; London: Frances Pinter, 1986); Donald Rothchild and E. Gyimah-Boadi, "Ghana's Economic Decline and Development Strategies," in John Ravenhill (ed.), *Africa in Economic Crisis* (New York: Columbia University Press, 1986); and Toye, "Ghana's Economic Reforms."

6. For a similar interpretation, see Toye, "Ghana's Economic Reforms," pp. 9–16.

7. See Rothchild and Gyimah-Boadi, "Ghana's Economic Decline and Development Strategies," pp. 270, 273–274; also based on confidential interviews.

8. On these characteristics, see Callaghy, "Lost Between State and Market," p. 39, and *Africa Confidential*, December 12, 1984, p. 3.

9. Green, "Ghana: Progress, Problematics and Limitations," discusses the Cocobod, and Rothchild and Gyimah-Boadi, "Ghana's Economic Decline and Development Strategies," discuss the civil service.

10. This description is simplified. Reginald Herbold Green, *Stabilisation and Adjustment Policies and Programmes: Country Study 1—Ghana* (Helsinki: World Institute for Development Economics Research, 1987), and Richard Pearce, E. Amonoo, and L. Honny, *The Impact of Economic Recovery Programmes on Smallholder Farmers and the Rural Poor in Sub-Saharan Africa: Ghana* (IFAD/ODI Working Paper No. 2, January 1989, draft, mimeo), provide excellent detailed analyses of the complex effects on the incomes of different groups.

11. See Kwame Asiedu-Saforo, "Economic Reform Programmes and Agricultural Development: Macro Policy Sequencing in Ghana, 1983–88," *Food Policy* (November 1989), pp. 359–370; Green, "Ghana: Progress, Problematics and Limitations"; Cord Jakobeit in this book, Chapter 12; Andrew Norton, "Ghana Social Profile" (London: Overseas Development Administration, 1988, mimeo); Pearce et al., *The Impact of Economic Recovery Programmes*; and Douglas Rimmer, "The Political Economy of Poverty, Equity and Growth: Ghana Study" (Washington, D.C.: World Bank Research Project RPO 67373, 1989, mimeo).

12. See also Nicholas Van Hear, "Labour and Structural Adjustment in Nigeria and Ghana," paper for ASAUK conference, September 1988, mimeo.

13. See Asiedu-Saforo, "Economic Reform Programmes"; John Loxley, *Ghana: Economic Crisis and the Long Road to Recovery* (Ottawa: North-South Institute, 1988); and Pearce et al., *The Impact of Economic Recovery Programmes*.

14. Rimmer, "The Political Economy of Poverty, Equity and Growth," p. 350.

15. This point is based on confidential IMF and World Bank documents but is also made by Green, "Ghana: Progress, Problematics and Limitations," and Toye, "Ghana's Economic Reforms."

16. Toye, "Ghana's Economic Reforms," pp. 52–54.

17. See also E. Gyimah-Boadi in this book, Chapter 10.

18. On the role of the weather, see also Sheetal K. Chand and Reinold Van Til, "Ghana: Towards Successful Stabilisation and Recovery," *Finance and Development* 25, 1 (March 1988), p. 34; Green, *Stabilisation and Adjustment Policies and Programmes*; and Loxley, *Ghana: Economic Crisis*.

19. For more details of savings and investment developments during 1980–1988, see the excellent study by Ernest Aryeetey, Erick Asante, Fritz Gockel, and Alexander Kyei, "Mobilizing Domestic Savings for African Development and Industrialization: A Ghanaian Case," paper presented to Harare workshop of the International Development Centre, Oxford University, December 1989, draft, mimeo.

20. Such management is acknowledged and praised in confidential IMF and World Bank documents. See also Loxley, *Ghana: Economic Crisis*, pp. 12–13.

21. This is confirmed by Callaghy, "Lost Between State and Market"; Green, *Stabilisation and Adjustment Policies and Programmes*; and Loxley, *Ghana: Economic Crisis*.

22. Data in this section do not necessarily accord with published figures. They are taken from more accurate semiconfidential and confidential IMF, PNDC, and World Bank documents prepared for programs in 1985–1988, including the following World Bank Country Economic Memoranda documents: *Ghana: Managing the Transition* (World Bank Report No. 5289-GH, November 7, 1984, 2 vols.); *Ghana: Towards Structural Adjustment* (World Bank Report No. 5854-GH, October 7, 1985, 2 vols.); *Ghana: Policies and Issues of Structural Adjustment* (World Bank Report No. 6635-GH, March 30, 1987).

23. Evidence for this paragraph is taken from confidential IMF and World Bank documents and interviews with all sides. For similar conclusions, see Ravi Gulhati and Raj Nallari, "Structural Adjustment of Foreign Aid to Africa: The Issue of Inter-Country Allocation" (Washington, D.C.: World Bank Economic Development Institute, July 1987, mimeo), p. 33.

24. Based on interviews with IMF, World Bank, and PNDC officials and potential investing companies in London. See also *South* magazine, February 1990, pp. 26–27, for a similar account.

25. Green, *Stabilisation and Adjustment Policies and Programmes*, p. 52, confirmed in interviews with Ghanaian and IMF and World Bank officials.

26. These reforms and the reasons behind them are discussed briefly in Tony Killick and Matthew Martin, *Current Initiatives on Developing Country Debt* (London: Overseas Development Institute Briefing Paper, April 1990), and Martin, *The Crumbling Facade of Africa's Debt Negotiations*, ch. 7.

27. On PAMSCAD, see Norton, "Ghana Social Profile," and *Africa Economic Digest* (January 30, 1989). Sources for the other social- and food-oriented measures are confidential documents and interviews with IMF, Bank, and PNDC officials.

28. A comprehensive plan for improving negotiating procedure is presented in Martin, *The Crumbling Facade of Africa's Debt Negotiations*, ch. 8.

29. The methods of calculating such true financing gaps, filling them, and keeping them filled, are the subject of the research project I am currently managing at the International Development Centre, Oxford.

# Selected Bibliography

Adda, William. "Privatization in Ghana." In V. V. Ramanadham, ed., *Privatization in Developing Countries*. London and New York: Routledge, Chapman and Hall, 1989.

Agyeman-Duah, Baffour. "Ghana, 1982–1986: The Politics of the P.N.D.C." *Journal of Modern African Studies* 25, 4 (1987).

Ahiakpor, James C. W. "The Success and Failure of Dependency Theory: The Experience of Ghana." *International Organization* 39, 3 (Summer 1985).

Alberti, Charles E. "Ghana's Educational Program: A Model for African Countries?" *Journal of the Midwest History of Education Society* 8 (1980).

Anin, T. E. *Gold in Ghana*. Accra: Selwyn Publishers, 1987.

Ansa-Asare, K. "Legislative History of the Legal Regime of Price Control in Ghana." *Journal of African Law* 39 (1985).

Arhin, Kwame. *Traditional Rule in Ghana, Past and Present*. Accra: Sedco Publishing, 1985.

Atim, Chris B., and Ahmed S. Gariba. "Ghana: Revolution or Counter-Revolution?" *Journal of African Marxists*, no. 10 (June 1987).

Austin, Dennis. "The Ghana Armed Forces and Ghanaian Society." *Third World Quarterly* 7, 1 (1985).

Azarya, Victor, and Naomi Chazan. "Disengagement from the State in Africa: Reflections on the Experience of Ghana and Guinea." *Comparative Studies in Society and History* 19 (1987).

Bank of Ghana. "Ghana's Stabilisation Measures and the IMF: A Case Study." *Africa Development* 10 (1985).

Bates, Robert H. *Essays on the Political Economy of Rural Africa*. Berkeley: University of California Press, 1983.

Beckman, Bjorn. *Organizing the Farmers: Cocoa Politics and National Development in Ghana*. Uppsala: Scandinavian Institute of African Studies, 1976.

Bing, Adotey. "Popular Participation Versus People's Power: Notes on Politics and Power Struggles in Ghana." *Review of African Political Economy* 31 (December 1984).

Callaghy, Thomas M. "Lost Between State and Market: The Politics of Economic Adjustment in Ghana, Zambia and Nigeria." In Joan M. Nelson, ed., *The Politics of Economic Adjustment in Developing Nations*. Princeton: Princeton University Press, 1990.

Chand, Sheetal K., and van Til, Reinold. "Ghana: Toward Successful Stabilisation and Recovery." *Finance and Development* 25, 1 (March 1988).
Chazan, Naomi. *An Anatomy of Ghanaian Politics: Managing Political Recession, 1969–1982*. Boulder: Westview Press, 1983.
———. "Ghana: Problems of Governance and the Emergence of Civil Society." In Larry Diamond, Juan J. Linz, and Seymour Martin Lipset, eds., *Democracy in Developing Countries: Africa*. Boulder: Lynne Rienner Publishers, 1988.
———. "Planning Democracy in Africa: A Comparative Perspective on Nigeria and Ghana." *Policy Sciences* 22 (1989).
———. "Liberalization, Governance and Political Space in Ghana." In Michael Bratton and Goran Hyden, eds., *Governance and Politics in Africa*. Boulder: Lynne Rienner Publishers, forthcoming.
Commander, S., J. Howell, and Wayo Seini. "Ghana 1983–7." In S. Commander, ed., *Structural Adjustment and Agriculture: Theory and Practice in Africa and Latin America*. London: James Currey/ODI, 1989.
Cook, Paul, and Colin Kirkpatrick. *Privatisation in Less Developed Countries*. Brighton, Sussex: Wheatsheaf Books, 1988.
Crook, Richard. "Legitimacy, Authority and the Transfer of Power in Ghana." *Political Studies* 35 (1987).
Damachi, Ukandi Godwin. *The Role of Trade Unions in the Development Process with a Case Study of Ghana*. New York: Praeger, 1974.
Dell, Sidney. "Stabilization: The Political Economy of Overkill." In Charles Wilber, ed., *The Political Economy of Development and Underdevelopment*, 3d ed. New York: Random House, 1984.
Economic Commission for Africa. *African Alternative to Structural Adjustment Programmes (AA-SAP)*. 1989.
Ewusi, Kodwo. *Economic Inequality in Ghana*. Legon, Ghana: Institute of Statistical, Social, and Economic Research, 1977.
———. *Structural Adjustment and Stabilisation Policies in Developing Countries: A Case Study of Ghana's Experience in 1983–1986*. Legon, Ghana: Institute of Statistical, Social, and Economic Research, 1987.
———. *Trends in the Economy of Ghana, 1986–88*. Legon, Ghana: Institute of Statistical, Social, and Economic Research, 1988.
George, Betty Stein. *Education in Ghana*. Washington, D.C.: U.S. Government Printing Office, 1976.
Green, Reginald Herbold. *Stabilisation and Adjustment Policies and Programmes: Country Study 1—Ghana*. Helsinki: World Institute for Development Economics Research, 1987.
———. "Ghana: Progress, Problematics and Limitations of the Success Story." *IDS Bulletin* 19, 1 (January 1988).
Gyimah-Boadi, E., and Donald Rothchild. "Ghana." In V. Subramaniam, ed., *Public Administration in the Third World*. New York: Greenwood Press, 1990.
Hansen, E. "The State and Popular Struggles in Ghana, 1982–86." In Peter Anyang' Nyong'o, ed., *Popular Struggles for Democracy in Africa*. London: Zed Books, 1987.
Hansen, E., and K. A. Ninsin, eds. *The State, Development and Politics in Ghana*. London: Codesria Book Series, 1989.
Harris, Laurence. "Conceptions of the IMF's Role in Africa." In Peter Laurence, ed., *World Recession and the Food Crisis in Africa*. London: James Currey; Boulder: Westview Press, 1986.
Haynes, Jeffrey. "Ghana: Indebtedness, Recovery, and the IMF, 1977–87." In

Trevor W. Parfitt and Stephen P. Riley, eds., *The African Debt Crisis.* London: Routledge, 1989.

Helleiner, Gerald. "The Question of Conditionality." In Carol Lancaster and John Williams, eds., *African Debt and Financing.* Washington, D.C.: Institute of International Economics, 1986.

Herbst, Jeffrey. "Economic Reform in Africa: The Lessons of Ghana." *UFS Field Staff Reports*, Africa/Middle East 1989–90, No. 15. Indianapolis: Universities Field Staff International, 1990.

Hodges, Tony. "Ghana's Strategy for Adjustment with Growth." *Africa Recovery* 2 (August 1988).

Howard, Rhoda. *Colonialism and Underdevelopment in Ghana.* London: Croom Helm, 1978.

Huq, M. M. *The Economy of Ghana: The First 25 Years Since Independence.* New York: St. Martin's Press, 1989.

Hutchful, Eboe. "IMF Adjustment Policies in Ghana Since 1966." *Africa Development* 10 (1985).

———. *The IMF and Ghana: The Confidential Record.* London: Zed Books, 1987.

———. "From 'Revolution' to Monetarism in Ghana." In Bonnie K. Campbell and John Loxley, eds., *Structural Adjustment in Africa.* London: Macmillan, 1989.

Hyden, Goran, "Prospects and Problems of State Coherence in Africa." In Donald Rothchild and Victor Olorunsola, eds., *State Versus Ethnic Claims: African Policy Dilemmas.* Boulder: Westview Press, 1983.

"Is Ghana Turning the Corner Economically?" *Washington Report on Africa* 7 (July 15, 1989).

Jeffries, Richard. *Class, Power and Ideology in Ghana: The Railwaymen of Sekondi.* Cambridge: Cambridge University Press, 1978.

———. "Rawlings and the Political Economy of Underdevelopment in Ghana." *African Affairs* 81, 384 (July 1982).

———. "The Labour Aristocracy? Ghana Case Study." *Review of African Political Economy*, No. 3 (May–October 1985).

———. "Ghana: The Political Economy of Personal Rule." In Donald B. Cruise O'Brien, John Cunn, and Richard Rathbone, eds., *Contemporary West African States.* Cambridge: Cambridge University Press, 1989.

Jonah, Kwesi. "Changing Relations Between the IMF and the Government of Ghana, 1960–1987." In E. Hansen and K. A. Ninsin, eds., *The State, Development and Politics in Ghana.* London: Codesria Book Series, 1989.

Kennedy, Paul. *African Capitalism: The Struggle for Ascendancy.* Cambridge: Cambridge University Press, 1988.

Killick, Tony. *Development Economics in Action: A Study of Economic Policies in Ghana.* London: Heinemann, 1978.

———, ed. *The Quest for Economic Stabilisation.* London: Heinemann, 1984.

———. "State Divestiture as a Policy Instrument in Developing Countries." *World Development* 16, 2 (December 1988).

Kraus, Jon. "Ghana's Shift from Radical Populism." *Current History* 86 (1987).

———. "The Political Economy of Agrarian Regression in Ghana." In Stephen Commins, Michael Lofchie, and Rhys Payne, eds., *Africa's Agrarian Crisis.* Boulder: Lynne Rienner Publishers, 1986.

Leith, J. Clark. *Foreign Trade Regimes and Economic Development: Ghana.* New York: National Bureau of Economic Research, 1974.

Le Vine, Victor. *Political Corruption: The Ghana Case.* Stanford: Hoover Institution Press, 1975.

Loxley, John. "The IMF and World Bank Conditionality and Sub-Saharan Africa." In Peter Laurence, ed., *World Recession and the Food Crisis in Africa*. London: James Currey; Boulder: Westview Press, 1986.
———. *Ghana: Economic Crisis and the Long Road to Recovery*. Ottawa: North-South Institute, 1988.
———. *The IMF and the Poorest Countries*. Ottawa: North-South Institute, 1988.
Martin, Matthew. *No Winners: The Crumbling Facade of Africa's Debt Negotiations* (London: Macmillan, 1991).
———. "Neither Phoenix nor Icarus: Negotiating IMF Programmes in Ghana and Zambia, 1983–1989." In Thomas M. Callaghy and John Ravenhill, eds., *Hemmed In: Responses to Africa's Economic Dilemma*. New York: Columbia University Press, 1990.
May, Ernesto. *Exchange Controls and Parallel Market Economies in Sub-Saharan Africa: Focus on Ghana*. World Bank Staffing Paper No. 711. Washington, D.C.: World Bank, 1985.
Migdal, Joel. *Strong Societies and Weak States: State-Society Relations and State Capabilities in the Third World*. Princeton: Princeton University Press, 1988.
Mikell, Gwendolyn. *Cocoa and Chaos in Ghana*. New York: Paragon House, 1989.
———. "Peasant Politicization and Economic Recuperation in Ghana: Local and National Dilemmas." *Journal of Modern Economic Studies* 27 (1989).
Ndu, Eme. "Ghana: Transition to Socialism?" *Labour, Capital and Society* 21, 1 (1988).
Nelson, Joan M. "The Political Economy of Stabilization: Commitment, Capacity and Public Response." In Robert H. Bates, ed., *Toward a Political Economy of Development*. Berkeley: University of California Press, 1988.
———, ed. *Fragile Coalitions: The Politics of Economic Adjustment*. New Brunswick, N.J.: Transaction Books, 1989.
———, ed. *Economic Crisis and Policy Choice: The Politics of Adjustment in the Third World*. Princeton: Princeton University Press, 1990.
Ninsin, Kwame A. "Ghanaian Politics After 1981: Revolution or Evolution?" *Canadian Journal of African Studies* 21, 1 (1987).
———. "The Impact of IMF-World Bank Policies on Ghanaian Society and Politics, 1982–88." *African Journal of Political Economy*, forthcoming.
———. *Political Struggles in Ghana*. Accra: Tornado Publications, forthcoming.
Ninsin, Kwame A., and F. K. Drah, eds. *The Search for Democracy in Ghana*. Accra: Assempa Publishers, 1987.
Norton, Andrew. "Ghana Social Profile." London: Overseas Development Administration, mimeo, 1988.
Oppong, Christine, Christine Okali, and Beverly Houghton. "Woman Power, Retrograde Steps in Ghana." *African Studies Review* 18 (1975).
Oquaye, M. *Politics in Ghana, 1972–1979*. Accra: Tornado Publications, 1980.
Owusu, Maxwell. "Rebellion, Revolution and Tradition: Reinterpreting Coups in Ghana." *Comparative Studies in Society and History* 31, 2 (1989).
Pearce, Richard, E. Amonoo, and L. Honny. *The Impact of Economic Recovery Programmes on Smallholder Farmers and the Rural Poor in Sub-Saharan Africa: Ghana*. IFAD/ODI Working Paper No. 2, January 1989, draft, mimeo.
Pellow, Deborah, and Naomi Chazan. *Ghana: Coping with Uncertainty*. Boulder: Westview Press, 1986.
Price, Robert M. "Neocolonialism and Ghana's Economic Decline: A Critical Assessment." *Canadian Journal of African Studies* 18, 1 (1984).

Rado, Emil. "Notes Towards a Political Economy of Ghana Today." *African Affairs* 85, 341 (1986).
Rawlings, Jerry John. *A Revolutionary Journey: Selected Speeches of Flt.-Lt. Jerry John Rawlings*, vol. 1. Accra: Ghana Publishing Corp., n.d.
Ray, Donald. *Ghana: Politics, Economy and Society*. Boulder: Lynne Rienner Publishers; London: Frances Pinter, 1986.
Republic of Ghana. *Economic Recovery Programme, 1984–1986*. Accra: Government Printer, 1983.
———. *Summary of the PNDC's Budget Statement and Economic Policy for 1983*. Accra: Government Printer, 1983.
———. *District Political Authority and Modalities for District Level Elections*. Accra: Ghana Publishing Corporation, July 1987.
———. *Programme of Actions to Mitigate the Social Costs of Adjustment*. Accra: Government Printer, November 1987.
———. *National Programme for Economic Development (Revised)*. Accra: Ghana Publishing Corporation, 1987.
———. *Revolution Brings Progress to Ghana*. Accra: Information Services Department, 1988.
———. *Ghana Living Standards Survey: Preliminary Results 1988*. Accra: Statistical Service, 1988.
———. *Towards a New Dynamism*. Accra: Government Printer, 1989.
———. "Decentralisation in Ghana." Accra: Information Services Department, n.d.
Rimmer, Douglas. "Ghana's Economic Decline." *Africa Insight* 18, 3 (1989).
———. "The Political Economy of Poverty, Equity and Growth: Ghana Study." Washington, D.C.: World Bank Research Project RPO 67373, mimeo, 1989.
Rothchild, Donald. "The Rawlings Revolution in Ghana: Pragmatism with Populist Rhetoric." *CSIS Africa Notes*, no. 42 (May 2, 1985).
Rothchild, Donald, and E. Gyimah-Boadi. "Ghana's Economic Decline and Development Strategies." In John Ravenhill, ed., *Africa in Economic Crisis*. New York: Columbia University Press, 1986.
———. "Populism in Ghana and Burkina Faso." *Current History* 88, 538 (1989).
Toye, John. "Ghana's Economic Reforms and World Bank Policy-Conditioned Lending, 1983–88." University of Sussex: Institute of Development Studies, mimeo, draft, March 1989.
United States Government. *Report of a Staff Study Mission to Great Britain, Ghana, Senegal, Côte d'Ivoire, and France, November 29–December 20, 1988, to the Committee on Foreign Affairs, U.S. House of Representatives*. Washington, D.C.: U.S. Government Printing Office, 1989.
———, Department of Labor. *Foreign Labor Trends: Ghana*. Washington, D.C.: U.S. Department of Labor, 1898.
Weissman, Steve. "Structural Adjustment in Africa: Insights from the Experiences of Ghana and Senegal: Report of Staff Study Mission." Committee on Foreign Relations, U.S. House of Representatives, March 1989.
World Bank. *Accelerated Development in Sub-Saharan Africa: An Agenda for Action*. Washington, D.C.: World Bank, 1981.
———. *Ghana: Managing the Transition*. Report No. 5398-GH, 2 vols. Washington, D.C.: World Bank, November 7, 1984.
———. *Ghana: Policies and Program for Adjustment*. Washington, D.C.: World Bank, April 1984.
———. *Toward Sustained Development in Sub-Saharan Africa*. Washington, D.C.: World Bank, 1984.

———. *Ghana: Towards Structural Adjustment.* Report No. 5854-GH, 2 vols. Washington, D.C.: World Bank, October 7, 1986.
———. *Ghana: Policies and Issues of Structural Adjustment.* Report No. 6635-GH. Washington, D.C.: World Bank, March 30, 1987.
———. *Ghana: Structural Adjustment for Growth.* Report No. 7515-GH. Washington, D.C.: World Bank, 1989.
———. *Sub-Saharan Africa: From Crisis to Sustainable Growth.* Washington, D.C.: World Bank, November 1989.
Yeebo, Zaya. "Ghana: Defence Committees and the Class Struggle." *Review of African Political Economy* 32 (April 1985).

# About the Contributors

*Kwasi Anyemedu* is a lecturer in economics at the University of Ghana, Legon. Prior to that appointment, he worked at the Ministry of Finance and Economic Planning, the Ghana Industrial Holding Corporation, and the State Enterprises Commission. In addition, he served for a brief period as chief executive of the State Goldmining Corporation.

*Naomi Chazan* is professor of political science and African studies at the Hebrew University of Jerusalem, where she also is chairperson of the Harry S. Truman Research Institute for the Advancement of Peace. She is the author of several books and numerous articles on comparative politics and African political development, including *Ghana: Coping with Uncertainty* (1986) and (with Robert Mortimer, John Ravenhill, and Donald Rothchild) *Politics and Society in Contemporary Africa* (1988).

*James Cobbe* is professor of economics and associate dean of the College of Social Sciences at Florida State University. His interests lie in public policy in developing countries, especially with respect to human resources. In addition to West and Southern Africa (where he spent four years, based in Lesotho), he has worked in Southeast Asia and the Caribbean. He is the author of *Governments and Mining Companies in Developing Countries* (1979) and (with J. E. Bardill) *Lesotho: Dilemmas of Development in Southern Africa* (1985).

*E. Gyimah-Boadi* is a lecturer in political science at the University of Ghana, Legon. He has researched and written extensively on the political dimensions of Ghana's Economic Recovery and Structural Adjustment Programs. He is currently editing a book on Ghana under the PNDC regime.

*Jeffrey Herbst* is assistant professor of politics and international affairs at

Princeton University's Woodrow Wilson School. He is the author of *State Politics in Zimbabwe* (1990). A Robert S. McNamara Fellowship from the World Bank funded his research.

*Cord Jakobeit* is assistant professor in political science at the Free University of Berlin, and visiting assistant professor at Stanford University's Overseas Studies Program in Berlin. He has been a consultant for the World Bank (IBRD) and the West German government. He has published articles on economic and political developments in Equatorial Guinea, Cameroon, and Côte d'Ivoire, and is coeditor of a forthcoming book on the cocoa world market.

*Richard Jeffries* is lecturer in politics with reference to Africa at the School of Oriental and African Studies, University of London. He is author of *Class, Power and Ideology in Ghana: The Railwaymen of Sekondi* (1978), and of numerous articles on Ghanaian politics.

*Jon Kraus* is professor of political science at the State University of New York at Fredonia. He researches and writes on West African issues. His most recent publication dealing with agriculture in Ghana appears in S. Commins (ed.), *Africa's Agrarian Crisis* (1986) and N. Chazan and T. Shaw (eds.), *Coping with Africa's Food Crisis* (1988). He also has a chapter on political parties in K. Lawson and P. Merkl (eds.), *When Parties Fail* (1988), and another on African trade unions in R. Southall (ed.), *Labour and Unions in Asia and Africa* (1988).

*Matthew Martin* is project manager of External Finance for Africa at the International Development Centre (Queen Elizabeth House), Oxford University. He has worked on debt and adjustment for the Overseas Development Institute, the Swedish International Development Agency, the UN Africa Recovery Programme, UNCTAD, and the World Bank. His forthcoming book, *The Crumbling Facade of Africa's Debt Negotiations: No Winners*, will be published by Macmillan in 1991.

*Gwendolyn Mikell* is associate professor of anthropology at Georgetown University, where she teaches in the Sociology Department and specializes in the study of rural populations, changing gender relations, and political change. She is the author of *Cocoa and Chaos in Ghana* (1989) and the editor of the 1985 issue of *Rural Africana*, "African Women and Development in the 1980s." Currently she is working on a book on state policy and Ghanaian women.

*Kwame A. Ninsin* is senior lecturer in political science at the University of

Ghana, Legon. He recently coedited (with Emmanuel Hansen) *The State, Development and Politics in Ghana* (1989). His book *Political Struggles in Ghana, 1966–81* will be published shortly.

*Paul Nugent* is lecturer in African history at the University of Edinburgh. Much of his chapter is based on fieldwork done in Ghana's Volta region in 1985 and 1986.

*Donald Rothchild* is professor of political science at the University of California, Davis. He was a visiting professor of political science at the University of Ghana, Legon, in 1975–1977, and in 1985. His books include *Racial Bargaining in Independent Kenya* (1973), (coauthor) *Scarcity, Choice and Public Policy in Middle Africa* (1978), and (coauthor) *Politics and Society in Contemporary Africa* (1988). Among his edited works are (coeditor) *State Versus Ethnic Claims: African Policy Dilemmas* (1983), (coeditor) *Afro-Marxist Regimes: Ideology and Public Policy* (1987), and (coeditor) *The Precarious Balance: State and Society in Africa* (1988).

# Index

Ababio, Shirley, 198
Abbey, Joe, 30
Abbott Laboratories, 196
Aboagye, E. K., 181
Abodakpi, Dan, 198, 204, 208(n23)
Accumulation, 49, 50
Acheampong, Ignatius K., 71, 73, 88, 145, 194; and state-owned enterprises, 196–197
Achimota Brewery Company, 199
ADC. *See* Agricultural Development Corporation
Adda, William, 198, 201, 205
Adu, Pandit, 198, 205
AFRC. *See* Armed Forces Revolutionary Council
African Bar Association, 13
African Development Bank, 257
AGC. *See* Ashanti Goldfields Corporation
AGI. *See* Association of Ghana Industries
Agricultural Development Corporation (ADC), 194, 195, 196
Agricultural Produce Marketing Board, 194
Agriculture, 6, 7, 85, 90, 93, 99(nn17, 18), 100(n24), 195, 247–248, 249; economic factors in, 57–58; exports, 215, 220(n8); and politics, 87–88; production in, 4, 9, 129–130; rural culture, 96–97; World Bank, 130–131. *See also various crops*
Aid. *See* Assistance
Akata-Pore, Alolga, 163
Akuafo Cheque System, 60, 75, 225
ALU. *See* Association of Local Unions
Amissah-Arthur, K. B., 198
Amoah and Associates, G. E., 199
Annan, D. F., 29, 149, 188
Archer Committee, 225
Armed Forces Revolutionary Council (AFRC), 73, 159, 160, 195, 197, 199, 204
Aryee, E. J. A., 198
Asamoah, Obed, 75, 84(n19)
Asante, 87
A. S. Electrical Clips, 195
Ashanti Goldfields Corporation (AGC), 134, 194, 213, 217
Assasie, J. Y., 185
Assistance, 9, 96, 163, 227, 251, 257, 258; attracting, 124–125
Association of Ghana Industries (AGI), 135
Association of Local Unions (ALU), 161
Associations, 26, 52; expansion of, 21, 32–34
Atim, Chris, 75, 163
Auction: foreign exchange, 185–186, 237–238, 249, 254

Baiden, Richard, 161
Balance of payments, 10, 126
Bank for Housing and Construction, 201
Bank of Ghana, 134
Banks, 125, 134, 201
Bast Fibres Board, 194
Bauxite, 5, 134
Biney, J. E., 213
Black market, 161; and currency rates, 75–77. *See also* Informal sector; Smuggling
BMB. *See* Borenschot-Moret-Bosboom
Boateng, D. S., 198, 208(n23)
Border Guards, 75, 77, 83(n11); as smugglers, 73–74, 76, 83(n12)

275

Borders: surveillance of, 75, 77
Borenschot-Moret-Bosboom (BMB), 197
Botchwey, Kwesi, 8, 30, 81, 127, 135, 142, 147, 164, 181, 185, 208(n23); economic policy of, 128–129, 204–205, 236
Briscoe, R. T., 195
Brown, J. P., 213
Budget, 181, 259; deficits, 10, 121, 125, 139, 248; reform in, 6–7
Burkina Faso: smuggling into, 70, 73
Bushfires, 223–224
Busia, Kofi A., 4, 194

Cade, E. H., 213
Cameroon, 230
Canada, 217, 239, 251, 252
Canadian Bogosu Resources, 216
Capital: foreign, 63(n4), 65(n21), 126, 163; in mining sector, 212–214
CDO. *See* Civil Defence Organisation
CDRs. *See* Committees for the Defence of the Revolution
CEPS. *See* Customs, Excise and Preventive Services
Chiefdoms, 30, 89, 125
Churches, 13, 52
Church of Jesus Christ of Latter-Day Saints, 13
Citizens' Vetting Committees, 24, 51, 124, 140–141
Civil Defence Organisation (CDO), 77, 81
Civilian courts, 29–30
Civil liberties, 13, 36
Civil Servants' Association, 55, 60
Civil service, 11, 12, 31, 145–146, 246
Clergy, 125

CMB. *See* Cocoa Marketing Board
Cocoa Board, 124, 132, 139, 145, 147, 184, 199, 225; reform in, 140, 177. *See also* COCOBOD
Cocoa Marketing Board (CMB), 60, 71, 75, 76, 194, 225
Cocoa production, 24, 92, 98(nn9, 10), 99(n15), 210, 232(n6); and economy, 78–79; exports, 5–6, 97(n1), 211, 217–218, 254, 255, 257; managing, 221–222; markets for, 60, 194; policy reform in, 223–226; prices for, 9, 11, 57–58, 77, 78(table), 79–80, 90, 123(table), 125, 129, 138, 229–231; regional, 86–87; rehabilitation of, 131, 226–229; smuggling in, 70, 71, 83(n10); World Bank program, 131–133. *See also various marketing boards*
Cocoa Services Division (CSD), 91
COCOBOD, 78, 91, 197, 200, 205, 240, 242; management of, 202, 227, 247. *See also* Cocoa Board
Coffee, 194
Committee of Secretaries, 198–199, 206
Committees for the Defence of the Revolution (CDRs), 29, 30, 37, 51, 59, 64(n13), 91, 96, 149; government support of, 53, 55
Communication: intergovernmental, 51–52
Community, 26, 91; rural organization of, 89–90

Consolidated African Selection Trust, 194
Construction, 133, 134
Consultative Group of Donors, 9, 250, 251, 259
Consumer goods: smuggling of, 71–72, 84(nn27, 28)
Convention People's party (CPP), 59, 67(n53), 87; regime legitimacy, 62–63; and state-owned enterprises, 194, 196
Cooperatives, 87, 90, 93, 96, 98(n11), 205; gold mining, 216–217; women's, 94, 95
Corporations: state, 140, 194. *See also* State-owned enterprises
Corporatism, 60; in rural sector, 89–90
Corruption, 14, 25, 50
Côte d'Ivoire: cocoa production, 71, 225, 227, 230; smuggling into, 70, 72(table), 76, 132, 222
Coups d'état: attempts at, 27, 126, 169
CPP. *See* Convention People's party
Credit, 135–136, 219
Crimes: economic, 51, 74
CSD. *See* Cocoa Services Division
Currency, 6, 249; devaluation of, 4, 125, 131, 134, 137–139, 176–177, 237–238, 243, 245, 257; and smuggling, 70–71; valuation of, 75–77. *See also* Exchange rate; Foreign exchange
Customs, Excise and Preventive Services (CEPS), 56

DANIDA. *See* Danish International

INDEX 277

Development Agency
Danish International
  Development Agency
  (DANIDA), 201
Darkmak Farms, 195
Darkmak Houses Properties,
  195
DAs. *See* District
  Assemblies
Day care centers, 95
Debt, 253, 256; external,
  12, 34, 55; increase in,
  10–11; relief, 119, 252
Debt servicing, 11, 245,
  254, 258, 259–260
Defense committees. *See*
  Committees for the
  Defence of the
  Revolution; National
  Defence Committee;
  People's Defence
  Committees
Dei, Henry, 198
Democracy, 29;
  establishing, 35, 38, 39,
  164–165, 257–258
Dependency, 162, 258
Development, 29, 96, 97,
  257; community, 61–62;
  economic, 85, 94–95;
  government spending
  and, 140, 142
Diamond Marketing
  Corporation, 214
Diamonds, 5, 121, 133,
  214
DIC. *See* Divestiture
  Implementation
  Committee
Diseases, 6, 143–144
District Assemblies (DAs),
  35, 149, 189, 205, 226;
  elections for, 14,
  17(n36), 36–37, 59,
  66(n31), 85, 91–92,
  165; use of, 59–60
District Councils, 168
Divestiture: of state-owned
  enterprises, 193, 195,
  196, 198, 199, 200–206
Divestiture Implementation
  Committee (DIC):

operations of, 198–202,
  205–206
DL Steel Company, 199
Doctors: in public sector,
  142–143
Donors, 9, 12, 96, 127,
  226, 251, 255, 257, 259
Drought, 91, 121, 145,
  180, 257; and bushfires,
  223–224

Eastern Europe, 180
ECA. *See* Economic
  Commission for Africa
Economic Advisory
  Committee, 124–125
Economic Commission for
  Africa (ECA), 119–120,
  210
Economic Community of
  West African States
  (ECOWAS), 219
Economic growth, 3, 16,
  35, 65(n23), 126, 150–
  151; and reform policies,
  128–136
Economic policy, 258–
  259; under Botchwey,
  204–205
Economic Recovery
  Program (ERP), 8, 14,
  29, 30, 31, 32, 34, 58,
  76, 85, 90, 105, 158,
  166–167, 193, 209,
  211, 217, 219, 223;
  external orientation of,
  54–55; and government
  legitimacy, 50–51;
  impacts of, 94, 177–
  178; indebtedness, 10–
  11; policies in, 57, 126–
  127; response to, 181–
  182
Economy, 3, 13, 21, 26,
  34, 41(n12), 49, 76, 77,
  128(table), 162;
  agricultural sector of,
  57–58; alternative, 4–5,
  33; capacity of, 256–
  257; collapsed, 120,
  121; decline in, 240–
  241;diversity of, 85–86;

external sector, 54–55,
  65(n24), 91; recovery of,
  163–164; reform of, 6–
  7, 8, 28, 124–125, 163,
  204–205, 241–243,
  248–249; and
  smuggling, 74, 81–82;
  stabilization of, 88–89;
  women in, 98(n14),
  99(nn22, 23)
ECOWAS. *See* Economic
  Community of West
  African States
EDSAC. *See* Educational
  Sector Adjustment Credit
Education, 12, 107,
  115(nn1–3); curriculums,
  108–109; investment in,
  141–142; reform in, 58,
  104–106, 112, 114,
  115(n5); spending on,
  103–104, 109–110,
  144; system of, 101,
  110–111
Educational Sector
  Adjustment Credit
  (EDSAC), 105
EFF. *See* Extended Fund
  Facility
Elections, 39, 47(n94),
  168, 243; district
  assembly, 14, 17(n36),
  36–37, 66(n31), 85, 91,
  165; of PNDC members,
  91–92
Electricity, 133, 134,
  254
Electricity Corporation of
  Ghana, 197
Elites, 32, 33, 71, 108,
  161; education system,
  101, 107, 111; rural
  sector, 91, 93; in
  secondary schools, 110,
  114
Ellis, J. E., 213
Emigration, 26, 160, 241.
  *See also* Migration
Employment, 31,
  101(table), 103, 115(n1)
Enhanced SAF (ESAF), 235,
  246, 251, 258, 260

Enterprises. *See* State-owned enterprises
Equatorial Guinea, 230
Equity, 85, 132
Erbynn, K. G., 198, 208(n23)
ERP. *See* Economic Recovery Program
ESAF. *See* Enhanced SAF
Europe, 26, 215
Ewes, 188
Exchange rate, 185, 211–212, 222, 237–238, 240; adjusting, 8–9, 137
Expatriates, 31
Export Promotion Council, 214
Export Rehabilitation Technical Assistance Project, 217
Exports, 8, 30, 97(n1), 121, 124, 127, 131, 133, 151, 176, 194, 209, 247, 257; declining values in, 10, 12; devaluation, 137–139; diversification of, 4, 10, 210–211, 217–219, 258; foreign markets, 5–6; nontraditional, 212, 214–216, 220(n8), 254; reform, 230–231
Extended Fund Facility (EFF), 235, 250

Famekwa Trading Company, 199, 201
Famine, 145
Farmers. *See* Peasants
Fattal Brothers, 195
Finance, 9; external, 259–260; and foreign exchange, 250–256
Firestone Corporation, U.S., 196
Fiscal policy, 238, 240, 246, 248
Food crops, 133, 247–248, 257; in informal sector, 26–27, 70; trade in, 131–132
Food Distribution Corporation, 130, 194, 195
Food Production Corporation, 199, 201
Foreign exchange, 211–212, 254; allocation for, 185–186; earning, 209–210; and finance policy, 250–256. *See also* Exchange rate
Front for National Unity, Democracy, and Development, 150

Gakakuma, E. K., 198, 205
Garment industry, 135
GBC. *See* Ghana Broadcasting Corporation
GDP. *See* Gross domestic product
GEA and Associates, 200
GEA General Chemicals, 200
GEA Packaging Gava Farms, 200
General Transport and Chemical Workers Union, 181
GES. *See* Ghana Education Service
Ghamot Enterprises, 200
Ghamot Motor Engineering, 200
Ghamot Textiles, 200
Ghana Airways, 9
Ghana Bar Association, 150
Ghana Bauxite Company, 194
Ghana Broadcasting Corporation (GBC), 56
Ghana Education Service (GES), 107
Ghana Employers' Association, 134
Ghana Export Promotion Council, 212
Ghanaian General Establishment Ltd, 195
Ghanaian Marine and Industrial Maduries, 195
Ghanaians, 30; expelled from Nigeria, 21, 27, 130, 180
Ghanaian Wood Industries, 195
Ghana Industrial Holding Corporation (GIHOC), 196, 199
Ghana Institute of Management and Public Administration (GIMPA), 197, 198
Ghana Investment Center, 218, 254
Ghana Minerals Commission, 218
Ghana National Procurement Agency, 195
Ghana National Trading Corporation, 149
Ghana Oil Palm Development Corporation, 195
Ghana Private Road Transport Union (GPRTU), 55–56, 60
Ghana Textile Printing (GTP) Company, 56, 204
Ghana Textile Products Company, 180
Ghana Water and Sewerage Corporation, 143
GIHOC. *See* Ghana Industrial Holding Corporation
GIMPA. *See* Ghana Institute of Management and Public Administration
Global 2000 small farmer projects, 130
Gold Coast Ordinance No. 38, 194
Gold production, 121, 133, 134, 218, 254, 255, 257; exports, 5, 10, 97(n1), 211; prices, 11, 138; small scale, 213–214, 216–217
Gonja Development Company, 194, 196
Government, 4, 29, 51, 53, 66–67(nn30, 42), 69,

121, 147, 186; legitimacy of, 49–50; populist, 24–25; social support, 56–57; spending by, 139–140
GPRTU. *See* Ghana Private Road Transport Union
Grants, 7, 126. *See also* Loans
Gross domestic product (GDP), 30, 104, 124, 131, 133, 139, 140, 141, 244, 258; decline in, 5, 74, 121; growth in, 3, 9, 129; and structural adjustment, 119–120
GTP. *See* Ghana Textile Printing
Guggisberg, Gordon, 210, 218
Guinea worm infection, 143–144

Handicrafts, 215
Health care, 12, 141, 142–143, 249
Households, 102(table), 103–104, 133
Hughes, Thomas, 213
Human rights, 32, 36
Hyperinflation, 145, 146

IBRD. *See* International Bank for Reconstruction and Development
ICCO. *See* International Cocoa Organization
ICU. *See* Industrial and Commercial Workers' Union
IDA. *See* International Development Association
IDC. *See* Industrial Development Corporation
IFC. *See* International Finance Corporation
IMF. *See* International Monetary Fund
Immunization, 143

Imports, 5, 9, 77, 129, 135, 138–139, 209, 223, 238, 248, 253, 254–255, 259; and economic programs, 251–252
Income, 58, 107, 115(n2), 226, 257; real, 161, 186
Industrial and Commercial Workers' Union (ICU), 56
Industrial Development Corporation (IDC), 194, 195, 196
Industry, 8, 129, 195; growth in, 10, 133; rehabilitation in, 134–135
Infant mortality, 121
Inflation, 132, 135, 145, 147–148, 151, 238, 240, 243, 257; rate of, 10, 58, 121, 123(table); reducing, 30, 137–138
Informal sector, 21–22, 26–27, 33. *See also* Black market
Infrastructure, 6, 8, 34, 120, 151, 223, 229
Intelligentsia: Neo-Marxist, 24, 31, 149, 160
Interest groups, 32
Interest rates, 135
Interim Management Committee, 161, 180
Interim National Coordinating Committee, 158
Internal Revenue Department, 60
International Bank for Reconstruction and Development (IBRD), 251
International Cocoa Organization (ICCO), 221
International Development Association (IDA), 7, 132, 217, 260
International Finance Corporation (IFC), 217
International Monetary Fund (IMF), 7, 9, 32, 124, 129, 139, 151, 223, 252, 254, 256, 258, 259, 260; credit, 135–136; and exchange rate, 137, 249; loans, 29, 64(n16), 65(nn21, 22), 119, 127, 245–246, 250–251, 255; negotiations with, 53–54, 125, 127, 238–239; problems, 244–245, 248, 249; programs, 126, 158, 178, 180, 235, 237, 241, 242, 243
Investment, 8, 25, 137, 229, 238, 254, 257; education, 141–142; export sectors, 127, 224; foreign, 54, 218–219; mining sector, 213, 216; private, 10, 135–136, 248
Issifu, Secretary-General, 161
Ivory Coast. *See* Côte d'Ivoire

Jehovah's Witnesses, 13
JFM. *See* June Fourth Movement
JSS. *See* Junior secondary schools
Juapong Textile Printing Company, 199, 204
Judicial system, 13, 52; restructuring, 29–30, 51. *See also* Civilian courts; Public Tribunals
June Fourth Movement (JFM), 23, 24, 64(n16), 124, 160, 161, 162, 165; economic recovery, 163–164
Junior secondary schools (JSS), 104, 105, 106, 110, 112, 113(table), 114; curriculums, 108–109

KNRG. *See* Kwame Nkrumah Revolutionary Guards
Kool Bottling Factory, 195
Kwahu Dairy Farms, 200, 195
Kwame Nkrumah Revolutionary Guards (KNRG), 24, 25, 162

Labor, 88, 130, 186, 224, 247; organized, 52, 55, 203; and PNDC, 178–180; power of, 173–175. *See also* Unions; Working class
Land Valuation Board (LVB), 202, 205
Legal system, 60–61. *See also* Judicial system
Legislative Instrument No. 457, 196
Legitimacy: of CPP regime, 62–63; and Economic Recovery Program, 50–51; government, 49–50
Libya, 163, 216
Licensing, 214
Limann, Hilla, 23, 74, 159
Liquidation: of state-owned enterprises, 147, 195, 196, 198, 199–200
Liquidity, 135, 136
Loans, 53, 133, 138, 249; access to, 253–254; cocoa production, 132, 278; IMF-World Bank, 235, 250–251, 252; repayment of, 126–127
Lonrho, 217
Lower classes, 50, 51, 52, 66–67(n42). *See also* Peasants
Loyalty Group of Companies, 194–195
Loyalty Industries Ltd., 201
LVB. *See* Land Valuation Board

Machinery, 5
Malnutrition, 143, 146
Management, Development, and Productivity Institute (MDPI), 197, 198
Manganese, 5, 121, 133, 211
Manufacturing, 4, 5, 133, 134, 135–136, 196
MDPI. *See* Management, Development, and Productivity Institute
Meat Marketing Board, 195
Mercury Law (PNDCL 217), 214
Mercury Ordinance (Cap. 184), 214
Metalico Ghana, 199
Middle class, 160
Middle East, 26
MIGA. *See* Multilateral Investment Guarantee Agency
Migration, 34, 89, 91
Military, 139, 149, 241. *See also* Border Guards
Mineral production, 70, 121, 129, 131, 133–134, 175; concessions, 212–213
Minerals and Mining Law (PNDC Law 153), 212–213
Minerals Commission, 213
Minerals Law, 216
Mine Workers' Union, 55, 60
Ministry of Agriculture, 130, 131
Ministry of Education, 106, 107, 109
Ministry of Finance and Economic Planning, 202
Ministry of Industries and Technology, 198
Mobisquads, 29, 37, 60, 92, 93, 94, 96, 205; community reaction to, 90–91
Monetarist policies, 14
Monetary policy, 238, 240, 243, 246, 252
Mortar Regiment, 80

Movement for Freedom and Justice, 150
Multilateral Investment Guarantee Agency (MIGA), 218–219, 254
Multinational corporations, 162
Mutual aid societies, 26

National Alliance of Liberals, 59
National Chamber of Commerce, 135
National Commission on Democracy (NCD), 14, 29, 30
National Council on Women in Development (NCWD), 94, 99(n22)
National Defence Committee (NDC), 29, 76, 126, 166; organization of, 124, 158
National Economic Review Committee, 51
National Industrial Companies (NIC), 197
National Industrial Companies Farms, 199
National Investigations Committee, 51
National Investment Bank, 201
Nationalism: economic, 202
Nationalization, 23, 125, 194–195
National Labor Advisory Committee, 135
National Liberation Council (NLC), 194, 196, 199, 202
National Liberation Movement, 87
National Mobilisation Programme, 29, 91–92
National Policy Implementation Monitoring Secretariat, 51
National Programme for

INDEX 281

Economic Development, 35
National Redemption Council (NRC), 73, 88, 194–195, 199
National Service Secretariat, 200
National Union of Ghana Students (NUGS), 55
NCD. *See* National Commission on Democracy
NCWD. *See* National Council on Women in Development
NDC. *See* National Defence Committee
NDM. *See* New Democratic Movement
Negotiating Sub-Committee, 198, 202
Neocolonialism, 162
Neo-Marxists, 24, 31, 149, 158, 160
New Democratic Movement (NDM), 23, 24, 55, 160, 162, 163, 164
NIC. *See* National Industrial Companies
Nigeria, 26, 53, 231(n4), 253; expellees from, 21, 27, 130, 180, 224, 241
Nkrumah, Kwame, 62, 63, 87, 175, 202, 204; as symbol, 67(n51), 189
Nkwakubew Animal Husbandry, 199
NLC. *See* National Liberation Council
NLC decree 207, 196
*Nnoboa*. *See* Work groups
NRC. *See* National Redemption Council
NSC. *See* Negotiating Sub-Committee
NUGS. *See* National Union of Ghana Students

Obeng, P. V., 29, 127, 135, 199, 206
Obimpeh, Stephen, 130
Obuasi mines, 213

OECD. *See* Organization for Economic Cooperation and Development
Office of Revenue Collection, 141
OFY. *See* Operation-Feed-Yourself
Oil. *See* Petroleum
Operation-Feed-Yourself (OFY), 88
Organization for Economic Cooperation and Development (OECD), 239, 250, 252, 256, 260; loan access, 253–254
Overseas Knitwear Fabrics, 199

Palm kernels, 194
PAMSCAD. *See* Programme of Actions to Mitigate the Social Costs of Adjustment
Parastatals, 6, 9, 31, 145, 201, 222. *See also* State-owned enterprises
Patronage, 25, 27
PDCs. *See* People's Defence Committees
Peasants, 60, 90, 91, 92, 97, 130, 175; and cocoa production, 225–226; income of, 147–148; political agitation of, 86–87, 125; in political economy, 85–86; smuggling by, 71, 73
People's Defence Committees (PDCs), 24, 29, 75, 76, 79, 126, 149, 158; establishment of, 124, 162, 179; opposition to, 165–166
People's Militia, 77–78, 80–81, 84(n30)
People's Revolutionary League of Ghana, 162
People's Shops, 76, 125
Petroleum, 5, 254
Phillips, J. V. L., 134–135

PIB. *See* Prices and Incomes Board
PNDC. *See* Provisional National Defence Council
PNDC law 219, 214
Police Task Force, 75
Politics, 3, 13, 21, 50, 52, 59, 64(n8), 66(n30), 85, 148, 157, 169; alternative, 4–5; control, 167–168; farmers and, 86–87; reform in, 34–35, 38–39, 45(n66)
Populism, 21, 60, 125; in PNDC, 23–28; radical, 8, 121, 124
Poverty, 4, 14, 26, 133, 257; and education, 103(table), 112; rural sector, 11–12, 34
Power, 21, 39, 41(n11), 51, 61, 86; reduction in, 27–28; structural changes in, 25, 148–150
Precious Minerals Marketing Corporation, 214, 217
Press, 52
Prices, 8, 10, 24, 99(n18), 126, 177, 183, 249; cocoa, 9, 57–58, 75, 76, 77, 78(table), 79–81, 125, 218, 229–231; decontrol of, 125, 237; producer, 6, 14, 34, 85, 90; reduction of, 131–132; World Bank policy, 132–133
Prices and Incomes Board (PIB), 177
Price Waterhouse, 198
Primary schools, 108, 113(table), 114(table), 144
Privatization, 31, 92, 193, 238, 240; of state-owned enterprises, 9, 147; support for, 202–203, 204
Professionals, 56
Programme of Actions to Mitigate the Social Costs

of Adjustment (PAMSCAD), 12, 35, 61–62, 90, 96, 148, 257
Progress party, 59, 194
Provisional National Defence Council (PNDC), 7, 13, 21, 22, 37, 50, 61, 63, 69, 95, 146, 148, 165, 178, 182, 257, 258, 259; criticism of, 168–169; debt, 252–253; economic capacity of, 139–140; economic recovery program, 11, 34–35, 57, 76–77, 121, 124–125, 144–145, 204–205, 235–237, 240–243, 248, 250; elections, 91–92; finance negotiations by, 238–239, 255–256; and labor, 179–180; policies of, 27, 35–36; populism, 23–28; radicals in, 125–126; restructuring by, 29, 31; rural sector, 90–91, 187–188; state-owned enterprises, 197–199; support of, 30–31, 149–150, 152(n13); and urban sector, 189–190
Public sector, 167
Public Service Workers' Union, 56
Public Tribunals, 24, 29, 51, 75, 161

Queen-mothers, 95

Radical movements, 162–163
Railways, 134, 174
Railway Workers' Union, 55, 60
Rawlings, Jerry T., 14, 23, 24, 31, 53, 63, 69, 74, 82, 90, 121, 143, 149, 163, 190, 241; on defense committees, 165–166; economic reform, 6–7, 28, 76, 88–89, 126, 127, 180, 181, 189, 195, 223, 224, 236; foreign assistance, 95–96; leadership of, 28–29, 39, 169–170, 240; political reform, 34, 35, 37–38; power of, 27, 120, 157, 158–160, 168, 182; structural reform, 8–9
Rawlings, Nana Agyeman, 95
RCCs. See Regional Coordinating Committees
Regional Coordinating Committees (RCCs), 124
Regional Development Corporations, 195
Religion, 13, 26
Roads, 12, 130, 131, 136
Rubber estates, 196
Ruling class, 52, 53; power, 49, 50; as smugglers, 74–75
Rural sector, 4, 33, 37, 60, 91, 187–188; agriculture in, 96–97; corporatism in, 89–90; economic development in, 92–93; economic reform in, 57–58, 164, 243–244; finances in, 75–76; government linkage to, 25, 61; informal sector in, 26–27; politics in, 87–88; standard of living in, 11–12; stratification of, 87, 98(n9); women's roles in, 94–95

SAF. See Structural Adjustment Facility
São Tomé, 230
SAP. See Structural adjustment program
Savings, 8, 10, 135
SDA. See Social Dimensions of Adjustment
SDR. See Special drawing rights
SEC. See State Enterprises Commission
Secondary schools, 143–144; classification of, 104, 105, 106, 112; curriculums of, 108–109, 110. See also Junior secondary schools; Senior secondary schools
Security, 165
Sekondi-Takoradi strikes, 174
Self-reliance, 25, 164
Senior secondary schools (SSS), 104, 105, 113(table), 115(n5); curriculums, 108–109; reforms, 112, 114; students in, 110–111
Service sector, 136
SES. See State Enterprises Secretariat
SFC. See State Fishing Corporation
SGMC. See State Gold Mining Corporation
Siaw, J. K., 199
Small-Scale Gold Mining Law (PNDCL 218), 214
SMC. See Supreme Military Council
Smuggling, 69, 83(n10), 84(nn27, 28), 132, 222; economy, 81–82; history of, 70–74; process of, 79–80; ruling class, 74–75
Social associations, 26
Social classes, 14, 24, 33, 49, 125; and economic recovery program, 54, 55, 57
Social Dimensions of Adjustment (SDA), 257
Socialism, 162
Social organizations. See Associations
Social Security and National Insurance Trust (SSNIT), 145
Social services, 33, 125
Society, 27; civil, 25–26, 39–40; consolidation of,

# INDEX

21–22; reform in, 28, 35
SOEs. *See* State-owned enterprises
Southern Cross Mining, 216
Soviet Union, 163, 180
SPA. *See* Special Program of Assistance for Africa
Special drawing rights (SDR), 7, 260
Special Program of Assistance for Africa (SPA), 251, 252
SSNIT. *See* Social Security and National Insurance Trust
SSS. *See* Senior secondary schools
Stabilization programs: impacts of, 120, 126–128, 131, 145, 148, 157
Standard Chartered Bank, 249, 252, 254
Standards of living, 11–12, 132, 133, 257
State, 63(nn3, 4); autonomy of, 22–23, 25; as economic manager, 12–13; empowerment of, 39–40; power of, 27–28; restructuring, 31–32
State agencies, 25
State Bakery, 196
State Commission for Economic Cooperation, 51
State Enterprises Commission (SEC), 197, 198, 200–201
State Enterprises Secretariat (SES), 196
State Farms Corporation, 196, 199
State Fishing Corporation (SFC), 147, 199, 201, 207(n15), 208(nn20, 21)
State Furniture and Joinery Corporation, 196
State Gold Mining Corporation (SGMC), 134, 217
State Hotels, 205

State Laundry Service, 196
State Match Factory, 196
State Metal Works, 196
State-owned enterprises (SOEs), 9, 56, 126, 147, 177; divestiture of, 193, 200–206; history of, 194–195; reforms in, 195–199
State Textile Manufacturing Company, 196
State Tobacco Products Corporation, 196
State Tyre Services Corporation, 196
Strikes, 34, 174–175, 179(table)
Structural Adjustment Facility (SAF), 126, 235, 246, 250, 251, 258
Structural adjustment program (SAP), 3, 4, 15, 30, 31, 34, 105, 145, 176, 178, 193, 242, 243, 251; adoption of, 157–158; and agricultural sector, 130–131; conditions required by, 119–120; impacts of, 126–128, 131, 148; working class, 183–184, 186–187
Students, 31, 55, 149, 167; protests by, 57, 141; radical, 23, 160
Subsidies, 125
Subversion Decree, 73
Sugar Estates and Units, 196
Supreme Military Council (SMC), 73, 199

Tamale Secondary School, 143–144
Tarek Trading Company, 195
Tata Brewery, 199
Tawiah, Ebo, 204, 205, 208(n23)
Taxation, 7, 60, 71, 175
Tax revenues, 124, 140–141, 197, 212, 213

Teachers, 58, 105, 106, 111; university, 107–108
Technical Sub-Committee (TSC), 198, 200, 202
Telecommunications, 219
Tema Cement Works, 196
Tema Textile Printing Company, 199, 204
Terberebie Goldfields, 216
31st December Revolution, 24
31st December Women's Movement, 60, 92, 95, 96, 99(n22)
Timber production, 5, 70, 121, 129, 131, 133; exports, 97(n1), 211, 254, 257
Togo, 71, 79, 230; smuggling into, 70, 72(table), 73, 76
Trade, 10, 26, 53, 54, 55, 70, 79, 123, 125, 136, 219, 233, 254; and food farmers, 131–132; liberalization of, 135, 238; rural-urban, 15, 34, 58. *See also* Exports; Imports; Smuggling
Trades Union Congress (TUC), 55, 56, 66(n29), 146, 150, 166, 177, 178, 180, 188, 198, 203; leadership in, 161, 184
Trans Africa Engineering and Motors, 195
Transport sector, 30, 136, 219, 223
Tribalism, 87
TSC. *See* Technical Sub-Committee, 198, 200, 202
Tsikata, Kojo, 31, 159, 163, 165
Tsikata, Tsatsu, 163, 205, 208(n23)
TUC. *See* Trades Union Congress
Two Worlds Manufacturing Company, 199

UGFC. *See* United Ghana Farmers' Council
Underemployment, 136, 147
UNDP. *See* United Nations Development Program
Unemployment, 12, 147, 151
UNICEF, 148, 249, 257
Unions, 23, 125, 145, 152(n13), 173, 181; antagonism toward, 179–180; government support of, 55–56, 161; repression of, 182–183
United Africa Company, 201
United Ghana Farmers' Council (UGFC), 87
United Kingdom, 216, 239, 252
United Nations Development Program (UNDP), 197, 257
United party, 59
United Soaps Industries (Ghana), 195
United States, 215–216, 251, 252
Universities, 111, 144; autonomy of, 107–108
University of Ghana, 162
University of Science and Technology, 202
Upper Volta. *See* Burkina Faso
Urban sector, 21, 31, 34, 37, 58, 60, 130, 144, 162, 189–190; labor in, 173–175; standard of living in, 11–12; unemployment in, 151, 160–161; workers in, 175–176
U.S. Agency for International Development (USAID), 88
USAID. *See* U.S. Agency for International Development
Utuka, Major General, 73

Valco, 163
Victory Industries, 200
Violence: PNDC, 182, 183
Volta River Authority, 194

Wages, 9, 11, 24, 121, 123(table), 136, 166, 177, 186, 248, 257, 259; daily costs, 146–147; stabilization program, 145–146
Water supply, 133, 134, 143
WDCs. *See* Workers' Defence Committees
Welfare, 4, 26, 29, 257
West Africa, 26
West African Chemical and Metal Industries, 195
West African Produce Marketing Board, 194
West Germany, 251, 252
Whab Incandescent Lamps Enterprises, 195
WID. *See* Women in Development programs
Women, 26, 125; in development projects, 94–95; economic roles of, 98(nn10, 14), 99(nn22, 23)
Women in Development (WID) programs, 94–95, 99(n21)
Workers' Defence Committees (WDCs), 24, 29, 124, 162, 165, 166, 179
Work groups: cooperative, 90–91
Working classes, 107, 167; activism of, 161–162, 174–175; structural adjustment program, 183–184, 186–187; urban sector, 175–176
World Bank, 3, 7, 9, 148, 151, 136, 137, 217, 218, 223, 251, 252, 254, 257, 258, 259, 260; agricultural sector, 130–131, 230, 232(n6), 249; assistance, 124–125, 235; education reform, 105, 106, 111; foreign exchange auction, 248–249; loans, 29, 53, 65(nn21, 22), 119, 129, 255; negotiations with, 126, 127, 238–239; price reductions, 131–133; programs, 178, 180, 237, 241, 243, 244, 246, 248; reform, 140, 256; state-owned enterprises, 195, 197

Yankey, A. K., 66(n29), 184
Youth, 26: in work groups, 90–91. *See also* Students

# About the Book

Ghana, the pacesetter in terms of African independence from colonial rule, has now emerged as the test case of what structural adjustment can achieve in overcoming economic stagnation and administrative deficiencies. Since Jerry Rawlings implemented IMF/World Bank-recommended reforms, the results in terms of economic growth and institutional development in the short term have been impressive. The long-term impact, however, remains uncertain, making it far from clear whether Ghana can be considered a model for other countries.

The authors of this book look at the issues involved in Ghana's current reform program. For example, can meaningful export diversification be achieved? Must structural adjustment programs necessarily involve heavy social costs for the general public? How does such a reform program affect the regime's support base? What is the likely impact of structural adjustment on state reform? Although there is a healthy difference of opinion among the authors on the implications of structural adjustment in Ghana, the book as a whole conveys a concise picture of the effort to achieve self-sustaining political, economic, and social development under Rawlings's leadership in the mid-1980s and into the 1990s.

# The SAIS African Studies Library
(available from Lynne Rienner Publishers)

*Tunisia: The Political Economy of Reform*, edited by I. William Zartman

*Ghana: The Political Economy of Recovery*, edited by Donald Rothchild

*Europe and Africa: The New Phase*, edited by I. William Zartman


Other SAIS Studies on Africa:

*The Political Economy of Ethiopia* (1990)

*The Political Economy of Senegal Under Structural Adjustment* (1990)

*The Political Economy of Morocco* (1987)

*The Military in African Politics* (1987)

*The Political Economy of Kenya* (1987)

*The Political Economy of Cameroon* (1986)

*The OAU After Twenty Years* (1984)

*The Political Economy of Zimbabwe* (1984)

*The Political Economy of Ivory Coast* (1984)

*The Political Economy of Nigeria* (1983)